MW00342004

Saab Automotive Repair Manual

A K Legg T Eng (CEI), AMIMI

Models covered
Saab 900 Sedan and Hatchback; 2.0 liter

Covers Turbo and 16-valve models

ISBN 1 85010 567 7

(9Z6 - 84010)
(980)

ABCDEF

2

Haynes Publishing Group
Sparkford Nr Yeovil
Somerset BA22 7JJ England

Haynes North America, Inc
861 Lawrence Drive
Newbury Park
California 91320 USA

Acknowledgements

Thanks are due to the Champion Sparking Plug Company Limited who supplied the illustrations showing the sparking plug conditions. Certain other illustrations are the copyright of Saab (Great Britain) Limited, and are used with their permission. Special thanks are also due to Saab (Great Britain) Limited and Saab-Scania of Sweden for the supply of technical information, to Sykes-Pickavant who provided some of the workshop tools, and to all those people at Sparkford who assisted in the production of this Manual.

About this manual

Its aim

The aim of this manual is to help you get the best value from your vehicle. It can do so in several ways. It can help you decide what work must be done (even should you choose to get it done by a garage), provide information on routine maintenance and servicing, and give a logical course of action and diagnosis when random faults occur. However, it is hoped that you will use the manual by tackling the work yourself. On simpler jobs it may even be quicker than booking the car into a garage and going there twice, to leave and collect it. Perhaps most important, a lot of money can be saved by avoiding the costs a garage must charge to cover its labour and overheads.

The manual has drawings and descriptions to show the function of the various components so that their layout can be understood. Then the tasks are described and photographed in a step-by-step sequence so that even a novice can do the work.

Its arrangement

The manual is divided into thirteen Chapters, each covering a logical sub-division of the vehicle. The Chapters are each divided into Sections, numbered with single figures, eg 5; and the Sections into paragraphs (or sub-sections), with decimal numbers following on from the Section they are in, eg 5.1, 5.2, 5.3 etc.

It is freely illustrated, especially in those parts where there is a detailed sequence of operations to be carried out. There are two forms of illustration: figures and photographs. The figures are numbered in sequence with decimal numbers, according to their position in the Chapter – eg Fig. 6.4 is the fourth drawing/illustration in Chapter 6. Photographs carry the same number (either individually or in related groups) as the Section or sub-section to which they relate.

There is an alphabetical index at the back of the manual as well as a contents list at the front. Each Chapter is also preceded by its own individual contents list.

References to the 'left' or 'right' of the vehicle are in the sense of a person in the driver's seat facing forwards.

Unless otherwise stated, nuts and bolts are removed by turning anti-clockwise, and tightened by turning clockwise.

Vehicle manufacturers continually make changes to specifications and recommendations, and these, when notified, are incorporated into our manuals at the earliest opportunity.

Whilst every care is taken to ensure that the information in this manual is correct, no liability can be accepted by the authors or publishers for loss, damage or injury caused by any errors in, or omissions from, the information given.

Introduction to the Saab 900, 99 and 90

The Saab 900 was first introduced in early 1979 and was similar to the existing 99 Combi Coupe, but with a longer more sloping bonnet, front spoiler and deeper windscreen. The body is of rigid construction employing safety beams in the doors and a reinforced roof.

The in-line mounted engine is located over the gearbox or automatic transmission providing drive to the front wheels. Unlike the more conventional layout, the engine is positioned with the flywheel at the front of the car, but this facilitates removal of the clutch without having to remove either the engine or gearbox.

Being of an up market design, the car incorporates many extras to add to comfort and driveability.

The Saab 90 replaced the 99 in the UK in 1984. Details of this vehicle are explained in the introduction to the supplementary chapter at the end of this manual.

Contents

Saab 900 Turbo 5-door

Saab 99 GL 2-door

General dimensions, weights and capacities

Dimensions in (mm)
Overall length – 99 models:
   Saloon – early 1979 .... 174.01 in (4420 mm)
   Saloon – late 1979 on .... 176.26 in (4477 mm)
   Combi Coupe .... 178.35 in (4530 mm)
Overall length – 900 models:
   Saloon and Combi Coupe .... 186.57 in (4739 mm)
Overall width:
   All models .... 66.54 in (1690 mm)
Overall height (at curb weight):
   99 models .... 56.69 in (1440 mm)
   900 models .... 55.91 in (1420 mm)

Track – 99 models:	Front	Rear
Non-Turbo pre-1982	55.12 in (1400 mm)	56.30 in (1430 mm)
Turbo and 1982 on models	55.51 in (1410 mm)	56.69 in (1440 mm)
Track – 900 models	55.91 in (1420 mm) or 56.30 in (1430 mm)	56.30 in (1430 mm) or 56.69 in (1440 mm)

Wheelbase – 99 models:
   Pre-1982 models .... 97.36 in (2473 mm)
   1982 on models .... 97.05 in (2465 mm)
Wheelbase – 900 models:
   Pre-1982 models .... 99.41 in (2525 mm)
   1982 on models .... 99.09 in (2517 mm)
Turning circle – 99 models .... 208.66 in (5300 mm)
Turning circle – 900 models:
   Pre-1981 models .... 208.66 in (5300 mm)
   1981 on models .... 220.47 in (5600 mm)

Weights lb (kg)
99 models:
   1979 Saloon .... 2645 to 2755 lb (1200 to 1250 kg)
   1979 Combi Coupe .... 2711 to 2910 lb (1230 to 1320 kg)
   1980 Saloon .... 2545 to 2733 lb (1200 to 1240 kg)
   1981 Saloon .... 2618 to 2706 lb (1190 to 1230 kg)
   1982 on models .... 2574 to 2651 lb (1170 to 1205 kg)
900 models:
   1979 Combi Coupe .... 2650 to 2820 lb (1200 to 1280 kg)
   1980 Combi Coupe .... 2610 to 2860 lb (1185 to 1295 kg)
   1981 on models .... 2687 to 2974 lb (1220 to 1350 kg)
Maximum roof rack load .... 220 lb (100 kg)
Maximum trailer weight .... 3300 lb (1500 kg)

Capacities
Engine oil (including filter) .... 6.2 Imp pt; 3.7 US qt; 3.5 litre
Cooling system (including heater):
   99 models .... 14.1 Imp pt; 8.5 US qt; 8.0 litre
   900 models .... 17.6 Imp pt; 10.6 US qt; 10.0 litre
Fuel tank – 99 models:
   Pre-1982 models .... 12.1 Imp gal; 58.1 US qt; 55.0 litre
   1982 models .... 12.8 Imp gal; 61.3 US qt; 58.0 litre
Fuel tank – 900 models:
   Pre-1981 models .... 12.1 Imp gal; 58.1 US qt; 55.0 litre
   1981 on models .... 13.9 Imp gal; 66.6 US qt; 63.0 litre
Manual gearbox:
   4-speed .... 4.4 Imp pt; 2.6 US qt; 2.5 litre
   5-speed .... 5.3 Imp pt; 3.2 US qt; 3.0 litre
Automatic transmission:
   Transmission fluid .... 14.1 Imp pt; 8.5 US qt; 8.0 litre
   Final drive oil – type 35 .... 2.2 Imp pt; 1.3 US qt; 1.25 litre
   Final drive oil – type 37 .... 2.5 Imp pt; 1.5 US qt; 1.4 litre

Use of English

As this book has been written in England, it uses the appropriate English component names, phrases, and spelling. Some of these differ from those used in America. Normally, these cause no difficulty, but to make sure, a glossary is printed below. In ordering spare parts remember the parts list may use some of these words:

English	American	English	American
Accelerator	Gas pedal	Locks	Latches
Aerial	Antenna	Methylated spirit	Denatured alcohol
Anti-roll bar	Stabiliser or sway bar	Motorway	Freeway, turnpike etc
Big-end bearing	Rod bearing	Number plate	License plate
Bonnet (engine cover)	Hood	Paraffin	Kerosene
Boot (luggage compartment)	Trunk	Petrol	Gasoline (gas)
Bulkhead	Firewall	Petrol tank	Gas tank
Bush	Bushing	'Pinking'	'Pinging'
Cam follower or tappet	Valve lifter or tappet	Prise (force apart)	Pry
Carburettor	Carburetor	Propeller shaft	Driveshaft
Catch	Latch	Quarterlight	Quarter window
Choke/venturi	Barrel	Retread	Recap
Circlip	Snap-ring	Reverse	Back-up
Clearance	Lash	Rocker cover	Valve cover
Crownwheel	Ring gear (of differential)	Saloon	Sedan
Damper	Shock absorber, shock	Seized	Frozen
Disc (brake)	Rotor/disk	Sidelight	Parking light
Distance piece	Spacer	Silencer	Muffler
Drop arm	Pitman arm	Sill panel (beneath doors)	Rocker panel
Drop head coupe	Convertible	Small end, little end	Piston pin or wrist pin
Dynamo	Generator (DC)	Spanner	Wrench
Earth (electrical)	Ground	Split cotter (for valve spring cap)	Lock (for valve spring retainer)
Engineer's blue	Prussian blue	Split pin	Cotter pin
Estate car	Station wagon	Steering arm	Spindle arm
Exhaust manifold	Header	Sump	Oil pan
Fault finding/diagnosis	Troubleshooting	Swarf	Metal chips or debris
Float chamber	Float bowl	Tab washer	Tang or lock
Free-play	Lash	Tappet	Valve lifter
Freewheel	Coast	Thrust bearing	Throw-out bearing
Gearbox	Transmission	Top gear	High
Gearchange	Shift	Torch	Flashlight
Grub screw	Setscrew, Allen screw	Trackrod (of steering)	Tie-rod (or connecting rod)
Gudgeon pin	Piston pin or wrist pin	Trailing shoe (of brake)	Secondary shoe
Halfshaft	Axleshaft	Transmission	Whole drive line
Handbrake	Parking brake	Tyre	Tire
Hood	Soft top	Van	Panel wagon/van
Hot spot	Heat riser	Vice	Vise
Indicator	Turn signal	Wheel nut	Lug nut
Interior light	Dome lamp	Windscreen	Windshield
Layshaft (of gearbox)	Countershaft	Wing/mudguard	Fender
Leading shoe (of brake)	Primary shoe		

Buying spare parts and vehicle identification numbers

Buying spare parts

Replacement parts are available from many sources, which generally fall into one of two categories – authorized dealer parts departments and independent retail auto parts stores. Our advice concerning these parts is as follows:

Retail auto parts stores: Good auto parts stores will stock frequently needed components which wear out relatively fast, such as clutch components, exhaust systems, brake parts, tune-up parts, etc. These stores often supply new or reconditioned parts on an exchange basis, which can save a considerable amount of money. Discount auto parts stores are often very good places to buy materials and parts needed for general vehicle maintenance such as oil, grease, filters, spark plugs, belts, touch-up paint, bulbs, etc. They also usually sell tools and general accessories, have convenient hours, charge lower prices and can often be found not far from home.

Authorized dealer parts department: This is the best source for parts which are unique to the vehicle and not generally available elsewhere (such as major engine parts, transmission parts, trim pieces, etc.).

Warranty information: If the vehicle is still covered under warranty, be sure that any replacement parts purchased – regardless of the source – do not invalidate the warranty!

To be sure of obtaining the correct parts, have engine and chassis numbers available and, if possible, take the old parts along for positive identification.

Vehicle identification numbers

Modifications are a continuing and unpublicized process in vehicle manufacture quite apart from major model changes. Spare parts manuals and lists are compiled upon a numerical basis, individual vehicle numbers being essential to correct identification of the component required.

The *engine number* is located on the front left side of the cylinder block (photo).

The *chassis number* is located on top of the right side front wheel arch except on early 99 models where it is located on the left side (photo). It is also punched into the body in the luggage compartment or beneath the rear seat cushion.

The *gearbox number* is located on top of the primary gear casing (photo).

The *body and trim color codes* are either on the right or left side of the engine compartment.

Engine number on an H type engine

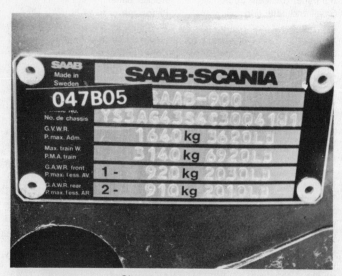

Chassis number plate

Gearbox number (as seen from front of car)

Tools and working facilities

Introduction

A selection of good tools is a fundamental requirement for anyone contemplating the maintenance and repair of a motor vehicle. For the owner who does not possess any, their purchase will prove a considerable expense, offsetting some of the savings made by doing-it-yourself. However, provided that the tools purchased are of good quality, they will last for many years and prove an extremely worthwhile investment.

To help the average owner to decide which tools are needed to carry out the various tasks detailed in this manual, we have compiled three lists of tools under the following headings: *Maintenance and minor repair, Repair and overhaul,* and *Special.* The newcomer to practical mechanics should start off with the *Maintenance and minor repair* tool kit and confine himself to the simpler jobs around the vehicle. Then, as his confidence and experience grow, he can undertake more difficult tasks, buying extra tools as, and when, they are needed. In this way, a *Maintenance and minor repair* tool kit can be built-up into a *Repair and overhaul* tool kit over a considerable period of time without any major cash outlays. The experienced do-it-yourselfer will have a tool kit good enough for most repair and overhaul procedures and will add tools from the *Special* category when he feels the expense is justified by the amount of use to which these tools will be put.

It is obviously not possible to cover the subject of tools fully here. For those who wish to learn more about tools and their use there is a book entitled *How to Choose and Use Car Tools* available from the publishers of this manual.

Maintenance and minor repair tool kit

The tools given in this list should be considered as a minimum requirement if routine maintenance, servicing and minor repair operations are to be undertaken. We recommend the purchase of combination spanners (ring one end, open-ended the other); although more expensive than open-ended ones, they do give the advantages of both types of spanner.

Combination spanners - 10, 11, 12, 13, 14 & 17 mm
Adjustable spanner - 9 inch
Gearbox/final drive drain plug key
Spark plug spanner (with rubber insert)
Spark plug gap adjustment tool
Set of feeler gauges
Brake bleed nipple spanner
Screwdriver - 4 in long x $\frac{1}{4}$ in dia (flat blade)
Screwdriver - 4 in long x $\frac{1}{4}$ in dia (cross blade)
Combination pliers - 6 inch
Hacksaw (junior)
Tyre pump
Tyre pressure gauge
Oil can
Fine emery cloth (1 sheet)
Wire brush (small)
Funnel (medium size)
Carburettor adjusting tool (photo)

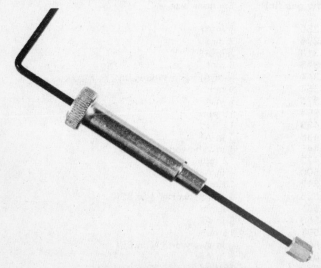

Carburettor adjusting tool

Tool kit provided with the car

Repair and overhaul tool kit

These tools are virtually essential for anyone undertaking any major repairs to a motor vehicle, and are additional to those given in the *Maintenance and minor repair* list. Included in this list is a comprehensive set of sockets. Although these are expensive they will be found invaluable as they are so versatile - particularly if various drives are included in the set. We recommend the $\frac{1}{2}$ in square-drive type, as this can be used with most proprietary torque wrenches. If you cannot afford a socket set, even bought piecemeal, then inexpensive tubular box spanners are a useful alternative.

The tools in this list will occasionally need to be supplemented by tools from the *Special* list.

Sockets (or box spanners) to cover range in previous list
Reversible ratchet drive (for use with sockets)
Extension piece, 10 inch (for use with sockets)
Universal joint (for use with sockets)
Torque wrench (for use with sockets)
'Mole' wrench - 8 inch
Ball pein hammer
Soft-faced hammer, plastic or rubber
Screwdriver - 6 in long x $\frac{5}{16}$ in dia (flat blade)
Screwdriver - 2 in long x $\frac{5}{16}$ in square (flat blade)
Screwdriver - 1$\frac{1}{2}$ in long x $\frac{1}{4}$ in dia (cross blade)
Screwdriver - 3 in long x $\frac{1}{8}$ in dia (electricians)
Pliers - electricians side cutters
Pliers - needle nosed
Pliers - circlip (internal and external)
Cold chisel - $\frac{1}{2}$ inch
Scriber
Scraper
Centre punch
Pin punch
Hacksaw
Valve grinding tool
Steel rule/straight-edge
Allen keys
Selection of files
Wire brush (large)
Axle-stands
Jack (strong scissor or hydraulic type)

Special tools

The tools in this list are those which are not used regularly, are expensive to buy, or which need to be used in accordance with their manufacturers' instructions. Unless relatively difficult mechanical jobs are undertaken frequently, it will not be economic to buy many of these tools. Where this is the case, you could consider clubbing together with friends (or joining a motorists' club) to make a joint purchase, or borrowing the tools against a deposit from a local garage or tool hire specialist.

The following list contains only those tools and instruments freely available to the public, and not those special tools produced by the vehicle manufacturer specifically for its dealer network. You will find occasional references to these manufacturers' special tools in the text of this manual. Generally, an alternative method of doing the job without the vehicle manufacturers' special tool is given. However, sometimes, there is no alternative to using them. Where this is the case and the relevant tool cannot be bought or borrowed, you will have to entrust the work to a franchised garage.

Valve spring compressor
Piston ring compressor
Balljoint separator
Universal hub/bearing puller
Impact screwdriver
Micrometer and/or vernier gauge
Dial gauge
Stroboscopic timing light
Dwell angle meter/tachometer
Universal electrical multi-meter
Cylinder compression gauge
Lifting tackle
Trolley jack
Light with extension lead

Buying tools

For practically all tools, a tool factor is the best source since he will have a very comprehensive range compared with the average garage or accessory shop. Having said that, accessory shops often offer excellent quality tools at discount prices, so it pays to shop around.

Remember, you don't have to buy the most expensive items on the shelf, but it is always advisable to steer clear of the very cheap tools. There are plenty of good tools around at reasonable prices, so ask the proprietor or manager of the shop for advice before making a purchase.

Care and maintenance of tools

Having purchased a reasonable tool kit, it is necessary to keep the tools in a clean serviceable condition. After use, always wipe off any dirt, grease and metal particles using a clean, dry cloth, before putting the tools away. Never leave them lying around after they have been used. A simple tool rack on the garage or workshop wall, for items such as screwdrivers and pliers is a good idea. Store all normal wrenches and sockets in a metal box. Any measuring instruments, gauges, meters, etc, must be carefully stored where they cannot be damaged or become rusty.

Take a little care when tools are used. Hammer heads inevitably become marked and screwdrivers lose the keen edge on their blades from time to time. A little timely attention with emery cloth or a file will soon restore items like this to a good serviceable finish.

Working facilities

Not to be forgotten when discussing tools, is the workshop itself. If anything more than routine maintenance is to be carried out, some form of suitable working area becomes essential.

It is appreciated that many an owner mechanic is forced by circumstances to remove an engine or similar item, without the benefit of a garage or workshop. Having done this, any repairs should always be done under the cover of a roof.

Wherever possible, any dismantling should be done on a clean, flat workbench or table at a suitable working height.

Any workbench needs a vice: one with a jaw opening of 4 in (100 mm) is suitable for most jobs. As mentioned previously, some clean dry storage space is also required for tools, as well as for lubricants, cleaning fluids, touch-up paints and so on, which become necessary.

Another item which may be required, and which has a much more general usage, is an electric drill with a chuck capacity of at least $\frac{5}{16}$ in (8 mm). This, together with a good range of twist drills, is virtually essential for fitting accessories such as mirrors and reversing lights.

Last, but not least, always keep a supply of old newspapers and clean, lint-free rags available, and try to keep any working area as clean as possible.

Spanner jaw gap comparison table

Jaw gap (in)	Spanner size
0.250	$\frac{1}{4}$ in AF
0.276	7 mm
0.313	$\frac{5}{16}$ in AF
0.315	8 mm
0.344	$\frac{11}{32}$ in AF; $\frac{1}{8}$ in Whitworth
0.354	9 mm
0.375	$\frac{3}{8}$ in AF
0.394	10 mm
0.433	11 mm
0.438	$\frac{7}{16}$ in AF
0.445	$\frac{3}{16}$ in Whitworth; $\frac{1}{4}$ in BSF
0.472	12 mm
0.500	$\frac{1}{2}$ in AF
0.512	13 mm
0.525	$\frac{1}{4}$ in Whitworth; $\frac{5}{16}$ in BSF
0.551	14 mm
0.563	$\frac{9}{16}$ in AF
0.591	15 mm
0.600	$\frac{5}{16}$ in Whitworth; $\frac{3}{8}$ in BSF
0.625	$\frac{5}{8}$ in AF
0.630	16 mm

Jaw gap (in)	Spanner size	Jaw gap (in)	Spanner size
0.669	17 mm	1.260	32 mm
0.686	$\frac{11}{16}$ in AF	1.300	$\frac{3}{4}$ in Whitworth; $\frac{7}{8}$ in BSF
0.709	18 mm	1.313	$1\frac{5}{16}$ in AF
0.710	$\frac{3}{8}$ in Whitworth; $\frac{7}{16}$ in BSF	1.390	$\frac{13}{16}$ in Whitworth; $\frac{15}{16}$ in BSF
0.748	19 mm	1.417	36 mm
0.750	$\frac{3}{4}$ in AF	1.438	$1\frac{7}{16}$ in AF
0.813	$\frac{13}{16}$ in AF	1.480	$\frac{7}{8}$ in Whitworth; 1 in BSF
0.820	$\frac{7}{16}$ in Whitworth; $\frac{1}{2}$ in BSF	1.500	$1\frac{1}{2}$ in AF
0.866	22 mm	1.575	40 mm; $\frac{15}{16}$ in Whitworth
0.875	$\frac{7}{8}$ in AF	1.614	41 mm
0.920	$\frac{1}{2}$ in Whitworth; $\frac{9}{16}$ in BSF	1.625	$1\frac{5}{8}$ in AF
0.938	$\frac{15}{16}$ in AF	1.670	1 in Whitworth; $1\frac{1}{8}$ in BSF
0.945	24 mm	1.688	$1\frac{11}{16}$ in AF
1.000	1 in AF	1.811	46 mm
1.010	$\frac{9}{16}$ in Whitworth; $\frac{5}{8}$ in BSF	1.813	$1\frac{13}{16}$ in AF
1.024	26 mm	1.860	$1\frac{1}{8}$ in Whitworth; $1\frac{1}{4}$ in BSF
1.063	$1\frac{1}{16}$ in AF; 27 mm	1.875	$1\frac{7}{8}$ in AF
1.100	$\frac{5}{8}$ in Whitworth; $\frac{11}{16}$ in BSF	1.969	50 mm
1.125	$1\frac{1}{8}$ in AF	2.000	2 in AF
1.181	30 mm	2.050	$1\frac{1}{4}$ in Whitworth; $1\frac{3}{8}$ in BSF
1.200	$\frac{11}{16}$ in Whitworth; $\frac{3}{4}$ in BSF	2.165	55 mm
1.250	$1\frac{1}{4}$ in AF	2.362	60 mm

General repair procedures

Whenever servicing, repair or overhaul work is carried out on the car or its components, it is necessary to observe the following procedures and instructions. This will assist in carrying out the operation efficiently and to a professional standard of workmanship.

Joint mating faces and gaskets

Where a gasket is used between the mating faces of two components, ensure that it is renewed on reassembly, and fit it dry unless otherwise stated in the repair procedure. Make sure that the mating faces are clean and dry with all traces of old gasket removed. When cleaning a joint face, use a tool which is not likely to score or damage the face, and remove any burrs or nicks with an oilstone or fine file.

Make sure that tapped holes are cleaned with a pipe cleaner, and keep them free of jointing compound if this is being used unless specifically instructed otherwise.

Ensure that all orifices, channels or pipes are clear and blow through them, preferably using compressed air.

Oil seals

Whenever an oil seal is removed from its working location, either individually or as part of an assembly, it should be renewed.

The very fine sealing lip of the seal is easily damaged and will not seal if the surface it contacts is not completely clean and free from scratches, nicks or grooves. If the original sealing surface of the component cannot be restored, the component should be renewed.

Protect the lips of the seal from any surface which may damage them in the course of fitting. Use tape or a conical sleeve where possible. Lubricate the seal lips with oil before fitting and, on dual lipped seals, fill the space between the lips with grease.

Unless otherwise stated, oil seals must be fitted with their sealing lips toward the lubricant to be sealed.

Use a tubular drift or block of wood of the appropriate size to install the seal and, if the seal housing is shouldered, drive the seal down to the shoulder. If the seal housing is unshouldered, the seal should be fitted with its face flush with the housing top face.

Screw threads and fastenings

Always ensure that a blind tapped hole is completely free from oil, grease, water or other fluid before installing the bolt or stud. Failure to do this could cause the housing to crack due to the hydraulic action of the bolt or stud as it is screwed in.

When tightening a castellated nut to accept a split pin, tighten the nut to the specified torque, where applicable, and then tighten further to the next split pin hole. Never slacken the nut to align a split pin hole unless stated in the repair procedure.

When checking or retightening a nut or bolt to a specified torque setting, slacken the nut or bolt by a quarter of a turn, and then retighten to the specified setting.

Locknuts, locktabs and washers

Any fastening which will rotate against a component or housing in the course of tightening should always have a washer between it and the relevant component or housing.

Spring or split washers should always be renewed when they are used to lock a critical component such as a big-end bearing retaining nut or bolt.

Locktabs which are folded over to retain a nut or bolt should always be renewed.

Self-locking nuts can be reused in non-critical areas, providing resistance can be felt when the locking portion passes over the bolt or stud thread.

Split pins must always be replaced with new ones of the correct size for the hole.

Special tools

Some repair procedures in this manual entail the use of special tools such as a press, two or three-legged pullers, spring compressors etc. Wherever possible, suitable readily available alternatives to the manufacturer's special tools are described, and are shown in use. In some instances, where no alternative is possible, it has been necessary to resort to the use of a manufacturer's tool and this has been done for reasons of safety as well as the efficient completion of the repair operation. Unless you are highly skilled and have a thorough understanding of the procedure described, never attempt to bypass the use of any special tool when the procedure described specifies its use. Not only is there a very great risk of personal injury, but expensive damage could be caused to the components involved.

Jacking and towing

The jack supplied with the car tool kit should only be used for changing roadwheels and must always be engaged with the recesses located on the sills (photos). When using a trolley jack the front of the car can be raised beneath the engine compartment crossmember, and the rear raised beneath the reinforced bracket immediately behind the fuel tank.

Towing eyes are provided at the front and rear of the car (photos).

The ignition key must be inserted and neutral selected. On automatic transmission models the transmission must contain the correct quantity of fluid, the towing speed must not exceed 25 mph (40 kph), and the towing distance must not exceed 25 miles (40 km). For longer distances the front of the car must be lifted clear of the ground. Push or tow starting is not possible on cars fitted with automatic transmission.

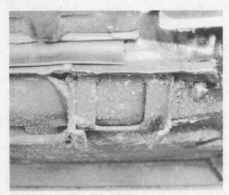

Recess for lifting jack

Tool kit jack in position

Spare wheel

Front towing eye

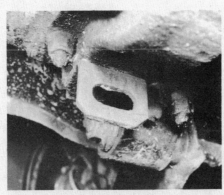

Alternative front towing eye on engine crossmember

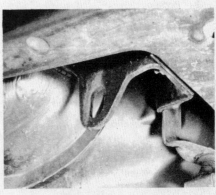

Rear towing eye

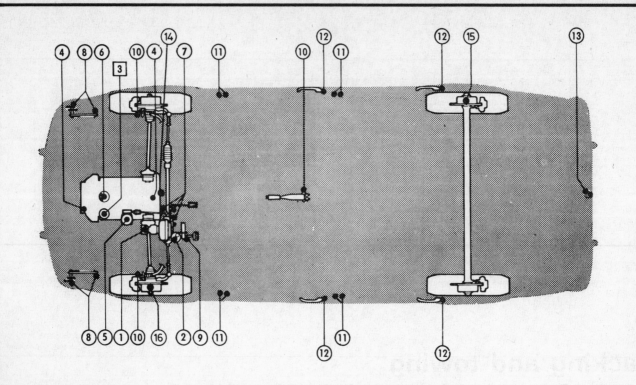

Recommended lubricants and fluids

Component or system	Lubricant type or specification
1 Brake hydraulic system	DOT 4 or SAE J1703
2 Clutch hydraulic system	DOT 4 or SAE J1703
3 Engine	SAE 10W/30, 10W/40 or 5W/30
4 Manual transmission Automatic transmission Final drive (automatic transmission)	SAE 10W/30 or 10W/40 Automatic transmission fluid SAE EP 80
5 Carburettor (damper oil)	Automatic transmission fluid
6 Distributor: Breaker cam Felt	 Bosch Ft1 v 4 grease Engine oil
7 Throttle control	Engine oil
8 Bonnet hinges	Engine oil
9 Pedals	Engine oil
10 Handbrake linkage	Chassis grease
11 Door hinges	Engine oil
12 Door locks	Chassis grease
13 Luggage compartment lock	Thin penetrating oil
14 Power steering	Saginaw hydraulic fluid
15 Rear wheel hubs	Special chassis grease
16 Front wheel bearings	Molybdenum paste

Safety first!

Regardless of how enthusiastic you may be about getting on with the job at hand, take the time to ensure that your safety is not jeopardized. A moment's lack of attention can result in an accident, as can failure to observe certain simple safety precautions. The possibility of an accident will always exist, and the following points should not be considered a comprehensive list of all dangers. Rather, they are intended to make you aware of the risks and to encourage a safety conscious approach to all work you carry out on your vehicle.

Essential DOs and DON'Ts

DON'T rely on a jack when working under the vehicle. Always use approved jackstands to support the weight of the vehicle and place them under the recommended lift or support points.

DON'T attempt to loosen extremely tight fasteners (i.e. wheel lug nuts) while the vehicle is on a jack — it may fall.

DON'T start the engine without first making sure that the transmission is in Neutral (or Park where applicable) and the parking brake is set.

DON'T remove the radiator cap from a hot cooling system — let it cool or cover it with a cloth and release the pressure gradually.

DON'T attempt to drain the engine oil until you are sure it has cooled to the point that it will not burn you.

DON'T touch any part of the engine or exhaust system until it has cooled sufficiently to avoid burns.

DON'T siphon toxic liquids such as gasoline, antifreeze and brake fluid by mouth, or allow them to remain on your skin.

DON'T inhale brake lining dust — it is potentially hazardous (see Asbestos below)

DON'T allow spilled oil or grease to remain on the floor — wipe it up before someone slips on it.

DON'T use loose fitting wrenches or other tools which may slip and cause injury.

DON'T push on wrenches when loosening or tightening nuts or bolts. Always try to pull the wrench toward you. If the situation calls for pushing the wrench away, push with an open hand to avoid scraped knuckles if the wrench should slip.

DON'T attempt to lift a heavy component alone — get someone to help you.

DON'T rush or take unsafe shortcuts to finish a job.

DON'T allow children or animals in or around the vehicle while you are working on it.

DO wear eye protection when using power tools such as a drill, sander, bench grinder, etc. and when working under a vehicle.

DO keep loose clothing and long hair well out of the way of moving parts.

DO make sure that any hoist used has a safe working load rating adequate for the job.

DO get someone to check on you periodically when working alone on a vehicle.

DO carry out work in a logical sequence and make sure that everything is correctly assembled and tightened.

DO keep chemicals and fluids tightly capped and out of the reach of children and pets.

DO remember that your vehicle's safety affects that of yourself and others. If in doubt on any point, get professional advice.

Asbestos

Certain friction, insulating, sealing, and other products — such as brake linings, brake bands, clutch linings, torque converters, gaskets, etc. — contain asbestos. *Extreme care must be taken to avoid inhalation of dust from such products since it is hazardous to health.* If in doubt, assume that they *do* contain asbestos.

Fire

Remember at all times that gasoline is highly flammable. Never smoke or have any kind of open flame around when working on a vehicle. But the risk does not end there. A spark caused by an electrical short circuit, by two metal surfaces contacting each other, or even by static electricity built up in your body under certain conditions, can ignite gasoline vapors, which in a confined space are highly explosive. Do not, under any circumstances, use gasoline for cleaning parts. Use an approved safety solvent.

Always disconnect the battery ground (–) cable *at the battery* before working on any part of the fuel system or electrical system. Never risk spilling fuel on a hot engine or exhaust component.

It is strongly recommended that a fire extinguisher suitable for use on fuel and electrical fires be kept handy in the garage or workshop at all times. Never try to extinguish a fuel or electrical fire with water.

Torch (flashlight in the US)

Any reference to a "torch" appearing in this manual should always be taken to mean a hand-held, battery-operated electric light or flashlight. It DOES NOT mean a welding or propane torch or blowtorch.

Fumes

Certain fumes are highly toxic and can quickly cause unconsciousness and even death if inhaled to any extent. Gasoline vapor falls into this category, as do the vapors from some cleaning solvents. Any draining or pouring of such volatile fluids should be done in a well ventilated area.

When using cleaning fluids and solvents, read the instructions on the container carefully. Never use materials from unmarked containers.

Never run the engine in an enclosed space, such as a garage. Exhaust fumes contain carbon monoxide, which is extremely poisonous. If you need to run the engine, always do so in the open air, or at least have the rear of the vehicle outside the work area.

If you are fortunate enough to have the use of an inspection pit, never drain or pour gasoline and never run the engine while the vehicle is over the pit. The fumes, being heavier than air, will concentrate in the pit with possibly lethal results.

The battery

Never create a spark or allow a bare light bulb near a battery. They normally give off a certain amount of hydrogen gas, which is highly explosive.

Always disconnect the battery ground (–) cable *at the battery* before working on the fuel or electrical systems.

If possible, loosen the filler caps or cover when charging the battery from an external source (this does not apply to sealed or maintenance-free batteries). Do not charge at an excessive rate or the battery may burst.

Take care when adding water to a non maintenance-free battery and when carrying a battery. The electrolyte, even when diluted, is very corrosive and should not be allowed to contact clothing or skin.

Always wear eye protection when cleaning the battery to prevent the caustic deposits from entering your eyes.

Mains electricity (household current in the US)

When using an electric power tool, inspection light, etc., which operates on household current, always make sure that the tool is correctly connected to its plug and that, where necessary, it is properly grounded. Do not use such items in damp conditions and, again, do not create a spark or apply excessive heat in the vicinity of fuel or fuel vapor.

Secondary ignition system voltage

A severe electric shock can result from touching certain parts of the ignition system (such as the spark plug wires) when the engine is running or being cranked, particularly if components are damp or the insulation is defective. In the case of an electronic ignition system, the secondary system voltage is much higher and could prove fatal.

Routine maintenance

For modifications, and information applicable to later models, see Supplement at end of manual

Maintenance is essential for ensuring safety and desirable for the purpose of getting the best in terms of performance and economy from the car. Over the years the need for periodic lubrication – oiling, greasing and so on – has been drastically reduced if not totally eliminated. This has unfortunately tended to lead some owners to think that because no such action is required the items either no longer exist or will last for ever. This is certainly not the case; it is essential to carry out regular visual examination as comprehensively as possible in order to spot any possible defects at an early stage before they develop into major expensive repairs.

Every 250 miles (400 km) or weekly – whichever comes first

Engine
Check the oil level and top up if necessary (photos)
Check the coolant level and top up if necessary

Tyres
Check the tyre pressures and adjust if necessary (photo)

Every 5000 miles (7500 km) on UK models – additional

Engine
Change engine oil on Turbo models
Clean fuel pump filter on carburettor engines
Renew spark plugs on Turbo models

Every 10 000 miles (15 000 km) on UK models – additional

Engine
Change oil and filter
Clean air cleaner element
Renew air cleaner element on Turbo models
Check fuel lines for security
Top up damper oil level on carburettor engines
Adjust slow running
Check exhaust system
Check cooling system hoses and antifreeze strength
Check all hoses and pipes for security
Adjust deceleration valve where applicable
Synchronise twin carburettors where applicable
Check and adjust choke control
Check all nuts and bolts for tightness
Check Turbo charging pressure and operation

Electrical
Check all drivebelts for condition and tension (photo)
Adjust headlamp alignment
Renew spark plugs
Check ignition leads
Renew contact breaker points where applicable

Adjust ignition timing
Check battery terminals and electrolyte level where applicable
Check operation of electrical components

Gearbox/transmission
Check oil/fluid level and top up if necessary (photos)
Check differential oil level and top up if necessary (automatic transmission models only)

Brakes
Check brake fluid level and top up if necessary
Check disc pads for wear
Check hydraulic system for security
Grease front brake caliper yokes with special grease
Check handbrake operation

Steering and suspension
Check toe-in and adjust if necessary
Check power steering fluid level and top up if necessary
Check suspension balljoints and rubbers
Check driveshaft joint bellows
Check steering track rod end joints and rubbers

Body
Lubricate door and bonnet locks and hinges
Check wiper blades and washer system (photo)

Every 20 000 miles (30 000 km) on UK models – additional

Engine
Check and adjust valve clearances on 99 models only
Renew delay valve

Automatic transmission
Renew fluid, clean filter, and adjust downshift and selector cables at first 20 000 miles (30 000 km) only

Body
Renew air filter for passenger compartment on 900 models only

Every 30 000 miles (45 000 km) on UK models – additional

Engine
Renew air cleaner element
Check and adjust valve clearances
Renew the fuel filter on fuel injection engines
Clean Turbo charge pressure regulator on 99 models only

Automatic transmission
Change final drive oil

Brakes
 Change brake fluid (at least once every two years)

Steering
 Check camber and caster

**Every 5000 miles (7500 km) on 1979 North American models –
additional**

Engine
 Check exhaust system
 Check all hoses
 Check coolant level and strength of antifreeze
 Change oil and filter on Turbo models

Gearbox/transmission
 Check manual gearbox oil level and top up if necessary

 Check automatic transmission fluid level and differential oil level
 and top up if necessary

Electrical system
 Check battery terminals for security
 Check operation of electrical components
 Check headlamp alignment

Brakes
 Check handbrake operation
 Check hydraulic system for security
 Check disc pads for wear
 Check brake and clutch fluid level and top up if necessary

Steering and suspension
 Check power steering fluid level and top up if necessary
 Check driveshaft joint bellows
 Check toe-in and adjust if necessary

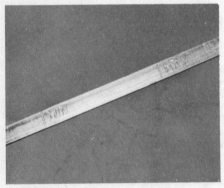
Engine oil level dipstick markings

Topping up the engine oil level

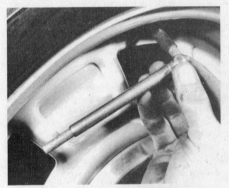
Checking the tyre pressures

Checking power steering gear drivebelt tension

Removing manual gearbox oil level dipstick

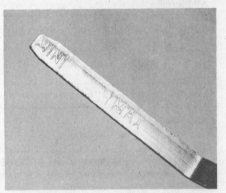
Manual gearbox level dipstick markings

Washer fluid reservoir

Using $\frac{3}{8}$ inch square key to remove manual gearbox drain plug

Checking the tyre tread depth

Every 15 000 miles (24 000 km) on 1979 North American models – additional

Engine
Check and adjust all drivebelts
Check and adjust valve clearances
Tighten cylinder head bolts
Renew spark plugs
Renew contact breaker points and condenser where applicable
Adjust ignition timing and clean ignition leads
Check distributor cap and rotor
Renew air cleaner element
Check fuel lines and lubricate throttle control
Check charcoal canister
Adjust slow running
Clean EGR components and check operation
Check pulse air system
Check deceleration valve
Renew oxygen sensor
Check Turbo system

Gearbox/transmission
Change manual gearbox oil (photo)
Change differential oil on automatic transmission models

Steering and suspension
Check suspension balljoints and rubbers
Check driveshaft joint bellows
Check steering track rod end joints and rubbers
Check camber and caster angles
Check steering gear oil level and top up if necessary

Body
Lubricate door and bonnet locks and hinges

Every 30 000 miles (48 000 km) on 1979 North American models – additional

Engine
Renew the distributor cap and rotor
Renew charcoal canister
Clean Turbo pressure regulator

Every 2 years on 1979 North American models – additional

Engine
Renew coolant and antifreeze

Every 7500 miles (12 000 km) on non-Turbo models or 5000 miles (7500 km) on Turbo models or every 6 months, on 1980 on North American models – additional

Engine
Change oil and filter
Tighten cylinder head and manifold bolts (1981 on)
Check cooling system hoses and antifreeze content
Check exhaust system

Gearbox/transmission
Check oil/fluid level and top up if necessary
Check differential oil level and top up if necessary

Electrical
Check battery terminals and electrolyte level where applicable
Check operation of electrical components

Steering and suspension
Check toe-in and adjust if necessary
Check power steering fluid level and top up if necessary
Check suspension balljoints and rubbers
Check driveshaft joint bellows
Check steering track rod end joints and rubbers

Brakes
Check hydraulic system for security
Check vacuum servo unit
Check handbrake operation
Check disc pads for wear
Check brake fluid level and top up if necessary

Every 15 000 miles (24 000 km) or every 12 months on 1980 on North American models – additional

Engine
Check fuel injection system where applicable
Check Turbo charging pressure and over-pressure switch operation
Check and adjust valve clearances

Electrical
Check headlamp alignment

Brakes
Grease front brake caliper yokes with special grease

Steering and suspension
Check wheel alignment
Check suspension balljoints and rubbers
Check driveshaft joint bellows
Check steering track rod end joints and rubbers
Check tyre tread depth (photo)

Automatic transmission
Change hydraulic fluid (once only at 15 000 miles)

Body
Renew passenger compartment air filter
Lubricate door and bonnet locks and hinges

Every 30 000 miles (48 000 km) on 1980 on North American models – additional

Engine
Change coolant and antifreeze
Check and adjust drivebelts
Renew spark plugs
Renew air cleaner element
Renew fuel filter (1980)
Clean ignition wires
Renew oxygen sensor

Brakes
Change brake fluid

Every 50 000 miles (80 000 km) on 1980 on North American models – additional

Engine
Renew the fuel filter

Every 60 000 miles (96 000 km) on 1980 on North American models – additional

Engine
Check fuel evaporative emission control system
Renew charcoal canister
Check resistance of ignition HT leads
Renew distributor cap and rotor
Adjust slow running
Check deceleration system
Check ignition timing advance operation
Clean EGR system

Under-bonnet view (fuel injection model)

1 Chassis number plate
2 Interior air filter
  location
3 Power steering pump
4 Engine oil filler cap

5 Distributor
6 Thermostat housing
7 Injector
8 Water pump
9 Inlet manifold

10 Brake/clutch fluid
   reservoir
11 Coolant expansion tank
12 Fuse box

13 Fuel filter
14 Fuel distributor
15 Gearbox
16 Coil

17 Warm up regulator
18 Electric cooling fan
19 Battery
20 Washer fluid reservoir

View of front underside of car

| 1 Exhaust system | 3 Shock absorber | 5 Brake caliper | 7 Engine oil drain plug | 9 Steering gear |
| 2 Steering track rod | 4 Lower control arm | 6 Crossmember | 8 Gearbox oil drain plug | 10 Jacking point |

View of rear underside of car

1	Trailing arm	5	Brake caliper
2	Exhaust system	6	Link
3	Shock absorber	7	Fuel tank
4	Rear axle tube	8	Fuel accumulator
		9	Brake hydraulic hoses
		10	Jacking point

Fault diagnosis

Introduction

The vehicle owner who does his or her own maintenance according to the recommended schedules should not have to use this section of the manual very often. Modern component reliability is such that, provided those items subject to wear or deterioration are inspected or renewed at the specified intervals, sudden failure is comparatively rare. Faults do not usually just happen as a result of sudden failure, but develop over a period of time. Major mechanical failures in particular are usually preceded by characteristic symptoms over hundreds or even thousands of miles. Those components which do occasionally fail without warning are often small and easily carried in the vehicle.

With any fault finding, the first step is to decide where to begin investigations. Sometimes this is obvious, but on other occasions a little detective work will be necessary. The owner who makes half a dozen haphazard adjustments or replacements may be successful in curing a fault (or its symptoms), but he will be none the wiser if the fault recurs and he may well have spent more time and money than was necessary. A calm and logical approach will be found to be more satisfactory in the long run. Always take into account any warning signs or abnormalities that may have been noticed in the period preceding the fault – power loss, high or low gauge readings, unusual noises or smells, etc – and remember that failure of components such as fuses or spark plugs may only be pointers to some underlying fault.

The pages which follow here are intended to help in cases of failure to start or breakdown on the road. There is also a Fault Diagnosis Section at the end of each Chapter which should be consulted if the preliminary checks prove unfruitful. Whatever the fault, certain basic principles apply. These are as follows:

Verify the fault. This is simply a matter of being sure that you know what the symptoms are before starting work. This is particularly important if you are investigating a fault for someone else who may not have described it very accurately.

Don't overlook the obvious. For example, if the vehicle won't start, is there petrol in the tank? (Don't take anyone else's word on this particular point, and don't trust the fuel gauge either!) If an electrical fault is indicated, look for loose or broken wires before digging out the test gear.

Cure the disease, not the symptom. Substituting a flat battery with a fully charged one will get you off the hard shoulder, but if the underlying cause is not attended to, the new battery will go the same way. Similarly, changing oil-fouled spark plugs for a new set will get you moving again, but remember that the reason for the fouling (if it wasn't simply an incorrect grade of plug) will have to be established and corrected.

Don't take anything for granted. Particularly, don't forget that a 'new' component may itself be defective (especially if it's been rattling round in the boot for months), and don't leave components out of a fault diagnosis sequence just because they are new or recently fitted. When you do finally diagnose a difficult fault, you'll probably realise that all the evidence was there from the start.

Electrical faults

Electrical faults can be more puzzling than straightforward mechanical failures, but they are no less susceptible to logical analysis if the basic principles of operation are understood. Vehicle electrical wiring exists in extremely unfavourable conditions – heat, vibration and chemical attack – and the first things to look for are loose or corroded connections and broken or chafed wires, especially where the wires pass through holes in the bodywork or are subject to vibration.

All metal-bodied vehicles in current production have one pole of the battery 'earthed', ie connected to the vehicle bodywork, and in nearly all modern vehicles it is the negative (–) terminal. The various electrical components – motors, bulb holders etc – are also connected to earth, either by means of a lead or directly by their mountings. Electric current flows through the component and then back to the battery via the bodywork. If the component mounting is loose or corroded, or if a good path back to the battery is not available, the circuit will be incomplete and malfunction will result. The engine and/or gearbox are also earthed by means of flexible metal straps to the body or subframe; if these straps are loose or missing, starter motor, generator and ignition trouble may result.

Assuming the earth return to be satisfactory, electrical faults will be due either to component malfunction or to defects in the current supply. Individual components are dealt with in Chapter 10. If supply wires are broken or cracked internally this results in an open-circuit, and the easiest way to check for this is to bypass the suspect wire temporarily with a length of wire having a crocodile clip or suitable connector at each end. Alternatively, a 12V test lamp can be used to verify the presence of supply voltage at various points along the wire and the break can be thus isolated.

If a bare portion of a live wire touches the bodywork or other earthed metal part, the electricity will take the low-resistance path thus formed back to the battery: this is known as a short-circuit. Hopefully a short-circuit will blow a fuse, but otherwise it may cause burning of the insulation (and possibly further short-circuits) or even a fire. This is why it is inadvisable to bypass persistently blowing fuses with silver foil or wire.

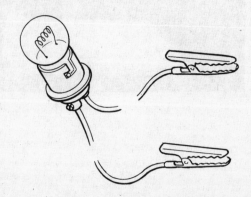

A simple test lamp is useful for tracing electrical faults

Spares and tool kit

Most vehicles are supplied only with sufficient tools for wheel changing; the *Maintenance and minor repair* tool kit detailed in *Tools and working facilities*, with the addition of a hammer, is probably sufficient for those repairs that most motorists would consider attempting at the roadside. In addition a few items which can be fitted without too much trouble in the event of a breakdown should be carried. Experience and available space will modify the list below, but the following may save having to call on professional assistance:

Spark plugs, clean and correctly gapped
HT lead and plug cap – long enough to reach the plug furthest from the distributor
Distributor rotor, condenser and contact breaker points
Drivebelt(s) – emergency type may suffice
Spare fuses
Set of principal light bulbs
Tin of radiator sealer and hose bandage
Exhaust bandage
Roll of insulating tape
Length of soft iron wire
Length of electrical flex
Torch or inspection lamp (can double as test lamp)
Battery jump leads
Tow-rope
Ignition waterproofing aerosol
Litre of engine oil
Sealed can of hydraulic fluid
Emergency windscreen
'Jubilee' clips
Tube of filler paste

If spare fuel is carried, a can designed for the purpose should be used to minimise risks of leakage and collision damage. A first aid kit and a warning triangle, whilst not at present compulsory in the UK, are obviously sensible items to carry in addition to the above.

When touring abroad it may be advisable to carry additional spares which, even if you cannot fit them yourself, could save having to wait while parts are obtained. The items below may be worth considering:

Choke and throttle cables
Cylinder head gasket
Alternator brushes
Fuel pump repair kit
Tyre valve core

One of the motoring organisations will be able to advise on availability of fuel etc in foreign countries.

Engine will not start

Engine fails to turn when starter operated

Flat battery (recharge, use jump leads, or push start where possible)
Battery terminals loose or corroded
Battery earth to body defective
Engine earth strap loose or broken
Starter motor (or solenoid) wiring loose or broken
Automatic transmission selector in wrong position, or inhibitor switch faulty
Ignition/starter switch faulty
Major mechanical failure (seizure)
Starter or solenoid internal fault (see Chapter 10)

Starter motor turns engine slowly

Partially discharged battery (recharge, use jump leads, or push start)
Battery terminals loose or corroded
Battery earth to body defective
Engine earth strap loose
Starter motor (or solenoid) wiring loose
Starter motor internal fault (see Chapter 10)

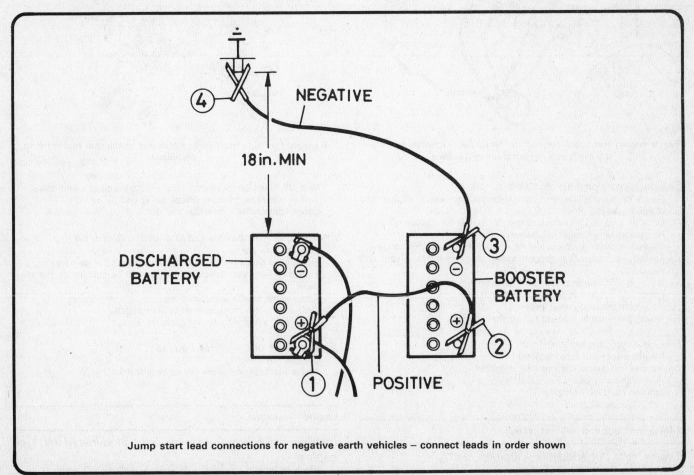

Jump start lead connections for negative earth vehicles – connect leads in order shown

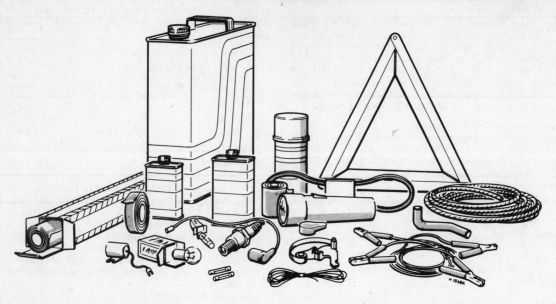

Carrying a few spares can save you a long walk!

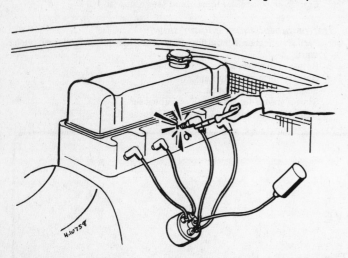

Crank engine and check for a spark. Note use of insulated pliers – dry cloth or a rubber glove will suffice

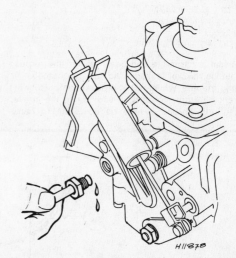

Remove fuel pipe from carburettor and check that fuel is being delivered

Engine turns normally but fails to start
Damp or dirty HT leads and distributor cap (crank engine and check for spark)
Dirty or incorrectly gapped distributor points (if applicable)
No fuel in tank (check for delivery)
Excessive choke (hot engine) or insufficient choke (cold engine)
Fouled or incorrectly gapped spark plugs (remove, clean and regap)
Other ignition system fault (see Chapter 4)
Other fuel system fault (see Chapter 3)
Poor compression (see Chapter 1)
Major mechanical failure (eg camshaft drive)

Engine fires but will not run
Insufficient choke (cold engine)
Air leaks at carburettor or inlet manifold
Fuel starvation (see Chapter 3)
Ignition fault (see Chapter 4)

Engine cuts out and will not restart

Engine cuts out suddenly – ignition fault
Loose or disconnected LT wires

Wet HT leads or distributor cap (after traversing water splash)
Coil or condenser failure (check for spark)
Other ignition fault (see Chapter 4)

Engine misfires before cutting out – fuel fault
Fuel tank empty
Fuel pump defective or filter blocked (check for delivery)
Fuel tank filler vent blocked (suction will be evident on releasing cap)
Carburettor needle valve sticking
Carburettor jets blocked (fuel contaminated)
Other fuel system fault (see Chapter 3)

Engine cuts out – other causes
Serious overheating
Major mechanical failure (eg camshaft drive)

Engine overheats

Ignition (no-charge) warning light illuminated (H type engine)
Slack or broken drivebelt – retension or renew (Chapter 2)

Ignition warning light not illuminated

Coolant loss due to internal or external leakage (see Chapter 2)
Thermostat defective
Low oil level
Brakes binding
Radiator clogged externally or internally
Electric cooling fan not operating correctly
Engine waterways clogged
Ignition timing incorrect or automatic advance malfunctioning
Mixture too weak

Note: *Do not add cold water to an overheated engine or damage may result*

Low engine oil pressure

Gauge reads low or warning light illuminated with engine running

Oil level low or incorrect grade
Defective gauge or sender unit
Wire to sender unit earthed
Engine overheating
Oil filter clogged or bypass valve defective
Oil pressure relief valve defective
Oil pick-up strainer clogged
Oil pump worn or mountings loose
Worn main or big-end bearings

Note: *Low oil pressure in a high-mileage engine at tickover is not necessarily a cause for concern. Sudden pressure loss at speed is far more significant. In any event, check the gauge or warning light sender before condemning the engine.*

Engine noises

Pre-ignition (pinking) on acceleration

Incorrect grade of fuel
Ignition timing incorrect
Distributor faulty or worn
Worn or maladjusted carburettor
Excessive carbon build-up in engine

Whistling or wheezing noises

Leaking vacuum hose
Leaking carburettor or manifold gasket
Blowing head gasket

Tapping or rattling

Incorrect valve clearances
Worn valve gear
Worn timing chain
Broken piston ring (ticking noise)

Knocking or thumping

Unintentional mechanical contact
Worn drivebelt
Peripheral component fault (generator, water pump etc)
Worn big-end bearings (regular heavy knocking, perhaps less under load)
Worn main bearings (rumbling and knocking, perhaps worsening under load)
Piston slap (most noticeable when cold)

Chapter 1 Engine

For modifications, and information applicable to later models, see Supplement at end of manual

Contents

Specifications

Type	Four cylinder in-line, single overhead camshaft engine mounted with flywheel at front of car
Identification:	
Type B engine	Pre-October 1981
Type H engine	October 1981 on

Compression ratio

UK models

B engine:
Turbo	7.2 to 1
Non-Turbo	9.2 to 1

H engine:
Turbo (except APC)	7.2 to 1
Turbo APC	8.5 to 1
Non-Turbo	9.5 to 1

North American models

B engine:
Turbo	7.2 to 1
1979 with catalyst	8.7 to 1
1979 without catalyst	9.25 to 1
1980 on models excluding Turbo	9.25 to 1

H engine:
Turbo	7.2 to 1
USA excluding Turbo	9.25 to 1
Canada excluding Turbo	9.5 to 1

General

Bore	3.543 in (90.0 mm)
Stroke	3.071 in (78.0 mm)
Capacity	121.0 cu in (1985 cm³)
Firing order (number 1 at rear)	1–3–4–2

B engine

Front

H engine

Cylinder location and distributor rotation

Idling speed – B engine:
    Single carburettor and Turbo 99 models .... 875 ± 50 rpm
    99 models except single carburettor and Turbo .... 850 ± 50 rpm
    900 models .... 850 ± 50 rpm
Idling speed – H engine:
    UK models .... 850 ± 50 rpm
    North American models .... 875 ± 50 rpm
Engine weight (approx) .... 308 lb (140 kg)

Cylinder block
Bore:
    Standard A type .... 3.5433 to 3.5437 in (90.000 to 90.010 mm)
    Standard B type .... 3.5437 to 3.5441 in (90.010 to 90.020 mm)
    1st oversize .... 3.5630 in (90.500 mm)
    2nd oversize .... 3.5827 in (91.000 mm)

Cylinder head
Maximum grinding .... 0.016 in (0.4 mm)
Depth .... 3.652 ± 0.002 in (92.75 ± 0.05 mm)

Pistons
Number of rings .... 2 compression, 1 oil scraper
Clearance of piston .... 0.001 to 0.002 in (0.025 to 0.051 mm)
Gudgeon pin diameter .... 0.9447 to 0.9449 in (23.996 to 24.000 mm)

Piston rings
Gap (in new cylinder):
    Top compression .... 0.014 to 0.022 in (0.35 to 0.55 mm)
    Bottom compression .... 0.012 to 0.018 in (0.30 to 0.45 mm)
    Oil scraper .... 0.015 to 0.055 in (0.38 to 1.40 mm)
Clearance in groove:
    Top compression .... 0.002 to 0.003 in (0.050 to 0.076 mm)
    Bottom compression .... 0.0016 to 0.0028 in (0.040 to 0.072 mm)

Connecting rods
Small-end bush diameter .... 0.9450 to 0.9453 in (24.004 to 24.010 mm)
Maximum difference in weight .... 6.0 grams

Crankshaft
Number of main bearings 5
Crankpin diameter:
    Standard .... 2.0465 to 2.0472 in (51.981 to 52.000 mm)
    1st undersize .... 2.0367 to 2.0374 in (51.731 to 51.750 mm)
    2nd undersize .... 2.0268 to 2.0276 in (51.481 to 51.500 mm)
    3rd undersize .... 2.0172 to 2.0177 in (51.237 to 51.250 mm)
    4th undersize .... 2.0074 to 2.0079 in (50.987 to 51.000 mm)
Main bearing pin diameter:
    Standard .... 2.2827 to 1.2835 in (57.981 to 58.000 mm)
    1st undersize .... 2.2729 to 2.2736 in (57.731 to 57.750 mm)
    2nd undersize .... 2.2630 to 2.2638 in (57.481 to 57.500 mm)
    3rd undersize .... 2.2534 to 2.2539 in (57.237 to 57.250 mm)
    4th undersize .... 2.2436 to 2.2441 in (56.987 to 57.000 mm)
Endfloat .... 0.003 to 0.011 in (0.08 to 0.28 mm)
Main bearing running clearance .... 0.0008 to 0.0024 in (0.020 to 0.062 mm)
Big-end bearing running clearance .... 0.0010 to 0.0024 in (0.026 to 0.062 mm)

Camshaft
Number of bearings 5
Endfloat .... 0.003 to 0.010 in (0.08 to 0.25 mm)

Valve timing
B engine

	Carburettor	Injection	Turbo
Inlet opens	10° BTDC	10° BTDC	12° BTDC
Inlet closes	54° ABDC	54° ABDC	40° ABDC
Exhaust opens	54° BBDC	46° BBDC	62° BBDC
Exhaust closes	10° ATDC	18° ATDC	12° ATDC

H engine

	Standard	Turbo	Turbo APC
Inlet opens	10° BTDC	12° BTDC	10° BTDC
Inlet closes	54° ABDC	40° ABDC	54° ABDC
Exhaust opens	46° BBDC	62° BBDC	46° BBDC
Exhaust closes	18° ATDC	12° ATDC	18° ATDC

Valves
Valve head angle .... 44.5°
Valve seat angle .... 45.0°
Valve seat width .... 0.039 to 0.079 in (1 to 2 mm)

1

Maximum valve play in guide	0.020 in (0.5 mm)
Valve guide length	1.837 in (46.65 mm)
Valve spring free length	1.697 in (43.1 mm)
Valve clearances – cold (at least 30 minutes after switching off):	
Inlet	0.008 to 0.010 in (0.20 to 0.25 mm)
Exhaust – non-Turbo	0.016 to 0.018 in (0.40 to 0.45 mm)
Exhaust – Turbo	0.018 to 0.020 in (0.45 to 0.50 mm)
Idler shaft endfloat (B engine only)	0.002 to 0.005 in (0.05 to 0.13 mm)

Lubrication system

Type	Forced flow with bi-rotor oil pump driven by idler shaft (B engine) or crankshaft (H engine)
Oil pump (B engine) – Rotor to housing clearance	0.002 to 0.003 in (0.05 to 0.09 mm)
Pressure relief valve open pressure:	
B engine	4 to 5 bar (57 to 71 lbf/in^2)
H engine	3.6 to 5.2 bar (51 to 74 lbf/in^2)
Pressure warning light operating pressure	0.3 to 0.5 bar (4.2 to 7.1 lbf/in^2)
Minimum oil pressure at 2000 rpm	3.0 bar (43.0 lbf/in^2)
Oil capacity (including filter)	6.0 Imp pt; 3.7 US qt; 3.5 litre

Torque wrench settings

	lbf ft	Nm
Main bearings	79	108
Big-end bearings	40	54
Camshaft bearing caps	13	18
Valve cover (B engine)	1.4	2.0
Crankshaft pulley bolt	137	190
Crankshaft oil seal housing	14	20
Idler shaft plate (B engine)	14	20
Flywheel	43	59
Oil pump	13	18
Cylinder head bolts:		
Stage 1	44	60
Stage 2	65	90
Stage 3	Run engine to normal operating temperature and allow to cool	
Stage 4	65	90
Stage 5	Further ¼ turn (90°)	
Sprocket (idler shaft on B engine)	18	25
Sprocket (camshaft)	14	20
Valve cover (H engine)	3.6	4.9
Timing cover (H engine)	14	20
Oil filter	7.2	10
Oil pressure switch	7.2	10

1   General description

The engine is of four cylinder in-line, single overhead camshaft type mounted at the front of the car with the flywheel facing forwards. Drive to the front wheels is through the gearbox attached to the bottom of the engine.

The type B engine fitted up to October 1981 was modified to the lighter type H engine. The engines are similar, but the type B engine incorporates an idler shaft to drive the distributor, water pump, oil pump, and fuel pump.

The crankshaft incorporates five main bearings with thrust washers fitted to the centre main bearing in order to control crankshaft endfloat.

Fig. 1.1 B type engine (Sec 1)

Fig. 1.2 H type engine (Sec 1)

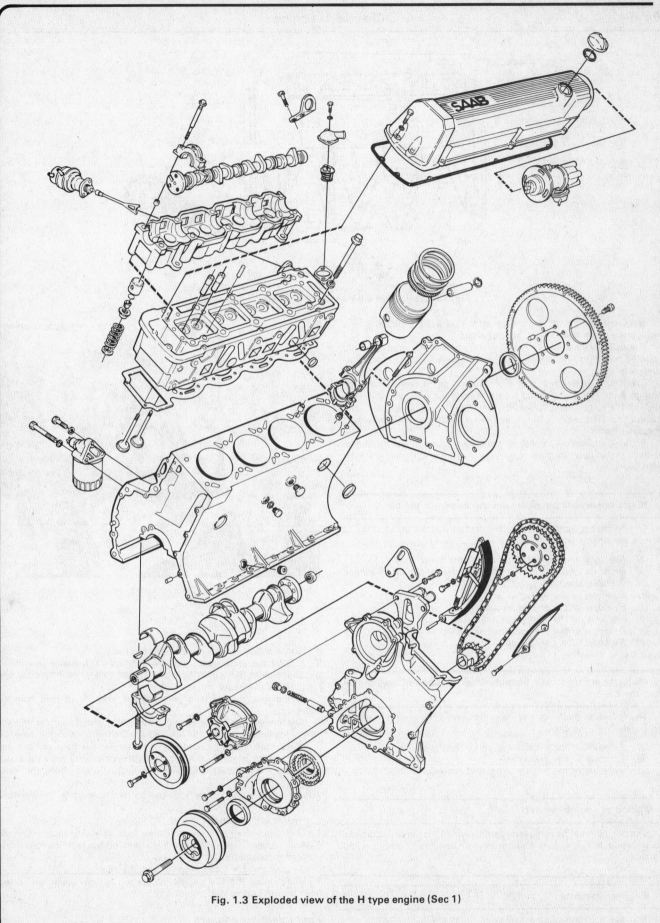

Fig. 1.3 Exploded view of the H type engine (Sec 1)

1

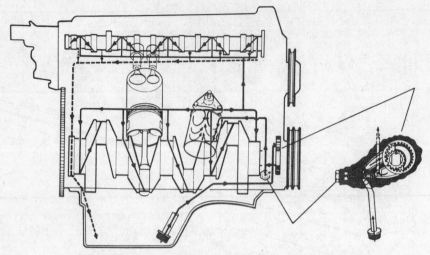

Fig. 1.4 Lubrication diagram for the H type engine (Sec 1)

The camshaft is driven by chain from the crankshaft, and on B type engines the chain also drives the idler shaft.

The cylinder head is of crossflow design with the inlet manifold mounted on the left-hand side and the exhaust manifold on the right-hand side.

Lubrication is by means of a bi-rotor oil pump which draws oil through a strainer and pick-up tube and forces it through a full-flow filter to the crankshaft, camshaft, idler shaft (type B engine), and timing chain. The pistons, bores, and valve mechanism are lubricated by splash feed.

A fully enclosed crankcase ventilation system is employed whereby piston blow-by gases are drawn into the inlet manifold via the valve cover.

2   Major operations possible with the engine in the car

The following operations can be carried out without having to remove the engine from the car:

(a) Removal and servicing of the cylinder head
(b) Removal of the camshaft (after removal of the cylinder head if necessary)
(c) Removal of the oil pump
(d) Removal of the engine mountings
(e) Removal of the clutch and flywheel
(f) Removal of the crankshaft oil seals
(g) Removal of the timing chain

3   Major operations only possible after removal of the engine from the car

The following operations can only be carried out after removal of the engine from the car:

(a) Removal of the pistons and connecting rods
(b) Removal of the crankshaft
(c) Renewal of the main and big-end bearings

4   Method of engine removal

The engine must be removed together with the gearbox/automatic transmission then the two units separated from each other on the bench.

5   Engine – removal

1   Remove the battery as described in Chapter 10.
2   Drain the cooling system as described in Chapter 2.
3   Remove the bonnet as described in Chapter 12.

5.5 Engine earth strap location showing front engine mounting

4   Loosen the clip and remove the top hose.
5   Unbolt the earth strap from the gearbox/transmission (photo).
6   Disconnect the wiring from the starter motor. Identify each lead for location to ensure correct refitting.
7   Disconnect the HT lead from the coil, and the LT lead from the distributor.
8   Disconnect the wiring from the water temperature sender unit and where applicable detach the wiring harness from the clutch cover.
9   If the clutch is to be removed (ie for engine overhaul) remove it at this stage with reference to Chapter 5. Alternatively, remove the clutch cover then disconnect and plug the hydraulic line from the slave cylinder.
10 Loosen the clip and remove the bottom hose from the radiator.

Carburettor engines
11 Remove the air cleaner and intake hose with reference to Chapter 3. Also remove the preheater hose and disconnect the crankcase ventilation hose(s).
12 Disconnect the accelerator and choke cables.
13 Disconnect the fuel supply and return (where applicable) hoses from the fuel pump and carburettor.

Fuel injection engines
14 Disconnect the hot air hose and the air inlet hose.
15 Disconnect the accelerator cable.

Fig. 1.5 Disconnecting the automatic transmission selector rod (Sec 5)

16 Identify the fuel injection system wiring then disconnect it from the warm-up regulator/boost control, cold start valve, thermo-time switch and auxiliary air valve.
17 Disconnect the fuel supply pipes from the mixture control unit and warm-up regulator.
18 If necessary for additional working room remove the air cleaner and mixture control unit.
19 Where applicable on APC versions disconnect the wiring from the solenoid valve and remove the valve, connector, and knock detector.
20 Where applicable on North American models disconnect the wiring from the oxygen sensor on the lambda system and also disconnect the wiring from the throttle valve switch.

All engines
21 Disconnect the wiring from the oil pressure sender unit.
22 Disconnect the hose from the expansion tank, and heater – note that the top heater hose connects to the water pump, the bottom hose to the inlet manifold.
23 Disconnect the vacuum hoses from the brake servo and heater control supply.
24 Disconnect the wiring from the radiator cooling fan motor and thermo-switch, and where applicable the headlights and headlight wipers.
25 On automatic transmission models disconnect the wiring from the switch on the transmission.
26 Identify for location then disconnect the wiring from the alternator.
27 Disconnect the main wiring harness connector and remove the harness from the engine.

99 models
28 Disconnect the headlight wiper linkage.
29 Remove the grille, disconnect the bonnet cable, then remove the retaining screws and withdraw the complete front panel and radiator from the car (photo).

All models
30 Where applicable disconnect and plug the hydraulic hoses from the oil cooler.
31 Jack up the front of the car and support it on axle stands. Chock the rear wheels.
32 Loosen the clips and disconnect the rubber bellows from the inner ends of the driveshafts.
33 Disconnect the speedometer cable from the rear of the gearbox/transmission (photo).
34 Remove both front wheels then jack up the suspension on each side in turn and place a metal or hardwood block between the upper control arm and the body. Lower the jack.
35 Unscrew and remove the bolts securing the lower control arms to the lower balljoints then pull out each driveshaft and disconnect them from the inner driveshafts.

Manual gearbox models
36 With the gear lever in neutral unscrew the nut from the gearshift rod, tap out the tapered pin, and separate the two rods (photo).

5.29 Removing the front panel and radiator on 99 models

5.33 Speedometer cable connection on the gearbox

5.36 Gearshift rod connection on manual gearbox models

1

5.41 Right-hand side rear engine mounting on a 900 model

5.43 Lifting out the engine

Automatic transmission models

37 Unscrew the screw for the selector cable at the transmission, then withdraw the cable with the selector rod fully forward in position P. Slide back the sleeve and unhook the cable.

All models

38 Disconnect the exhaust downpipe from the manifold.
39 Where applicable remove the power steering pump belt with reference to Chapter 11 then with the mounting bolts/nuts loosened detach the pump and place it to one side of the engine compartment. Do not disconnect the hydraulic hoses.
40 Attach a suitable hoist to the engine hangers and take the weight of the unit.
41 Unscrew and remove the rear engine mounting bolts (photo).
42 Loosen only the front engine mounting bolt – do not remove the bolt as the bracket has open ended slots.
43 Lift the engine from the engine compartment taking care not to damage components on the bulkhead and side panels (photo).

6 Engine – separation from gearbox/automatic transmission

1 Clean the engine and gearbox/automatic transmission and wipe dry.
2 Unscrew the drain plugs and drain the engine oil and gearbox/automatic transmission oil/fluid (photo).
3 Unbolt the cover from the flywheel if still fitted, then remove the starter motor as described in Chapter 10.
4 On manual gearbox models remove the clutch as described in Chapter 5 if still fitted. Unscrew the bolts securing the gearbox to the engine then lift up the engine and remove the gasket. Note the location of stays and brackets (photo).
5 On automatic transmission models disconnect the downshift cable then unscrew the bolts securing the transmission to the engine. Unscrew the bolts securing the flywheel/driveplate to the torque converter. To do this turn the flywheel until the bolts are accessible just above the oil pump. Turn the driveplate so that the angles are horizontal then lift the engine from the transmission. Retain the torque

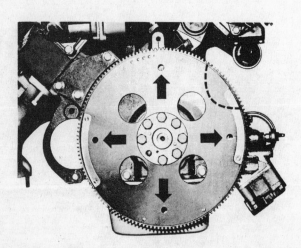

Fig. 1.6 Torque converter bolt locations on the driveplate on automatic transmission models (Sec 6)

Fig. 1.7 Torque converter support plate on automatic transmission models (Sec 6)

6.2 Removing the engine oil drain plug

6.4 Inlet manifold stay location on a fuel injection model

converter in the transmission by fitting a support plate to it (Fig. 1.7). Remove the gasket.

7 Engine dismantling – general

1   It is best to mount the engine on a dismantling stand, but if this is not available, stand the engine on blocks of wood on a strong bench at a comfortable working height.
2   Cleanliness is most important, and the engine should be thoroughly cleaned before commencing work.
3   Avoid working with the engine directly on a concrete floor, as grit presents a real source of trouble.
4   As parts are removed, clean them in a paraffin bath. However do not immerse parts with internal oilways in paraffin as it is difficult to remove, usually requiring a high pressure hose. Clean oilways with nylon pipe cleaners.
5   It is advisable to have suitable containers to hold small items according to their use, as this will help when reassembling the engine and also prevent possible losses.
6   Always obtain complete sets of gaskets when the engine is being dismantled, but retain the old gaskets with a view to using them as a pattern to make a replacement if a new one is not available.
7   When possible refit nuts, bolts, and washers in their location after being removed as this helps protect the threads and will also be helpful when reassembling the engine.
8   Retain unserviceable components in order to compare them with the new parts supplied.

8 Ancillary components – removal

   Before dismantling the main engine components, the following externally mounted ancillary components can be removed. The removal sequence need not necessarily follow the order given:

Alternator (Chapter 10) and mounting bracket (photo)
Inlet and exhaust manifolds (Chapter 3)
Distributor (Chapter 4)
Emission control components (Chapter 3)
Fuel injection components (Chapter 3)
Oil filter (Section 19 of this Chapter)
Water pump (Chapter 2)
Thermostat (Chapter 2) and housing (photo)
Engine mountings
Oil pump pick-up tube and O-ring (type H engine) (photo)
Oil pump on type B engine (Section 20 of this Chapter)
Oil filter housing and gasket on type H engine (photo)
Engine and gearbox/automatic transmission dipstick tubes (photos)

8.1 Showing the alternator and mounting bracket

8.2 Removing the thermostat housing on a fuel injection model

1

8.3 Oil pump pick up tube on H type engine

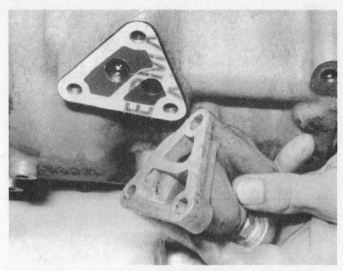

8.4 Removing oil filter housing on H type engine

8.5 Removing the engine oil level dipstick tube

9.2 Using an Allen key to remove the valve cover

9 Cylinder head – removal

If the engine is still in the car disconnect the various components from the cylinder head as described in Sections 5 and 8.

1   Turn the flywheel until the TDC 0° mark is aligned with the timing mark on the housing cover and with number 1 piston at TDC firing position.

2   Unbolt and remove the valve cover (photo). Remove the gasket.

3   On B type engines, unscrew one of the bolts from the camshaft sprocket and insert it through the mounting plate into the centre of the sprocket. Tighten the bolt securely as otherwise the chain tensioner will take up a new position making it impossible to refit the sprocket. Unscrew the remaining sprocket bolts.

4   On H type engines unscrew the camshaft sprocket bolts and lower the sprocket between the timing chain guide and tensioner, keeping the chain in its original position on the sprocket. Also remove the two bolts securing the timing cover to the cylinder head (photo).

5   On all engines unscrew and remove the cylinder head bolts using a reversal of the sequence given in Fig. 1.16.

6   Lift the cylinder head from the cylinder block taking care not to disturb the camshaft sprocket and timing chain (photo). If necessary tap the cylinder head free with a wooden mallet. *Do not use a lever otherwise the mating surfaces will be damaged.*

7   Remove the cylinder head gasket from the block.

9.4 Timing cover to cylinder head bolts

9.6 Removing the cylinder head (H type engine)

Fig. 1.8 Securing the camshaft sprocket to the mounting plate on B type engines (Sec 9)

10 Camshaft – removal

1   It is not necessary to remove the cylinder head in order to remove the camshaft, but this is advisable if the head is to be worked on.
2   Follow paragraphs 1 to 4 in Section 9.
3   Unscrew the bolts from the camshaft bearing caps evenly and in diagonal sequence.
4   Identify the bearing caps for position then remove them and lift the camshaft from the head (photos).

11 Cylinder head – dismantling

1   With the camshaft removed lift out the tappets keeping them identified for position (photo). If necessary use a valve grinding suction tool or a magnet to remove them.
2   Remove the shims from the tops of the valves again keeping them identified for position (photo).
3   Remove the camshaft bearing housing from the cylinder head (photo).

10.4A No 1 camshaft bearing cap

10.4B No 5 camshaft bearing cap

10.4C Lifting the camshaft from the cylinder head

11.1 Removing a tappet

11.2 Removing a shim from the top of a valve

11.3 Lifting the camshaft bearing housing from the cylinder head

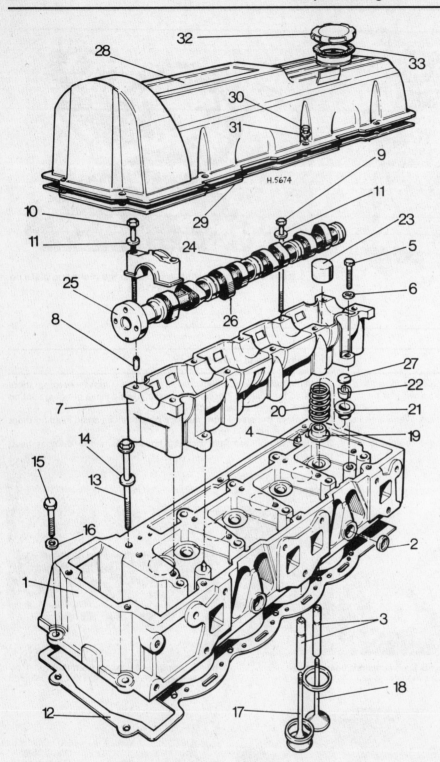

H.5674

Fig. 1.9 Exploded view of the cylinder head on B type engines (Secs 10 and 11)

1 Cylinder head
2 Core plug
3 Valve guide
4 Locating pin
5 Bolt
6 Washer
7 Camshaft bearing carrier
8 Sleeve
9 Bolt
10 Bolt
11 Washer
12 Cylinder head gasket
13 Cylinder head bolt
14 Washer
15 Bolt
16 Washer
17 Valve
18 Valve
19 Spring seat
20 Valve spring
21 Retainer
22 Split collets
23 Tappet
24 Camshaft bearing
25 Camshaft
26 Cam
27 Shim
28 Camshaft cover
29 Cover gasket
30 Screw
31 Washer
32 Oil filler cap
33 Seal

4 Using a valve spring compressor, compress each valve spring in turn until the split collets can be removed. Release the compressor and remove the cap, spring and seat then remove the valve (photos). Keep each component identified for position. If the caps are difficult to release do not continue to tighten the compressor, but gently tap the top of the tool with a hammer. Always make sure that the compressor is held firmly over the cap.

12 Timing chain and sprockets (B type engine) – removal

1 Remove the cylinder head as described in Section 9.

2 Hold the crankshaft stationary by inserting a metal bar in the starter ring gear or placing a block of wood between a crankshaft web and the cylinder block (engine removed) then unscrew the crankshaft pulley bolt and remove the pulley. Use a puller if necessary.

3 Unbolt the timing chain cover.

4 Note how the tensioner is fitted then unbolt and remove it. Remove the guide plate (photos).

5 Unbolt the camshaft sprocket mounting plate and guide and withdraw them together with the chain.

6 Using a suitable puller, remove the sprocket from the front of the crankshaft. Remove the shims.

11.4A Compress the valve spring with a compressor and remove the collets ...

11.4B ... then remove the cap ...

11.4C ... spring and seat ...

11.4D ... and valve

12.4A Timing chain tensioner on B type engine

12.4B Removing the timing chain tensioner guard plate on B type engine

1

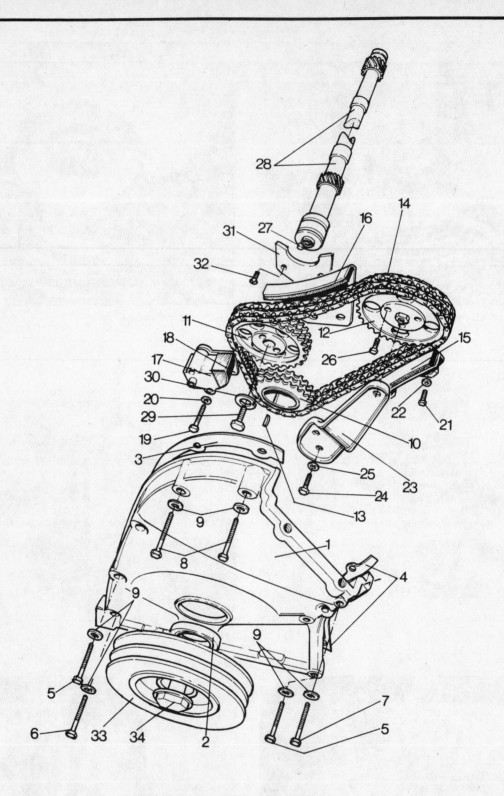

Fig. 1.10 Timing chain components on B type engines (Sec 12)

1	Timing cover	10	Crankshaft sprocket	19	Bolt	27	Dowel pin
2	Oil seal	11	Idler shaft sprocket	20	Washer	28	Idler shaft
3	Gasket	12	Camshaft sprocket	21	Bolt	29	Bolt
4	Gasket	13	Woodruff key	22	Washer	30	Washer
5	Bolt	14	Chain	23	Mounting plate	31	Retainer plate
6	Bolt	15	Fixed guide	24	Bolt	32	Socket screw
7	Bolt	16	Adjustable guide	25	Washer	33	Pulley
8	Bolt	17	Chain tensioner	26	Bolt	34	Bolt
9	Washer	18	Guide plate				

13.3A Remove the idler shaft locking plate on B type engines ...

13.3B ... and withdraw the idler shaft

14.1 Removing the crankshaft pulley bolt

13 Idler shaft (B type engine) – removal

1　Remove the timing chain as described in Section 12.
2　Hold the idler shaft sprocket stationary with a screwdriver inserted through one of the holes then unscrew the bolt and remove the sprocket.
3　Remove the two socket-head screws from the locking plate, extract the plate and withdraw the idler shaft from the cylinder block (photos). Note that the shaft cannot be removed until the distributor, water pump, oil pump, and fuel pump have first been removed.

14 Oil pump (H type engine) – removal

1　Hold the crankshaft stationary by inserting a metal bar in the starter ring gear or placing a block of wood between a crankshaft web and the cylinder block (engine removed). Then unscrew the crankshaft pulley bolt and remove the pulley using a puller if necessary (if the engine is in the car the drivebelts must first be disconnected) (photo).
2　Unscrew the bolts and remove the oil pump from the front of the timing cover (photos).
3　Prise the rubber sealing ring from the groove in the oil pump (photo).

15 Timing chain and sprockets (H type engine) – removal

1　Remove the oil pump as described in Section 14.
2　Remove the water pump and disconnect the hoses as described in Chapter 2.
3　It is preferable though not essential to remove the cylinder head as described in Section 9.
4　Unbolt and remove the timing cover and remove the gasket and pick-up tube O-ring. Note the location of the alternator link (photos).

1

14.2A Oil pump on H type engine

14.2B Removing the oil pump on H type engine

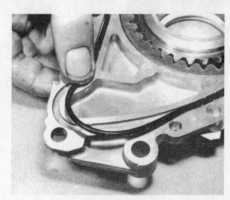

14.3 Removing the oil pump rubber sealing ring

15.4A Alternator link location on the timing cover on H type engine

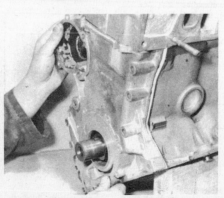

15.4B Removing the timing cover on H type engine

15.4C Showing timing cover gasket locations on H type engine

15.5 Removing the timing chain and sprockets (H engine)

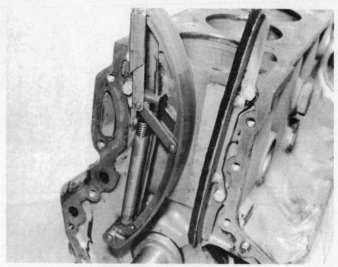

15.6A Timing chain guide and tensioner on H type engine

15.6B Removing the timing chain tensioner on H type engine

16.2 Removing the flywheel

5   Remove the timing chain together with the camshaft and crankshaft sprockets (photo).
6   Unbolt the chain guide and tensioner from the 'front' of the cylinder block (photos).

16 Flywheel/driveplate – removal

1   With the clutch or torque converter removed, hold the crankshaft stationary by inserting a metal bar in the starter ring gear or placing a block of wood between a crankshaft web and the cylinder block (engine removed).
2   Unscrew the bolts and withdraw the flywheel/driveplate from the crankshaft (photo).

17 Pistons and connecting rods – removal

1   Before removing the pistons the engine must be separated from the gearbox/automatic transmission and the cylinder head removed. On B type engines unbolt the oil pick up tube and remove the gasket. On H type engines unbolt the oil pick up tube, withdraw it from the timing cover and remove the O-ring.
2   Check that the big-end caps are marked for position so that they can be refitted correctly (photo).

17.2 Connecting rod and big-end cap markings

17.3 Removing a big-end bearing cap

18.1 Removing the engine plate

18.2A No 2 main bearing cap

18.2B No 3 main bearing cap showing holes for oil pump pick up tube bolts on H type engine

18.3 Using a feeler blade to check the crankshaft endfloat

18.4 Removing a main bearing cap

18.5 Removing the crankshaft

18.6 Removing the centre main bearing shell

19.2 Oil filter and housing on H type engine

3   Clean any carbon deposits from the tops of the cylinder bores, then working on each piston in turn, rotate the crankshaft so that the crankpin is at its lowest point. Unscrew the nuts and tap off the cap making sure that the bearing shells remain in the cap and connecting rod (photo). Using the handle of a hammer, push the piston and connecting rod up the bore and withdraw from the top of the cylinder block. Loosely refit the cap to the connecting rod.

18 Crankshaft and main bearings – removal

1   With the flywheel/driveplate removed unbolt the 'rear' engine plate from the block and remove the gasket (photo).
2   Check that the main bearing caps are marked for position so that they can be refitted correctly (photos).
3   Before removing the crankshaft check that the endfloat is within the specified limits by inserting a feeler blade between the centre crankshaft web and the thrust washers (photo). This will indicate whether new thrust washers are required or not.
4   Unscrew the bolts and tap off the main bearing caps complete with bearing shells (photo). If the thrust washers are to be re-used identify them for location.
5   Lift the crankshaft from the crankcase (photo).
6   Extract the bearing shells and thrust washers keeping them identified for location (photo).

19 Oil filter – renewal

1   The oil filter should be renewed every 10 000 miles (15 000 km) on UK models or every 15 000 miles (22 500 km) on North American models.
2   Place a container directly beneath the oil filter, then using a strap wrench, unscrew and remove the filter (photo). If a strap wrench is not

available it may be possible to unscrew the filter by driving a screwdriver through the filter canister and using it as a lever.

3   Wipe clean the filter face on the housing.

4   Smear a little oil on the new filter seal and screw on the filter until it just contacts the housing, then tighten it a further half a turn. Wipe clean the exterior of the filter.

20 Oil pump (B type engine) – removal

1   Unscrew the through bolts and withdraw the oil pump from the cylinder block.

2   Extract the sealing ring which is between the pump and the intermediate plate. The driveshaft will remain in the crankcase attached to the distributor drivegear.

21 Crankcase ventilation system – description and maintenance

1   The system is of fully enclosed type. The blow-by gases are drawn from the crankcase up through the block and cylinder head and then through a hose to the air cleaner, from where they are drawn into the engine and burnt in the combustion chambers. A small bore hose also feeds the gases direct to the inlet manifold on all but Turbo models (photo).

2   On carburettor engines a flame guard is fitted to the hose at the air cleaner.

3   Maintenance consists of periodically cleaning the hoses and where applicable the flame guard, and also checking the hoses for security.

22 Examination and renovation – general

With the engine completely stripped, clean all the components and examine them for wear. Each part should be checked, and where necessary renewed or renovated as described in the following Sections. Renew main and big-end shell bearings as a matter of course, unless you know that they have had little wear and are in perfect condition.

23 Crankshaft and main bearings – examination and renovation

1   Examine the crankpin and main journal surfaces for signs of scoring or scratches. Check the ovality of the crankpins at different positions with a micrometer. If more than 0.002 in (0.05 mm) out of round, the crankshaft will have to be reground. It will also have to be reground if there are any scores or scratches present. Also check the journals in the same fashion.

2   If it is necessary to regrind the crankshaft and fit new bearings your local Saab garage or engineering works will be able to decide how much metal to grind off and the size of new bearing shells. The crankshaft can only be reground once before hardening will be required.

3   Full details of crankshaft regrinding tolerances and bearing undersizes are given in Specifications.

4   The main bearing clearances may be established by using a strip of Plastigage between the crankshaft journals and the main bearing/shell caps. Tighten the bearing cap bolts to the specified torque. Remove the cap and compare the flattened Plastigage strip with the index provided (photo). The clearance should be compared with the tolerances in Specifications.

5   If the crankshaft endfloat as previously checked is more than the maximum specified amount, new thrust washers should be fitted to the centre main bearing, however these are usually supplied together with the main and big-end bearings on a reground crankshaft.

24 Cylinder block and bores – examination and renovation

1   The cylinder bores must be examined for taper, ovality, scoring and scratches. Start by carefully examining the top of the cylinder bores. If they are at all worn a very slight ridge will be found on the thrust side. This marks the top of the piston ring travel. The owner will have a good indication of the bore wear prior to dismantling the

21.1 Crankcase ventilation hoses on the valve cover

23.4 Using Plastigage to check bearing running clearances

engine, or removing the cylinder head. Excessive oil consumption accompanied by blue smoke from the exhaust is a sure sign of worn cylinder bores and piston rings.

2   Measure the bore diameter just under the ridge with a micrometer and compare it with the diameter at the bottom of the bore, which is not subject to wear. If the difference between the two measurements is more than 0.008 in (0.2032 mm) then it will be necessary to fit special pistons and rings or to have the cylinders rebored and fit oversize pistons. If no micrometer is available remove the rings from the piston and place each piston in each bore in turn about three-quarters of the way down the bore. If an 0.0005 to 0.002 in (0.014 to 0.040 mm) feeler gauge slid between the piston and cylinder wall requires less than a pull of between 1.8 to 2.6 lbf (0.8164 to 1.179 kgf) to withdraw it, using a spring balance, then remedial action must be taken. Oversize pistons are available as listed in Specifications.

3   These are accurately machined to just below the indicated measurements so as to provide correct running clearances in bores bored out to the exact oversize dimensions.

4   If the bores are slightly worn but not so badly worn as to justify reboring them, then special oil control rings and pistons can be fitted which will restore compression and stop the engine burning oil. Several different types are available and the manufacturer's instructions concerning their fitting must be followed closely.

24.6 Core plug in the cylinder block

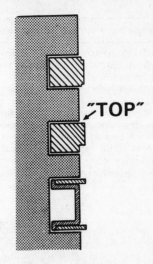

"TOP"

Fig. 1.11 Cross-section diagram of the piston rings (Sec 25)

5   If new pistons are being fitted and the bores have not been reground, it is essential to slightly roughen the hard glaze on the sides of the bores with fine glass paper so the new piston rings will have a chance to bed in properly.
6   Thoroughly examine the crankcase and cylinder block for cracks and damage and use a piece of wire to probe all oilways and waterways to ensure they are unobstructed. Check that the core plugs are secure and not leaking (photo).

25 Pistons and rings – examination and renovation

1   If new pistons are to be installed, they will be selected from grades available after measuring the cylinder bores as described in the preceding Section or will be provided in the appropriate oversize by the repairer who has rebored the cylinder block.
2   If the original pistons are to be refitted, carefully remove the piston rings being careful not to over expand them otherwise they will snap as they are very brittle (photo). The best method to remove them is to slide two or three old feeler blades behind them and pull the rings upwards off the piston using a twisting motion. The feeler blades will prevent the lower rings dropping into an empty groove.
3   Clean the grooves and rings free from carbon, taking care not to scratch the aluminium surfaces of the pistons.
4   If new rings are to be fitted, then order the top compression ring to be stepped to prevent it impinging on the 'wear ring' which will almost certainly have been formed at the top of the cylinder bore.
5   Before fitting the rings to the pistons, push each ring in turn down to the bottom of its respective cylinder bore (use an inverted piston to do this and to keep the ring square in the bore) and measure the ring end-gap, using a feeler blade (photo). The gap should be as listed in Specifications.

6   The piston rings should now be tested in their respective grooves for side clearance which again should be as shown in Specifications.
7   Where necessary a piston ring which is slightly tight in its groove may be rubbed down holding it perfectly squarely on an oilstone or a sheet of fine emery cloth laid on a piece of plate glass. Excessive tightness can only be rectified by having the grooves machined out.
8   The pistons can be removed from the connecting rods after extracting the circlips from each end of the gudgeon pin and pushing the gudgeon pin out using finger pressure. Heat the pistons in hot water first if necessary. The gudgeon pin should be a push fit into the piston at room temperature. If it appears slack, then both the piston and gudgeon pin should be renewed.

26 Connecting rods – examination and renovation

1   Big-end bearing failure is indicated by a knocking from within the crankcase and a slight drop in oil pressure.
2   Examine the big-end bearing surfaces for pitting and scoring. Renew the shells as a set where necessary. Where the crankshaft has been reground, the correct undersize big-end shell bearings will be supplied by the repairer (photo).
3   Should there be any suspicion that a connecting rod is bent or twisted or the small end bush no longer provides a push fit for the gudgeon pin then the complete connecting rod assembly should be exchanged for a reconditioned one but ensure that the comparative weight of the two rods is within 0.212 oz (6.0 g).
4   Measurement of the big-end bearing clearances may be carried out in a similar manner to that described for the main bearings in Section 23 but tighten the securing nuts on the cap bolts to the specified torque.

1

25.2 Showing piston rings and gudgeon pin retaining circlip

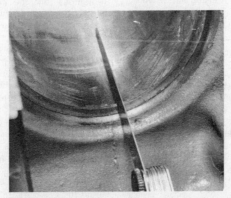

25.5 Checking piston ring gaps with a feeler gauge

26.2 Big-end bearing components

27 Flywheel/driveplate – examination and renovation

1   If the teeth of the starter ring gear on either the flywheel or
driveplate (automatic transmission) are worn or chipped, the complete
assembly should be renewed. Reconditioning of the flywheel or
driveplate is not recommended due to the balancing which is carried
out during manufacture of the components.
2   Where applicable check the clutch driven plate mating surface of
the flywheel for deep scoring and if evident renew the flywheel.
3   Check the spigot bearing in the flywheel on manual gearbox
models for roughness and if necessary use metal tubing to drive out
the old bearing and drive in the new bearing (photo). The metal tube
should only contact the outer race of the new bearing.

27.3 Spigot bearing located in the centre of the flywheel

28 Idler shaft (B type engine) – examination and renovation

1   Examine the bearing surfaces of the idler shaft; if these are scored
or worn, renew the shaft.
2   If the fuel pump cam or the gears which drive the water pump, oil
pump or distributor are worn then the idler shaft will have to be
renewed.

29 Camshaft and bearings – examination and renovation

1   Examine the camshaft bearing surfaces and cam lobes for wear
and scoring. If evident renew the camshaft.
2   Examine the bearing surfaces of the bearing housing and if worn
excessively renew the housing.

30 Timing sprockets, chain and tensioner – examination and renovation

1   Examine the teeth on the crankshaft, camshaft and idler shaft
(type B engine) sprockets for wear. If worn the side of each tooth will
be slightly concave in shape and in this case the sprockets should be
renewed.
2   Examine the links of the chain for side slackness and renew the
chain if any slackness is noticeable when compared with a new chain.
It is a sensible precaution to renew the chain at about 30 000 miles
(48 000 km) and at a lesser mileage if the engine is stripped down for
a major overhaul. The actual rollers on a very badly worn chain may be
slightly grooved.
3   Examine the chain tensioner and guide for wear and renew them
as necessary.

31 Valves and valve seats – examination and renovation

1   Examine the heads of the valves for pitting and burning, especially
the heads of the exhaust valves. The valve seatings should be
examined at the same time. If the pitting on valve and seat is very
slight the marks can be removed by grinding the seats and valves
together with coarse and then fine, valve grinding paste.
2   Where bad pitting has occurred to the valve seats it will be
necessary to recut them and fit new valves. If the valve seats are so
worn that they cannot be recut, then it will be necessary to fit new
valve seat inserts. These latter two jobs should be entrusted to the
local Saab agent or engineering works. In practice it is very seldom
that the seats are so badly worn that they require renewal. Normally,
it is the valves that are worn, and the owner can easily purchase a new
set of valves and match them to the seats by valve grinding.
3   Valve grinding is carried out as follows. Smear a trace of coarse
carborundum paste on the seat face and apply a suction grinder tool
to the valve head. With a semi-rotary motion, grind the valve head to
its seat, lifting the valve occasionally to redistribute the grinding paste.
When a dull matt even surface finish is produced on both the valve
seat and the valve, wipe off the paste and repeat the process with fine
carborundum paste, lifting and turning the valve to redistribute the
paste as before. A light spring placed under the valve head will greatly
ease this operation. When a smooth unbroken ring of light grey matt
finish is produced, on both valve and valve seat faces, the grinding
operation is complete.
4   Scrape away all carbon from the valve head and the valve stem.
Carefully clean away every trace of grinding compound, taking great
care to leave none in the ports or in the valve guides. Clean the valves
and valve seats with a paraffin soaked rag then with a clean rag, and
finally, if an air line is available, blow the valves, valve guides and valve
ports clean.
5   Note that fuel injection engines are fitted with sodium filled
exhaust valves which could be dangerous if cut open or melted with
other substances.

32 Valve guides and springs – examination and renovation

1   To estimate wear in the valve guides fully insert a new valve then
pull it out approximately 0.12 in (3.0 mm) and attempt to rock it side
to side. If the deflection is more than the maximum amount given in
Specifications the valve guide must be renewed by a Saab dealer or
engineering works.
2   Check that the valve springs free length is as given in the
Specifications and renew them as a set if necessary. In any event it is
worthwhile to renew them if they have been in use for 30 000 miles
(48 000 km) or more.

33 Cylinder head – decarbonising and examination

1   With the cylinder head removed, use a blunt scraper to remove all
traces of carbon and deposits from the combustion spaces and ports.
Remember that the cylinder head is aluminium alloy and can be
damaged easily during the decarbonising operations. Scrape the
cylinder head free from scale or old pieces of gasket or jointing
compound. Clean the cylinder head by washing it in paraffin and take
particular care to pull a piece of rag through the ports and cylinder
head bolt holes. Any grit remaining in these recesses may well drop
onto the gasket or cylinder block mating surfaces as the cylinder head
is lowered into position and could lead to a gasket leak after
reassembly is complete.
2   With the cylinder head clean test for distortion if a history of
coolant leakage has been apparent. Carry out this test using a straight
edge and feeler gauges or a piece of plate glass. If the surface shows
any warping in excess of 0.0039 in (0.1 mm) then the cylinder head
will have to be resurfaced which is a job for a specialist engineering
company.
3   Clean the pistons and top of the cylinder bores. If the pistons are
still in the block then it is essential that great care is taken to ensure
that no carbon gets into the cylinder bores as this could scratch the
cylinder walls or cause damage to the piston and rings. To ensure this

does not happen, first turn the crankshaft so that two of the pistons are at the top of their bores. Stuff rag into the other two bores or seal them off with paper and masking tape. The waterways should also be covered with small pieces of masking tape to prevent particles of carbon entering the cooling system and damaging the water pump. Press a little grease into the gap between the cylinder walls and the two pistons which are to be worked on. With a blunt scraper carefully scrape away the carbon from the piston crown, taking care not to scratch the aluminium. Also scrape away the carbon from the surrounding lip of the cylinder wall. When all carbon has been removed, scrape away the grease which will now be contaminated with carbon particles, taking care not to press any into the bores. To assist prevention of carbon build-up the piston crown can be polished with a metal polish. Remove the rags or masking tape from the other two cylinders and turn the crankshaft so that the two pistons which were at the bottom are now at the top. Place rag or masking tape in the cylinders which have been decarbonised and proceed as just described.

34 Oil pump – examination and renovation

Type B engine
1   Remove the two screws which secure the cover to the housing.

2   Remove the cover and extract the rotors and O-ring.
3   The pressure relief valve can be removed if the split pin is first withdrawn.
4   The endfloat of the rotors should be between 0.002 and 0.004 in (0.05 and 0.09 mm). If it exceeds this tolerance, the end face of the oil pump housing can be rubbed down by holding it squarely on a sheet of abrasive placed on a piece of plate glass. Excessive wear between the rotors can only be rectified by renewing the pump.
5   Reassembly is a reversal of dismantling but note that the chamfered edge of the outer rotor is nearest the driveshaft.

Type H engine
6   Remove the two rotors from the pump housing and check both the rotors and housing for wear. Modifications have been made to the oil pump so it is worthwhile making a thorough inspection. Note also that wear on the timing cover can cause noise from the pressure relief valve by the introduction of air into the oil. An air leak at the pick up tube connection to the timing cover can also cause the same noise (photos).
7   Clean the components then refit the rotors with the indentation on the outer rotor facing out of the pump.
8   Using a straightedge and feeler gauge check that the rotor endfloat is within the limits given in the Specifications. Renew the oil pump if not.
9   Lubricate the rotor liberally with engine oil.

34.6A Removing early type inner rotor from the oil pump on H type engine

34.6B Removing late type inner rotor from the oil pump on H type engine

34.6C Removing the outer rotor from the oil pump on H type engine

34.6D Dismantled oil pump on H type engine

34.6E Showing the two types of crankshaft sprocket necessary for early and late oil pumps on H type engine

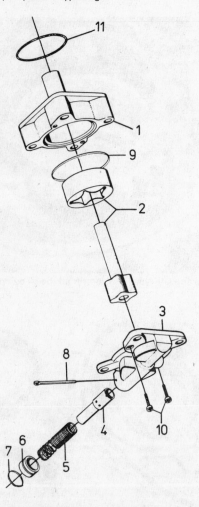

Fig. 1.12 Exploded view of the oil pump on B type engines (Sec 34)

1	Pump body	7	Seal
2	Rotors	8	Split pin
3	Cover	9	Seal
4	Piston	10	Screws
5	Spring	11	Seal
6	Stop		

35 Engine reassembly – general

1   To ensure maximum life with minimum trouble from a rebuilt engine, not only must everything be correctly assembled, but everything must be spotlessly clean, all the oilways must be clear, locking washers and spring washers must always be fitted where indicated and all bearing and other working surfaces must be thoroughly lubricated during reassembly.

2   Before assembly begins, renew any bolts or studs with damaged threads.

3   Gather together a torque wrench, oil can, clean rag, and a set of engine gaskets and oil seals, together with a new oil filter.

36 Crankshaft and main bearings – refitting

1   Clean both sides of the main bearing shells and fit them the correct way round in the crankcase recesses.

2   Smear a little grease on the inner surfaces of the thrust washers and stick them on each side of the centre main bearing with the lubrication grooves facing outwards (photo).

3   Lubricate the bearing shells with oil then lower the crankshaft into position (photo).

4   Fit the bearing shells and thrust washers to the main bearing caps then oil them and fit the caps in their correct positions.

5   Insert and tighten evenly the main bearing cap bolts to the specified torque (photo). Make sure that the crankshaft rotates freely.

6   Using a feeler gauge between the centre crankshaft web and the thrust washers check that the endfloat is within the specified limits.

7   Prise the oil seal from the 'rear' engine plate, clean the recess, then drive in the new seal using a block of wood (photo). Make sure that the seal lips will face into the engine.

8   Apply sealing compound to the cylinder block and fit the engine plate gasket (photo). Locate the engine plate on the dowels then insert the belts and tighten them evenly in diagonal sequence. To prevent damage to the oil seal smear a little grease on the lips first.

9   Trim the excess gasket from the bottom face of the engine plate (photo).

37 Pistons and connecting rods – refitting

1   Clean the bearing recesses in the connecting rods and big-end caps then press in the bearing shells after thoroughly cleaning them. Lubricate the shells with oil.

2   Position the compression ring gaps opposite each other and in line with the gudgeon pin, then position the oil scraper segments gaps approximately 60° from the gudgeon pin (Fig. 1.14). Lubricate the rings with oil.

3   The notch on the piston crown must face the timing chain end of the engine and on type B engines the figures on the connecting rods

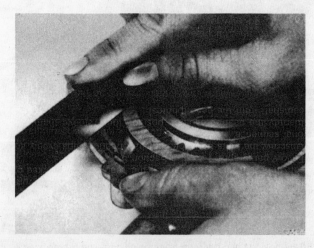

Fig. 1.13 Checking the oil pump rotor endfloat on H type engines (Sec 34)

36.2 Centre main bearing and thrust washers

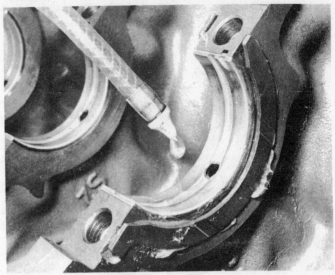

36.3 Oiling the main bearing shells

36.5 Tightening the main bearing cap bolts

36.7 Prising the oil seal from the engine plate

36.8 'Rear' engine plate gasket on the block

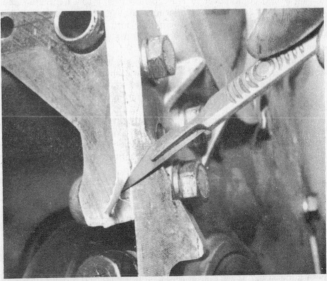

36.9 Trimming the 'rear' engine plate gasket

1

37.3 Piston crown showing notch which faces the timing chain end of the engine

37.5 Using a ring compressor when installing the pistons

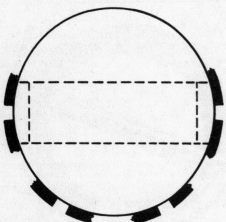

Fig. 1.14 Correct location of piston ring gaps (Sec 37)

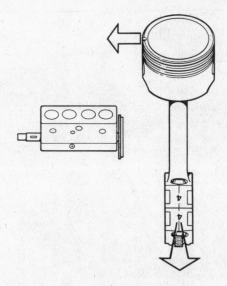

Fig. 1.15 Correct location of piston and connecting rod in the engine (Sec 37)

and caps must face away from the idler shaft (photo). The bearing shell location tabs must be adjacent to each other.

4 Lubricate the cylinder bores with engine oil.

5 Fit a ring compressor to No 1 piston then insert the piston and connecting rod into No 1 cylinder (photo). With No 1 crankpin at its lowest point, drive the piston carefully into the cylinder with the wooden handle of a hammer, and at the same time guide the connecting rod onto the crankpin.

6 Oil the crankpin then fit the big-end bearing cap in its previously noted position, and tighten the nuts to the specified torque.

7 Check that the crankshaft turns freely.

8 Repeat the procedure given in paragraphs 5 to 7 for the remaining pistons.

9 Refit the oil pick up tube together with a new gasket (B type engine) or O-ring (H type engine). Make sure that the O-ring is correctly fitted on the H type engine otherwise the pressure relief valve may cause a noise through air being present in the oil.

38 Flywheel/driveplate – refitting

1 Clean the mating faces then locate the flywheel/driveplate on the end of the crankshaft. A locating dowel ensures fitting in only one position.

2 Apply locking fluid to the threads of the bolts then insert them and tighten to the specified torque while holding the crankshaft stationary with a metal bar in the starter ring gear or by placing a block of wood between a crankshaft web and the block (photos).

39 Timing chain and sprockets (H type engine) – refitting

1 Fit the chain guide and tensioner to the 'front' of the cylinder block and insert and tighten the bolts (photo). Flat washers should be fitted beneath the bolt heads for the chain guide.

2 Turn the crankshaft so that Nos 1 and 4 pistons are at top dead centre (TDC) – the 0° mark on the flywheel/driveplate should also be aligned with the engine plate upper bolt (photo).

3 Locate the camshaft and crankshaft sprockets in the timing chain with the key slot and TDC pointer uppermost.

4 Slide the sprocket onto the crankshaft over the Woodruff key and place the camshaft sprocket between the tensioner and guide.

5 Apply sealing compound to the mating faces then refit the timing cover together with a new gasket. If applicable fit a new pick up tube O-ring and make sure that the tube is correctly seated. Insert and tighten the bolts.

6 Refit the cylinder head, water pump and oil pump.

40 Oil pump (H type engine) – refitting

1 Prise the oil seal from the oil pump and fit a new seal using a block of wood. Also fit a new O-ring seal (photos).

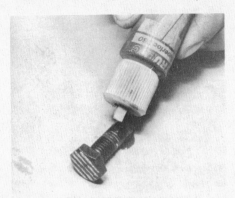

38.2A Applying locking fluid to the flywheel bolts

38.2B Tightening the flywheel bolts

39.1 Timing chain tensioner on the 'front' of the cylinder block

39.2 TDC marks on the flywheel and 'rear' engine plate

40.1A Prising the oil seal from the oil pump on H type engines

40.1B Oil seal fitted to the oil pump on H type engines

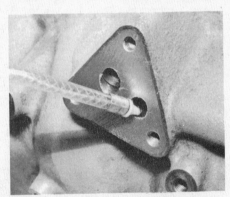

40.4 Priming the oil pump-to-filter oilway on H type engines

40.6 One method of holding the crankshaft stationary

2   Fit the oil pump to the timing cover and insert the bolts loosely.
3   If centring holes are provided, insert close fitting pins then tighten the bolts. Otherwise use Saab centring tool 83 93 589 before tightening the bolts. It is most important to centralise the oil pump correctly otherwise damage may occur.
4   Prime the oil pump by filling the oilway from the filter with oil while turning the crankshaft slowly (photo).
5   Smear a little grease on the seal contact face then locate the pulley on the crankshaft.
6   Insert and tighten the crankshaft pulley bolt while holding the crankshaft stationary (photo).
7   If the engine is already in the car, refit the drivebelts.

41 Idler shaft (B type engine) – refitting

1   Oil the bearing surfaces of the idler shaft then insert it into the cylinder block.

2   Fit the locking plate then insert and tighten the two socket-head screws.
3   Locate the sprocket on the idler shaft, insert the bolt together with a new lockwasher, and tighten the bolt while inserting a screwdriver through one of the holes. Bend the lockwasher onto one of the bolt head flats.
4   Refit the timing chain.

42 Cylinder head – reassembly

1   Working on each valve in turn first oil the valve stem and insert the valve in its correct guide.
2   Fit the seat, spring, and cap then compress the springs with a valve spring compressor and insert the split collets.
3   Release the compressor and remove it. Tap the end of the valve stem with a wooden mallet to settle the collets.

43.2 Tightening camshaft bearing cap bolts

44.1 Cylinder head gasket on the cylinder block on H type engine

44.4 Tightening cylinder head bolts

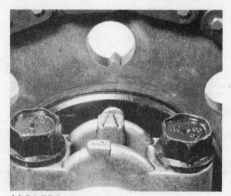

44.5A TDC alignment marks on the camshaft sprocket and bearing cap (H type engine)

44.5B Tightening the camshaft sprocket bolts (H type engine)

4   Locate the camshaft bearing housing on the cylinder head with the feeler gauge apertures on the inlet side.
5   Fit the shims in their correct positions in the tops of the valves.
6   Oil the tappets and insert them in the bearing housing in their correct locations. Keep the cylinder head upright until the camshaft has been refitted otherwise the shims may be displaced.

43 Camshaft – refitting

1   Oil the bearing surfaces then lower the camshaft into the bearing housing with the lobe peaks for No 1 cylinder pointing upwards.
2   Fit the bearing caps in their correct positions, then insert the bolts and tighten them evenly and in diagonal sequence to the specified torque (photo).

44 Cylinder head – refitting

1   Make sure that the mating faces of the cylinder head and block are perfectly clean. Locate the new gasket on the block making sure that all internal holes are aligned. *Do not use jointing compound* (photo).
2   Check that the camshaft is positioned with the lobe peaks for No 1 cylinder pointing upwards (ie No 1 cylinder TDC firing position).
3   Lower the cylinder head onto the block and insert the bolts.
4   Tighten the bolts to the specified torques given in the first two stages in Specifications and in the order shown in Fig. 1.16 (photo).
5   On H type engines insert and tighten the two bolts securing the timing cover to the cylinder head. Lift the camshaft sprocket and at the same time release the timing chain tensioner using a screwdriver or hooked tool. Fit the sprocket and chain to the camshaft and insert the bolts. Check that the TDC marks are aligned on the camshaft sprocket, bearing cap, and flywheel/driveplate rim as previously set. Tighten the bolts (photos).
6   On B type engines refit the timing chain and sprockets as described in Section 45.
7   Adjust the valve clearances as described in Section 48, then refit the valve cover together with a new gasket/O-ring.

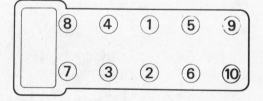

Fig. 1.16 Cylinder head bolt tightening sequence (Sec 44)

Fig. 1.17 Showing method of releasing the timing chain tensioner on H type engines (Sec 44)

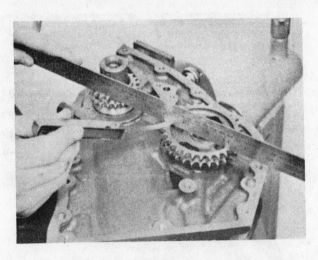

Fig. 1.18 Checking the sprocket alignment on B type engines
(Sec 45)

Fig. 1.19 Showing TDC alignment marks on the camshaft on B
type engines (Sec 45)

Fig. 1.21 Timing chain tensioner components on B type engines
(Sec 45)

A Reynolds type   *B JWIS type*

Fig. 1.20 Align the bulge in the idler sprocket with the TDC mark
on B type engines (Sec 45)

Fig. 1.22 Fit the Reynolds type tensioner with a spacer ('B' type
engines) (Sec 45)

45 Timing chain and sprockets (B type engine) – refitting

1   Locate the sprocket on the front of the crankshaft together with
the shims removed. If the crankshaft or camshaft sprocket has been
renewed use a steel rule or straightedge to determine the shim
thickness required to align both sprockets.

2   Check that the camshaft and flywheel TDC marks are aligned, and
turn the idler shaft so that the bulge in the sprocket hole is aligned
with the mark on the locking plate.

3   Fit the camshaft sprocket to the mounting plate if removed then
locate the sprocket in the timing chain.

4   Lower the chain and sprocket through the head aperture and align
the sprocket holes with the camshaft with the hole bulge uppermost.
Carefully loop the chain over the crankshaft and idler shaft sprockets
without misaligning them and insert the sprocket bolts and tighten
them.

5   Locate the chain guide then position the mounting plate and insert
the bolts. Slightly depress the chain guide to pre-tension the chain,
then tighten the mounting bolts.

6   Check that the timing marks are still aligned.

7   Where a Reynolds type chain tensioner is fitted first remove the
pad, spring, and ratchet from the housing then fit the spring and
ratchet to the pad and use an Allen key to fully compress the spring

while turning the ratchet clockwise. Fit the pad and spring in the
housing with a 0.020 in (0.5 mm) spacer (Fig. 1.22).

8   Where a JWIS type chain tensioner is fitted press and turn the pad
until it is fully entered in the housing. Keep the pad in this position until
fitted and the timing chain tensioned.

9   Fit the chain tensioner and guide plate to the block and insert and
tighten the bolts.

Fig. 1.23 Checking the timing chain tensioner setting on B type engines (Sec 45)

45.10 Checking timing chain tensioner gap on B type engines

10 Loosen the bolts then depress the chain guide to take up any slack. Remove the spacer where applicable and adjust the chain guide until the gap between the pad and the housing is 0.020 in (0.5 mm) (photo). Tighten the bolts.
11 Unscrew the camshaft sprocket centre bolt and refit it to the sprocket.
12 Turn the crankshaft two complete turns making sure that the gap on the chain tensioner does not exceed 0.060 in (1.5 mm) or decrease to less than 0.020 in (0.5 mm).
13 Using a steel rule measure the distance from the tensioner pad to the upper face of the cylinder head (Fig. 1.23). If it is less than 11.8 in (300 mm) either the chain has not been adjusted correctly or the chain and/or tensioner are worn excessively.
14 Fit the timing chain cover together with a new gasket, insert and tighten the bolts. Trim any excess gasket from the lower face. Do not forget to fit the alternator link.
15 Fit the pulley on the crankshaft then insert and tighten the bolt while holding the crankshaft stationary.

46 Oil pump (B type engine) – refitting

1 Clean the mating faces then fit the oil pump to the cylinder block together with a new O-ring.
2 Insert and tighten the through bolts.

47 Ancillary components – refitting

Refer to Section 8 and refit the listed components with reference to the Chapters indicated where applicable.

48 Valve clearances – adjustment

1 The valve clearances must be adjusted with the engine cold. First unbolt and remove the valve cover. On H type engines it will be necessary to turn the engine until the TDC 0° mark on the flywheel is aligned with the mark on the housing cover otherwise the distributor drive will prevent the removal of the valve cover.
2 Turn the engine until No 1 cam lobe peak is pointing away from the tappet.
3 Using a feeler gauge check that the clearance between the heel of the cam and the tappet is as given in the Specifications. The feeler blade should be a firm sliding fit (photo). If not, record the actual clearance.
4 Check the remaining clearances using the same procedure and record them as necessary.
5 If adjustment is required remove the camshaft with reference to Section 10 then remove the tappets and shims from the relevant valves, keeping them identified. Measure the thickness of the existing

48.3 Checking the valve clearances

48.5 Using a micrometer to check the tappet shim thickness

shims and by comparison with the correct clearances determine the thickness of the new shims. Use a micrometer to measure the shims (photo).

6 Fit the correct shims followed by the tappets and camshaft (Section 43).

7 Rotate the engine several times then recheck the clearances.

8 Refit the valve cover after positioning the flywheel at TDC on H type engines.

49 Engine – refitting to gearbox/automatic transmission

Reverse the procedure given in Section 6 but note the following additional points:

(a) Always fit a new gasket
(b) Apply sealing compound to both sides of the gasket in the shaded areas shown in Fig. 1.24
(c) Apply sealing compound to the threads of the six bolts shown in Fig. 1.24
(d) On automatic transmission models take care not to damage the torque converter centre stub
(e) Refill the engine with oil and the gearbox/automatic transmission with oil/fluid

50 Engine – refitting

Reverse the procedure given in Section 5, but note the following additional points (photo):

(a) Tension the power steering pump belt with reference to Chapter 11
(b) Refit the clutch as described in Chapter 5
(c) Refit the bonnet as described in Chapter 12
(d) Fill the cooling system as described in Chapter 2

51 Engine – adjustment after major overhaul

1 With the engine installed in the car, make a final visual check to see that everything has been reconnected and that no loose rags or tools have been left within the engine compartment.

2 Turn the idling speed adjusting screw in about $\frac{1}{2}$ turn to ensure that the engine will have a faster than usual idling speed during initial start up and operation.

3 On carburettor models fully pull out the choke control.

4 Start the engine and allow it to run at a fast idle speed. Starting may take a little longer than usual as the fuel circuit will need to be primed.

5 Check that the oil pressure warning light goes out then check the oil filter, fuel hoses and water hoses for leaks.

6 Run the engine to normal operating temperature then adjust the slow running as described in Chapter 3.

7 Switch off the engine and allow it to cool for approximately 30 minutes, then remove the valve cover and tighten the cylinder head bolts to the torque given in the Specifications, stages 4 and 5.

8 If new pistons and bearings have been fitted, the engine must be run-in for the first 500 miles (800 km).

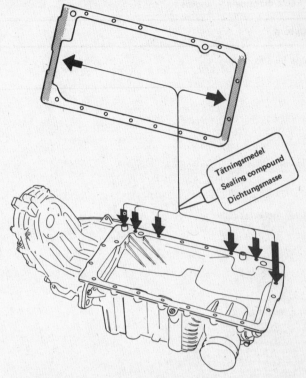

Fig. 1.24 Apply sealing compound as indicated when fitting the engine to the gearbox/automatic transmission (Sec 49)

50.1 Installing the engine

Fault diagnosis overleaf

52 Fault diagnosis – engine

Symptom	Reason(s)
Engine fails to start	Discharged battery
	Loose battery connection
	Loose or broken ignition leads
	Moisture on spark plugs, distributor cap or HT leads
	Incorrect spark plug gap
	Cracked distributor cap or rotor
	Dirt or water in carburettor (if applicable)
	Empty fuel tank
	Faulty fuel pump
	Faulty starter motor
	Low cylinder compression
	Faulty ignition system
Engine idles erratically	Inlet manifold air leak
	Leaking cylinder head gasket
	Incorrect valve clearances
	Loose crankcase ventilation hoses
	Incorrect slow running adjustment
	Uneven cylinder compressions
	Incorrect ignition timing
Engine misfires	Incorrect spark plug gap
	Faulty ignition system
	Distributor cap cracked
	Uneven cylinder compressions
	Moisture on spark plugs, distributor cap or HT leads
Engine stalls	Incorrect slow running adjustment
	Inlet manifold air leak
	Incorrect ignition timing
Excessive oil consumption	Worn pistons and cylinder bores
	Valve guides worn
	Oil leaking from gasket or oil seal

Chapter 2 Cooling system

Contents

Specifications

System type	Pressurised, with pump, crossflow radiator and expansion tank, electric cooling fan, and thermostat. On type B engines the water pump is driven by a skew gear on the idler shaft. On type H engines the water pump is driven by a drivebelt from the crankshaft pulley
Expansion tank cap pressure	12.8 to 17.0 lbf/in^2 (0.9 to 1.2 bar)

Thermostat opening temperature (engine coolant)

99 models with type B engine	87° to 91°C (189° to 196°F)
99 models with type H engine	89°C (192°F)
900 models with type B engine	88°C (190°F)
900 models with type H engine:	
UK	87° to 91°C (189° to 196°F)
USA and Canada	88°C (190°F)

Thermostat opening temperature (engine oil cooler)	75°C (165°F)
Water pump/alternator drivebelt tension (type H engines)	0.4 to 0.6 in (10.0 to 15.0 mm)

Electric cooling fan thermo-switch

Cut-in temperature	90° to 95°C (194° to 203°F)
Cut-out temperature	85° to 90°C (185° to 194°F)

System capacity (including heater)

99 models	14.0 Imp pt; 8.5 US qt; 8.0 litre
900 models	17.6 Imp pt; 10.6 US qt; 10.0 litre

Torque wrench settings	lbf ft	Nm
Thermostat housing	13	18

2

1 General description

The cooling system is of pressurised type and consists of a front mounted crossflow radiator, gear driven (B type engine) or belt driven (H type engine) water pump, thermo-switch controlled electric cooling fan, wax type thermostat, and an expansion tank. Some models are equipped with the following additional cooling systems where the car is operated under severe conditions:

Twin row radiator
Additional electric cooling fan
Engine oil or automatic transmission oil cooler located in the radiator to water pump hose

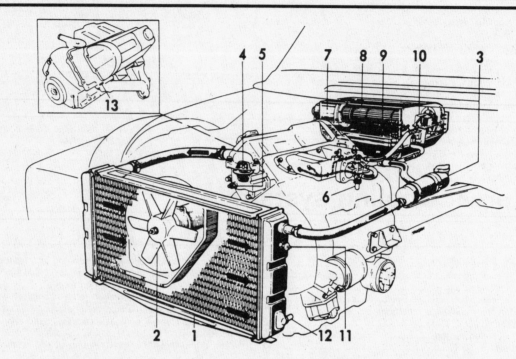

Fig. 2.1 Cooling system components on 99 models fitted with type B engine (Sec 1)

1	Radiator	5	Temperature transmitter	9	Heater matrix	12	Drain valve (radiator)
2	Electric cooling fan	6	Water pump	10	Heater control valve	13	Drain valve (cylinder
3	Expansion tank	7	Heater motor	11	Thermo-switch		block)
4	Thermostat	8	Impeller				

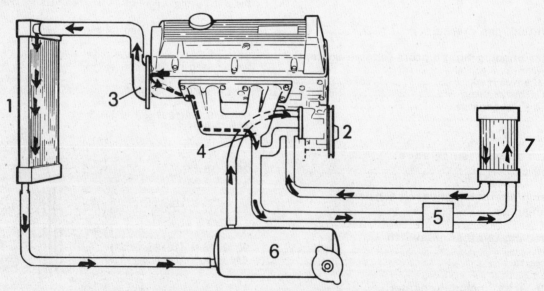

Fig. 2.2 Cooling system components on 99 models fitted with type H engine (Sec 1)

1	Radiator	3	Thermostat	5	Heater control valve	7	Heater matrix
2	Water pump	4	Inlet manifold	6	Expansion tank		

Engine oil or automatic transmission oil cooler (air flow type) located below the left-hand headlamp and incorporating a thermostat in the oil filter adaptor or on the automatic transmission

The thermostat is located at the front of the cylinder head, and its purpose is to ensure rapid engine warm-up by restricting the flow of coolant in the engine when cold, and also to assist in regulating the normal operating temperature of the engine.

The expansion tank incorporates a pressure cap which effectively pressurises the cooling system as the coolant temperature rises, thereby raising the boiling point temperature of the coolant.

A drain plug is provided on the left-hand side (99 models) or right-hand side (900 models) of the radiator. A drain plug is also provided on the engine cylinder block.

The system functions as follows. With the engine cold the thermostat is shut and circulation is from the water pump through the cylinder block, cylinder head, inlet manifold and returning to the pump. With the heater valve open, the water returning to the pump passes through the interior heater matrix. With the engine at normal operating temperature circulation is also through the radiator, however at high engine temperature, when the thermostat is fully open, the circulation through the inlet manifold is closed by the bottom of the thermostat and all coolant passes through the radiator. On 99 models the return from the radiator is via the expansion tank, however on 900 models a separate return hose is fitted.

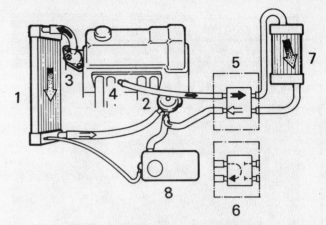

Fig. 2.3 Cooling system components on 900 models fitted with type B engine (Sec 1)

1	Radiator	6	Heater control valve
2	Water pump		(shut)
3	Thermostat	7	Heater matrix
4	Inlet manifold	8	Expansion tank
5	Heater control valve		
	(open)		

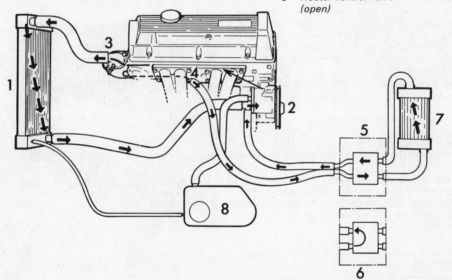

Fig. 2.4 Cooling system components on 900 models fitted with type H engine (Sec 1)

1	Radiator	4	Inlet manifold	6	Heater control valve	7 Heater matrix
2	Water pump	5	Heater control valve		(shut)	8 Expansion tank
3	Thermostat		(open)			

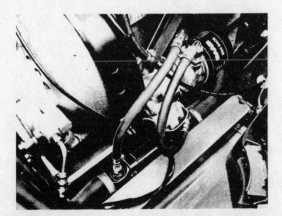

Fig. 2.5 Showing engine oil cooler located in bottom hose (Sec 1)

Fig. 2.6 Showing air type engine oil cooler located below the left-hand headlamp (Sec 1)

Fig. 2.7 Showing oil filter adaptor connections for the air type engine oil cooler (Sec 1)

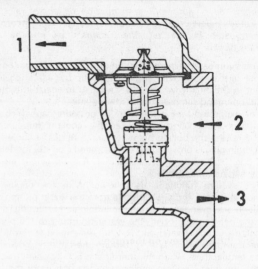

Fig. 2.8 Coolant flow through the thermostat (Sec 1)

1 To radiator	3 To water pump
2 From cylinder head	

2   Cooling system – draining

1   It is preferable to drain the cooling system with the engine cold. If this is not possible, place a thick cloth over the expansion tank filler cap and turn it slowly anti-clockwise until all the pressure has been released. Be prepared for the emission of very hot steam, as the release of pressure may cause the coolant to boil.

2   Remove the filler cap then position a suitable container beneath the radiator drain plug – on 99 models the plug is on the left-hand side, on 900 models it is on the right-hand side.

3   Set the heater control to maximum heat then unscrew the drain plug and drain the coolant.

4   Position another container beneath the right-hand side of the cylinder block, unscrew the drain plug, and drain the coolant from the block.

5   On 900 models loosen the clip and disconnect the bottom hose from the radiator in order to drain the remaining coolant (photo). Any remaining coolant on 99 models can only be drained after removing the radiator and inverting it, however this will only be necessary where severe contamination has occurred.

3   Cooling system – flushing

1   After some time the radiator and engine waterways may become restricted or even blocked with scale or sediment. When this occurs, the coolant will appear rusty and dark in colour and the system should then be flushed. In severe cases, reverse flushing may be required.

2   Disconnect the top hose from the radiator then insert a hose and allow water to circulate through the radiator until it runs clear from the bottom hose outlet (900 models) or drain plug (99 models).

3   Insert the hose in the expansion tank filler neck and allow water to run out of the cylinder block, bottom hose (900 models) and through the vent hose to the radiator until clear.

4   Disconnect the hose from the inlet manifold, insert the hose, and allow water to run through the heater and out of the bottom hose (900 models) or cylinder block (99 models).

5   In severe cases of contamination the system should be reverse flushed. To do this, remove the radiator as described in Section 6, invert it, and insert a hose in the bottom hose outlet (900 models) or drain plug aperture (remove first on 99 models). Continue flushing until clear water runs from the inlet.

6   The engine should also be reverse flushed. To do this, remove the thermostat as described in Section 7 and insert a hose into the cylinder head (photo). Continue flushing until clear water runs from the cylinder block drain plug.

7   Disconnect the heater supply and return hoses and reverse flush the heater until the water is clear.

8   The use of chemical cleaners should only be necessary as a last resort, and the regular renewal of antifreeze at the recommended intervals should prevent the contamination of the system.

2.5 Radiator bottom hose connection on 900 models

3.6 Top hose connection to thermostat housing

Fig. 2.9 Bleed screw on thermostat housing on late 99 models with H engine (Sec 4)

Fig. 2.10 Bleed screw located on heater temperature control valve on late 99 models (Sec 4)

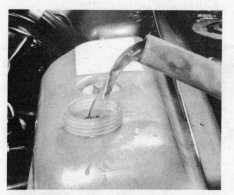

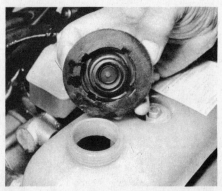

4.3A Topping up the expansion tank with coolant

4.3B Bleed screw on the thermostat housing

4.4 Refitting the filler cap to the expansion tank

4 Cooling system – filling

1 Refit the radiator and thermostat as applicable, reconnect the hoses and tighten the clips, and refit and tighten the radiator and cylinder block drain plugs.
2 Loosen the bleed screw on the thermostat cover (all models except late 99 with H engine) or thermostat housing (late 99 models with H engine).
3 Poor coolant into the expansion tank filler neck until it reaches the maximum level mark. Tighten the bleed screw when coolant free of air bubbles comes out (photos).
4 Top up the coolant level and refit the filler cap (photo).
5 Run the engine at a fast idling speed for several minutes – at the same time on late 99 models loosen the bleed screw at the heater temperature control valve until air-free coolant comes out then tighten the screw.
6 Stop the engine and top up the coolant level as necessary, being careful to release pressure from the system before removing the filler cap.

5 Antifreeze mixture – general

Antifreeze mixture is toxic, and precautions must be taken to prevent it contacting the skin and clothing. It can also cause permanent damage to paintwork.
1 The antifreeze mixture concentration should be checked and the mixture renewed at the intervals given in the Routine Maintenance section at the beginning of this manual. This is particularly necessary where the mixture contains a corrosion inhibitor as otherwise scale and sediment will accumulate.
2 Before adding the mixture, the cooling system should be com-

pletely drained and flushed, and all hose connections checked for tightness.
3 The correct concentration will depend on the lowest ambient temperature likely to be encountered, but it should be a minimum of 40% and a maximum of 60% as shown in the following chart.

Protection to	Antifreeze	Water
−25°C (−13°F)	40%	60%
−35°C (−31°F)	50%	50%
−50°C (−58°F)	60%	40%

4 Mix the required quantity in a clean container then fill the cooling system with reference to Section 4.
5 After filling, a label should be attached to the radiator stating the type of anti-freeze and the date installed. Any subsequent topping up should be made with the same type and concentration of antifreeze.

6 Radiator – removal, inspection, cleaning and refitting

1 Disconnect the battery negative lead.
2 Drain the cooling system as described in Section 2.
3 Loosen the clips and disconnect the top hose and expansion tank hose from the radiator (photo).
4 Remove the ignition coil as described in Chapter 4.
5 Disconnect the wiring from the electric cooling fan and thermo switch (photo).

99 models (except Turbo)
6 Disconnect the headlamp lens wiper pushrod from the wiper motor crank in front of the radiator.
7 Disconnect the wiring from the headlamp wiper motor and temperature sensing switch, and unclip the harness from the electric cooling fan cowling.

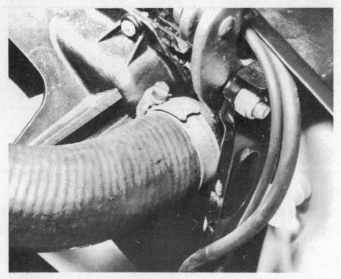

6.3 Top hose connection to the radiator

6.5 Cooling fan thermo-switch location on the radiator

6.12A Radiator upper mounting screw on 900 models

6.12B Removing the radiator on 900 models

6.12C Electric cooling fan location on radiator

6.12D Removing the electric cooling fan assembly

Fig. 2.11 Removing the radiator on an early 99 model (Sec 6)

Fig. 2.12 Removing the electric cooling fan from the radiator on an early 99 model (Sec 6)

8   Unscrew the radiator securing screws and lift the radiator from the engine compartment. The fan motor and the wiper motor can be released from the radiator if required, by removing the attachment bolts.

99 models (Turbo)
9   Disconnect the wiring from the headlamp wiper motors and temperature sensing switch, and unclip the harness from the electric cooling fan cowling.
10   Remove the screws securing the front panel section then lift away the panel and radiator assembly.
11   The fan motor can be removed after undoing the bolts which secure the fan cover to the radiator frame. If the fan blades are being removed from the motor shaft note that the securing nut has a left-hand thread.

900 models
12   Unscrew and remove the two upper mounting bolts, move the top of the radiator slightly rearwards, and lift the radiator from the engine compartment. For better access remove the electric cooling fan first (photos).

All models
13   Radiator repair is best left to a specialist, however minor repairs may be made using a proprietary repair kit, soldering, or using a coolant additive.
14   Clear the matrix of flies and small leaves with a soft brush or by hosing. Reverse flush the radiator as described in Section 3. Examine the hoses and clips and renew them if they are damaged or deteriorated. Also check the mounting rubbers and renew them if necessary. If necessary unscrew and remove the thermo-switch and remove the gasket.
15   Refitting is a reversal of removal. Fit the thermo switch together with a new gasket. Fill the cooling system as described in Section 4.

7   Thermostat – removal, testing and refitting

1   The thermostat is located on the front of the cylinder head. First partially drain the cooling system with reference to Section 2 so that the coolant level is below the thermostat housing.
2   Unscrew the bolts from the thermostat cover and remove the cover from the housing – there is no need to disconnect the top hose (photo).
3   Remove the sealing ring and extract the thermostat (photo).
4   To test the thermostat suspend it with a piece of string in a container of water. Gradually heat the water and note the temperature at which the thermostat starts to open. Remove the thermostat from the water and check that it is fully closed when cold.

7.2 Remove the cover ...

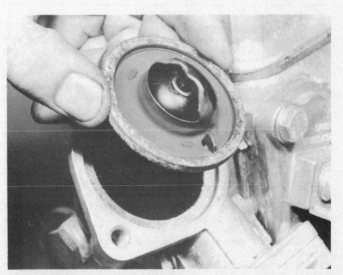

7.3 ... and withdraw the thermostat

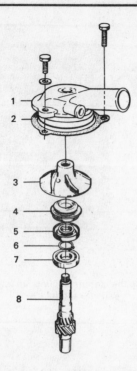

Fig. 2.13 Exploded view of the water pump fitted to the B type engine (Sec 8)

1	Cover	5	Bearing seal
2	Gasket	6	Circlip
3	Impeller	7	Ball bearing
4	Pump seal	8	Driveshaft

5   Renew the thermostat if the opening temperature is not as given in the Specifications or if the unit does not fully close when cold.

6   Clean the mating faces of the cover and housing.

7   Refitting is a reversal of removal, but use a new sealing ring and tighten the bolts to the specified torque. The arrow on the thermostat must face the cover. Refill the cooling system as described in Section 4.

8 Water pump (type B engine) – removal, overhaul and refitting

1   Disconnect the battery negative lead.

2   Drain the cooling system as described in Section 2.

3   Remove the inlet manifold and gasket as described in Chapter 3 and use masking tape to cover the inlet ports and water passage in the cylinder head.

4   Remove the alternator and bracket as described in Chapter 10. On some models it will be necessary to unbolt both rear engine mountings and jack up the rear of the engine/gearbox unit in order to remove the alternator bracket bolt from the gearbox cover – also pivot the bracket away from the engine without removing the lower bracket bolt.

5   Unscrew the remaining bolts and remove the outer pump cover and gasket from the cylinder block.

6   Remove the *left-hand threaded* bolt retaining the impeller. In order to remove the pump it may be necessary to use the SAAB extractor tool as illustrated. Alternatively, re-insert the left-hand threaded bolt with a large washer beneath the head and screw it in about 4 turns; then apply leverage at opposite points to extract the pump. Shock loads, as applied from a slide hammer, should be avoided to prevent damage to the bearing.

7   Support the underside of the impeller and drive out the shaft using a soft metal drift.

8   Note the location of the seals then remove them from the driveshaft.

9   Extract the circlip then support the bearing with the drivegear downwards and drive out the shaft using a soft metal drift.

Fig. 2.14 Removing the water pump cover on the B type engine (Sec 8)

Fig. 2.15 Using Saab tool number 83 92 649 to remove the water pump from the cylinder block on the B type engine (Sec 8)

Fig. 2.16 Inserting the water pump driveshaft in the cylinder block on the B type engine (Sec 8)

9.4 Water pump

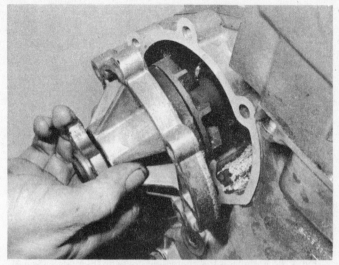
9.6A Removing the water pump from the timing cover

10 Clean all the components in paraffin and wipe dry. Spin the bearing by hand and check it for roughness and excessive play. Examine the driveshaft and gear teeth for wear and damage. Check the impeller for corrosion. Renew the components as necessary and obtain a set of seals.

11 Commence reassembly by driving the bearing fully onto the shaft using a length of metal tubing on the inner race.

12 Fit the bearing retaining circlip to the shaft.

13 Clean the cylinder block seating then insert the water pump shaft and engage the gear with the idler shaft.

14 Using a length of metal tubing on the bearing outer race, drive the bearing and shaft fully into the cylinder block.

15 Locate the bearing seal over the shaft and use metal tubing to position the seal in the block.

16 Locate the pump seal over the shaft and use metal tubing to position it in the block.

17 Clean the end of the shaft and the impeller bore then locate the impeller on the shaft.

18 Using tool 83 92 649 or a home made equivalent carefully press the impeller onto the shaft taking care not to push the shaft through the bearing inner race. Press on the impeller a little at a time and make sure that the shaft turns freely. Check that the impeller is fully home by temporarily fitting the cover and checking that there is clearance. If the shaft jams, it has probably moved through the bearing against the cylinder block in which case the pump must be removed and the bearing repositioned.

19 Clean the mating faces then fit the water pump cover to the cylinder block together with a new gasket.

20 Fit the alternator bracket then insert the bolts in the cover and tighten them evenly. Where applicable lower the engine/gearbox unit and reconnect the rear engine mountings.

21 Refit the alternator as described in Chapter 10 and tension the drivebelt as described in Section 10.

22 Remove the masking tape then refit the inlet manifold together with a new gasket as described in Chapter 3.

23 Reconnect the battery negative lead.

24 Fill the cooling system as described in Section 4.

9.6B Water pump location in the timing cover

9 Water pump (type H engine) – removal and refitting

1 Disconnect the battery negative lead.

2 Drain the cooling system as described in Section 2.

3 Remove the drivebelt(s) as described in Section 10.

4 Unscrew the bolts and remove the pulley from the water pump flange (photo).

5 On 99 models unbolt the cover from the heater unit.

6 Unscrew the bolts and remove the water pump from the timing cover (photos). Remove the gasket.

9.7 Hose connections to the water pump cover

Fig. 2.17 Removing the heater unit cover on 99 models (Sec 9)

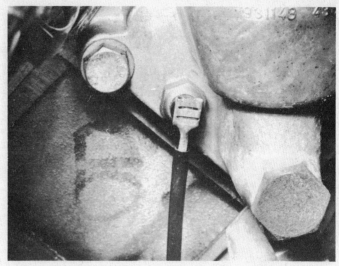

11.1 Temperature gauge transmitter location on the thermostat housing on 900 models

7   If necessary, loosen the clips and disconnect the hoses from the water pump cover (photo). Identify the hoses for location to ensure correct refitting. Unbolt the cover from the timing cover and remove the gasket. Note that the rear engine hanger is located on the upper bolts.
8   No repairs are possible, and if the water pump is faulty it should be renewed.
9   Clean the mating faces of the timing cover, water pump and cover as applicable.
10 Refitting is a reversal of removal, but fit new gaskets and tighten the bolts evenly. Tension the drivebelt(s) as described in Section 10, and fill the cooling system as described in Section 4.

10 Water pump/alternator drivebelt (type H engine) – checking, renewal and adjustment

1   The drivebelt should be checked and if necessary re-tensioned every 10 000 miles (15 000 km) on UK models or every 15 000 miles (22 500 km) on USA and Canada models. Check the full length of the drivebelt for cracks and deterioration and renew it if necessary.
2   On models equipped with power steering and/or air conditioning first remove the pump/compressor drivebelts with reference to Chapters 11 and 12 respectively.
3   Disconnect the battery negative lead.
4   Loosen the alternator pivot and adjustment bolts and swivel the alternator in toward the cylinder block.
5   Slip the drivebelt from the alternator, water pump and crankshaft pulleys.
6   Fit the new drivebelt over the pulleys, then lever the alternator away from the cylinder block until the specified tension is achieved. Lever the alternator on the drive end bracket to prevent straining the brackets. It is helpful to semi-tighten the adjustment link bolt before tensioning the drivebelt.
7   Tighten the alternator pivot and adjustment bolts.
8   Reconnect the battery negative lead.
9   Refit and tension the pump/compressor drivebelts if applicable with reference to Chapters 11 and 12.

11 Temperature gauge transmitter – removal and refitting

1   The temperature gauge transmitter is located on the thermostat housing (photo). First partially drain the cooling system with reference to Section 2 so that the coolant level is below the thermostat housing.
2   Disconnect the wire from the terminal on the transmitter.
3   Unscrew and remove the transmitter from the thermostat housing.
4   Refitting is a reversal of removal. Fill the cooling system with reference to Section 4.

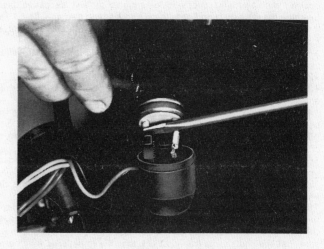

Fig. 2.18 Using a screwdriver to bridge the thermo-switch terminals (Sec 12)

12 Electric cooling fan thermo-switch – testing, removal and refitting

1   The electric cooling fan thermo-switch is located on the left-hand side of the radiator beneath the expansion tank hose connection.
2   To test the switch pull back the cover to expose the two terminals, then, with the ignition switched on, use a screwdriver to bridge the two terminals. The cooling fan should operate proving that the circuit is in order. Switch off the ignition.
3   Partially drain the cooling system with reference to Section 2 so that the coolant level is below the thermo-switch.
4   Disconnect the wires from the terminals then unscrew the switch and remove the gasket.
5   Suspend the switch with a piece of string in a container of water and connect a test lamp and leads with 12 volt supply to the two terminals. Gradually heat the water and check that the test lamp lights up at the cut-in temperature given in the Specifications. Allow the water to cool and check that the light goes out at the cut-out temperature given in the Specifications. Renew the switch if it is faulty.
6   Refitting is a reversal of removal, but always fit a new gasket. Fill the cooling system with reference to Section 4.

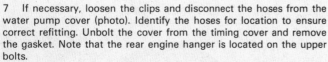

13 Fault diagnosis – cooling system

Symptom	Reason(s)
Overheating	Low coolant level
	Faulty expansion tank pressure cap
	Thermostat sticking shut
	Water pump drivebelt slipping,
	(type H engine only)
	Clogged radiator matrix
	Retarded ignition timing
	Electric cooling fan or thermo-switch faulty
Slow warm up	Thermostat sticking open
	Electric cooling fan operating
	continuously due to short circuit
	in wiring or faulty thermo-switch
Coolant hose	Deteriorated hose or loose clip
	Leaking water pump or thermostat
	housing gasket
	Blown cylinder head gasket
	Leaking radiator
	Cracked cylinder head
	Leaking core plug

2

Chapter 3
Fuel, exhaust and emission control systems

For modifications, and information applicable to later models, see Supplement at end of manual

Contents

Specifications

Air cleaner

Type	Automatic air temperature control with renewable paper element
Temperature rating – B type engine:	
Non-Turbo models	8° to 18°C (43° to 64°F)
Turbo models	-5° to + 5°C (23° to 41°F)
Temperature rating – H type engine:	
Non-Turbo models	23° to 37°C (73° to 99°F)
Turbo models	-5° to + 5°C (23° to 41°F)

Fuel pump (carburettor models)

Type	Mechanical, diaphagm, operated from idler shaft on B type engines or camshaft on H type engines
Fuel pressure at starter speed	2.4 to 3.6 lbf/in² (0.17 to 0.25 bar)

Fuel tank

Capacity	According to model between 12.1 and 15.3 Imp gal; 14.5 and 18.4 US gal; 55.0 and 69.6 litre

Carburettor
Single carburettor engines

Type	Zenith 175 CD
Diameter	1.75 in
Metering needle	B1 DS
Float setting	0.63 to 0.67 in (16.0 to 17.0 mm)
Float valve	0.08 in (2.0 mm)
Damper oil level (min)	0.4 in (10.0 mm) below upper edge
Float idle cam clearance (B type engine)	0.04 in (1.0 mm)
Fast idling speed (H type engine)	1100 rpm
Idling speed	850 ± 50 rpm
CO content (with distributor vacuum and crankcase ventilation hoses disconnected)	1.75 ± 0.25 % at 2000 rpm
Jet position	0.1 in (2.5 mm) from seating
Initial metering needle position	Shoulder level with bottom of piston
Temperature compensator opening at 20° (60°F)	0.004 to 0.012 in (0.1 to 0.3 mm)
Piston return spring colour coding	Red

Twin carburettor engines

Type	Zenith 150 CD
Diameter	1.5 in
Metering needle:	
1979 models	B5 EJ
1980 on models	B5 EQ
Float setting	0.63 to 0.67 in (16.0 to 17.0 mm)
Float valve	0.08 in (2.0 mm)
Damper oil level (min)	0.4 in (10.0 mm) below upper edge
Fast idle cam clearance (B type engine)	0.04 in (1.0 mm)
Fast idling speed (H type engine)	1100 rpm
Idling speed	850 ± 50 rpm
CO content (with distributor vacuum and crankcase ventilation hoses disconnected)	1.5 ± 1.0% at 850 rpm
Jet position:	
B type engine	0.1 in (2.5 mm) from seating
H type engine	0.090 ± 0.004 in (2.3 ± 0.1 mm) from seating
Initial metering needle position	Shoulder level with bottom of piston
Temperature compensator opening at 20°C (60°F)	0.004 to 0.012 in (0.1 to 0.3 mm)
Piston return spring colour coding	Blue

Fuel injection system

Type	Bosch CI (continuous injection)
Fuel pump capacity (return pipe discharge in 30 seconds)	900 cc
Control pressure (warm engine)	48.5 to 54.0 lbf/in^2 (3.4 to 3.8 bar)
Full load control pressure (Turbo models)	36.3 to 42.1 lbf/in^2 (2.5 to 2.9 bar)
Line pressure:	
Non-Turbo models	66.9 to 69.7 lbf/in^2 (4.7 to 4.9 bar)
Turbo models	76.8 to 79.7 lbf/in^2 (5.4 to 5.6 bar)
Minimum leakage pressure after 20 minutes	21.8 lbf/in^2 (1.5 bar)
Injection valve opening pressure:	
1979 models to date code 828	36.3 to 52.2 lbf/in^2 (2.5 to 3.6 bar)
1979 models from date code 829	39.2 to 55.1 lbf/in^2 (2.7 to 3.8 bar)
1980 models	43.5 to 55.1 lbf/in^2 (3.0 to 3.8 bar)
1981 on models	43.5 to 59.5 lbf/in^2 (3.0 to 4.1 bar)
Maximum variation	8.7 lbf/in^2 (0.6 bar)
Idling speed:	
UK models	850 ± 50 rpm
North American models	875 ± 50 rpm
CO content (at idling speed) – UK models:	
Pre-1982	1.5 ± 1.0%
1982 on – Non-Turbo models	1.0 ± 0.5%
1982 on Turbo models	1.0 ± 0.5% (see also Turbo system)
CO content (at idling speed) – USA models:	
B type engine – without catalyst	0.75 ± 0.25%
B type engine – with catalyst (1979)	0.75 + 0.25%, − 0.5%
B type engine – with catalyst (1980)	1.0 ± 0.25%
H type engine – checking	Oxygen sensor pulse relation within 10 to 90% with warm engine
H type engine – setting	Oxygen sensor pulse relation within 55 to 65% with warm engine
CO content (at idling speed) – Canada models	1.5 ± 0.5%

Turbo system

Type	Garrett Airesearch
Maximum charging pressure:	
UK models	10.2 ± 0.7 lbf/ft^2 (0.7 ± 0.05 bar)
North American models	7.3 ± 0.7 lbf/in^2 (0.5 ± 0.05 bar)
Pressure regulator spring length (approx):	
UK models	0.709 in (18.0 mm)
North American models	0.717 in (18.2 mm)
Pressure switch actuating pressure:	
UK models	13.1 ± 1.5 lbf/in^2 (0.9 ± 0.1 bar)
North American models	10.2 ± 1.5 lbf/in^2 (0.7 ± 0.1 bar)
Turbo shaft bearing clearance:	
Endfloat	0.001 to 0.040 in (0.025 to 0.100 mm)
Radial play	0.003 to 0.007 in (0.075 to 0.180 mm)

Turbo fuel boost (1979 models)

Type	Full-load enrichment, speed and throttle controlled
Throttle valve switch (valve opening with circuit closed)	62° (except Turbo APC)
Speed transmitter (closing speed)	80 ± 3 mph (130 ± 5 kph)
Regulator reduced control pressure	35.6 to 41.2 lbf/in^2 (2.5 to 2.9 bar)
CO value with throttle valve switch depressed and idling CO value 1.0 to 2.0%	4.0 to 6.0%

Turbo fuel boost (1980 on models)

Type ....   Charging pressure controlled full-load enrichment
Warm up regulator/boost control simulated charging pressure when
control pressure reduced:
    Standard ....   4.7 to 5.7 lbf/in^2 (0.33 to 0.40 bar)
    APC ....   2.1 to 4.5 lbf/in^2 (0.15 to 0.32 bar)
Reduced pressure with charging pressure over 5.7 lbf/in^2
(0.4 bar) ....   35.0 to 41.2 lbf/in^2 (2.5 to 2.9 bar)

Exhaust emission control system

B type engine

Two port EGR valve opening speed:
    Manual transmission ....   2600 to 3200 rpm
    Automatic transmission ....   2300 to 2900 rpm
Oxygen sensor system pulse relation:
    Opening interval at fixed regulation ....   60 ± 5%
    Opening interval with earthed sensor cable ....   Greater than 75%
    Opening interval with throttle valve fully open:
        1979 Standard ....   45 ± 5%
        1979 Turbo ....   80 ± 5%
        1980 Standard ....   65 ± 5%
        1980 Turbo ....   85 ± 5%
Oxygen sensor renewal interval:
    B type engine ....   15 000 miles (24 000 km)
    H type engine ....   30 000 miles (48 000 km)
CO value with evaporative canister purge pipe disconnected:
    Disconnected sensor, maximum deviation during checking ....   0.25 to 1.0%
    Disconnected sensor, value for checking 0.75%
    Connected sensor, value for checking ....   0.4% max

Torque wrench settings

	lbf ft	Nm
Oxygen sensor	29	40
Knock detector	5	8
Inlet manifold	13	18
Throttle valve housing	13	18
Exhaust manifold	18	25
EGR valve	11	15

1 General description

The fuel system consists of a rear mounted fuel tank, fuel pump, and either a side draught carburettor (single or twin) or fuel injection system.

The air cleaner is of automatic temperature control type with a renewable paper element.

The exhaust system is in three sections and on certain North American versions incorporates a catalytic converter.

Turbo models incorporate an exhaust driven compressor to supercharge the induction air/fuel mixture.

Before working on the fuel system read the precautions given in 'Safety first' at the front of this manual.

2 Air cleaner and element – removal and refitting

1 The air clear is located on the left-hand side of the engine compartment and it incorporates an automatic air temperature control. On non-Turbo models the air cleaner element should be cleaned every 10 000 miles (15 000 km) and renewed every 30 000 miles (45 000 km). On Turbo models the element should be renewed every 10 000 miles (15 000 km).
2 To remove the element either release the clips or remove the screws from the air cleaner cover, move the cover to one side, and withdraw the element (photos).
3 If cleaning the element, tap it to release the accumulated dust and if available use an air line. Do not attempt to wash the element.
4 Wipe clean the inside surfaces of the air cleaner.
5 To remove the air cleaner loosen the clips and withdraw the air ducts and crankcase ventilation hose, then release the unit from the mounting bracket.
6 Refitting is a reversal of removal.

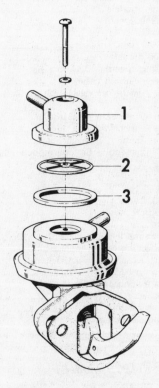

Fig. 3.1 Fuel pump fitted to B type engines (Sec 4)

   1 Cover   *3 Gasket*
   2 Filter

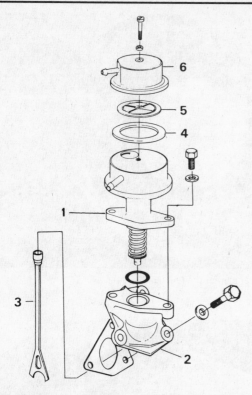

Fig. 3.2 Fuel pump fitted to H type engines (Sec 4)

1	Body	4	Seal
2	Adaptor	5	Filter
3	Pushrod	6	Cover

3 Air cleaner temperature control – testing

1 With the engine cold disconnect the cold air duct from the unit and check that the control flap is positioned correctly, in accordance with the ambient temperature, with reference to the Specifications.

2 For a more accurate test loosen the clips and remove the unit from the air cleaner body (photo). On non-Turbo models remove the thermostat from in front of the carburettor/throttle housing with the cable.

3 Check the operation of the unit by immersing the thermostat in water (mixed with anti-freeze where applicable) and checking the operating temperatures with reference to the Specifications (photo). At the lower temperature or under, the flap must admit only heated air and at the higher temperature or over, only cold air.

4 When refitting the unit on non-Turbo models make sure that the flap is over the cold air aperture at room temperature. If not loosen the plastic nut on the cable and turn the cable through 180° as necessary. Tighten the nut afterwards.

4 Fuel pump (carburettor engines) – testing, servicing, removal and refitting

1 The fuel pump is located on the left-hand side of the cylinder block (B type engines) or cylinder head (H type engines) (photo). To test its operation disconnect the outlet hose and hold a wad of rag by the outlet. Disconnect the low tension negative wire from the ignition coil, then have an assistant spin the engine on the starter and check that well defined spurts of fuel are ejected.

2 If a pressure gauge is available check that the fuel pump delivers the specified pressure at starter speed.

3 The fuel pump filter should be cleaned every 5000 miles (7500 km). To do this mark the cover in relation to the body then remove the central screw and lift off the cover.

4 Remove the gauze filter and rubber seal and clean them in fuel. Also clean the cover and body. Check the seal for condition and renew it if necessary.

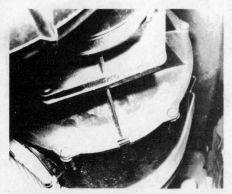

2.2A Air cleaner unit on a fuel injection model

2.2B Removing the air cleaner element

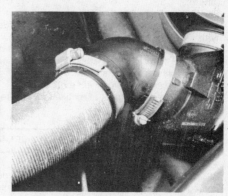

3.2 Air cleaner temperature control unit

3

3.3 Air cleaner temperature control unit thermostat location

4.1 Removing the fuel pump on a B type engine

5   Refit the filter and cover together with the seal, and insert and tighten the screw.

6   To remove the fuel pump, identify then disconnect the two hoses. Unscrew the mounting bolts and withdraw the pump from the cylinder block (B type engines) or cylinder head (H type engines). Remove the gasket.

7   On H type engines withdraw the pushrod from the cylinder head, and also unbolt the pump from the adaptor.

8   Clean away all traces of gasket from the mating surfaces. If the fuel pump is faulty it must be renewed as it is not possible to dismantle it.

9   Refitting is a reversal of removal, but always fit a new gasket, and on H type engines a new seal between the adaptor and pump. On B type engines locate the pump operating lever on the idler shaft cam. On H type engines make sure that the pushrod is correctly located in the groove on the camshaft and hold it in this position with a small screwdriver while fitting the pump.

5   Fuel tank – removal, servicing and refitting

Note: *For safety the fuel tank must always be removed in a well ventilated area, never over a pit.*

1   Disconnect the battery negative lead.

2   Jack up the rear of the car and support on axle stands. Apply the handbrake.

3   Remove the filler cap then syphon or pump all the fuel from the tank into a suitable container (photo). Alternatively the tank fuel outlet hose can be disconnected and on fuel injection models the pump located in the tank can be used to remove the fuel.

4   Remove the floor panel (or carpet on some 99 models) from the luggage compartment, then remove the screws and withdraw the fuel level transmitter cover plate and where applicable the pump cover plate.

5   Disconnect the wiring from the fuel level transmitter and where applicable the pump, noting their location for correct refitting.

6   Disconnect the filler and ventilation hoses, and the fuel supply and return hoses (photo). Remove the fuel line clips where applicable.

7   Support the tank then release the straps by unscrewing the nuts (photo).

8   Lower the fuel tank and withdraw it from under the car.

9   Remove the fuel level transmitter and fuel pump (if applicable) with reference to Sections 6 and 4.

10   If the tank is contaminated with sediment or water, swill it out with clean fluid. If the tank leaks or is damaged, it should be repaired by specialists or alternatively renewed. *Do not, under any circumstances, solder or weld a fuel tank.*

11   Refitting is a reversal of removal, but make sure that all hoses are securely fitted.

6   Fuel level transmitter – removal and refitting

1   Disconnect the battery negative lead.

2   Remove the floor panel (or carpet on some 99 models) from the luggage compartment, then remove the screws and withdraw the transmitter cover plate (photo).

3   Disconnect the wiring and hose.

4   Remove the screws or unscrew the plastic cap as applicable, then carefully withdraw the transmitter unit from the tank. On pre-1981 models the unit incorporates a float and lever, whereas on later models the float is sealed in a plastic tube.

5   Refitting is a reversal of removal, but always fit a new seal.

7   Choke cable (carburettor engines) – removal and refitting

1   Note the fitted position of the choke cable for correct refitting.

2   Disconnect the inner cable from the carburettor lever, and unclip the outer cable from the bracket.

3   Release the cable from the clips in the engine compartment.

Pre-1982 900 models

4   Remove the gear lever housing cover screws and lift it sufficiently to disconnect the inner and outer cables. Where applicable disconnect the cable from the intermediate lever.

5   Release the grommet from the bulkhead and withdraw the cable.

5.3 Filler cap for the fuel tank

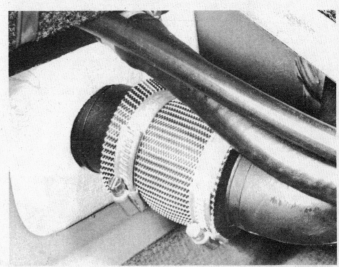
5.6 Fuel tank filler hose beneath the rear floor

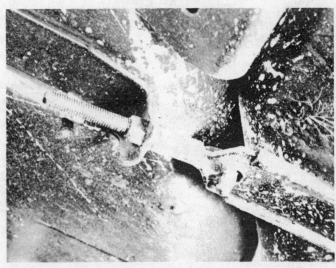
5.7 Fuel tank securing strap

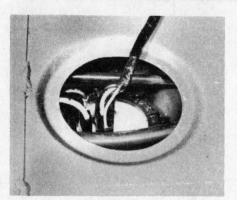

6.2 Fuel tank transmitter beneath the rear floor

8.1 Showing throttle lever and cable on a fuel injection model

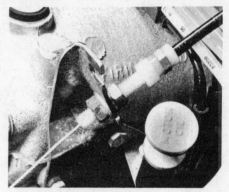

8.2 Accelerator cable and bracket on a fuel injection model

1982 on 900 models

6   Unscrew the choke control knob then remove the gear lever housing cover screws and lift it sufficiently to disconnect the cable and wiring.
7   Release the grommet from the bulkhead and withdraw the cable.

99 models

8   Remove the lower facia panel then unscrew the control knob and the plastic washer on the warning light.
9   Disconnect the warning light wiring and unscrew the cable nut.
10   Release the grommet from the bulkhead and withdraw the cable.

All models

11   Refitting is a reversal of removal, but adjust the cable to remove all slackness.

8   Accelerator cable – removal and refitting

1   Turn the throttle lever at the engine and disconnect the inner cable (photo).
2   Loosen the nuts and disconnect the outer cable from the bracket (photo).

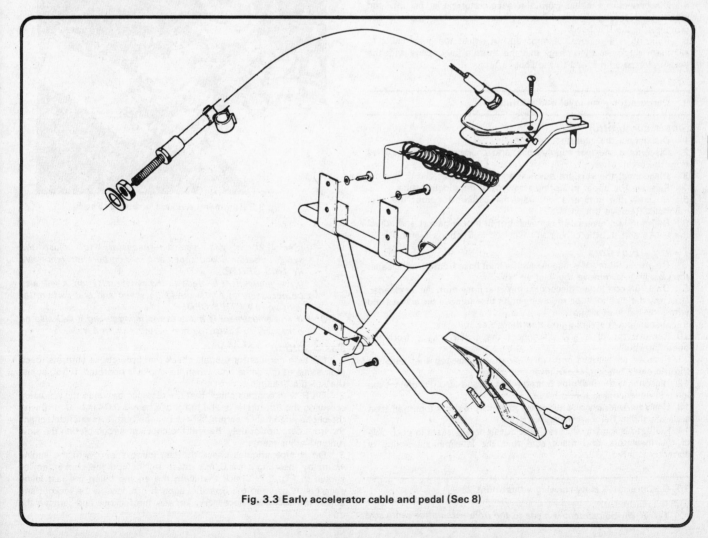

Fig. 3.3 Early accelerator cable and pedal (Sec 8)

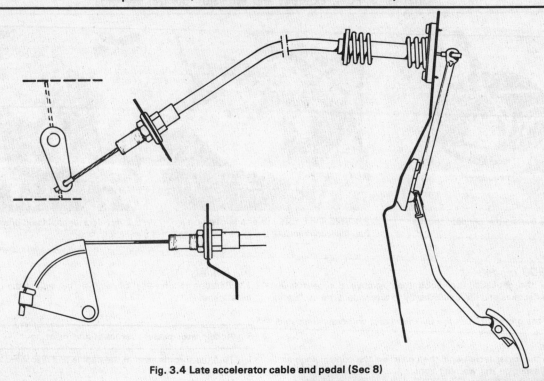

Fig. 3.4 Late accelerator cable and pedal (Sec 8)

3   Remove the lower facia panel.
4   Disconnect the cable from the accelerator pedal or arm and withdraw it through the bulkhead. Where applicable unscrew the grommet in the bulkhead.
5   Refitting is a reversal of removal, but adjust the outer cable to eliminate slackness then check that the throttle fully opens with the accelerator pedal pressed to the floor.

9   Carburettor – removal and refitting

Single carburettor
1   Disconnect the inlet duct.
2   Disconnect the fuel supply hose, and choke and throttle cables from the carburettor.
3   Disconnect the vacuum advance and retard hose.
4   Remove the upper mounting screw from the dipstick tube.
5   Unscrew the nuts and withdraw the carburettor from the inlet manifold. Remove the gasket.
6   Refitting is a reversal of removal, but fit a new gasket and adjust the choke and throttle cables as described in Sections 7 and 8.

Twin carburettors
7   On pre-1983 models disconnect the inlet hose from the air cleaner then unclip and remove the inlet air box.
8   On 1983 on models disconnect the inlet hose from the air cleaner. Unscrew the dipstick tube mounting bolts then remove the screws and withdraw the inlet air box.
9   Disconnect the choke and throttle cables.
10 Remove the clips and disconnect the choke linkage from the operating rod.
11 Remove the screws and withdraw the air box together with the throttle cable bracket, choke lever and gasket.
12 Disconnect the fuel pipe from the hoses, and also disconnect the ignition advance and retard hoses.
13 Unscrew the nuts and withdraw both carburettors together, then separate them. Remove the gaskets.
14 Refitting is a reversal of removal, but fit new gaskets to each side of the insulators, and make sure that the intermediate spring is correctly located.

10   Carburettor – slow running adjustment

1   *If any adjustment is made to the front carburettor vent valve*

Fig. 3.5 Removing twin carburettors (Sec 9)

(Sec 12), it will also be necessary to adjust the synchronisation, idling speed and rear carburettor vent valve IN THIS ORDER.
2   *If any adjustment is made to the synchronisation, it will also be necessary to adjust the idling speed and rear carburettor vent valve IN THIS ORDER.*
3   *If any adjustment is made to the idling speed it will also be necessary to adjust the rear carburettor vent valve.*

Basic setting – choke
1   On twin carburettor models check that both choke controls touch their stops at the same time when the choke is operated. If not, adjust the spindle linkages.
2   On B type engines check that the distance between the adjusting screw on the throttle lever and the choke cam is 0.04 in (1.0 mm) with the choke knob fully inserted. Where twin carburettors are fitted check the front carburettor only. Repeat the check after completing the slow running adjustments.
3   On H type engines check the fast idling speed with the engine warm by inserting an 8.0 mm twist drill behind the choke cam as shown in Fig. 3.7. Check that with the engine idling the fast idling speed is as given in the Specifications. If not, loosen the locknut and adjust the screw as necessary. Tighten the locknut and remove the drill.

Fig. 3.6 Basic choke setting clearance on the carburettor (Sec 10)

Fig. 3.7 Adjusting the choke fast idling setting using a drill (Sec 10)

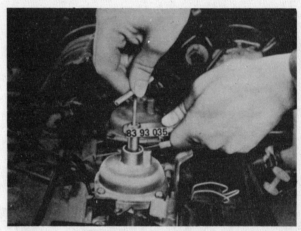

Fig. 3.8 Using the special tool to adjust the mixture (Sec 10)

Fig. 3.9 Carburettor adjusting screw locations (Sec 10)

Basic setting — metering needle

4 Unscrew the damper and cap.

5 Mark the vacuum chamber cover in relation to the carburettor body then remove the screws and withdraw the cover and spring.

6 Lift out the piston and diaphragm then using Saab tool 83 93 035 adjust the metering needle so that its shoulder is level with the bottom of the piston.

7 Refit the piston, diaphragm, and cover together with the spring making sure that the diaphragm tab engages the cut-out. Top up the damper with oil to within 0.4 in (10.0 mm) of the top.

Twin carburettors — synchronisation and idling

8 Run the engine to normal operating temperature and allow it to idle.

9 Adjust the idle speed screw on the front carburettor so that the engine is running at the specified idling speed.

10 If an air flow balancer is available check that the air flow through both carburettors is identical. Alternatively a rough check can be made using a short length of plastic tube positioned in each carburettor inlet in turn — the amount of hiss should be identical. If necessary loosen the locknut and adjust the screw on the intermediate linkage. Tighten the locknut afterwards.

CO content (mixture) setting

11 Run the engine to normal operating temperature and make sure that the choke control is fully off.

12 Where the setting speed is 2000 rpm clamp the distributor vacuum hose, and disconnect the crankcase ventilation hoses.

13 Connect a CO meter and tachometer to the engine and check that the readings are as given in the Specifications with the engine idling.

14 If adjustment is necessary unscrew and remove the damper and cap and use tool 83 93 035 to raise or lower the metering needle as required. To use the tool hold the piston and diaphragm stationary with the sleeve and turn the spindle clockwise to richen the mixture or anti-clockwise to weaken the mixture.

15 Stop the engine and refit the hoses as necessary. Refit the damper and cap. Remove the CO meter and tachometer.

Other adjustments

16 Refer to Fig. 3.9. The float chamber vent valve on the front carburettor of twin carburettor models is set by the manufacturers and will not normally require adjustment. If it is altered it will affect the other slow running adjustments.

17 Similarly the vent valve on the rear carburettor will not normally require adjustment.

Pre-1984 models

1 Vent valve (front carburettor)	3 Engine idling speed
2 Synchronising adjustment	4 Vent valve (rear carburettor)

1984 models

1 Redundant tapped hole	4 Vent valve (rear carburettor)
2 Synchronising adjustment	5 Engine idling speed
3 Vent valve (front carburettor)	

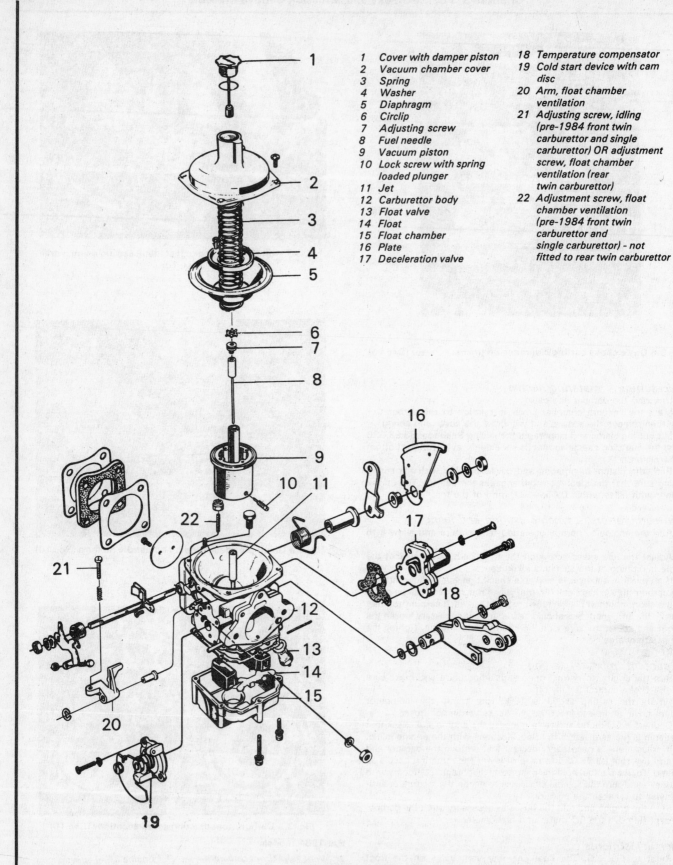

1 Cover with damper piston
2 Vacuum chamber cover
3 Spring
4 Washer
5 Diaphragm
6 Circlip
7 Adjusting screw
8 Fuel needle
9 Vacuum piston
10 Lock screw with spring loaded plunger
11 Jet
12 Carburettor body
13 Float valve
14 Float
15 Float chamber
16 Plate
17 Deceleration valve
18 Temperature compensator
19 Cold start device with cam disc
20 Arm, float chamber ventilation
21 Adjusting screw, idling (pre-1984 front twin carburettor and single carburettor) OR adjustment screw, float chamber ventilation (rear twin carburettor)
22 Adjustment screw, float chamber ventilation (pre-1984 front twin carburettor and single carburettor) - not fitted to rear twin carburettor

Fig. 3.10 Exploded view of front carburettor (twin carburettor engine) or single carburettor arrangement – typical pre-1984 arrangement (Sec 11)

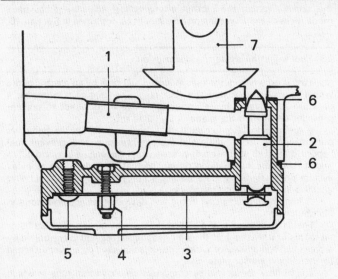

Fig. 3.12 Checking the float setting (Sec 11)

Fig. 3.11 Cross-section of the temperature compensator (Sec 11)

1 Air passage
2 Valve
3 Bi-metallic strip
4 Adjustment nut
5 Bi-metallic strip retaining screw
6 Seal
7 Jet bridge

11 Carburettor – overhaul

1 Clean the external surfaces of the carburettor.
2 Unscrew the damper and cap.
3 Mark the vacuum chamber cover in relation to the body then remove the screws and withdraw the cover and spring.
4 Lift out the piston and diaphragm.
5 If necessary remove the metering needle from the piston by unscrewing the screw then using Saab tool 83 93 035 and turning the spindle anti-clockwise.
6 Remove the screws from the top of the piston and withdraw the two washers followed by the diaphragm. Only one washer is fitted to the twin carburettors.
7 Remove the screws and withdraw the float chamber and gasket.
8 Unclip and remove the float and spindle.
9 Unscrew and remove the needle valve and washer.
10 Remove the countersunk screws and withdraw the choke mechanism.
11 Remove the screws and withdraw the temperature compensator. Recover the two O-ring seals.
12 Clean all the components and examine them for wear and damage. The diaphragm should be checked for distortion and cracks. Check that the temperature compensator valve moves freely. Clean the body using an air line or tyre pump.
13 Commence assembly by locating the diaphragm on the piston with the tab in the cut-out.
14 Fit the washer(s) then insert and tighten the screws taking care not to distort the diaphragm.
15 Insert the metering needle housing in the piston and use tool 83 93 035 to secure the needle. Fit and tighten the lock screw into the groove in the housing and use the tool to adjust the needle so that its shoulder is level with the bottom of the piston.
16 Fit the piston and diaphragm to the body making sure that the diaphragm rim locates in the body groove.
17 Fit the vacuum chamber cover in its previously noted position, then insert and tighten the screws.
18 Clip the float and spindle in position with the flat side of the float away from the body.
19 Invert the carburettor and use vernier calipers to check that the float setting is as given in the Specifications. The measurement is taken from the top of the float to the float chamber mating surface. If necessary bend the metal tab which contacts the needle valve.
20 Insert and tighten the needle valve and washer.

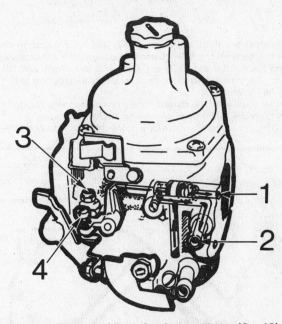

Fig. 3.13 Carburettor float chamber ventilation (Sec 12)

1 To air cleaner
2 To atmosphere
3 Vent valve adjustment (pre-1984 front carburettor)
4 Idle speed adjustment (pre-1984 front carburettor) OR vent valve adjustment (rear carburettor) OR vent valve adjustment (1984 front carburettor)

21 Fit the float chamber together with a new gasket and slide on the chamber until the O-ring makes contact. Insert all the screws loosely then press down the chamber and tighten them all evenly.
22 Fit the choke unit and tighten the screws.
23 Fit the temperature compensator together with two new O-ring seals and tighten the screws evenly.

12 Carburettor vent valve – checking and adjustment

1 The vent valve facilitates good starting when the engine is hot by preventing vaporized fuel entering the inlet manifold. On twin carburettor engines it also prevents 'run-on' after the ignition has been switched off.
2 To check the valve first connect a hose to the atmosphere air aperture (Fig. 3.13). If the carburettor is removed from the engine and the fuel inlet pipe disconnected, plug the fuel inlet.

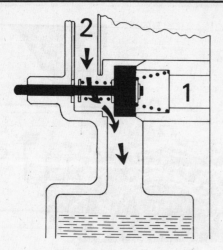

Fig. 3.14 Position of carburettor vent valve with throttle closed (Sec 12)

1   To air cleaner   *2   From atmosphere*

3   Fully close the throttle and check that it is not possible to blow through the hose (ie the float chamber is open to the atmosphere).
4   Open the throttle lever 0.02 to 0.04 in (0.5 to 1.0 mm) and check that it is now possible to blow through the hose prooving that the valve is half open.
5   Further opening of the throttle should prevent blowing through the hose as the valve will only allow venting to the air cleaner.
6   If necessary adjust the valve by loosening the locknut and turning

the screw. Tighten the locknut afterwards. If adjustment has been made recheck the slow running adjustment as described in Section 10.

13   Fuel injection system – description

Fuel is drawn from the rear mounted fuel tank by an electric pump which is mounted within the fuel tank. The pump incorporates a pressure relief valve and a non-return valve in its outlet to prevent pressure drop when the pump is switched off.

A fuel accumulator is mounted in the fuel line from the pump, its purpose being (i) to maintain system pressure and prevent fuel vaporizing and so ensure an easy start when the engine is warm, (ii) to absorb pressure fluctuations during normal operation, (iii) to delay system pressure rise at cold starting to prevent too much fuel being injected into the engine cylinders.

A fuel line filter is fitted in the line between the accumulator and distributor unit.

Fuel is distributed to the engine cylinders by means of a distributor unit. This unit meters fuel through injector valves and is controlled by a pressure regulator valve which in turn is actuated by a lever attached to the airflow sensor plate.

The airflow sensor device comprises an air venturi tube in which an air flow sensor plate moves. The plate is connected through a lever to the fuel distributor and automatically controls the quantity of fuel injected according to the engine speed and load.

The remaining components of the system are refinements and include a warm-up regulator, a cold start valve, a line pressure regulator and an auxiliary air valve to compensate for losses due to condensation in the inlet manifold and combustion chambers at cold starting.

Turbo models incorporate a fuel boosting system to provide extra fuel for rapid acceleration and to assist internal cooling of the engine during sustained periods of load.

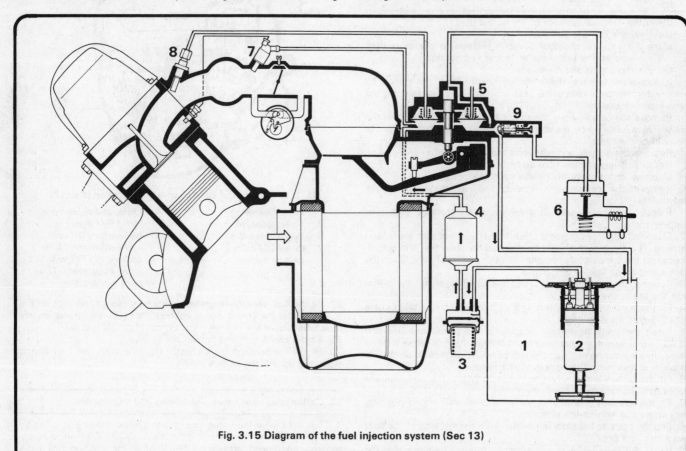

Fig. 3.15 Diagram of the fuel injection system (Sec 13)

1	*Fuel tank*	*4*	*Fuel filter*	*6*	*Warm up regulator*
2	*Fuel pump*	*5*	*Fuel distributor*	*7*	*Cold start valve*
3	*Fuel accumulator*				

8	*Injection valves*
9	*Line pressure regulator*

15.1 Air inlet duct on fuel injection models

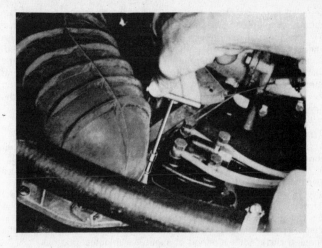

Fig. 3.16 Adjusting the idling mixture on fuel injection models
(Sec 15)

14 Fuel injection system – maintenance

1   Every 30 000 miles (45 000 km) renew the fuel filter.
2   At the same time check the security of all wiring, pipes and hoses in the system.

15 Fuel injection system – adjustments

These adjustments are not to be regarded as routine but are only required if engine performance or idling quality deteriorate and are not the result of other engine components (ignition, valves etc) needing adjustment or overhaul.

Throttle valve
1   Remove the air hose and check that the throttle valve is central in its bore (photo).
2   Loosen the locknut and unscrew the throttle stop screw so that the valve is completely closed.
3   Turn the screw until it just touches the lever, then turn it a further third of a turn and tighten the locknut. The clearance between the valve and bore should now be approximately 0.002 in (0.05 mm).

Idling speed and mixture
4   A throttle valve bypass control screw is provided on the venturi housing to adjust engine idling speed. First run the engine to normal operating temperature then connect a CO meter and tachometer.
5   Allow the engine to idle and check that the idling speed is as given in the Specifications. If not, loosen the locknut and turn the adjusting screw as necessary, Tighten the locknut afterwards.
6   Adjustment of the mixture involves removing a plug from the fuel distributor and on late models a special tool is required. In some territories removal of the plug by unauthorised persons is illegal.
7   Run the engine to normal operating temperature and remove the plug from the fuel distributor. Obtain an Allen key or special tool and connect a CO meter and tachometer.

Non-catalyst North American models
8   Disconenct the 'pulse-air' hose and plug the air inlet to the return valves.
9   On Canadian and 1979 USA models disconnect the hose from the charcoal canister.
10 Insert the CO meter sond in the exhaust pipe.

Catalyst 1979 North American models
11 Disconnect the hose from the charcoal canister.
12 Insert the CO meter sond in the exhaust pipe.
13 Disconnect the oxygen sond wire and cover it with insulating tape.

Catalyst 1980 North American models
14 Remove the plug from the front exhaust pipe and insert the CO meter.
15 Disconnect the oxygen sond wire and cover it with insulating tape.

All models
16 Rev up the engine and allow it to idle for 30 seconds, then note the reading on the CO meter.
17 If adjustment is necessary turn the adjustment key clockwise to enrich or anti-clockwise to weaken the mixture. Note that the Allen key must be removed before increasing the engine speed otherwise damage may occur.

Catalyst North American models
18 Connect the oxygen sond wire and check that the CO reading after the catalyser is less than 0.4% with the catalyser at normal operating temperature.

All models
19 Disconnect the CO meter and tachometer, and refit the plug. Reconnect the hoses as required.

16 Fuel injection system – testing components

1   The following components can be tested without the use of special equipment. Renewal is described in the next Section.

Fuel pump
2   Remove the cover plate within the luggage boot or compartment and using a voltmeter measure the voltage between the positive and

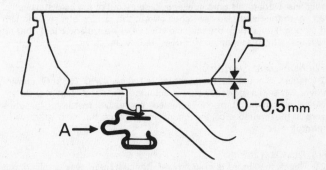

Fig. 3.17 Correct 'rest' position for air flow sensor plate (Sec 16)

A = wire clip

negative terminals of the fuel pump when it is operating (photo). The voltage should not be below 11.5V otherwise it must be renewed.
3   Fuel pump discharge can be checked by disconnecting the return fuel line at the fuel distributor provided the fuel filter is not clogged. Connect a hose to the return outlet at the fuel distributor and place the free end in a suitable container. Remove the fuel pump relay and connect terminals 30 and 87 with a wire link. Switch on the ignition for 30 seconds and check that the discharge is as given in the Specifications.

Auxiliary air valve
4   Make sure that the engine is cold and that the safety circuit connection at the airflow sensor is disconnected where applicable.
5   If the cold engine control pressure is also to be checked disconnect the wiring from the warm up regulator.
6   On H type engine models remove the fuel pump relay and connect terminals 30 and 87 with a wire brush. Switch on the ignition.
7   Using a torch and mirror, check that there is an opening (oval in shape) within the valve. Switch on the ignition and observe that the opening closes after a period of about five minutes (photos).

Warm up regulator
8   Disconnect the lead from the warm-up regulator and bridge the contacts in the lead plug with a voltmeter (photo).
9   On B type engines disconnect the safety circuit at the airflow sensor and switch on the ignition.
10 On H type engines remove the fuel pump relay and connect terminals 30 and 87 with a wire link. Switch on the ignition.
11 Check that the recorded voltage is at least 11.5 volt.

Fuel injection valves
12 Remove the flexible bellows from the airflow sensor.
13 Unscrew the injection valves from the inlet manifold (leaving the fuel lines connected) and place them in a clean container (photo).
14 On B type engines disconnect the safety circuit at the airflow sensor and switch on the ignition.
15 On H type engines remove the fuel pump relay and connect terminals 30 and 87 with a wire link. Switch on the ignition.
16 Raise the lever in the airflow sensor and observe the fuel spray from the injection nozzles. If the spray is restricted or poorly defined, the valves should be removed for cleaning by your dealer or renewed.
17 Switch off the ignition and wipe the ends of the injection valve nozzles dry. Lift the airflow sensor lever and check the nozzles for leakage of fuel. If a drop of fuel forms in under fifteen seconds, then the injection valves must be cleaned or renewed.

Cold start valve
18 Disconnect the lead from the cold start valve and unscrew it from the throttle valve housing. Do not disconnect the fuel line (photo).
19 Connect two leads between the cold start valve terminals and a main beam terminal of one of the headlamps and earth.
20 On B type engines disconnect the safety circuit at the airflow sensor and switch on the ignition.
21 On H type engines remove the fuel pump relay and connect terminals 30 and 87 with a wire link. Switch on the ignition.
22 Place the cold start valve in a container and have an assistant switch the headlamps to main beam for a period not exceeding thirty seconds. During this time, fuel should spray out of the cold start valve.
23 With the headlamps switched off but the ignition still switched on (fuel pump operating) dry the cold start valve nozzle and check that no fuel leaks from the valve. If it does, renew the valve.

Thermo-time switch
24 When the engine temperature is below 45°C (113°F) current flows while the starter motor is actuated. To check that the switch closes when the starter is actuated, connect a test-lamp in series across the contacts of the connector plug of the cold start valve (photo).

Air flow sensor
25 Check that there is a steady resistance as the lever is raised, but no resistance as it is lowered.
26 The plate should be central within the venturi and positioned as shown in Fig. 3.17 when at rest. Adjustment is made by bending the wire clip beneath the plate after removing the unit.

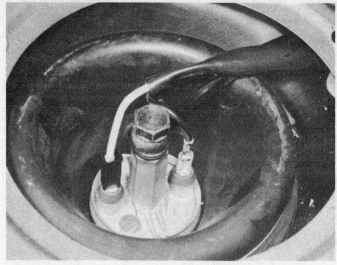
16.2 Fuel pump location beneath the rear floor on a fuel injection model

16.7A Disconnecting the auxiliary air valve top hose

16.7B Auxiliary air valve location

16.8 Warm up regulator lead connector

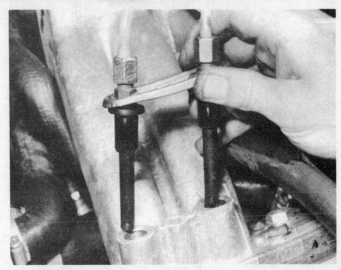
16.13 Removing the fuel injection valves

16.18 Cold start valve location

16.24 Cold start valve thermo time switch location

17 Fuel injection system – removal and refitting of components

1   *The fuel pump* is located on the top of the fuel tank. First disconnect the battery negative terminal.

2   Remove the cover plate from the luggage boot or compartment and disconnect the wiring from the pump.

3   Hold the pump stationary then disconnect the delivery pipe by unscrewing the union.

4   On early models turn the top plate anti-clockwise and withdraw the pump and O-ring.

5   On late models insert a jointed screwdriver through the special hole and release the clamp. Withdraw the pump.

6   Release the clips and remove the splash guard and mounting from the pump.

7   On early models when reassembling the splash guard to the pump and the pump to the mounting, make sure that the parts take up the attitude shown in Fig. 3.18.

8   Make sure that the height of the splash guard is also as illustrated in Fig. 3.19.

9   Install the pump using a new seal (early models) and reconnect the leads and fuel line to it. On later models the suction strainer inlet must be positioned facing to the rear and to the right at an angle of 45°.

10   *The fuel accumulator* is located on the side of the fuel tank (photo).

17.10 Fuel accumulator

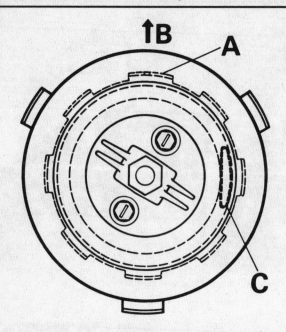

Fig. 3.18 End view of fuel pump fitted to early models (Sec 17)

A	Wide tongue	C	Splash guard indent
B	Front of car		

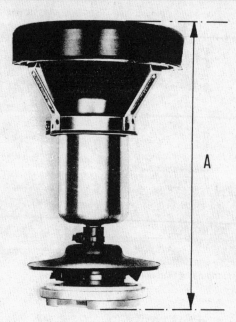

Fig. 3.19 Fuel pump dimension (Sec 17)

A = 8.58 in (218.0 mm) on pre-1980 models

A = 9.29 in (236.0 mm) on 1980 on models

Removal is carried out by disconnecting the fuel lines from it and pulling it from its bracket. Make sure that when installing the new accumulator the fuel lines are correctly connected (fuel pump line nearest the edge of the accumulator).

11 *The mixture control unit* is mounted on the air cleaner and consists of a *fuel distributor* and *the airflow sensor*. To remove the unit, disconnect the fuel lines from the fuel distributor and disconnect the lines to the injection valves then the control pressure line (photos).

12 Remove the flexible bellows which run between the airflow sensor and the throttle valve housing.

13 Remove the retaining bolts and lift the mixture control unit from the air cleaner. If the fuel distributor is to be separated from the airflow sensor, take care that the control plunger does not fall out. Do not handle the plunger but if this is unavoidable, clean it before installation with fuel. When refitting the fuel distributor (which is a sealed unit and must be renewed complete if faulty), check that the O-ring seal is in

position and tighten its three retaining bolts no tighter than 3lbf ft (4 Nm).

14 *The line pressure regulator* is screwed into the fuel distributor and should not be dismantled unless absolutely essential. Pressure adjustment is carried out by varying the thickness of the shims on the end of the spring.

15 *The airflow sensor* can be dismantled if the complete mixture control unit is first removed from the engine and the fuel distributor detached from it.

16 Remove the lower plastic section from the airflow sensor and extract the two stop bracket mounting screws. Remove the bracket, spring, insulation and connectors, as applicable.

17 Extract the retaining screws and remove the sensor plate.

18 Extract the circlips from the lever seating and remove the shims, seals, spring and balls.

19 Remove the counter-weight screw and press out the pivot.

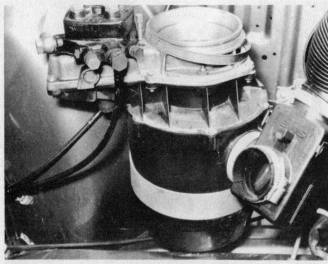

17.11A Mixture control unit and air cleaner unit

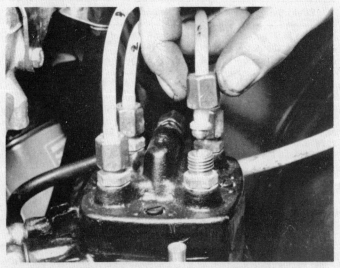

17.11B Disconnecting the fuel line from the fuel distributor

20 Withdraw the lever, counter-weight and adjustment arm.
21 Reassemble the stop bracket in the reverse order to dismantling. Tighten the screws only to 4 lbf ft (6 Nm).
22 Fit the counter-weight to the lever tightening the screw only fingertight. Place the adjustment arm in the lever so that the socket headed screw on the arm is visible.
23 Apply Silicone grease to both bearings and install the lever/arm assembly in the airflow sensor housing and insert the pivot.
24 Apply grease to the balls and fit them together with the spring, seals, shims and circlips. The spring goes on the side which has the longer bearing seat and the circlips should have their sharp edges facing outwards.
25 Centre the sensor plate in the air venturi and then centre the lever so that the threaded holes in both components are in alignment with each other.
26 Tighten the counter-weight screw to a torque of 4 lbf ft (6 Nm) and then fit the sensor plate screw and tighten it to a similar torque. Check that the lever can be moved without binding.
27 Adjust the rest position of the sensor plate by bending the wire loop on the stop bracket underneath the airflow sensor.
28 Now set the position of the adjustment arm. To do this, use a depth gauge and measure the distance between the face with which the fuel distributor mates and the needle bearing. This should be between 0.71 and 0.75 in. (18 to 19 mm), if not turn the mixture control screw using an Allen key.
29 With the mixture control unit (consisting of the fuel distributor and airflow sensor) installed to the engine, the mixture should be checked as described in Section 15.
30 *Fuel injection valves* must be removed only after cleaning away any surrounding dirt. Disconnect the fuel line using two spanners to prevent the valve turning, then remove the retaining plate.
31 *The warm up regulator* is located by the thermostat housing. Disconnect the fuel lines and wiring then unbolt and remove it (photo).
32 *The auxiliary air valve* is located by the distributor on B type engines and by the warm up regulator on H type engines. Disconnect the hoses and wiring and remove the mounting screws (photo).

18 Manifolds and exhaust system – general

1 The inlet and exhaust manifolds can be removed and refitted with the engine in the car. The cooling system will have to be drained before the inlet manifold can be removed. Always use new gaskets when refitting and tighten all nuts and bolts to the specified torque (photos).
2 The exhaust system is of three section type and varies slightly in design according to date of production and model.
3 The centre and rear mountings are of flexible type (photos).
4 Examination of the exhaust pipe and silencers at regular intervals is worthwhile as small defects may be repairable when, if left they will almost certainly require renewal of one of the sections of the system. Also, any leaks, apart from the noise factor, may cause poisonous exhaust gases to get inside the car which can be unpleasant, to say the least, even in mild concentrations. Prolonged inhalation could cause sickness and giddiness.
5 As the sleeve connections and clamps are usually very difficult to separate it is quicker and easier in the long run to remove the complete system from the car when renewing a section. It can be expensive if another section is damaged when trying to separate a bad section from it.
6 To remove the system first disconnect the rear mounting rubber.
7 Disconnect the centre mounting rubber.
8 Disconnect the manifold to downpipe connecting flange and then withdraw the complete exhaust system from below and out to the rear of the vehicle. If necessary, jack up the rear of the vehicle to provide more clearance (photo).
9 When separating the damaged section to be removed cut away the damaged part from the adjoining good section rather than risk damaging the latter.
10 If small repairs are being carried out it is best, if possible, not to try and pull the sections apart.
11 Refitting should be carried out after connecting the two sections together. De-burr and grease the connecting socket and make sure

17.31 Fuel lines on the warm up regulator

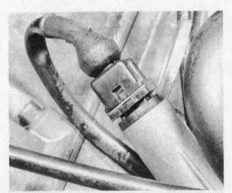
17.32 Lead connector on the auxiliary air valve

18.1A To remove the inlet manifold on a fuel injection model disconnect the vacuum hoses ...

18.1B ... coolant hoses ...

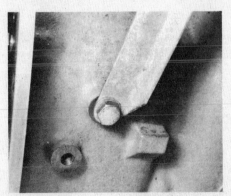
18.1C ... mounting bracket ...

18.1D ... mounting bolts ...

18.1E ... and remove the inlet manifold ...

18.1F ... and gasket

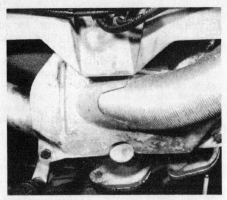

18.1G To remove the exhaust manifold disconnect the hot air hose ...

18.1H ... remove the power steering pump bracket (where applicable) ...

18.1I ... unbolt the gearbox oil dipstick tube ...

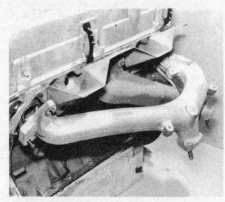

18.1J ... remove the nuts and withdraw the exhaust manifold ...

18.1K ... heat shield ...

18.1L ... and gaskets

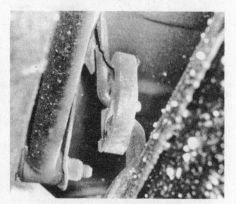

18.3A Exhaust centre mounting rubber

18.3B Exhaust rear mounting rubber

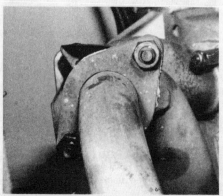

18.8 Exhaust downpipe flange

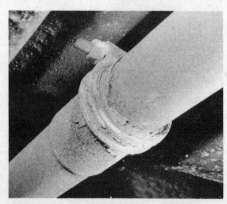

18.11 Exhaust section joint

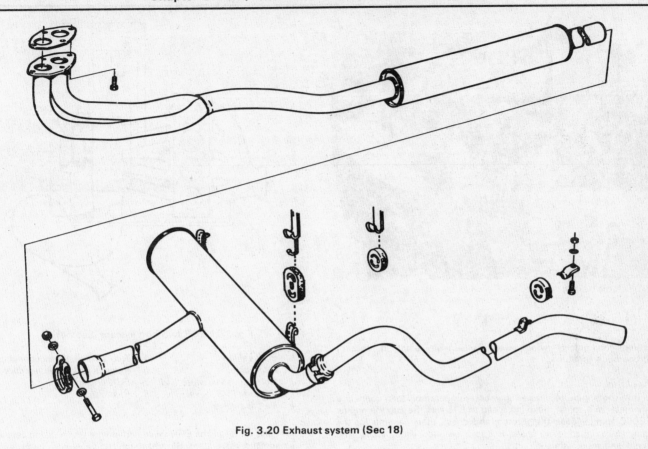

Fig. 3.20 Exhaust system (Sec 18)

that the clamp is in good condition and slipped over the front pipe but do not tighten it at this stage (photo).

12 Connect the system to the manifold and connect the rear support strap. Now adjust the attitude of the silencer. Fit a new flange gasket or ring.

13 Tighten the pipe clamps and flange bolts. Check that the exhaust system will not knock against any part of the vehicle when deflected slightly in a sideways or upwards direction.

14 Note that on Turbo models the joint between the downpipe and the charge pressure regulator incorporates a sealing ring instead of a gasket.

19 Fuel evaporative emission control system – general

1 This system is fitted to certain North American models and incorporates a charcoal filter which absorbs fuel vapour from the fuel tank. A roll-over valve is also incorporated to prevent fuel escaping into the engine compartment.

2 The charcoal canister must be renewed every 30 000 miles (48 000 km).

20 Exhaust emission control system – general

The following Sections 21 to 26 describe the exhaust emission control systems. The actual components fitted depend on the model, year of manufacture, and territory it is operated in. The crankcase ventilation system is described in Chapter 1.

21 Deceleration device system

General description

1 The device assists combustion during engine overrun in order to prevent the emission of unburned hydrocarbons.

2 The electric type incorporates an engine speed transmitter and a solenoid operated idling stop. During engine overrun the idling speed is increased to approximately 1550 rpm if the speed of the car exceeds 18 mph (30 kph).

3 The vacuum type incorporates a spring-loaded valve actuated by inlet manifold vacuum.

Checking

4 To check the electric type connect a tachometer and run the engine to normal operating temperature. Disconnect the positive solenoid cable and connect battery voltage. Rev the engine then release the throttle and check that the idling speed is maintained at 1550 rpm. If necessary adjust the solenoid with the screw. Connect a test lamp between the positive solenoid wire and earth, then drive the car at about 25 mph (40 kph) and declutch. Brake the car and check that the test lamp goes out at a speed of 18.6 mph (30 kph).

5 To check the vacuum controlled type run the engine to normal operating temperature and connect a tachometer. Adjust the idling speed to 875 rpm then rev up the engine to 3000 rpm, release the throttle, and check that the time for the engine to return to idling speed is 4 to 6 seconds. Unscrew the unit screw until the valve closes then adjust the idling speed of the engine in the normal way. Now screw in the unit screw until the engine speed is 1600 rpm and back off the screw two complete turns. Finally adjust the idling speed again. Note that the check should be completed without the radiator fan cutting in.

Component replacement

6 To remove the electric speed transmitter remove the lower facia panel and unplug the unit. The solenoid can be removed by disconnecting the wiring and unscrewing the unit.

7 To remove the vacuum valve disconnect the hose and unscrew the unit from the inlet manifold.

22 Dashpot system

General description

1 The dashpot system is a deceleration device to prevent the throttle

3

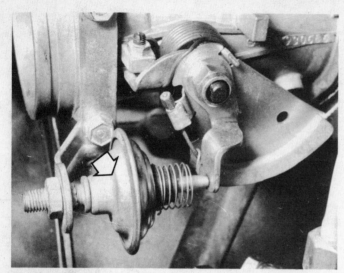

22.1 Throttle dashpot

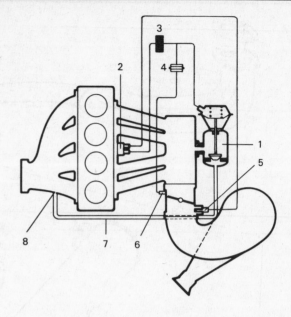

Fig. 3.21 EGR two-port system (Sec 24)

1 EGR valve	5 Two-port vacuum connection
2 PVS valve	6 Release vacuum connection
3 Holding valve (white end	7 EGR crosspipe
towards PVS valve)	8 Restriction
4 Release valve	

shutting too quickly which would otherwise result in unburnt hydrocarbons (photo).

Checking
2   Run the engine to normal operating temperature, then connect a tachometer and adjust the idling speed to 875 rpm. Rev up the engine to 3000 rpm, release the throttle, and check that the time for the engine to return to idling speed is 3 to 6 seconds. if not, loosen the locknut and reposition the unit.

Component replacement
3   Loosen the locknut and remove the unit from the bracket.

23 Delay valve system

General description
1   This unit is located in the distributor vacuum advance pipe and its purpose is to delay ignition advance during acceleration so reducing nitrous oxide emissions. Note that the white end of the valve must be towards the distributor.

Checking
2   Connect a tachometer and timing light and run the engine to normal operating temperature. Have an assistant open the throttle quickly so that the engine runs at 3000 rpm. Using the timing light check that the time from when the throttle was opened to when the ignition advances is between 4 and 8 seconds. If not, renew the delay valve.

Component replacement
3   Disconnect the hoses and remove the valve.

24 Exhaust gas recirculation (EGR) system

General description
1   In order to reduce nitrous oxide emissions a proportion of the exhaust gas is diverted into the inlet manifold and this inert gas prevents local hot spots in the combustion chambers. The EGR valve is operated by vacuum. The components are shown in Fig. 3.21 and the system operates in conjunction with engine temperature.

Checking
2   Remove the throttle valve housing, the EGR pipe, and the EGR valve.
3   Clean the pipe with a suitable solvent or piece of wire, and clean

the inlet and outlet of the EGR valve with a wire brush taking care not to damage the valve stem. Blow through the valve with compressed air.
4   Clean the calibrated hole in the exhaust manifold using a 0.20 in (5.0 mm) drill (manual transmission models) or 0.39 in (10.0 mm) drill (automatic transmission models).
5   Clean the calibrated hole in the inlet manifold using a 0.39 in (10.0 mm) drill.
6   Refit the unit using new gaskets and where applicable reset the warning counter unit.
7   To check the operation of the valve disconnect the PVS hose at the switch, suck the end of the hose and then release. The valve should be heard to close. Also suck on the hose with the engine idling and check that this causes the idling speed to drop.
8   To check the PVS valve disconnect the hoses and attempt to blow through the valve. With the engine cold the valve should be shut, but with the engine warm it should be open.
9   To check the cut-in speed on the two port system run the engine to normal operating temperature and connect a tachometer. Increase the engine speed and check that the valve opens at between 2600 and 3200 rpm on manual transmission models or between 2300 and 2900 rpm on automatic transmission models.
10 To check the holding valve on the two port system rev the engine to between 3000 and 3500 rpm then pinch the hose between the release valve and three-way nipple. Reduce the engine speed to idling and check that the EGR valve remains open for 6 more seconds.
11 To check the release valve in the two port system, rev the engine so that the EGR valve is open then reduce the speed to idling and check that the EGR valve closes immediately.

Component replacement
12 Removal of the EGR valve has been described already. Removal of the other components is straightforward, but it will be necessary to drain the cooling system before removing the PVS valve.

25 Pulse air system

General description
1   The pulse air system supplies air to the exhaust gases in order to facilitate complete combustion. The system utilises the brief vacuums

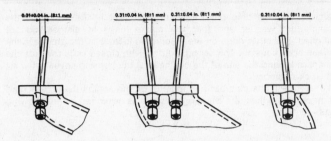

Fig. 3.22 Showing correct alignment of the pulse air inlet pipes (Sec 25)

which occur in the exhaust manifold during the engine cycle, to introduce air through check valves. There are two check valves, one to numbers 1 and 4 cylinders, and the other to numbers 2 and 3 cylinders.

Checking
2   Disconnect the hoses from the check valves and check that with the engine running at idling speed suction can be felt with the thumbs placed over the openings.

Component replacement
3   Unscrew the pipe unions and the mounting bracket and disconnect the air hose. Unscrew the mounting bracket bolt and withdraw the unit.
4   When refitting the inlet pipes to the exhaust manifold align them as shown in Fig. 3.22.

26 Oxygen sensor regulated system (Lambda)

General description
1   This system incorporates an oxygen sensor (Lambda sensor) in the exhaust manifold which controls the injection system electronically. The components are shown in Fig. 3.24 and it will be seen that a catalytic converter is also fitted in the exhaust system. The oxygen sensor must be renewed every 30 000 miles (48 000 km).

Checking
2   Checking the system is a complicated procedure involving the use of a pulse relation instrument, therefore it is recommended that a Saab dealer carries out the work.

Component replacement
3   To remove the oxygen sensor let the engine cool then disconnect the wiring and unscrew the unit. Handle the unit carefully as it is highly sensitive. When refitting coat the threads with an anti-seize compound, and reset the warning counter.
4   To remove the modulating valve disconnect the wiring, the small bore line to the valve and the return lines, and remove the valve. When refitting always use new seals and note that the rubber valve retainer is made of special rubber which must not be exposed to fuel.
5   To remove the control unit on early models slide back the passenger seat, remove the unit cover, disconnect the wiring and remove the screws. On later models tilt the rear seat forward to expose the unit.
6   To remove the throttle valve switch disconnect the wiring and remove the mounting screws. When refitting the switch position it so that with the throttle valve fully open there is a clearance of 0.008 to 0.020 in (0.2 to 0.5 mm) at the switch lever.
7   To remove the catalytic converter unbolt the flanges and remove the flat and conical seals.

27 Turbo system – general

General description
1   Some models are equipped with a turbocharger which provides an increase in power output and torque.

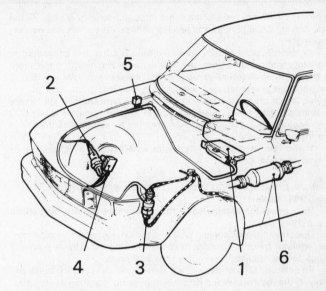

Fig. 3.23 Oxygen sensor regulated system component locations (Sec 26)

1	Electronic control unit	4	Throttle switch
2	Oxygen sensor	5	Relay
3	Modulating valve	6	Catalytic converter

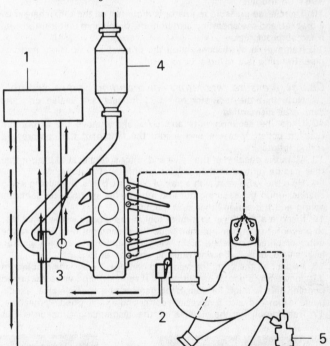

Fig. 3.24 Diagram of oxygen sensor regulated system (Sec 26)

1	Control unit	3	Oxygen sensor
2	Throttle valve switch, full-load enrichment	4	Catalytic converter
		5	Modulating valve

2   Turbocharging is achieved by installing a turbine in the exhaust system and using the exhaust gases to drive the turbine which in turn drives a compressor mounted on a common shaft. The compressor is located in the induction and therefore the charging pressure in the combustion chamber is increased.
3   The turbine shaft is mounted in a floating sliding-contact bearing and lubricating oil is supplied through a separate pipe from the oil

pump. The oil is returned to the sump through a large bore pipe. Piston type sealing rings provide the sealing between the shaft and bearing housing.

4   An overpressure switch, mounted on a bracket and connected to the inlet manifold by a hose, breaks the fuel pump circuit in the event of the charging pressure exceeding the pre-set limit. Over-revving of the engine is prevented by a rotor having a built-in centrifugal cut-out device which breaks the ignition circuit on B type engines. On H type engines the fuel pump relay cuts-out at engine speeds above 6000 rpm. A gauge indicating the charge pressure is mounted on the top of the instrument panel.

5   Some late models are fitted with an electronic APC system as described in Section 28.

Charge pressure regulator – removal and refitting
Pre-1981 models
6   Disconnect the battery leads, then remove the battery, heat shield and battery tray.

7   Disconnect the air cooling pipe and the exhaust pressure pipe from the regulator (photo). Remove the bolts securing the exhaust manifold flange to the regulator and collect the sealing ring.

8   Release the tabs of the locking plate, undo the securing bolts and remove the bellows pipe. Remove the turbo securing bolts, after releasing the lockplate tabs, and lift away the charge pressure regulator (photos).

9   Refitting is the reverse of the removal procedure. Always use a new gasket between the turbo and the charge pressure regulator and lock the nuts with the lockplates.

1981 on models
10   The charge pressure regulator is mounted on the turbocharger by a bracket, and the operating arm from the diaphragm unit is fitted with a tamperproof seal.

11   Removal is by disconnecting the bracket and housing, and link pipe. Refitting is a reversal of removal.

Charge pressure regulator – dismantling and reassembly
Note that the regulator on 1981 models is a sealed unit and cannot be dismantled.

12   Undo the securing nuts and bolts and remove the diaphragm housing cover. Measure and record the length of the compressed spring (photos).

13   Mark the position of the valve and outer spring seat to ensure that they can be refitted in their original positions at reassembly.

14   Hold the valve seat with a pair of pipe grip pliers, then using a ring spanner undo the securing nut and remove the spring outer seat, the spring and the spring inner seat (photos).

15   Insert a screwdriver or similar tool in the groove in the valve disc to prevent it from turning, then undo the diaphragm nut. Remove the outer diaphragm washer, plain washer, diaphragm housing, gasket, heat shield, gasket, bearing housing and gasket (photos).

16   Inspect all the parts for wear and damage. Renew the diaphragm if it shows any signs of deterioration. If the valve and valve seat need grinding this is a job for your Saab garage as a special valve spindle guide is required, also a valve seat cutter and a valve grinding machine.

17   Reassembly is the reverse of the dismantling procedure, but

ensure that the diaphragm inner ridge locates in the groove in the diaphragm washer and that the marks made at dismantling are aligned. The outer ridge on the diaphragm locates in the groove in the diaphragm housing. The spring is fitted with closed coils towards the diaphragm and the end of the coil nearest the housing cover at the six o'clock position.

18   Refit the charge pressure regulator on the engine then check, and if necessary adjust, the charging pressure as described in the following sub-section.

Charge pressure regulator – adjusting
19   On 1981 on models check the basic setting as follows. Hold the control arm in the 'closed' position with the operating arm disconnected, then adjust the length of the operating arm until it aligns with the control arm. Screw the end fitting onto the operating arm six turns then tighten the locknut. Connect the operating arm to the control arm and fit the circlip.

20   A pressure gauge and length of hose are required for checking the charge pressure. Connect the gauge to the connector on the inlet manifold by means of the hose and position the gauge beside the charge pressure gauge on the top of the instrument panel.

21   Drive the car to warm it up to normal operating temperature and then check the charging pressure as follows:

(a)   *Drive the car in 3rd gear (manual gearbox) or position 1 (automatic transmission) at an engine speed of less than 1500 rpm*

(b)   *Accelerate to full throttle, pedal right down to the floor, then as the engine speed approaches 3000 rpm apply the brakes (throttle pedal still pressed down) to put the car under full load at 3000 rpm and note the maximum pressure recorded on the pressure gauge*

22   If the pressure is not as given in the Specifications, adjust the regulator as follows.

Pre-1981 models

(a)   *Remove the heat shield and disconnect the exhaust pressure line from the diaphragm housing cover. Remove the diaphragm housing cover*

(b)   *Hold the spring seat with a pair of pipe grip pliers and slacken the locknut, then adjust the tension of the spring by turning the seat clockwise or anti-clockwise as required*

(c)   *After adjustment, tighten the locknut*

(d)   *Refit the diaphragm housing cover, use a new gasket, exhaust pressure line and heat shield*

(e)   *Recheck the charging pressure as described in paragraph 21 above*

1981 on models

(a)   *Disconnect the operating arm and lengthen it to reduce the pressure, shorten it to increase the pressure. Note that two turns are equivalent to 0.6 lbf/in^2 (0.04 bar).*

27.7 Turbo charge pressure regulator and connecting pipes

27.8A Removing the charge pressure regulator

27.8B Turbo unit with charge pressure regulator removed

27.12A To dismantle the charge pressure regulator remove the diaphragm housing cover ...

27.12B ... measure the length of the spring ...

27.14A ... remove the nut and outer seat ...

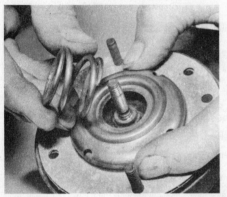

27.14B ... spring ...

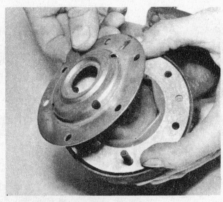

27.14C ... inner seat and gasket ...

27.15A ... nut, and washers ...

27.15B ... diaphragm ...

27.15C ... inner washer ...

27.15D ... diaphragm housing and heat shield ...

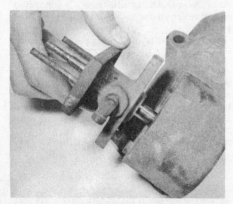

27.15E ... bearing housing ...

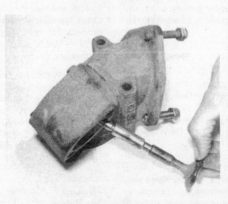

27.15F ... and valve

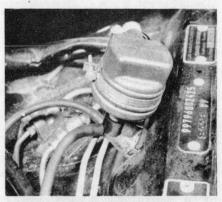

27.28 Turbo pressure switch location

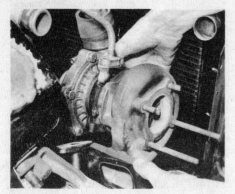
27.33A Removing the turbo unit

27.33B Engine with turbo unit removed

27.33C Showing the turbo unit oil return pipe on the cylinder block

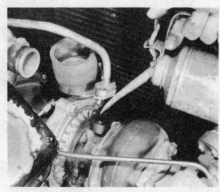
27.34A Priming the turbo unit with oil

27.34B Fitting the oil supply pipe to the turbo unit

Charge pressure regulator (pre-1981 models) – cleaning

23 The diaphragm housing of the charge pressure regulator should be cleaned every 30 000 miles (48 000 km).

24 Remove the heat shield. Disconnect the exhaust pressure line and remove the diaphragm housing cover.

25 Using a suitable brush, thoroughly clean the diaphragm housing.

26 Refit the cover, exhaust line and heat shield.

Pressure switch and gauge – checking

27 With the engine at idle speed, disconnect the inlet manifold to pressure gauge hose at the inlet manifold connector, then connect a pressure gauge and a suitable pump to the hose.

28 Use the pump to apply pressure to the switch and check that the engine cuts out at the specified pressure, see the Specifications at the beginning of this Chapter (photo).

29 The pressure gauge on the top of the instrument panel can be checked at the same time as the pressure switch. The needle should be within the wide orange zone at maximum charging pressure. At cut-out pressure the needle should be in front of the limit between the orange and red zones.

Turbo unit – removal and refitting

30 Remove the battery.

31 On pre-1981 models remove the charge pressure regulator as previously described and disconnect the hose between the compressor and throttle housing.

32 On 1981 on models remove the suction and pressure connections from the compressor and loosen the pre-heating hose. Remove the exhaust elbow.

33 On all models disconnect the oil supply and return lines then unbolt the turbo unit from the exhaust manifold (photos).

34 The turbo unit is not reparable, if it is defective, an exchange unit will have to be fitted. Refitting is the reverse of the removal procedure. Fill the oil inlet port with engine oil and always use new gaskets (photos). Disconnect the ignition coil and turn the engine over on the starter motor for about 30 seconds to prime the turbo unit lubricating system before starting the engine.

Fuel boost device – description and checking

1979 models

35 The fuel boost device is fitted in the fuel supply on turbocharged engines to supply extra fuel under heavy engine load conditions. It also improves engine cooling at continual high speed. The device consists of a solenoid valve and a pressure regulator which are connected in parallel with the control pressure regulator in the control pressure system.

36 The pressure regulator is preset approximately 14.5 lbf/ft^2 (1 kgf/cm^2) below the pressure of the control pressure regulator, therefore the control pressure will drop from 52.6 lbf/in^2 (3.7 kgf/cm^2) to 38.4 lbf/in^2 (2.7 kgf/cm^2) when the solenoid valve opens. This raises the position of the control plunger and thereby boosts the fuel supply to the engine. The solenoid is actuated either by a switch at the throttle valve or by means of the speed transmitter which is connected to the speedometer cable and which closes the circuit when the speed exceeds 80 mph (130 km/h).

37 The fuel boost device is checked when measuring the CO emission as follows:

- (a) *Warm up the engine to the normal operating temperature, connect a CO meter to the exhaust and check that the CO content is within the specification*
- (b) *Depress the actuating arm on the throttle valve switch and check that the CO value increases to the figure specified, refer to the Specification*
- (c) *Release the actuating arm and check that the CO value is to specification*

1980/81 models

38 The function of the system is similar to that for 1979 models, but the components are different as shown in Fig. 3.28.

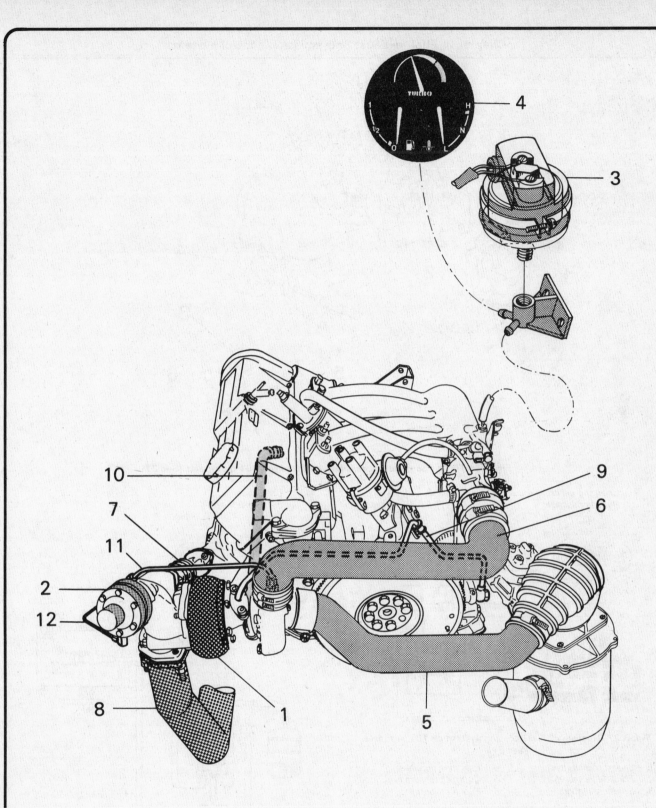

Fig. 3.25 Turbo system components (Sec 27)

1	Turbocharger	5	Hose, air cleaner to turbocharger
2	Wastegate boost control		
3	Pressure transducer	6	Hose, turbocharger to inlet manifold
4	Turbo gauge		

7	Bellows	10	Oil return line
8	Exhaust outlet pipe	11	Cooling air pipe
9	Oil supply line	12	Exhaust pressure line

3

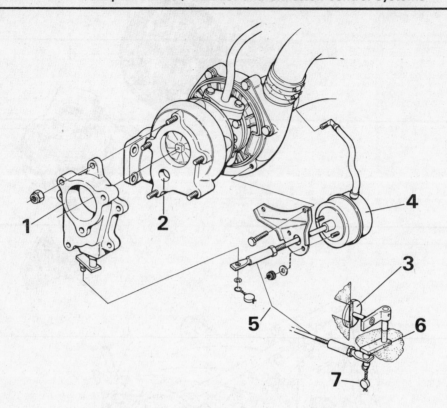

Fig. 3.26 Turbo charge pressure regulator fitted to 1981 on models (Sec 27)

1	Charging pressure regulator	3	Flap valve
2	Bypass passage	4	Diaphragm unit

5	Lever	7	Anti-tamper seal
6	Control arm		

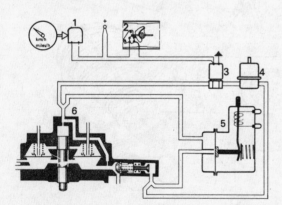

Fig. 3.27 Diagram of fuel boosting system on 1979 models (Sec 27)

1	Speed transmitter	4	Pressure regulator
2	Throttle valve switch	5	Control pressure regulator
3	Solenoid (valve)	6	Fuel distributor

39 To check the high load (partially open throttle) first run the engine to normal operating temperature and connect a CO meter. Remove the pressure hose from the butterfly housing and connect a pressure gauge and air pump to the hose. Plug the butterfly housing connection. With the engine idling increase the pressure to 11.6 lbf/in^2 (0.8 bar) and check that the CO reading is between 2 and 6%.

40 To check the wide-open throttle setting first remove the air pump and check that the CO reading returns to normal. Then depress the throttle valve switch and check that the CO reading is between 4 and 6%.

41 To check the residual pressure connect a pressure gauge between the non-return valve and the pressure tank. Using an air pump increase the pressure to 11.6 lbf/in^2 (0.8 bar) and check that the pressure does not drop below 8.7 lbf/in^2 (0.6 bar) after 2 minutes.

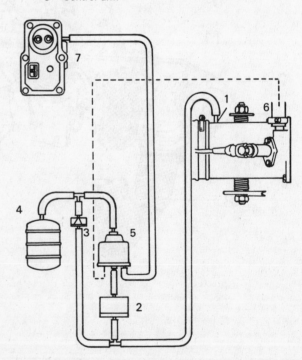

Fig. 3.28 Diagram of fuel boosting system on 1980/81 models (Sec 27)

1	Pressure outlet in the throttle housing (before the butterfly)	5	Electrical control valve
2	Delay valve	6	Throttle valve switch (62° throttle opening)
3	Non-return valve	7	Warm up regulator/boost control
4	Pressure tank		

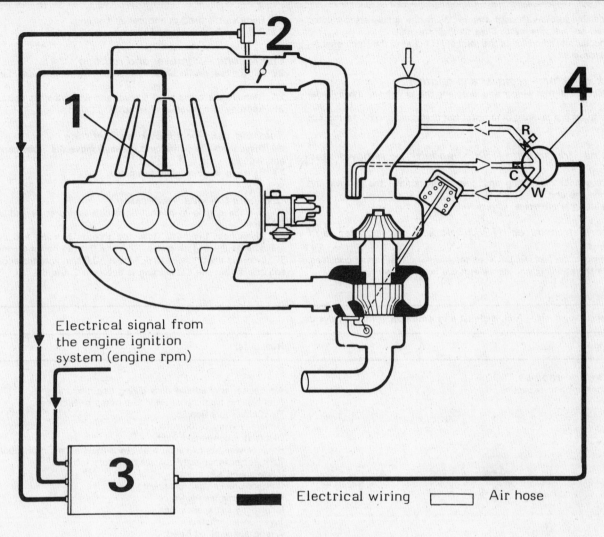

Electrical signal from the engine ignition system (engine rpm)

Electrical wiring   Air hose

Fig. 3.29 Diagram of the APC system (Sec 28)

1   Knock detector   2   Pressure transducer   3   Contol unit   4   Solenoid valve

28 APC system – general

General description

1   The automatic performance control (APC) system provides continual adjustment of the Turbo system by means of a knock detector which together wth other components controls the charge pressure. Differences in fuel octane rating can therefore be compensated for automatically to provide optimum performance.

2   Accurate testing of the system should be carried out by a Saab dealer as special instrumentation is required.

Charge pressure regulator – basic setting

3   This is identical to that described in Section 27 paragraphs 19 to 22 except that the operating arm end fitting should be screwed onto the operating arm $3\frac{1}{2}$ turns instead of 6 turns, and also the APC solenoid wires should be disconnected while checking the pressure on the road.

APC system – checking

4   Remove the pressure transducer from the inlet manifold and plug the aperture.

5   Connect a pressure gauge in the hose to the pressure transducer (1982 models) or pressure switch (1983 models).

6   Connect an air pump to the hose then start the engine and run it at 2000 rpm.

7   Increase the pressure with the air pump to 7.3 lbf/in² (0.5 bar) and check that the solenoid valve makes a 'chattering' sound. This proves the system is functioning correctly.

Pressure transducer – checking

8   On 1982 models disconnect the transducer hose at the inlet manifold and connect a pressure gauge. As from 1983 remove the bellows between the front and rear centre consoles, remove the padding and disconnect the transducer hose then connect the pressure gauge.

9   Connect an air pump to the transducer. Disconnect the wiring.

10 Connect an ohmmeter to the pressure switch terminals and check that the resistance is 10 ohm at atmospheric pressure.

11 Increase the pressure to 14.5 lbf/in² (1.0 bar) then reduce it to 8.7 lbf/in² (0.6 bar) while tapping the transducer.

12 Now measure the resistance which should be 88 ohm.

Solenoid valve – checking

13 Disconnect the wiring from the valve and the hose from the turbo compressor inlet to the valve R connection.

14 Connect a 12 volt supply to the solenoid terminals and check that

it is possible to blow through the unit. With the supply disconnected it should not be possible to blow through the unit.

15 Check that the orifice in the solenoid C outlet to the turbo charger is unobstructed.

Knock detector – removal and refitting

16 Disconnect the wiring and unscrew the unit from the cylinder block.

17 Refitting is a reversal of removal, but first clean and oil the threads of the unit.

Pressure transducer (1982 models) – removal and refitting

18 Disconnect the wiring and hose, then remove the screws and withdraw the unit.

19 Refitting is a reversal of removal.

Pressure transducer (1983 models) – removal and refitting

20 Remove the bellows between the front and rear centre consoles, remove the padding, and disconnect the hose and wiring.

21 Remove the bracket and unbolt the unit.

22 Refitting is a reversal of removal.

Control unit – removal and refitting

23 Lift the rear seat cushion and remove the multi-connector from the unit.

24 Remove the cross-head screws and withdraw the unit.

25 Refitting is a reversal of removal.

Solenoid valve – removal and refitting

26 Disconnect the wiring and hoses, remove the cross-head screws, and withdraw the unit.

27 Refitting is a reversal of removal.

Fuel boost device – checking

28 Run the engine to normal operating temperature and connect a CO meter.

29 Disconnect the hose from the throttle housing and connect a pressure gauge and air pump. Plug the throttle housing connection.

30 Increase the pressure to 8.7 lbf/in^2 (0.6 bar) with the engine idling and check that the CO reading is between 2 and 6%.

---

29 Fault diagnosis – fuel, exhaust and emission control systems

Symptom	Reason(s)
Carburettor engines	
Fuel consumption excessive	Air cleaner choked and dirty giving rich mixture.
	Fuel leaking from carburettor fuel pump or fuel lines.
	Float chambers flooding.
	Generally worn carburettor.
	Distributor condenser faulty.
	Balance weights or vacuum advance mechanism in distributor faulty.
	Carburettor incorrectly adjusted; mixture too rich.
	Idling speed too high.
	Contact breaker gap incorrect.
	Valve clearances incorrect.
	Incorrectly set spark plugs.
	Tyres under-inflated.
	Wrong spark plugs fitted.
	Brakes dragging.
	Emission control system faulty.
Insufficient fuel delivery or weak mixture due to air leaks	Partially clogged filters in pump and carburettor.
	Incorrectly seating valves in fuel pump.
	Fuel pump diaphragm leaking or damaged.
	Gasket in fuel pump damaged.
	Fuel pump valves sticking due to fuel gumming.
	Too little fuel in fuel tank (prevalent when climbing steep hills).
	Union joints or pipe connections loose.
	Split fuel pipe on suction side of fuel pump.
	Inlet manifold to block or inlet manifold to carburettor gaskets leaking.
	Fuel tank relief valve stuck closed.
Fuel injection engines	
Engine will not start (fuel pump not working)	Fuse blown.
	Faulty electrical connections to pump.
	Main pump relay not operating.
Engine will not start (fuel pump running)	Pressure sensor leads faulty.
	Temperature sensor (coolant) leads faulty.
	Defective pressure regulator.
Engine starts cold but stalls	Faulty (fuel injection) control contacts within distributor
	Pressure sensor defective.
Engine cuts out after misfiring at normal roadspeeds	Dirty (fuel injection) contacts within distributor.
	Lack of fuel pressure.
	Loose electrical plug connector.
Engine runs irregularly (white interior to exhaust tailpipe)	Insecure connection to injector.
	Injector sticking.

Symptom	Reason(s)
Lack of power	Low fuel pressure. Faulty pressure sensor. Throttle valve incorrectly adjusted.
Excessive fuel consumption	Incorrectly adjusted throttle valve switch. Incorrect fuel pressure. Sensors or control unit faulty.
Engine 'hunts' at idling	Leaking hose between auxiliary air regulator and inlet manifold. Throttle valve plate not closing correctly.
Engine misfires during acceleration	Throttle valve switch faulty or plug incorrectly connected to it (where applicable).
High idling speed cannot be reduced	System leaking air. Leaking seals under injector.

Turbo circuit

Symptom	Reason(s)
Noisy turbo unit	Defective turbo shaft bearing. Turbo shaft damaged and out of balance.
Charging pressure low	Defective seals and gaskets. Charging pressure setting incorrect. Charge pressure regulator valve sticking open. Air cleaner blocked.
Charging pressure too high	Exhaust pressure line loose and/or blocked. Defective charge pressure regulator diaphragm. Charge pressure regulator sticking closed. Charge pressure setting incorrect.
Engine knocking (pinking)	Charging pressure too high.
Turbo shaft oil seals leaking	Blocked oil return. Excessive crankcase pressure. Turbo unit seals defective.

EGR system

Symptom	Reason(s)
Poor idling or will not idle at all	EGR valve stuck open. Faulty vacuum signal switch (proportional system).
Engine runs erratically or accelerates slowly	Faulty EGR valve (proportional system). Incorrect residual pressure from amplifier (proportional system).
Poor engine response when engine cold	Faulty PVS valve (EGR proportional system).
Excessive exhaust gas CO emission	EGR valve stuck. Vacuum signal switch faulty. Incorrect residual pressure from amplifier (proportional system) or too high a signal. Incorrect calibrated EGR valve.

3

Chapter 4 Ignition system

For specifications applicable to later models, see Supplement at end of manual

Contents

Specifications

System type	Conventional with coil and contact breaker points, or electronic with coil, impulse generator, and control unit

Coil
Conventional system

Primary winding resistance (at 20°C/68°F)	2.6 to 3.1 ohm
Primary winding current (at 1000 distributor rpm)	1.9 amp

Electronic system – Inductive transmitter

Primary winding resistance (at 20°C/68°F)	1.0 to 1.4 ohm
Secondary winding resistance	55 000 to 85 000 ohm
Primary winding current (at 1000 distributor rpm)	3.2 amp

Electromagnetic – Hall transmitter

Primary winding resistance (at 20°C/68°F)	0.52 to 0.76 ohm
Secondary winding resistance	24 000 to 35 000 ohm (or 70 000 to 90 000 ohm)

Distributor

Firing order	1-3-4-2 (No 1 cylinder timing chain end)
Rotation (viewed from cap end)	Anti-clockwise
Lubricant type/specification:	
Breaker cam	Bosch Ft1 v 4 grease
Felt	Multigrade engine oil, viscosity range SAE 10W/30 to 15W/50 to API SF/CC, SF/CD or better (Duckhams QXR, Hypergrade, or 10W/40 Motor Oil)

Conventional system

Condenser capacity	0.2 mf ± 10%
Contact points gap	0.016 in (0.4 mm)
Dwell angle	50° ± 3°
Shaft endfloat	0.004 to 0.012 in (0.10 to 0.30 mm)
Rotor arm resistance	5000 ohm

Electronic system – Inductive transmitter

Rotor arm ignition cut-out speed	6000 rpm (engine)
Rotor arm resistance	5000 ohm
Compensating resistance	0.6 ohm (starter connected)
	1.0 ohm (engine running)

Electronic system – Hall transmitter

Rotor arm ignition cut-out speed	6000 rpm (engine)
Rotor arm resistance	5000 ohm

Ignition timing
UK 99 models

Conventional system	17° (type B) or 18° (type H) BTDC at maximum of 800 rpm (type B) or 2000 rpm (type H) and vacuum hose disconnected
Electronic system (ie Turbo models)	23° BTDC at 2000 rpm and vacuum hose disconnected and plugged

UK 900 models – Conventional system
To 1980 models .... 17° BTDC at maximum of 800 rpm and vacuum hose disconnected
1981 on models .... 20° BTDC at 2000 rpm and vacuum hose disconnected

UK 900 models – Electronic system
Induction transmitter (ie Turbo models) .... 23° BTDC at 2000 rpm and vacuum hose disconnected and plugged
Hall transmitter:
    Turbo models .... 23° BTDC at 2000 rpm and vacuum hose disconnected and plugged
    Turbo APC models .... 20° BTDC at 2000 rpm and vacuum hose disconnected and plugged

Canada 900 models
Conventional system:
    1979 and 1980 manual transmission models .... 20° BTDC at 2000 rpm and vacuum hose disconnected
    1979 and 1980 automatic transmission models .... 23° BTDC at 2000 rpm and vacuum hose disconnected
    1981 models .... 22° BTDC at 2000 rpm and vacuum hose disconnected
Electronic ststem:
    1979 and 1980 manual transmission models .... 20° BTDC at 2000 rpm and vacuum hose disconnected and plugged
    1979 and 1980 automatic transmission models .... 23° BTDC at 2000 rpm and vacuum hose disconnected and plugged
    1981 models .... 20° BTDC at 2000 rpm and vacuum hose disconnected and plugged

USA 900 models
Electronic system all models .... 20° BTDC at 2000 rpm and vacuum hose disconnected and plugged

Spark plugs
Type:
    All models except Turbo .... NGK BP-6ES
        Bosch W 175 T 30
        Champion N-9Y
    Turbo models without APC .... NGK BP-6ES
        NGK BP-7ES
        Champion N-7Y
    Turbo models with APC .... NGK BP-7ES
        Champion N-7Y
Gap .... 0.024 to 0.028 in (0.6 to 0.7 mm)

HT leads
Resistance:
    Leads to Nos 1 and 2 cylinders .... 3250 ohm (max)
    Leads to Nos 3 and 4 cylinders .... 3000 ohm (max)
    Lead from coil to distributor cap .... 1000 ohm (max)

Torque wrench settings

	lbf ft	Nm
Spark plugs	18 to 22	25 to 29

1 General description

The ignition system may be of either conventional or electronic type – all USA and all Turbo models are equipped with electronic ignition. Both systems use a coil, but on the conventional system the primary circuit is switched by contact points whereas on the electronic system the circuit is switched electronically.

In order that the engine can run correctly it is necessary for an electrical spark to ignite the fuel/air mixture in the combustion chamber at exactly the right moment in relation to engine speed and load. The ignition system is based on feeding low tension (LT) voltage from the battery to the coil where it is converted to high tension (HT) voltage. The high tension voltage is powerful enough to jump the spark plug gap in the cylinders many times a second under high compression pressures, providing that the system is in good condition.

The system functions in the following manner. Low tension voltage is changed in the coil to high tension voltage by the alternate switching on and off of the primary circuit by the contact points (conventional system) or impulse generator and control unit (electronic system). The high tension voltage is fed to the relevant spark plug via the distributor cap and rotor arm. The ignition is advanced and retarded automatically to ensure that the spark occurs at the correct instant in relation to engine speed and load.

The ignition advance in relation to engine speed is controlled by centrifugal weights in the distributor which turn the upper section of the driveshaft on the lower drive section. Advance (and retard on Turbo models) in relation to engine load is controlled by a vacuum unit on the distributor which moves the distributor base plate.

The electronic ignition may be of two alternative types. The

inductive transmitter type incorporates a rotor with four arms which rotate past four magnetic stator posts, and an induction coil transmits the electronic impulse to a control unit. The Hall transmitter type incorporates a slotted rotor, magnet, and a semi-conductor transmitter which again transmits the electronic impulse to a control unit.

When working on electronic ignition systems remember that the high tension voltage can be considerably higher than on a conventional system and in certain circumstances could prove fatal. Depending on the position of the distributor components it is also possible for a single high tension spark to be generated simply by knocking the distributor with the ignition switched on. It is therefore important to keep the ignition system clean and dry at all times, and to make sure that the ignition switch is off when working on the engine.

2 Routine maintenance

UK models
1 Spark plugs should be renewed every 10 000 miles (15 000 km) on all models except Turbo models where they should be renewed every 5000 miles (7500 km).
2 Every 10 000 miles (15 000 km) clean and check the plug HT leads and distributor cap, and lubricate the distributor driveshaft. Renew the contact breaker points where applicable, and adjust the dwell angle and ignition timing.

Canada and USA models
3 On 1979 models renew the spark plugs every 15 000 miles (22 500 km) and where applicable renew the contact breaker points

and condenser. Adjust the dwell angle where applicable, and adjust the ignition timing.

4   Lubricate the distributor where applicable, and clean and check the plug HT leads and distributor cap every 15 000 miles (22 500 km). Renew the distributor cap and rotor every 30 000 miles (45 000 km).

5   On 1980 and 1981 models renew the spark plugs every 15 000 miles (22 500 km) only under severe driving conditions, otherwise renew them every 30 000 miles (45 000 km).

6   Clean and check the plug HT leads and distributor cap every 12 months, and renew the distributor cap and rotor every 60 000 miles (90 000 km).

3   Contact breaker points – checking

There is no specific interval for checking the contact breaker points, but the following information is given for use in the event of breakdown. If the points are renewed at the recommended intervals it will not normally be necessary to check them.

1   Prise back the spring clips, remove the distributor cap and place it to one side.

2   Pull off the rotor arm and on type H engines remove the plastic dust cover (photo).

3   Prise open the contact points and examine the condition of their faces. If they are discoloured or pitted, remove them with reference to Section 4 and dress them using emery tape or a grindstone. If they are worn excessively, renew them.

4   If the contact points are in good condition, adjust them as described in Section 4.

5   Refit the plastic dust cover (if applicable), the rotor arm, and the distributor cap.

4   Contact breaker points – renewal and adjustment

1   Prise back the spring clips, remove the distributor cap and place it to one side.

2   Pull off the rotor arm.

3   On type H engines remove the plastic dust cover, then mark the bearing plate for position, loosen the screws and withdraw the plate (photo).

4   Disconnect the LT lead from the terminal inside the distributor (photo).

5   Unscrew the fixed contact retaining screw and withdraw the contact breaker points (photo).

6   Wipe clean the distributor base plate, the distributor cap and the HT leads. Check that the carbon brush moves freely in the distributor cap and that the metal HT segments are clean.

7   Apply one or two drops of oil to the felt pad at the top of the driveshaft.

8   Fit the new contact breaker points and tighten the fixed contact screws finger tight.

9   Connect the LT lead to the terminal.

10   Turn the engine with a spanner on the crankshaft pulley bolt until the heel of the moving contact is on the high point of one of the cam lobes.

11   Using a feeler blade check that the gap between the two points is as given in the Specifications (photo). If not, with the fixed contact screw finger tight use a screwdriver in the baseplate slot to reposition the fixed contact until the feeler blade is a firm sliding fit between the two points. When correct tighten the screw.

12   Connect a dwellmeter to the engine and turn the engine on the starter – the dwell angle should be within the limits given in the Specifications but if not, adjust the contact points gap as necessary. Reduce the gap to increase the angle or increase the gap to reduce the angle.

13   On type H engines refit the bearing plate and tighten the screws, and fit the plastic dust cover (photo). Note that adjustment of the contact points gap is possible with the bearing plate fitted if the points are being checked as in Section 2.

14   Refit the rotor arm and distributor cap.

5   Condenser – testing, removal and refitting

1   The condenser is fitted in parallel with the contact points, and its

3.2 Removing the plastic dust cover from the distributor on type H engines

4.3 Removing the distributor bearing plate on type H engines

4.4 Contact breaker points location on type H engines

4.5 Removing the contact breaker points retaining screw

4.11 Using a feeler blade to adjust the contact breaker points gap

4.13 Showing bearing plate location tab on the type H engine distributor

Fig. 4.1 Removing the contact breaker points on the type B engine (Sec 4)

Fig. 4.2 Adjusting the contact breaker points gap on the type B engine (Sec 4)

purpose is to reduce arcing between the points, and also to accelerate the collapse of the coil low tension negative field. A faulty condenser can cause the complete failure of the ignition system, as the points will be prevented from interrupting the low tension circuit.

2   To test the condenser, remove the distributor cap and on type H engines the rotor arm and plastic dust cover. Turn the engine until the points are closed then switch on the ignition and separate the points with a screwdriver. If this is accompanied by a *strong* blue flash, the condenser is faulty (a weak spark is normal).

3   A further test can be made for short circuiting by disconnecting the LT leads from the connector block and using a test lamp and leads connected to the terminal and body. If the test lamp lights, the condenser is faulty.

4   If the condenser is suspect, renew it and check whether the fault persists.

5   To remove the condenser first check that the ignition is switched off.

Type B engines

6   Prise back the spring clips, remove the distributor cap and place it to one side.

7   Mark the distributor body in relation to the cylinder block then loosen the mounting bolt and turn the distributor so that the condenser screw is visible.

8   Disconnect the LT leads then remove the screw and withdraw the condenser.

9   Refitting is a reversal of removal, but check and adjust the ignition timing as described in Section 8.

Type H engines

10   Disconnect the LT lead from the distributor terminal.

11   Remove the mounting screw, withdraw the condenser and disconnect the LT lead (photo).

12   Refitting is a reversal of removal.

---

6   Distributor – removal and refitting

Type B engines

1   Prise back the spring clips, remove the distributor cap and place it to one side.

2   Disconnect the coil to distributor wiring.

3   Disconnect the vacuum hose.

4   Turn the engine with a spanner on the crankshaft pulley bolt until the rotor arm is approaching the No 1 HT lead position of the distributor cap (No 1 cylinder is at the timing chain end of engine). Continue turning until the relevant ignition timing mark on the flywheel is aligned with the mark in the clutch housing cover timing hole. The rotor arm should now point towards the groove in the distributor rim (remove the plastic cover if applicable).

5.11 Condenser location on the type H engine distributor

4

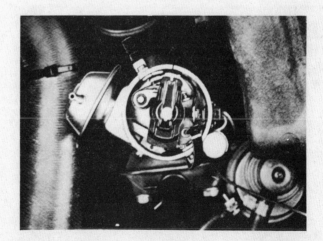

Fig. 4.3 Distributor rotor arm on the type B engine pointing to the timing groove (Sec 6)

Fig. 4.4 Unscrewing the distributor mounting bolt on the type B engine (Sec 6)

Fig. 4.5 Showing movement of the rotor arm when removing the distributor on the type B engine (Sec 6)

5   Mark the distributor body in relation to the cylinder block then unscrew the mounting bolt and lift out the distributor. As the distributor is being removed, the rotor arm will turn approximately 50° clockwise – make a pencil mark on the rim for this position.

6   To refit the distributor check that the ignition timing mark on the flywheel is still aligned with the mark in the clutch housing cover timing hole. Turn the rotor arm so that it is approximately 50° clockwise of the groove in the distributor rim.

7   Position the distributor over the hole in the block with the groove in the distributor rim facing the cylinder head, then insert it fully into the block so that the gears are engaged. It may be necessary to turn the engine slightly so that the oil pump shaft locates correctly. The rotor arm should now point towards the groove in the distributor rim.

8   Check that the previously made marks on the distributor body and block are aligned, then insert the mounting bolt and tighten slightly.

9   Reconnect the vacuum hose and LT lead, and refit the distributor cap.

10   Adjust the ignition timing as described in Section 8.

Type H engines

11   Prise back the spring clips, remove the distributor cap and place it to one side.

12   Disconnect the LT lead and the vacuum hose (photo).

13   Mark the distributor body in relation to the valve cover, then unscrew the mounting bolts and withdraw the distributor (photos).

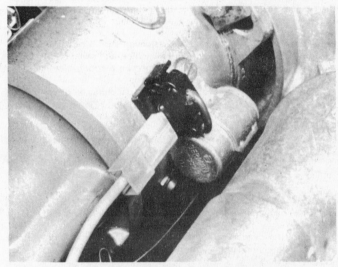

6.12 LT lead connection on the type H engine distributor

6.13A Distributor mounting bolts on the type H engine

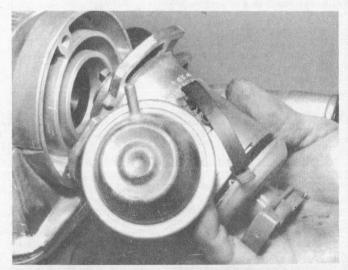

6.13B Removing the distributor on the type H engine

Common spark plug conditions

NORMAL
Symptoms: Brown to grayish-tan color and slight electrode wear. Correct heat range for engine and operating conditions.
Recommendation: When new spark plugs are installed, replace with plugs of the same heat range.

WORN
Symptoms: Rounded electrodes with a small amount of deposits on the firing end. Normal color. Causes hard starting in damp or cold weather and poor fuel economy.
Recommendation: Plugs have been left in the engine too long. Replace with new plugs of the same heat range. Follow the recommended maintenance schedule.

CARBON DEPOSITS
Symptoms: Dry sooty deposits indicate a rich mixture or weak ignition. Causes misfiring, hard starting and hesitation.
Recommendation: Make sure the plug has the correct heat range. Check for a clogged air filter or problem in the fuel system or engine management system. Also check for ignition system problems.

ASH DEPOSITS
Symptoms: Light brown deposits encrusted on the side or center electrodes or both. Derived from oil and/or fuel additives. Excessive amounts may mask the spark, causing misfiring and hesitation during acceleration.
Recommendation: If excessive deposits accumulate over a short time or low mileage, install new valve guide seals to prevent seepage of oil into the combustion chambers. Also try changing gasoline brands.

OIL DEPOSITS
Symptoms: Oily coating caused by poor oil control. Oil is leaking past worn valve guides or piston rings into the combustion chamber. Causes hard starting, misfiring and hesitation.
Recommendation: Correct the mechanical condition with necessary repairs and install new plugs.

GAP BRIDGING
Symptoms: Combustion deposits lodge between the electrodes. Heavy deposits accumulate and bridge the electrode gap. The plug ceases to fire, resulting in a dead cylinder.
Recommendation: Locate the faulty plug and remove the deposits from between the electrodes.

TOO HOT
Symptoms: Blistered, white insulator, eroded electrode and absence of deposits. Results in shortened plug life.
Recommendation: Check for the correct plug heat range, over-advanced ignition timing, lean fuel mixture, intake manifold vacuum leaks, sticking valves and insufficient engine cooling.

PREIGNITION
Symptoms: Melted electrodes. Insulators are white, but may be dirty due to misfiring or flying debris in the combustion chamber. Can lead to engine damage.
Recommendation: Check for the correct plug heat range, over-advanced ignition timing, lean fuel mixture, insufficient engine cooling and lack of lubrication.

HIGH SPEED GLAZING
Symptoms: Insulator has yellowish, glazed appearance. Indicates that combustion chamber temperatures have risen suddenly during hard acceleration. Normal deposits melt to form a conductive coating. Causes misfiring at high speeds.
Recommendation: Install new plugs. Consider using a colder plug if driving habits warrant.

DETONATION
Symptoms: Insulators may be cracked or chipped. Improper gap setting techniques can also result in a fractured insulator tip. Can lead to piston damage.
Recommendation: Make sure the fuel anti-knock values meet engine requirements. Use care when setting the gaps on new plugs. Avoid lugging the engine.

MECHANICAL DAMAGE
Symptoms: May be caused by a foreign object in the combustion chamber or the piston striking an incorrect reach (too long) plug. Causes a dead cylinder and could result in piston damage.
Recommendation: Repair the mechanical damage. Remove the foreign object from the engine and/or install the correct reach plug.

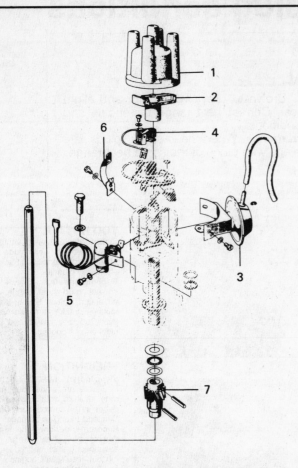

Fig. 4.6 Exploded view of the distributor on the type B engine with conventional ignition (Sec 7)

1	Distributor cap	5	Low-tension wire
2	Rotor arm	6	Spring clip
3	Vacuum control unit	7	Drivegear
4	Contact breaker points		

14 To refit the distributor hold it over the mounting hole with the previously made marks aligned. If a new distributor is being fitted, the vacuum capsule should face the exhaust manifold side of the engine.

15 Turn the distributor shaft to align the dogs with the offset groove in the camshaft, then fit the distributor to the valve cover.

16 Align the previously made marks then insert the mounting bolts and tighten them slightly.

17 Reconnect the vacuum hose and LT lead, and refit the distributor cap.

18 Adjust the ignition timing as described in Section 8.

7 Distributor – dismantling and reassembly

Complete dismantling of the distributor is not recommended, however if necessary refer to Figs 4.6 to 4.9 inclusive

Conventional ignition system vacuum control unit

1 Prise back the spring clips, remove the distributor cap and place it to one side. Pull off the rotor arm.

2 On type H engines remove the plastic dust cover then mark the bearing plate for position, loosen the screws and withdraw the plate.

3 Disconnect the vacuum hose.

4 Remove the retaining screws from the distributor body. Note on type B engines that one of the screws secures the distributor cap clip.

5 Extract the circlip from inside the distributor, disengage the control arm and withdraw the vacuum control unit.

6 Refitting is a reversal of removal.

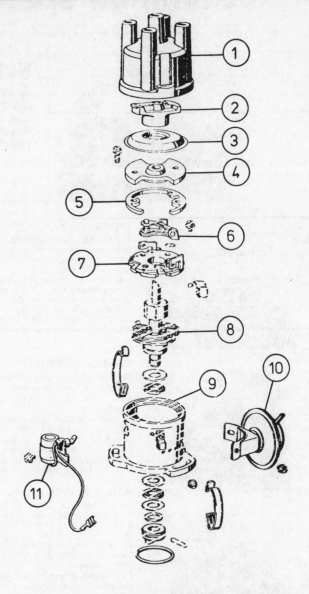

Fig. 4.7 Exploded view of the distributor on the type H engine with conventional ignition (Sec 7)

1	Distributor cap	7	Base plate
2	Rotor arm	8	Shaft and centrifugal
3	Dust cover		mechanism
4	Bearing plate	9	Body
5	Spring clip	10	Vacuum unit
6	Contact breaker points	11	Condenser

Electronic ignition (inductive) induction coil

7 Remove the distributor as described in Section 5.

8 Remove the rotor arm and plastic dust cover.

9 Remove the clip, unscrew the screw and withdraw the cable terminal.

10 Remove the screws, unhook the control arm and withdraw the vacuum control unit and pad noting the location of the distributor cap clip.

11 Remove the screws securing the transmitter plate and distributor cap clip and remove the clip.

12 Extract the circlip from the shaft, remove the washer, and prise off the rotor. Recover the lock pin.

13 Extract the circlip and withdraw the impulse transmitter.

14 Remove the screws and separate the induction coil from the transmitter plate.

15 Refitting is a reversal of removal.

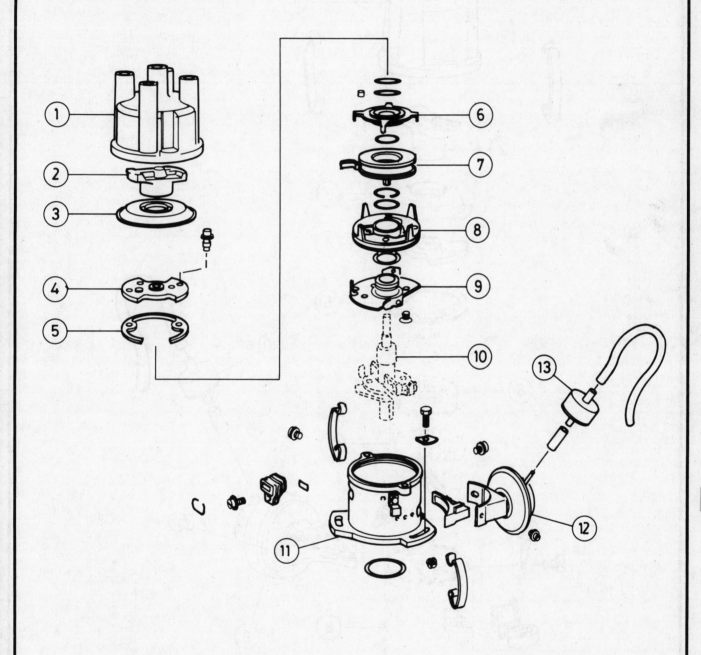

Fig. 4.8 Exploded view of the distributor on the type H engine with inductive electronic ignition
(Sec 7)

1 Distributor cap	6 Rotor	10 Shaft and centrifugal
2 Rotor arm	7 Induction coil	mechanism
3 Dust cover	8 Stator	11 Body
4 Bearing plate	9 Base plate	12 Vacuum unit
5 Spring clip		13 Delay valve

4

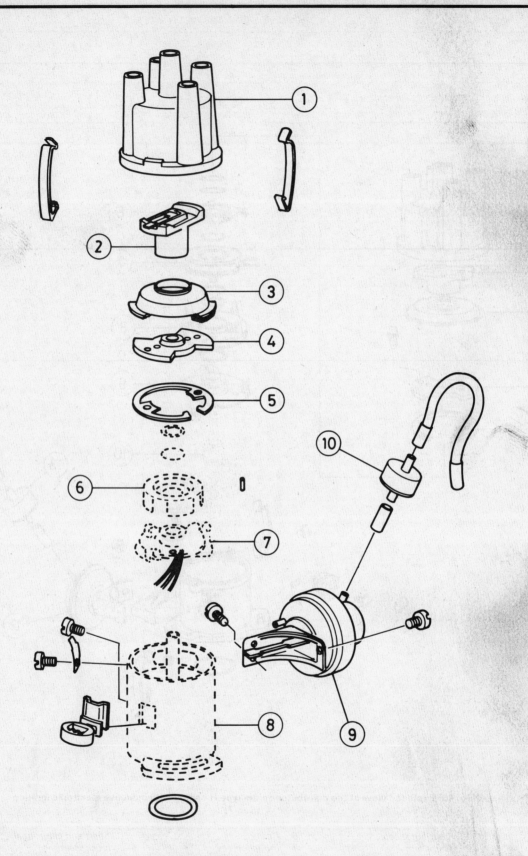

Fig. 4.9 Exploded view of the distributor on the type H engine with Hall effect electronic ignition (Sec 7)

1	Distributor cap	3	Dust cover	5	Spring clip	7	Hall transmitter	9	Vacuum unit
2	Rotor arm	4	Bearing plate	6	Slotted rotor	8	Body	10	Delay valve

8 Ignition timing – adjustment

Before adjusting the ignition timing on models equipped with a conventional ignition system, check and if necessary adjust the contact points dwell angle as described in Section 3. The initial setting method should be used in order to start the engine or for emergency roadside repairs, but the final setting must always be made using a stroboscopic timing light. The clutch housing cover incorporates an attachment point for a special instrument which gives an instant ignition timing read-out, but this instrument will not normally be available to the home mechanic.

Initial setting

1   Remove the No 1 spark plug (timing chain end of engine) and place a finger over the aperture.
2   Turn the engine in the normal running direction (clockwise viewed from timing chain end of engine, anti-clockwise from front of car) until pressure is felt in No 1 cylinder indicating that the piston is commencing its compression stroke. Use a spanner on the crankshaft pulley bolt or engage top gear and pull the car forwards (except automatic transmission models).
3   Continue turning the engine until the correct ignition timing mark appears opposite the mark on the clutch housing cover timing hole (photo).
4   Remove the distributor cap and check that the rotor arm is pointing in the direction of the No 1 terminal of the cap.
5   On conventional ignition models connect a 12 volt test lamp and leads between the coil terminal 1 (with blue wire attached) and a suitable earthing point on the engine. Loosen the distributor retaining bolt(s) and switch on the ignition. If the bulb is already lit turn the distributor body slightly anti-clockwise until the bulb goes out. Turn the distributor body clockwise until the bulb *just* lights up indicating that the points have just opened, then tighten the bolt(s). Switch off the ignition and remove the test lamp.
6   *On electronic ignition models* remove the rotor arm and dust cover and check that the rotor arms are aligned with the stator posts on the inductive transmitter type, or one of the rotor slots is aligned with the transmitter on the Hall effect type. If not, loosen the distributor retaining bolt(s) and turn the distributor body as necessary. Make sure that the rotor arm is still pointing in the direction of the No 1 terminal of the cap. Refit the dust cover and rotor arm.
7   Refit the distributor cap and No 1 spark plug and HT lead.
8   Once the engine has been started check the timing stroboscopically as follows.

Final setting

9   Disconnect and if necessary plug the vacuum hose at the distributor. Where a delay valve is fitted in the vacuum line do not disconnect the hose with the engine running otherwise foreign matter may cause the valve to be inoperative.

10   Connect a timing light and tachometer to the engine in accordance with the manufacturers' instructions.
11   Start the engine and run it at the speed given in the Specifications.
12   Point the timing light into the timing hole in the clutch housing cover. The correct timing mark on the flywheel should appear to be stationary and aligned with the mark on the cover. If not, loosen the distributor retaining bolt(s) and turn it clockwise to advance or anti-clockwise to retard the ignition. Tighten the bolt(s) when the setting is correct.
13   Gradually increase the engine speed while still pointing the timing light at the timing marks. The flywheel marks should appear to move clockwise when viewed from the front of the car proving that the distributor centrifugal weights are operating.
14   Run the engine at about 4000 rpm and note the ignition timing, then reconnect the vacuum hose. On non-Turbo models the timing should advance a few degrees, but on Turbo models it should retard a few degrees, proving that the vacuum unit is operating.
15   Switch off the engine and remove the timing light and tachometer. Check that the vacuum hose is secure.

9 Coil – description and testing

1   The coil is located on the radiator fan housing. The coil fitted to the electronic ignition system is different from the coil on the conventional system, and as from 1981 incorporates a safety fuse which blows if the coil overheats. Always keep the coil clean and dry.
2   To ensure the correct HT polarity at the spark plugs always connect the leads to the correct terminals (refer to the wiring diagrams in Chapter 10 if necessary).
3   To test the coil disconnect the wiring and release the clamp (photo). Connect an ohmmeter between terminals 1 and 15 (ie the primary windings) and check that the resistance is as given in the Specifications. On electronic ignition coils connect the ohmmeter between terminal 1 and the HT terminal, and check that the resistance is as given in the Specifications. If the coil is faulty, renew it. Refit the coil and reconnect the wires.

10 Spark plugs and HT leads – general

1   The correct functioning of the spark plugs is vital for the correct running and efficiency of the engine. The spark plugs should be renewed at the intervals given in Section 2, however, if misfiring or bad starting is experienced in the service period, they must be removed, cleaned, and regapped.
2   To remove the spark plugs, disconnect the HT leads by pulling on the connectors, not the leads. If necessary identify the leads for position (see Fig. 4.10).
3   Clean around each spark plug using a small brush, then using a

8.3 Ignition timing marks on the flywheel

9.3 Coil and wiring

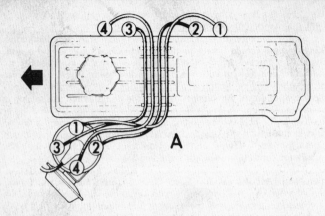

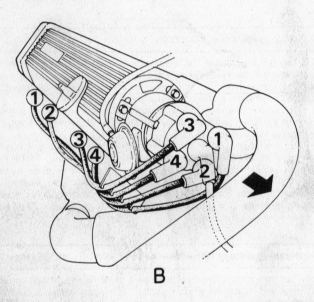

Fig. 4.10 Showing spark plug HT lead positions (Sec 10)

A   Type B engine   B   Type H engine

Arrow indicates flywheel end of engine

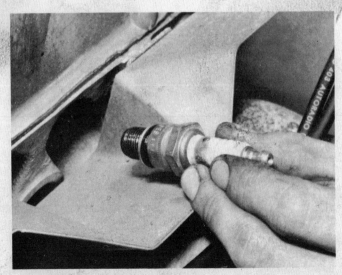

10.3 Removing a spark plug

plug spanner (preferably with a rubber insert) unscrew and remove the plugs (photo).

4   The condition of the spark plugs will tell much about the overall condition of the engine.

5   If the insulator nose of the spark plug is clean and white, with no deposits, this is indicative of a weak mixture, or too hot a plug. (A hot plug transfers heat away from the electrode slowly — a cold plug transfers it away quickly).

6   If the tip and insulator nose is covered with hard black looking deposits, then this is indicative that the mixture is too rich. Should the plug be black and oily, then it is likely that the engine is fairly worn, as well as the mixture being too rich.

7   If the insulator nose is covered with light tan to greyish brown deposits, then the mixture is correct and it is likely that the engine is in good condition.

8   If there are any traces of long brown tapering stains on the outside of the white portion of the plug, the plug will have to be renewed, as this shows that there is a faulty joint between the plug body and the insulator, and compression is being lost.

9   Plugs should be cleaned by a sand blasting machine, which will free them from carbon more thoroughly than cleaning by hand. The machine may also test the condition of the plugs under compression. Any plug that fails to spark at the recommended pressure should be renewed.

10   The spark plug gap is of considerable importance, as, if it is too large or too small the size of the spark and its efficiency will be seriously impaired. The spark plug gap should be set to the amount given in Specifications. To set it, measure the gap with a feeler gauge, and then bend open, or close, the outer plug electrode until the correct gap is achieved. The centre electrode should never be bent as this may crack the insulation and cause plug failure, if nothing worse.

11   Before fitting the spark plugs check that the threaded connector sleeves are tight and that the plug exterior surfaces and threads are clean. Check that the sealing washers are in good condition.

12   Screw in the spark plugs by hand then tighten them to the specified torque.

13   Push the HT lead connectors firmly onto their respective plug and check that the leads are fully entered into the plastic clips.

14   Clean or renew the HT leads and distributor cap at the interval given in Section 2. To test the HT leads remove them together with the distributor cap, then connect an ohmmeter to each end of the leads and the appropriate terminal within the cap in turn. If the resistance is greater than the maximum amount given in the Specifications, check that the lead connection in the cap is good before renewing the lead. Check the distributor cap and rotor for hairline cracks and signs of arcing.

11 Fault diagnosis – ignition system

Engine fails to start

1   If the engine fails to start and the car was running normally when it was last used, first check there is fuel in the fuel tank. If the engine turns over normally on the starter motor and the battery is evidently well charged, then the fault may be in either the high or low tension circuits. First check the HT circuit. **Note:** If the battery is known to be fully charged; the ignition light comes on and the starter motor fails to turn the engine, check the tightness of the leads on the battery terminals and also the secureness of the earth lead to its connection to the body. It is quite common for the leads to have worked loose, even if they look and feel secure. If one of the battery terminal posts gets very hot when trying to work the starter motor this is a sure indication of a faulty connection to that terminal.

2   One of the commonest reasons for bad starting is wet or damp spark plug leads and distributor. Remove the distributor cap. If condensation is visible internally, dry the cap with a rag and also wipe over the leads, then refit the cap.

3   If the engine still fails to start, disconnect an HT lead from any spark plug and hold the end of the cable approximately 0.2 in (5.0 mm) away from the cylinder head using *well insulated pliers*. While an assistant spins the engine on the starter motor, check that a regular blue spark occurs. If so, remove, clean, and re-gap the spark plugs as described in Section 10.

4   If no spark occurs, disconnect the main feed HT lead from the distributor cap and check for a spark as in paragraph 3. If sparks now

Fig. 4.11 Compensating resistor location on the left-hand side of the engine compartment on models equipped with inductive electronic ignition (Sec 11)

Fig. 4.12 Control unit location on the left-hand side of the engine compartment on models equipped with inductive electronic ignition (Sec 11)

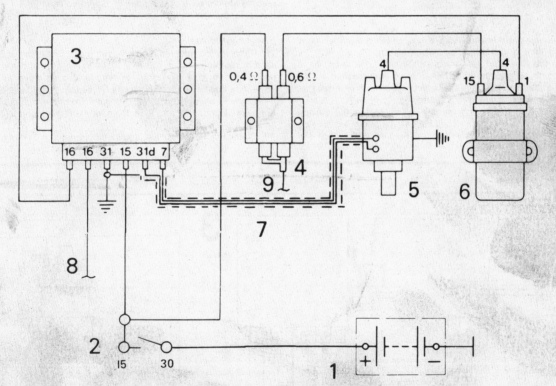

Fig. 4.13 Wiring diagram for the inductive electronic ignition (Sec 11)

1	Battery	4	Compensating resistor	7	Screened cable	9	To relay terminal 87a
2	Ignition switch	5	Distributor	8	To fuel pump relay, tachometer		(connected at start)
3	Electronic control unit	6	Ignition coil		and TSI test socket		

occur, check the distributor cap, rotor arm, and HT leads as described in Section 10 and renew them as necessary. Also check that all wiring and connectors are secure.

Conventional ignition system

5 Use a 12v voltmeter or a 12v bulb and two lengths of wire. With the ignition switch on and the points open test between the low tension wire to the coil (it is marked 15 or +) and earth. No reading indicates a break in the supply from the ignition switch. Check the connections at the switch to see if any are loose. Refit them and the engine should run. A reading shows a faulty coil or condenser, or broken lead between the coil and the distributor.

6 Take a reading between the low tension coil terminal marked 1 or – and earth. No reading indicates a faulty condenser (check as described in Section 5) or faulty coil. A reading shows a broken lead between the coil and distributor. For these tests it is sufficient to separate the points with a piece of dry paper while testing with the points open.

Electronic ignition system (inductive transmitter)

7 Disconnect the wires from the compensating resistor (located by the fusebox), and use an ohmmeter to check that its resistance is 0.6 ohm. If not, renew it.

8 Check that with the ignition on, current is available at the single

transmitter (located in distributor) air gaps between the rotor and stator posts are 0.010 in (0.25 mm).

11 Using an ohmmeter check that the resistance of the transmitter is between 895 and 1285 ohm. If not, renew the induction coil.

Electronic ignition system (Hall transmitter)

12 Locate the control unit on the left-hand side of the engine compartment. Remove the mounting bolt and turn the unit around the earthed bolt until the fuse is visible. Pull back the rubber cover (do not remove the fuse) and connect a voltmeter between terminals 4 and 2. If battery voltage is not available with the ignition switched on, check the ignition switch wiring.

13 Disconnect the wiring from the distributor and check that battery voltage is available with the ignition switched on. If not, check the wiring.

14 Connect a voltmeter between terminals 6 and 3 on the control unit, leaving the fuse connected. Remove the distributor cap and dust cover, then turn the engine until one of the gaps in the slotted rotor is aligned with the Hall transmitter. The voltage reading should be 0.4 volt or less. Now turn the engine so that the rotor covers the transmitter. The voltage reading should be 1.0 volt or more. If the voltage is incorrect renew the transmitter unit.

15 Disconnect the distributor wiring and connect a voltmeter across terminals 15 and 1 on the coil. When the ignition is turned on the reading should be 6 volt dropping to zero volt within 1 to 2 seconds. If not, renew the control unit.

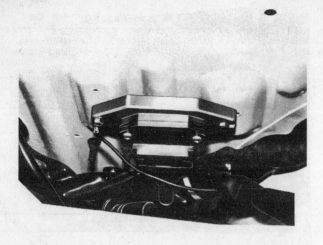

Fig. 4.14 Control unit location on the left-hand side of the engine compartment on models equipped with Hall effect electronic ignition (Sec 11)

terminal on the compensating resistor. If not, check the starter relay and connecting wire, and the ignition switch wiring.

9   Check that the wire from the control unit (located on the left-hand side of the engine compartment) terminal 31 is well earthed to the body. Check that battery voltage is available at terminal 15. Check that the wires on terminals 16 are well insulated.

10 Connect a voltmeter across terminals 7 and 31d at the control unit. Spin the engine on the starter and check that a minimum reading of 1 volt (AC) is obtained. If there is no reading check that the

Engine misfires

16 If the engine misfires regularly, run it at a fast idling speed. Pull off each of the plug caps in turn and listen to the note of the engine. *Hold the plug cap in a dry cloth or with a rubber glove as additional protection against a shock from the HT supply.* No difference in engine running will be noticed when the lead from the defective circuit is removed. Removing the lead from one of the good cylinders will accentuate the misfire.

17 Check the HT supply as described in paragraph 3. If in order, check

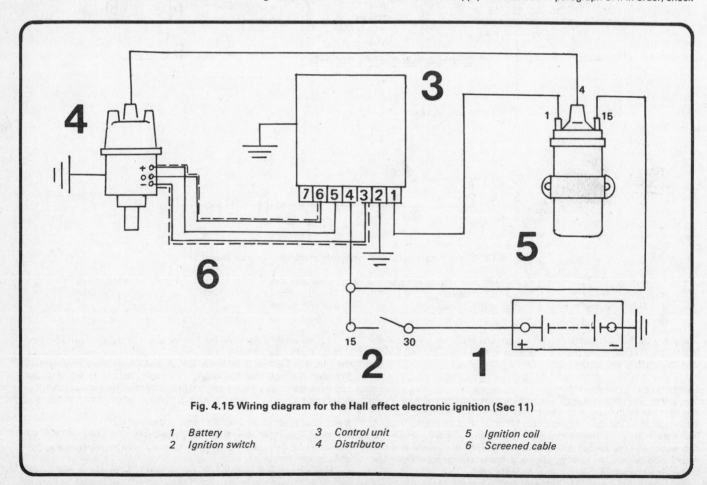

Fig. 4.15 Wiring diagram for the Hall effect electronic ignition (Sec 11)

1 Battery	3 Control unit	5 Ignition coil
2 Ignition switch	4 Distributor	6 Screened cable

the spark plug. The plug may be loose, the insulation may be cracked, or the points may have burnt away giving too wide a gap for the spark to jump. Worse still, one of the points may have broken off. Either renew the plug, or clean it, reset the gap, and then test it. If there is no spark at the end of the plug lead, or if it is weak and intermittent, check the HT lead from the distributor cap to the plug. If the insulation is cracked or perished, renew the lead. Check the connections at the distributor cap.

18 If there is still no spark, examine the distributor cap carefully for tracking. This can be recognised by a very thin black line running between two or more electrodes, or between an electrode and some other part of the distributor. These lines are paths which now conduct electricity across the cap thus letting it run to earth. The only answer is a new distributor cap.

19 Finally check the coil for tracking across the HT tower, and renew it if necessary.

4

Chapter 5 Clutch

Contents

Specifications

Clutch type .... Single dry plate with damper springs, diaphragm spring pressure plate, hydraulically operated

General
Clutch plate diameter:
    Standard models .... 8.0 in (204 mm)
    Turbo models .... 8.5 in (217 mm)
Clutch plate lining thickness (compressed by pressure plate):
    Standard models .... 0.28 to 0.30 in (7.11 to 7.62 mm)
    Turbo models .... 0.27 to 0.29 in (6.86 to 7.37 mm)
Pressure plate inner taper (max) .... 0.0012 in (0.03 mm)

Torque wrench settings

	lbf ft	Nm
Slave cylinder	4 to 10	6 to 14
Clutch shaft plastic propeller	0.75 to 1.5	1 to 2
Other 8 mm bolts	15 to 18	20 to 25

1 General description

The clutch is of single dry plate type with a diaphragm spring pressure plate. The clutch plate (or disc) incorporates a spring cushioned hub to absorb transmission shocks and ensure a smooth take up of drive. On five-speed gearbox models a pre-damper is also fitted to the hub. The clutch assembly is dowelled and bolted to the flywheel.

The clutch plate is splined to the clutch shaft and is held in position between the flywheel and pressure plate by the pressure of the diaphragm spring. Friction lining is riveted to both sides of the clutch plate.

The clutch is hydraulically operated. When the clutch pedal is depressed, the master cylinder piston is moved forwards and hydraulic fluid is forced through the hydraulic pipe to the slave cylinder. The slave cylinder is of annular type and is fitted over the clutch shaft – the release bearing is fitted to the end of the piston. The hydraulic pressure forces the release bearing against the diaphragm spring fingers which in turn pivot the outer edge of the spring plate and the pressure plate away from the clutch plate linings. The clutch plate slides clear of the flywheel and no drive is transmitted through the clutch.

When the clutch pedal is released, the clutch plate is gripped between the flywheel and pressure plate and drive is again transmitted through the clutch.

Wear of the clutch plate linings is compensated for automatically by friction of the slave cylinder seal and a plastic sleeve and circlip on the slave cylinder piston.

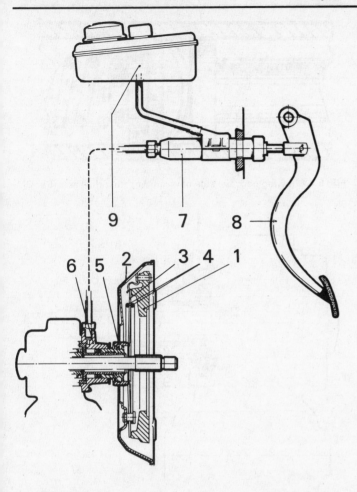

Fig. 5.1 Cross-section diagram of the clutch components (Sec 1)

1	Pressure plate	7	Master cylinder (different
2	Cover		on RHD 99 models)
3	Diaphragm spring	8	Clutch pedal
4	Fulcrum rings	9	Fluid reservoir (different
5	Release bearing		on RHD 99 models)
6	Slave cylinder		

2 Clutch pedal – removal and refitting

1 Working inside the car remove the lower facia panel – the screws/bolts are located in the engine compartment and behind the ashtray.

2 Extract the split pin and remove the washer and pivot pin securing the master cylinder clevis to the pedal. On RHD 900 models the pedal shaft is extended to the master cylinder which is located on the left-hand side of the car (photo).

3 Unhook and remove the pedal return spring.

4 On all models except RHD 900 models, unscrew the locknut, remove the pivot bolt and withdraw the clutch pedal.

5 On RHD 900 models prise the lockring from the left-hand end of the pedal shaft and remove the washer, then remove the right-hand bracket (three nuts) and withdraw the pedal and shaft. Temporarily refit the bracket to hold the brake pedal in place.

6 Remove the pivot centre tube where applicable and check the bushes for wear. If necessary drive out the old bushes with a soft metal drift and fit new ones, and also renew the footpad rubber.

7 Refitting is a reversal of removal, but lubricate the bushes with a molybdenum disulphide based grease.

3 Master cylinder – removal, overhaul and refitting

1 Working inside the car remove the lower facia panel where applicable – the screws/bolts are located in the engine compartment and behind the ashtray.

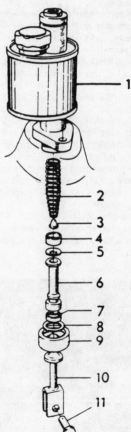

Fig. 5.2 Exploded diagram of the clutch master cylinder fitted to RHD 99 models (Sec 3)

1	Fluid reservoir and	6	Piston
	master cylinder body	7	Seal
2	Spring	8	Circlip
3	Seat	9	Rubber cap
4	Seal	10	Pushrod
5	Washer	11	Clevis pin

2.2 Rear view of the clutch slave cylinder from inside the car on RHD 900 models

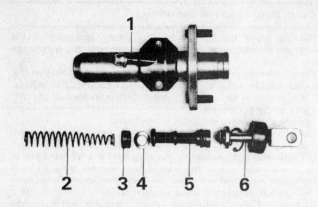

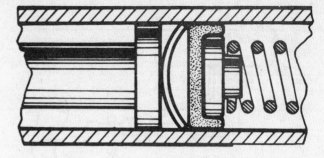

Fig. 5.4 Showing concave side of washer against the seals (Sec 3)

Fig. 5.3 Exploded view of the clutch master cylinder fitted to all models except RHD 99 models (Sec 3)

1	Body	4	Washer
2	Spring and seat	5	Piston and seal
3	Seal	6	Pushrod

2   Extract the split pin and remove the washer and pivot pin securing the master cylinder push rod clevis to the pedal. On RHD 900 models the pedal shaft is extended to the master cylinder which is located on the left-hand side of the car.

3   Working in the engine compartment place some rag around the master cylinder to absorb any spilt fluid. If any fluid is accidentally spilled onto the bodywork, wash off immediately with cold water otherwise damage will occur.

4   On all models except RHD 99 models disconnect and plug the fluid reservoir supply tube at the master cylinder.

5   Unscrew the union nut securing the slave cylinder hydraulic pipe to the master cylinder, remove the clip where applicable, and position the pipe to one side (photo).

6   Unscrew the retaining nuts/bolts and withdraw the master cylinder from the engine compartment side of the bulkhead (photo). Take care not to spill hydraulic fluid on the bodywork.

7   Pour the hydraulic fluid from the cylinder and discard it (remove the filler cap on RHD 99 models). Clean the exterior of the cylinder with paraffin or preferably methylated spirit, and wipe dry.

8   Prise off the rubber cap then extract the circlip from the mouth of the cylinder using circlip pliers.

9   Remove the pushrod and spacer.

10   Remove the piston together with the washer, seal and spring by tapping the cylinder on a block of wood. Note the position of the components.

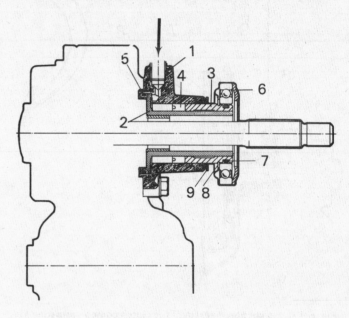

Fig. 5.5 Cross-section diagram of the clutch slave cylinder on early models (Sec 4)

1	Body	6	Release bearing
2	Sleeve	7	O-ring
3	Piston	8	Circlip
4	Seal	9	Circlip
5	O-ring		

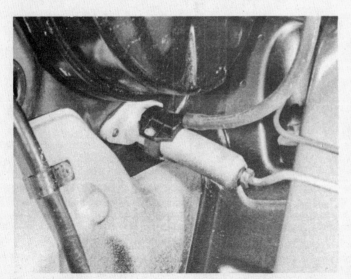

3.5 View of the clutch slave cylinder from the engine compartment on RHD 900 models

3.6 Removing the clutch master cylinder on a RHD 99 model

11 Prise the seal from the piston.

12 Clean all the components with methylated spirit then examine them for wear and damage. In particular check the cylinder bore for scoring and corrosion. If evident renew the complete master cylinder. If the bore is good, obtain a repair kit of seals.

13 Fit the new seal to the piston with the sealing lip towards the centre of the piston. Use the fingers only to manipulate the seal into position, and dip the seal in fresh hydraulic fluid first.

14 Locate the seat on the small diameter end of the spring then dip the seal in hydraulic fluid and locate it on the seat.

15 Insert the spring (large diameter end first), seat and seal in the cylinder until the spring touches the end of the bore.

16 Fit the washer with its concave side against the seal, then insert the pushrod and spacer together with a new rubber cap.

17 Depress the pushrod and insert the circlip in the groove in the mouth of the cylinder.

18 Fit the rubber cap in the groove on the cylinder.

19 Refitting is a reversal of removal, but bleed the hydraulic system as described in Section 5.

4 Slave cylinder – removal, overhaul and refitting

1 The slave cylinder must be removed together with the clutch assembly as described in Section 7, then withdrawn from the pressure plate assembly.

2 Disconnect and plug the hydraulic pipe (photo). Pour the fluid from the slave cylinder and discard it.

3 Remove the release bearing from the end of the piston and prise out the O-ring. If the bearing is tight, support it in a vice and tap the piston through it using a metal tube.

4 Support the cylinder body and push the inner sleeve out. Prise out the O-ring from the flange of the sleeve.

5 Push the piston and seal from the body. Remove the circlip from the piston on early models, or the plastic seal from the body on later models.

6 Clean all the components with methylated spirit then examine them for wear and damage. In particular check the internal surfaces for scoring and corrosion. If evident renew the complete slave cylinder, however if the surfaces are in good condition, obtain a repair kit.

7 Dip the O-ring in hydraulic fluid and fit it to the groove in the flange of the sleeve, using the fingers only to manipulate it.

8 Dip the piston seal in hydraulic fluid then slide it a little way onto the sleeve, sealing lips first.

9 Insert the sleeve in the cylinder body and press in fully, then push the piston seal about half way into the body.

4.2 Disconnecting the hydraulic pipe from the clutch slave cylinder

10 With the release bearing circlip fitted, locate the return circlip (early models) or plastic seal (later models) on the piston, then slide the piston onto the sleeve until it touches the seal.

11 Check the release bearing with reference to Section 8 and renew it if necessary. Fit the O-ring to the groove in the end of the piston, then press on the bearing making sure that the pressure plate side is facing away from the cylinder body.

12 Refit the slave cylinder as described in Section 9 and finally bleed the hydraulic system as described in Section 5.

5 Hydraulic system – bleeding

1 The need for bleeding the cylinders and fluid lines arises when air gets into them. Air gets in whenever a joint or seal leaks or part has to be dismantled. Bleeding is simply the process of venting the air out again.

2 Bleeding can only be carried out successfully on this car if the hydraulic system is pressurised. SAAB recommend the use of a

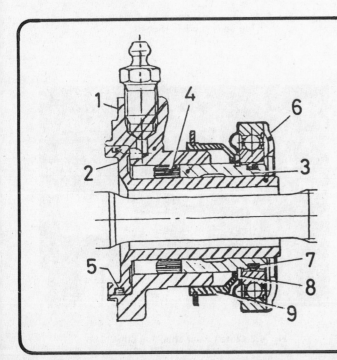

Fg. 5.6 Cross-section diagram of the clutch slave cylinder on later models (Sec 4)

1. Body
2. Sleeve
3. Piston
4. Seal
5. O-ring
6. Release bearing
7. O-ring
8. Circlip
9. Plastic sleeve with circlip

5

5.4 Clutch slave cylinder bleed nipple

6.1 Removing the clutch inspection cover from the main clutch cover

cooling system pressure tester; this is simply a hand pump with an adaptor enabling it to make an airtight seal when applied to (in this case) the hydraulic system reservoir filler neck. With a little ingenuity a bicycle pump could be used instead if a suitable adaptor were constructed, or alternatively a pressure bleeding kit may be obtained from a motor accessory shop.

3   Make sure that the reservoir is filled and obtain a piece of $\frac{1}{4}$ in (6 mm) bore diameter rubber or plastic tube about 2 to 3 feet (0.6 to 0.8 m) long. A clean glass jar and a quantity of fresh clean hydraulic fluid will also be needed.

4   Clean the area around the slave cylinder bleed nipple, slacken the nipple half a turn and fit one end of the rubber over it (photo). Place the other end of the tube in the glass jar, adding sufficient hydraulic fluid to cover the end of the tube.

5   Fit the pressurising device over the master cylinder filler neck and pump once or more. It is not necessary to touch the clutch pedal. Fluid will flow out of the bleed nipple. If the jar is placed so that it is visible whilst the pumping is carried out, it will be possible to see when the expelled fluid is free from air bubbles.

6   Pump until the emerging fluid is free from air bubbles. Pause to top up the master cylinder reservoir if necessary; if the level is allowed to fall too far, air will be introduced into the system and the bleeding procedure will have to be repeated.

7   When all air has been expelled, tighten the bleed nipple, top up the reservoir and check the operation of the clutch.

6   Clutch – checking for wear

1   Wear of the clutch plate linings can be checked before removing the clutch components. First prise the rectangular inspection cover from the main cover over the clutch (photo).

2   Fully depress and release the clutch pedal several times.

3   Look through the inspection hole at the slave cylinder and release bearing – on early models a circlip is located on the piston, but on later models a plastic sleeve will be visible.

4   Check that the circlip is in contact with the end of the slave cylinder body on early models, or that the plastic sleeve is contacting the release bearing on later models.

5   On early models check that the distance between the circlip on the piston and the release bearing retaining circlip is not less than 0.04 in (1.0 mm).

6   On later models check that the distance between the plastic sleeve and the turned surface of the slave cylinder is not less than 0.08 in (2.0 mm).

7   If the distance is less than the amount given in paragraph 5 or 6, the clutch plate linings are worn excessively and the clutch should be dismantled for further investigation. If the distance is more, refit the inspection cover.

MIN.1mm

Fig. 5.7 Clutch wear checking dimension on early models (Sec 6)

min2mm

Fig. 5.8 Clutch wear checking dimension on later models (Sec 6)

7 Clutch – removal

1 Remove the bonnet as described in Chapter 12.
2 On 99 models remove the radiator as described in Chapter 2.
3 On all models unbolt and remove the clutch housing cover (photo).
4 The clutch diaphragm spring must now be held in its depressed position until after the clutch is removed. To do this have an assistant keep the clutch pedal fully depressed and fit a spacer ring between the diaphragm spring and the pressure plate cover, then have the assistant release the pedal. Saab tool number 83 90 023 can be used, but if not available a home made spacer can be made out of plastic tube or similar (photo). If for some reason the clutch hydraulics are inoperative a lever must be made or tool 83 93 175 (Fig. 5.10) obtained in order to depress the diaphragm spring.
5 Remove the clip and withdraw the cap and seal from the front of the primary gear casing (photos).
6 Unscrew the plastic oil thrower propeller from the front of the clutch shaft (photo).

7 The clutch shaft must now be removed. To do this use an 8 mm bolt to attach a suitable length of metal bar to the front of the shaft, then tap the upper section of the bar until the shaft is released from the support bearing, clutch plate and primary gear (photo). Take care not to damage the radiator on 900 models.
8 Unscrew the bolts securing the slave cylinder to the primary gear casing using an Allen key where applicable (photo).
9 Hold the flywheel stationary with a lever inserted in the starter ring gear and resting on the starter, then unscrew the bolts securing the pressure plate to the flywheel in diagonal sequence.
10 Release the pressure plate from the dowels, then withdraw it together with the clutch plate and slave cylinder from the car (photo). Take care not to damage the slave cylinder components on the diaphragm spring fingers – there is no need to disconnect the hydraulic pipe from the slave cylinder.
11 If necessary place the pressure plate assembly on the bench, depress the diaphragm spring fingers with a lever, and remove the spacer or plastic tube.

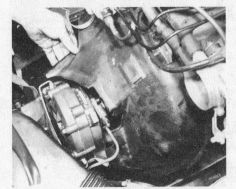
7.3 Removing the clutch housing cover

7.4 Fitting an old HT lead to the pressure plate to retain the diaphragm spring in the depressed position

7.5A Remove the clip ...

7.5B ... and cap from the primary case

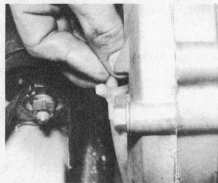
7.6 Unscrewing the plastic oil thrower

7.7 Using a metal bar and bolt to remove the clutch shaft

7.8 Removing the clutch slave cylinder bolts

7.10 Removing the clutch and slave cylinder

5

Fig. 5.9 Fitting the spacer ring, Saab tool
number 83 90 023 (Sec 7)

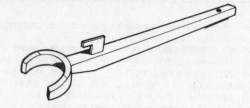

Fig. 5.10 Saab tool number 83 93 175
for depressing the clutch diaphragm
spring (Sec 7)

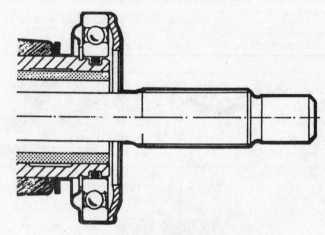

Fig. 5.11 Cross-section diagram of the
release bearing (Sec 8)

8   Clutch – inspection

1   Examine the surfaces of the pressure plate and flywheel for
scoring. If this is only light, the parts may be re-used, but if excessive
the pressure plate assembly must be renewed and the flywheel friction
face reground provided the amount of metal being removed is minimal.
If any doubt exists renew the flywheel.
2   Renew the clutch plate (disc) if the linings are worn down to or
near the rivets. If the linings appear oil stained, the cause of the oil leak
must be found and rectified – this is most likely to be a failed
crankshaft rear oil seal or primary gear casing oil seal. Check the clutch
plate hub, springs and centre splines for wear.
3   Check the pressure plate assembly for wear, particularly for
looseness of the diaphragm spring and discolouration of the spring
which would indicate overheating at some time. Place a straight edge
across the friction face and use feeler blades at the inner edges to
check for taper (photo). If the taper at any point exceeds the maximum
amount given in the Specifications or if the pressure plate is otherwise
damaged, it should be renewed.
4   Spin the release bearing by hand and check it for roughness. Hold
the outer race and attempt to move it laterally against the inner race.
If any excessive movement or roughness is evident renew the bearing
with reference to Section 4. Do not clean the bearing with paraffin or
any solvent.

9   Clutch – refitting

1   Check that the spacer or plastic tube is fitted between the
diaphragm spring and the pressure plate cover (photo).
2   Locate the clutch plate against the pressure plate with the
projecting side towards the slave cylinder (ie away from the flywheel).

Hold the slave cylinder with the release bearing against the diaphragm
spring fingers.
3   Lower the three components into position and locate the pressure
plate cover on the flywheel dowels. Insert two bolts loosely in the
flywheel to retain the assembly.
4   Smear a little molybdenum disulphide grease on the clutch shaft
splines, then insert the shaft through the primary gear, into
engagement with the clutch plate splines, and into the spigot bearing
located in the flywheel. Use a soft-face mallet to tap the shaft fully into
position so that the primary gear circlip engages the groove where
applicable.
5   Coat the threads of the slave cylinder bolts with a liquid locking
compound, locate the cylinder on the primary gear casing then insert
and tighten the bolts to the specified torque.
6   Insert all the pressure plate bolts and tighten them finger tight.
7   Insert and tighten the plastic propeller to the front of the clutch
shaft.
8   Fit the cap and seal to the front of the primary gear casing and
retain with the clip.
9   Hold the flywheel stationary with a lever inserted in the starter ring

8.3 Checking the clutch pressure plate for
taper

9.1 Showing plastic tube keeping
diaphragm spring depressed

9.11 Showing clutch slave cylinder return
limit sleeve

gear then tighten the pressure plate bolts evenly in diagonal sequence.
10 Have an assistant depress the clutch pedal just sufficient for the spacer or plastic tube to be removed from the pressure plate assembly. Do not fully depress the clutch pedal at this stage otherwise the piston could possibly be pushed out of the slave cylinder.
11 While the assistant holds the clutch pedal depressed, use two screwdrivers to slide the return movement circlip against the slave cylinder body (early models), or the plastic sleeve and circlip against the release bearing (later models) (photo).

12 Release the clutch pedal. The circlip (early models) or plastic sleeve (later models) will now take up its initial position. On early models the distance between the circlip on the piston and the release bearing circlip should be approximately 0.24 in (6.0 mm). On later models the distance between the plastic sleeve and the turned surface of the slave cylinder should be approximately 0.35 in (9.0 mm).
13 Refit the clutch housing cover and tighten the bolts.
14 On 99 models refit the radiator as described in Chapter 2.
15 Refit the bonnet as described in Chapter 12.

10 Fault diagnosis – clutch

Symptom	Reason(s)
Judder when taking up drive	Worn clutch plate friction surfaces or contamination with oil Worn splines on clutch plate or clutch shaft Loose or worn engine/gearbox mountings
Clutch drag (failure to disengage)	Clutch plate seized on splines Flywheel spigot bearing seized Air in hydraulic system
Clutch slip	Worn clutch plate friction surfaces or contamination with oil Slave cylinder piston sticking
Noise evident on depressing clutch pedal	Dry or worn release bearing Worn clutch plate or pressure plate assembly

Chapter 6 Manual gearbox and final drive

Contents

Specifications

Type .... Four or five forward speeds and reverse, synchromesh on all forward speeds

Ratios (various according to model)
Typical overall ratios:

	1983 900 GL	1983 900 GLS
1st	13.78 to 1	13.94 to 1
2nd	7.79 to 1	7.88 to 1
3rd	5.23 to 1	5.29 to 1
4th	3.55 to 1	3.80 to 1
5th	–	3.08 to 1
Reverse	15.15 to 1	15.34 to 1
Final drive	3.67 to 1	3.67 to 1

Oil capacity

4-speed	4.4 Imp pt; 2.6 US qt; 2.5 litre
5-speed	5.3 Imp pt; 3.2 US qt; 3.0 litre

Torque wrench settings

	lbf ft	Nm
Output shaft gear retaining nut	30 to 45	40 to 60
Output shaft bearing housing	15 to 18.5	20 to 25

---

1 General description

The gearbox incorporates four or five forward speeds according to model and reverse. Synchromesh engagement is on all forward speeds. Reverse gear engagement is assisted by a braking device which stops rotation of the output shaft. The device consists of a pressure spring on the selector shaft which forces the 1st/2nd selector fork against the synchro sleeve.

When overhauling the gearbox, due consideration should be given to the costs involved, since it is often more economical to obtain a service exchange or good secondhand gearbox rather than fit new parts to the existing gearbox.

Overhaul of the differential unit is not considered to be within the

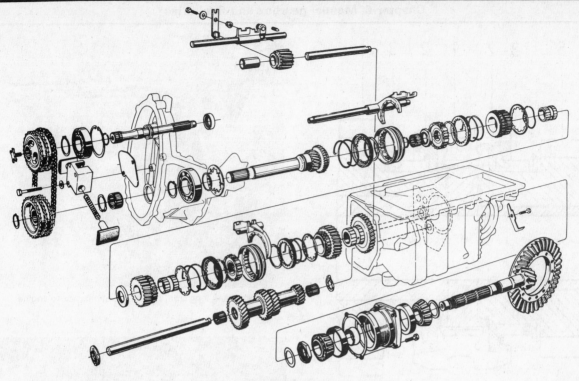

Fig. 6.1 Exploded view of the 4-speed
gearbox (Sec 1)

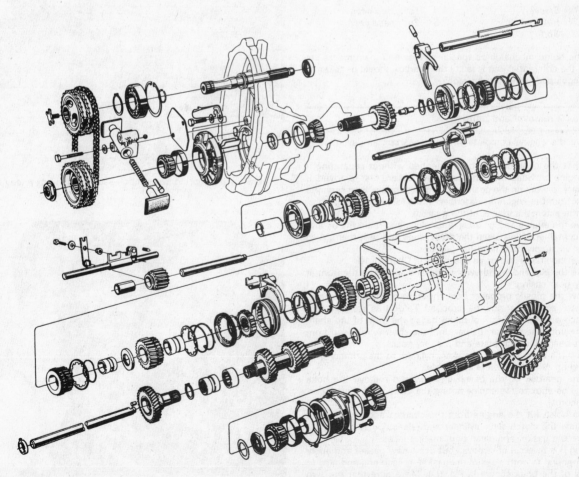

Fig. 6.2 Exploded view of the 5-speed
gearbox (Sec 1)

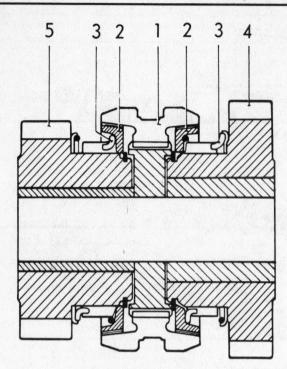

**Fig. 6.3 Cross-section diagram of a
synchromesh unit (Sec 1)**

1 Sleeve	4 1st speed gear
2 Ring	5 2nd speed gear
3 Spring	

2.10A Showing long front bolt securing gearbox to engine

2.10B Showing support bracket bolt securing gearbox to engine

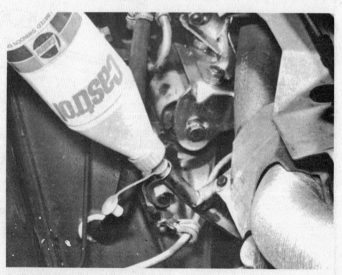

2.13 Refilling the gearbox with oil

scope of the home mechanic as special gauges and instruments are required. If the differential unit is faulty the gearbox should be taken to a suitably equipped workshop for repair.

2 Gearbox – removal and refitting

1   Remove the engine complete with the gearbox as described in Chapter 1.
2   Note that the gearbox may be dismantled without separating it from the engine provided the clutch and flywheel are first removed. If it is necessary to work on the gearbox casing separately, then separate the gearbox from the engine as described in the following paragraphs.
3   Clean the external surfaces of the gearbox.
4   Remove the engine and gearbox drain plugs and drain the oil into a suitable container. Wipe clean the drain plugs and refit them. Also remove the oil supply tube from the gearbox.
5   Remove the starter motor as described in Chapter 10.
6   Remove the clip and withdraw the cap and seal from the front of the primary gear casing.
7   Unscrew the plastic propeller from the front of the clutch shaft.
8   The clutch shaft must now be removed. To do this use an 8 mm bolt to attach a suitable length of metal bar to the front of the shaft, then tap the upper section of the bar until the shaft is released from the support bearing, clutch plate and primary gear.
9   Unscrew the bolts securing the slave cylinder to the primary gear casing using an Allen key where applicable.
10 With the gearbox on the bench unscrew and remove the bolts securing the gearbox to the engine noting the location of the support brackets (photos).
11 Using a hoist, lift the engine from the gearbox and at the same time withdraw the clutch slave cylinder and release bearing.
12 Remove the gasket and clean both mating faces.
13 Refitting is a reversal of removal, but use a new gasket and apply sealing compound to both sides of the gasket at each end and also to the threads of the bolts shown in Fig. 6.4. Make sure that the two guide dowels are fitted in the gearbox casing. After refitting the engine and gearbox to the car refill the engine and gearbox with the specified oil (photo).

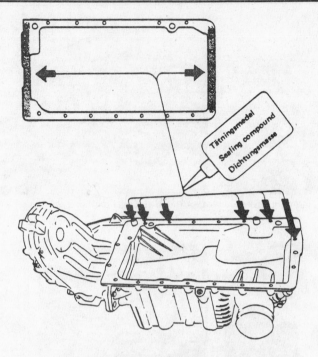

Fig. 6.4 Sealing compound application
craft (Sec 2)

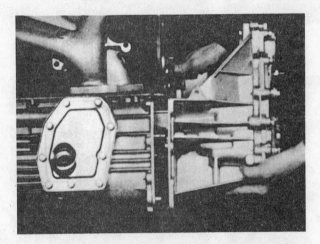

Fig. 6.5 Removing the primary gear
casing on 4-speed models (Sec 3)

3 Gearbox (four-speed) – dismantling into major assemblies

1 Unscrew the bolts and remove the differential cover from the rear of the gearbox. Remove the gasket.

2 Mark the differential bearing housings in relation to the gearbox casing then unscrew and remove the bolts.

3 Tap the bearing housings from the casing with a wooden mallet. If they are tight use a slide hammer in the slots provided. Keep all shims in their original position and recover the springs and plungers from the inner ends of the inner driveshafts.

4 Turn the differential so that the housing cut-out is parallel with the left-hand side of the gearbox casing, then move the differential to the left and withdraw it from the rear of the casing.

5 Unscrew the bolt and remove the layshaft and reverse gear shaft locking plate from the rear of the gearbox casing.

6 Extract the layshaft using tool 83 90 049 if necessary, and allow the laygear to drop down.

7 Unscrew the bolts and then separate the complete primary gear casing from the gearbox casing.

8 Remove the laygear from the gearbox together with the thrust washers and needle rollers.

9 Unscrew the bolts and remove the cover and filler plug from the right-hand side of the gearbox casing. Remove the gasket, then extract the detent spring and ball from the hole in the casing.

10 Using an Allen key unscrew the tapered retaining bolt then remove the outer shaft and reverse gear lever, at the same time disconnecting the lever from the selector dog.

11 Pull out the 1st/2nd and 3rd/4th selector shaft then remove the 3rd/4th synchro sleeve together with the selector fork. Keep the components identified for position.

12 Remove the reverse gear shaft and withdraw the reverse gear.

13 Remove the circlip and needle bearing from the end of the output shaft.

14 Hold the output shaft stationary by inserting a suitable bar in the teeth of the reverse gear on the output shaft, then unscrew the end nut.

15 Remove the 3rd/top synchro unit followed by 3rd gear.

16 Unscrew the four bolts from the rear of the output shaft then using a soft-faced mallet, drive the shaft assembly from the gearbox. At the same time remove the gears, synchro unit, washers and shims keeping them identified for position. Ideally reassemble the components to the shaft after it has been removed from the gearbox casing.

4 Gearbox (five-speed) – dismantling into major assemblies

1 Unscrew the bolts and remove the differential cover from the rear of the gearbox. Remove the gasket (photo).

2 Mark the differential bearing housings in relation to the gearbox casing then unscrew and remove the bolts (photo).

3 Tap the bearing housings from the casing with a wooden mallet. If they are tight use a slide hammer in the slots provided. Keep all shims in their original position and recover the springs and plungers from the inner ends of the inner driveshafts.

4 Turn the differential so that the housing cut-out is parallel with the

6

4.1 Removing the differential cover

4.2 Removing the differential bearing housings

4.4A Turn the differential to align the cut-out ...

4.4B ... then remove the differential

4.5 Removing the primary gear front cover

4.6A Removing the right-hand side cover

4.6B Removing the detent spring ...

4.6C ... and ball

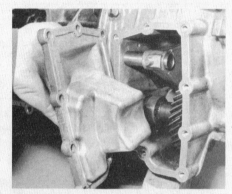

4.7 Removing the primary gear casing cover

4.8 Extracting the dowel from the 5th gear selector fork

4.9 Removing the lower sprocket nut

4.10A Chain tensioner location

left-hand side of the gearbox casing, then move the differential to the left and withdraw it from the rear of the casing (photos).

5   Unscrew the bolts and remove the primary gear front cover from the front of the gearbox. Remove the gasket (photo).

6   Unscrew the bolts and remove the cover and filler plug from the right-hand side of the gearbox casing. Remove the gasket, then extract the detent spring and ball from the hole in the casing (photos).

7   Unscrew the bolts and remove the cover from the side of the primary gear casing – use cloth to soak up the trapped oil. Remove the gasket (photo).

8   Extract the dowel from the 5th gear selector fork and use a screwdriver to lever the fork into the 5th gear position (photo).

9   Select reverse gear. The input shaft is now locked and the lower sprocket nut can be unscrewed and removed (photo). If fitted first release the lockwasher.

10   Unscrew the bolts securing the chain tensioner to the primary gear

casing, squeeze the tensioner pads together and withdraw the unit. Remove the backing plate (photos).

11   Using circlip pliers through the hole in the upper sprocket, expand the circlip and pull the sprocket out so that the circlip is resting on the casing shoulder. Now withdraw both the upper and lower sprockets simultaneously together with the chain (photos). If necessary use a puller or slide hammer.

12   Using circlip pliers expand the circlip on the laygear connector and slide the connector onto the input pinion (photos).

13   Working inside the rear of the gearbox unscrew the bolt and remove the locking plate for the layshaft and reverse gear shaft (photo).

14   Using a drift from the front of the gearbox, drive out the layshaft and remove it (photo).

15   Withdraw the input pinion together with the connector (and thrust washer if applicable) from the side of the gearbox. If there is

4.10B Removing the chain tensioner and backing plate

4.11A Upper sprocket retaining circlip location

4.11B Removing the sprockets and chain

4.12A Expand the laygear connector circlip ...

4.12B ... and slide the connector onto the input pinion

4.13 Layshaft and reverse gear shaft locking plate location

4.14 Driving out the layshaft

4.15 Laygear rear thrust washer location

4.16 Input shaft bearing housing showing oil catcher location

6

4.17A Removing the input shaft and bearing housing

4.17B Removing the plastic tube from the input shaft

4.18 Removing the 5th gear selector fork and synchro sleeve

insufficient room, first remove the thrust washer from the rear of the laygear so that the laygear can be moved slightly rearwards (photo). Take care not to allow the collar and rollers to fall out of the pinion.

16 Note how the oil catcher is fitted, then unscrew the bolts from the input shaft bearing housing (photo).

17 Withdraw the bearing and housing using a slide hammer on the end of the input shaft. Alternatively temporarily refit the sprocket nut and lever off the housing. Remove the plastic tube from the input shaft (photos).

18 Slide the 5th gear selector fork from the shaft together with the synchro sleeve and withdraw them from the gearbox (photo).

19 Up to and including gearbox number 436500 extract the circlip from the 5th gear synchro hub, and remove the hub, shims and spacer from the output shaft.

20 Extract the reverse gear shaft from the casing and remove the reverse gear idler (photo).

21 From gearbox number 436501 (ie 1982 models on) hold the output shaft stationary by inserting a suitable bar in the teeth of the reverse gear on the output shaft (photo).

22 Unscrew the nut, and remove the 5th gear synchro hub and spacer from the end of the output shaft (photos).

23 Unscrew the bolts and separate the primary gear casing from the gearbox casing (photo).

24 Remove the laygear from the gearbox together with the needle bearings and thrust washer (if applicable) (photo).

25 Remove the locking plunger from the side of the gearbox (photo).

26 Slide the 5th gear selector tube from the outer selector shaft (photo).

27 Unscrew the tapered bolt then pull out the outer selector shaft together with the reverse lever and dog (photos).

28 Pull out the inner selector shaft (photo).

29 Remove the selector shaft together with the selector dog (photo).

30 Unscrew the four bolts from the rear of the output shaft then using a soft-faced mallet, drive the shaft assembly from the gearbox

4.20 Reverse idler gear and lever

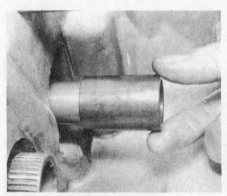

4.21 Metal bar for locking reverse gear and output shaft

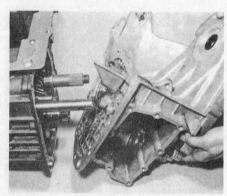

4.22A Unscrew the nut ...

4.22B ... remove the 5th gear synchro hub ...

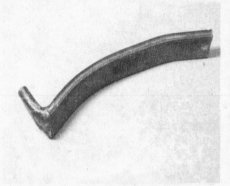

4.22C ... and slide off the spacer

4.23 Removing the primary gear casing

4.24 Removing the laygear

4.25 Removing the locking plunger

4.26 Slide the 5th gear selector tube from the selector shaft

4.27A Unscrew the tapered bolt ...

4.27B ... and withdraw the selector shaft with the reverse lever and dog

4.28 Removing the inner selector shaft

4.29 Removing the selector shaft and dog

4.30A Output shaft bearing retaining plate

4.30B Driving out the output shaft

4.30C Removing the output shaft

5.1 Output shaft and bearing housing

6

(photos). At the same time remove the gears, synchro units, washers and shims keeping them identified for position. Ideally reassemble the components to the shaft after it has been removed from the gearbox casing.

5 Output shaft and bearing – servicing

1　Examine the output shaft for wear and damage (photo). If the pinion gear teeth are worn excessively it will be necessary to renew both the output shaft and the differential unit, and a garage will need to set up the preload. In this case it will probably be more economical to obtain a new or secondhand gearbox.

2　Spin the output shaft in the bearing and check it for roughness and excessive play. If necessary renew the bearings as follows.

3　Mount the bearing housing in a vice then unscrew the nut.

4　Support the housing and press out the shaft then similarly remove the rear tapered bearing.

5　Drive the outer tracks from the housing.

6　Clean all the components then drive the outer tracks into the bearing.

7　Using a metal tube on the inner track drive the rear tapered bearing onto the shaft and fit the spacer.

8　Fit the housing then press on the front tapered bearing using a metal tube on the inner track, until the rollers just contact the outer tracks.

9　Apply a liquid locking agent to the nut threads then fit the nut and tighten it until the turning torque for the bearings is 2.0 lbf ft (2.5 Nm) for new bearings or 1.0 lbf ft (1.3 Nm) for bearings that have completed more than 1200 miles (2000 km). The correct preload can

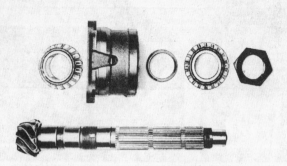

Fig. 6.6 Output shaft and bearing
components on 4-speed models (Sec 5)

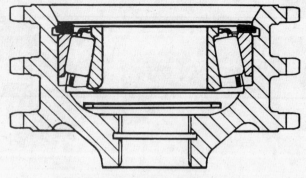

Fig. 6.7 Cross-section diagram of the
upper primary gear sprocket and bearing
(Sec 6)

be obtained by wrapping string around the housing and using a spring balance to record a reading of 10 to 15 lbf f (4.7 to 7.0 kg f) for new bearings and 4.2 to 9.2 lb f (1.9 to 4.3 kg f) for bearings that have completed more than 1200 miles (2000 km).
10 Lock the nut by peening the flange.

6 Primary gears and casing (four-speed) – servicing

1 Unscrew the bolts and remove the cover and gasket.
2 Unbolt and remove the chain tensioner and backing plate.
3 Extract the circlip from the lower sprocket then expand the upper circlip using circlip pliers through one of the holes and pull off the sprockets and chain. If necessary use a puller.
4 Extract the circlip from the upper sprocket then support the sprocket and drive out the bearing. Remove the circlip.
5 Remove the screws using an Allen key and withdraw the input shaft bearing retainer.
6 Drive out the input shaft using a soft-faced mallet.
7 Extract the circlip and press the bearing from the input shaft.
8 Extract the circlip and drive the needle bearing from the primary gear casing.
9 Prise out the clutch shaft seal.
10 Clean all the components and examine them for wear and damage.
11 Drive the new clutch shaft seal squarely into the casing using a block of wood.
12 Drive in the needle bearing with the mark facing outwards then fit the circlip.
13 Using a metal tube on the inner track drive the bearing onto the input shaft and fit the circlip.
14 Press the input shaft and bearing into the casing and locate the retainer. Apply sealing compound to the threads of the screws then insert and tighten them.
15 Locate the circlip in the upper sprocket then press in the bearing using a metal tube on the outer track and secure with the circlip. Make sure the bearing is the right way round (Fig. 6.7) and that the chamfer on the outer circlip faces outwards.
16 Locate the chain on the sprockets and fit them in the casing. Fit the circlips to secure the sprockets.
17 Squeeze the chain tensioner pads together and fit the assembly together with the backing plate between the chain. Locate them as shown in Fig. 6.8 then apply locking fluid to the threads, fit the bolts and tighten them.
18 Fit the cover with a new gasket and tighten the bolts.

7 Primary gears and casing (five-speed) – servicing

1 Using an Allen key unscrew the countersunk screws and remove the bearing retainer from the casing (photo).
2 Using a metal tube drive out the bearing and similarly drive out the layshaft needle bearing.
3 Prise the clutch shaft seal from the casing (photo).

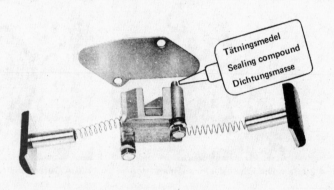

Tätningsmedel
Sealing compound
Dichtungsmasse

Fig. 6.8 Primary chain tensioner and
backing plate (Sec 6)

4 Extract the circlip from the upper sprocket then support the sprocket and drive out the bearing. Remove the inner circlip.
5 Spin the input shaft in its bearing and check it for roughness and excessive play. If necessary renew the bearings as follows.
6 Support the housing then drive the input shaft from its bearings noting the location of the spacer and shims. Support the rear bearing and press out the shaft.
7 Drive the outer tracks from the housing.
8 Clean the components and examine them for wear and damage.
9 Using a metal tube on the inner track drive the new bearing onto the input shaft.
10 Drive the outer tracks into the housing.
11 Fit the shims, spacer, housing and bearing to the shaft using a metal tube on the inner track. With a three tonne force applied there must be no play in the bearing, but the shaft should rotate freely. If necessary adjust the shim thickness.
12 Drive the new clutch shaft seal squarely into the casing using a block of wood.
13 Drive in the layshaft needle bearing with the numbered end facing the casing cover end.
14 Drive in the new ball bearing, fit the retainer and tighten the screws – the two through-screws should have sealing compound applied to their threads.
15 Locate the circlip in the upper sprocket then press in the bearing using a metal tube on the outer track and secure with the circlip. Make sure the bearing is the right way round (Fig. 6.7) and that the chamfer on the outer circlip faces outwards.

8 Gears, selectors and casing – servicing

1 Prise the oil seals from the differential bearing housings (photo).
2 Clean the housings then press in the new oil seals squarely with a socket or block of wood so that they project approximately 0.08 in (2.0 mm) above the housings (photos).

7.1 Inner view of the primary gear casing

7.3 Clutch shaft oil seal location in the primary gear casing

8.1 Prising an oil seal from a differential bearing housing

8.2 Fitting an oil seal to a differential bearing housing

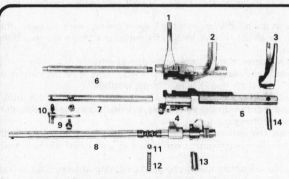

Fig. 6.9 Selector components on 5-speed models (Sec 8)

1	1st/2nd selector fork	8	Main selector shaft
2	3rd/4th selector fork	9	Reverse lever
3	5th selector fork	10	Taper screw
4	Selector shaft finger	11	Detent ball
5	5th selector tube	12	Detent spring
6	Inner selector shaft	13	Plunger
7	Outer selector shaft	14	Dowel

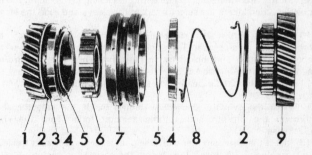

Fig. 6.10 1st/2nd gears and synchro unit (Sec 8)

1	2nd gear	6	Hub
2	Guide ring	7	Sleeve
3	Spring	8	Spring
4	Synchro ring	9	1st gear
5	Circlip		

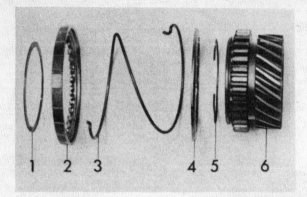

Fig. 6.11 3rd gear and synchro ring (Sec 8)

1	Circlip	4	Guide ring
2	Synchro ring	5	Circlip
3	Spring	6	3rd gear

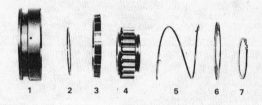

Fig. 6.12 5th synchro unit components (Sec 8)

1	Sleeve	5	Spring
2	Circlip	6	Guide ring
3	Synchro ring	7	Circlip
4	Hub		

3　Clean the gears, selector components and casing and check them for wear and damage.

4　To dismantle the synchromesh units extract the circlip and remove the synchro ring. Keep the components identified for position as each unit is different. Reassemble in reverse order.

5　Check the selector forks and shafts for excessive wear and renew them if necessary.

9　Gearbox (four-speed) – reassembly

1　Insert the output shaft into the gearbox casing and use temporary locating studs to align the housing. Make sure that the shims are in position.

2　Drive the housing into the casing using a soft-faced mallet, remove the studs, and insert and tighten the bolts.

3　Using a steel rule and straight edge determine the distance from the nut on the output shaft bearing to the mating face for the primary gear casing. If the distance is not 7.677 to 7.681 in (195.0 to 195.1 mm) shims must be fitted against the nut.

4　Locate the reverse gear on the output shaft and drive it on fully using a metal tube.

5　Slide the 1st gear on the reverse gear bearing sleeve.

6　Fit the 1st/2nd synchro hub, then locate the selector fork in the sleeve and slide the sleeve on the hub.

7　Drive the 2nd gear bearing sleeve onto the shaft and slide the 2nd gear onto it.

8　Fit the splined spacer then drive the 3rd gear bearing sleeve onto the shaft and slide the 3rd gear onto it.

9　Fit the 3rd/4the synchro hub with the locking holes facing the nut position, then locate the selector fork in the sleeve and slide the sleeve on the hub.

10　Hold the output shaft stationary by inserting a suitable bar in the teeth of the reverse gear. Then tighten the nut onto the shaft to the specified torque and lock it by peening the flange into the 3rd/4th synchro hub locking holes.

11　Locate the needle bearing on the end of the output shaft and fit the circlip.

12　With the synchro sleeves in neutral insert the selector shaft through the 3rd/4th and 1st/2nd selector forks. Turn the shaft clockwise.

13　Insert the outer shaft and reverse gear lever and connect the lever to the selector lug. Insert the shaft in the casing and secure with the tapered bolt using a liquid locking agent.

14　Turn the 1st/2nd and 3rd/4th selector shaft anti-clockwise and insert it in the casing.

15　Grease the needle rollers and locate them in the laygear, then place the laygear in the bottom of the gearbox.

16　Locate the laygear front thrust washer on the primary gear casing – if necessary this can be glued in place.

17　Check that the connecting tube is located in the input shaft recess.

18　Apply sealing compound to the mating faces then fit the primary

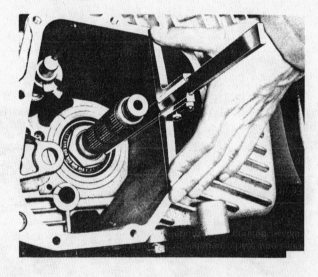

Fig. 6.13 Checking the output shaft dimension for fitting shims on 4-speed models (Sec 9)

gear casing to the gearbox casing. Do not fully tighten the bolts at this stage.

19　Invert the gearbox so that the laygear meshes with the gears, then fit the rear thrust washer and insert the layshaft from the rear of the gearbox.

20　Fully tighten the primary gear casing bolts.

21　Engage the reverse gear with the tab on the lever then insert the reverse gear shaft from the rear of the gearbox.

22　With the layshaft and reverse gear shaft aligned fit the locking plate and secure with the bolt. Apply locking fluid to the threads of the bolt before fitting it.

23　Insert the detent ball and spring in the casing hole then fit the cover and filler plug together with a new gasket. Insert and tighten the bolts.

24　Locate the differential in the gearbox casing, then smear the faces of the bearing housings with sealing compound and bolt them to the casing at the same time aligning the differential. Make sure that the shims are in their correct positions and that the springs and plungers are in the ends of the driveshafts.

25　Fit the differential cover together with a new gasket and tighten the bolts.

10　Gearbox (five-speed) – reassembly

1　Insert the output shaft into the gearbox casing and use temporary

locating studs to align the housing. Make sure that the shims are in position (photo).
2 Drive the housing into the casing using a soft-faced mallet, remove the studs and insert and tighten the bolts to the specified torque.
3 Using a steel rule and straight edge, determine the distance from the nut on the output shaft bearing to the mating face for the primary gear casing. If the distance is not 7.677 to 7.681 in (195.0 to 195.1 mm) shims must be fitted against the nut (photo).
4 Slide the 1st gear on the reverse gear bearing sleeve then locate the assembly on the output shaft and drive it on fully using a metal tube (photo).
5 Slide the sleeve on the 1st/2nd synchro hub, locate the selector fork on the sleeve then locate the assembly on the output shaft and drive it on fully using a metal tube if necessary (photo).
6 Fit the 2nd gear bearing sleeve using a metal tube, then slide the 2nd gear onto it (photos).

7 Fit the splined spacer followed by the 3rd gear and bearing sleeve (photos).
8 Fit the 3rd/4th synchro hub on the shaft, locate the selector fork on the sleeve and slide the sleeve on the hub (photos).
9 Fit the 4th gear bearing sleeve then slide the 4th gear onto it (photos).
10 Drive on the ball bearing bush using a metal tube (photos).
11 Fit the selector shaft together with the selector dog.
12 With the synchro sleeves in neutral, insert the inner selector shaft through the 1st/2nd and 3rd/4th selector forks and into the casing.
13 Insert the outer shaft and reverse gear lever and connect the lever to the selector dog. Insert the shaft in the casing and secure with the tapered bolt using locking fluid.
14 Slide the 5th gear selector tube on the outer selector shaft with the dog located inside the reverse dog.
15 Fit the locking plunger in the side of the gearbox making sure that it is the correct way round.

10.1 Showing shims located on the output shaft bearing housing

10.3 Fit the adjustment shims to the output shaft ...

10.4 ... followed by 1st and reverse gears ...

10.5 ... 1st/2nd synchro unit and selector fork ...

10.6A ... 2nd gear bearing sleeve

10.6B ... 2nd gear ...

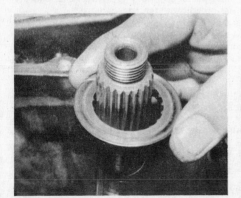
10.7A ... splined spacer ...

10.7B ... 3rd gear and bearing sleeve ...

10.8A ... 3rd/4th synchro hub ...

6

10.8B ... 3rd/4th synchro sleeve and selector fork ...

10.9A ... 4th gear bearing sleeve ...

10.9B ... 4th gear ...

10.10A .... and finally the ball bearing bush ...

10.10B ... using a metal tube

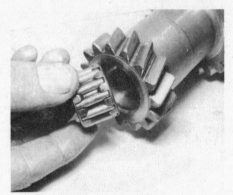

10.16 Locate the needle bearings in the laygear

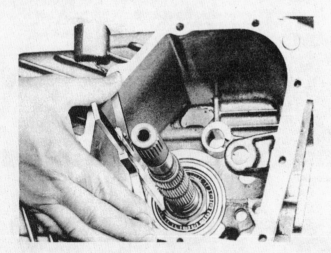

Fig. 6.14 Checking the output shaft dimension for fitting shims on 5-speed models (Sec 10)

16 Locate the needle bearings in the laygear and place the laygear in the bottom of the gearbox (photo).

17 Mesh the laygear with the output shaft and retain by temporarily inserting the layshaft from the rear of the gearbox. Do not fully insert it.

18 Up to and including gearbox number 436500 temporarily fit the spacer, shims, 5th synchro hub and circlip to the output shaft and check that there is no endplay. If necessary adjust the shim thickness then remove the components.

19 On all gearboxes apply sealing compound to the mating faces then fit the primary gear casing to the gearbox casing and tighten the bolts.

20 Up to and including gearbox number 436500 fit the spacer to the output shaft followed by the shims, 5th synchro hub and circlip.

21 From gearbox number 436501 (ie 1982 models on) fit the spacer to the output shaft followed by the 5th synchro hub and nut. Hold the shaft stationary by inserting a suitable bar in the teeth of the reverse gear then tighten the nut onto the shaft to the specified torque and lock it by peening the flange into the synchro hub locking holes.

22 Locate the selector fork on the 5th synchro sleeve then insert the components in the primary gear casing and slide the selector fork onto the selector shaft.

23 Check that the plastic tube is fitted to the input shaft bore, then fit the shaft and bearing housing to the casing using a soft-faced mallet to tap it into position. Make sure that the bolt holes are correctly aligned using guide pins if necessary. Insert and tighten the bolts together with the oil catcher.

24 On early models grease the laygear front thrust washer and locate it in the primary gear casing with the tab engaged.

25 Grease the rollers and locate them in the input pinion. On later models fit the collared sleeve (photo).

26 Fit the laygear connector and circlip on the input pinion, then insert the assembly in the primary gear casing and slide the connector onto the laygear until the circlip can be fitted.

27 Pull out the layshaft, move the laygear forwards and fit the rear thrust washer behind the laygear with the tab correctly located. Refit the layshaft and drive it fully into position.

28 Locate the reverse gear idler in the side of the casing with the gear lever tab engaged with the idler groove, then insert the reverse gear shaft (photo).

29 With the layshaft and reverse gear shaft aligned fit the locking plate and secure with the bolt. Apply locking fluid to the threads of the bolt before fitting it.

30 Locate the primary chain on the sprockets, and fit them in the casing — the tab holes on the bottom sprocket must be facing outwards (photo).

31 Secure the sprockets by fitting the circlips in their grooves.

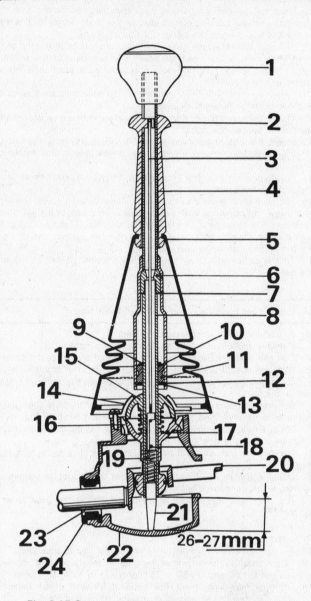

Fig. 6.15 Cross-section diagram of the gear lever and housing (Sec 11)

1 Knob	13 Lock ring
2 Carrier	14 Cover
3 Catch rod	15 Bearing
4 Gear lever	16 Gear lever bearing
5 Rubber boot	17 Carrier
6 Rubber bush	18 Tension pin
7 Washer	19 Spring
8 Hollow lever	20 Gear shift rod
9 Slot ring	21 Catch stud
10 Washer	22 Bottom part
11 Rubber bush	23 Bearing
12 Washer	24 Rubber bush

Fig. 6.16 Special key for removing the gear lever housing mounting screws (Sec 11)

10.25 Fitting the input pinion rollers and collared sleeve

10.28 Fitting the reverse idler gear

10.30 Primary chain and sprockets located in the casing

10.33 Tightening the lower sprocket nut

11.7 Gear lever housing

32 Squeeze the chain tensioner pads together and fit the assembly together with the backing plate between the chain. Apply locking fluid to the threads then fit the bolts and tighten them.

33 Select 5th and reverse gears simultaneously then fit the nut to the input shaft next to the lower sprocket and tighten it to the specified torque (photo). Using a round-nose punch peen the nut flange into the recess in the sprocket.

34 Select neutral gear then secure the 5th gear selector fork to the selector shaft by fitting the dowel.

35 Fit the primary gear casing cover together with a new gasket then insert and tighten the bolts.

36 Insert the detent ball and spring in the casing hole then fit the cover and filler plug together with a new gasket. Insert and tighten the bolts.

37 Fit the primary gear front cover together with a new gasket. Insert and tighten the bolts.

38 Locate the differential in the gearbox casing, then smear the faces of the bearing housings with sealing compound and bolt them to the casing at the same time aligning the differential. Make sure that the shims are in their correct positions and that the springs and plungers are in the ends of the driveshafts.

39 Fit the differential cover together with a new gasket and tighten the bolts.

11 Gear lever housing – removal and refitting

1   Disconnect the battery negative lead.

2   Remove the driver's seat as described in Chapter 12.

3   Pull the rubber boot up the gear lever and pull back the carpet.

4   Remove one of the heater ducts from in front of the housing.

5   Drive out the taper pin from the joint between the shift rod and the heater ducts.

6   On early models remove the heater control buttons then unbolt the gear lever cover and disconnect the warning lamp wiring.

7   On late models remove the centre console as described in Chapter 12 then unbolt the gear lever cover (photo).

8   Disconnect the wiring from the ignition lock and reverse lamp switch.

9   Using a special key (Fig. 6.16) remove the mounting screws and withdraw the gear lever housing from the car.

10   Refitting is a reversal of removal, but adjust the gear lever as follows.

Adjustment

11   Engage reverse gear and turn the ignition key to position 'L'.

12   Check that the movement of the gear lever forward and backward is between 0.120 and 0.160 in (3.0 and 4.0 mm). If not, loosen the mounting screws and move the housing forward or backward as required. Tighten the screws after making the adjustment.

12 Fault diagnosis – manual gearbox and final drive

Symptom	Reason(s)
Ineffective synchromesh	Worn synchro rings
Jumps out of gear	Weak detent spring
	Worn selector forks
	Worn gears
Noisy operation	Worn bearings or gears
Difficulty in engaging gears	Clutch fault
	Worn selector components
	Seized spigot bearing in the flywheel

Chapter 7 Automatic transmission and final drive

Contents

Specifications

Type .... Borg-Warner Type 35 (early models) or Type 37 (late models), three forward speeds and one reverse, epicyclic geartrain with hydraulic control, three element hydraulic torque converter

Ratios

1st	2.39 to 1
2nd	1.45 to 1
3rd	1.0 to 1
Reverse	2.09 to 1
Final drive	3.89 to 1

Stall speed

99 models	1900 to 2300 rpm
900 models:	
Type 489	2150 to 2550 rpm
Type 002	2100 to 2500 rpm
Type 001 Turbo UK	2500 to 2900 rpm at charging pressure of 0.7 bar
Type 001 Turbo USA	2100 to 2600 rpm at charging pressure of 0.5 bar
Type 001 Turbo Canada	2400 to 2900 rpm at charging pressure of 0.7 bar
Type 003 Turbo APC USA	2600 to 3000 rpm at charging pressure of 0.6 bar
Type 004 Turbo APC UK	2750 to 3150 rpm at charging pressure of 0.6 bar

Fluid capacity (transmission) .... 14 Imp pt; 8.5 US qt; 8.0 litre

Oil capacity (final drive)

Type 35	2.2 Imp pt; 1.3 US qt; 1.25 litre
Type 37	2.5 Imp pt; 1.5 US qt; 1.4 litre

Torque wrench settings

	lbf ft	Nm
Selector cable clamp bolt	1.8	2.5
Rear brake band adjusting screw locknut	29 to 40	40 to 55
Front brake band adjusting screw locknut	14 to 20	20 to 27
Torque converter to driveplate	24 to 29	33 to 39
Oil pan	6 to 9	8 to 12
Drain plug	4 to 6	5 to 8
Primary gear casing bottom cover	6 to 9	8 to 12
Oil cooler connector	5 to 7	7 to 10
Oil cooler connector nut	10 to 12	13 to 16
Line pressure plug	4 to 5	5 to 7

7

Fig. 7.1 Borg-Warner Type 35 automatic transmission (Sec 1)

Fig. 7.2 Borg-Warner Type 37 automatic transmission (Sec 1)

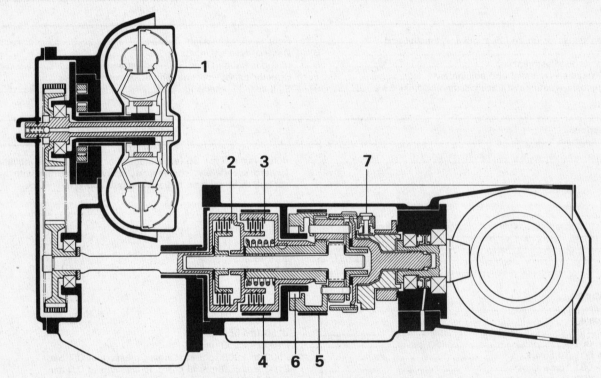

Fig. 7.3 Cross-section diagram of Type 37 transmission (Sec 1)

1 Torque converter	3 Rear clutch	5 Rear brake band	7 Governor
2 Front clutch	4 Front brake band	6 One-way clutch	

1   General description

The automatic transmission is of Borg-Warner Type 35 or Type 37 having three forward speeds and one reverse. The epicyclic geartrain is hydraulically controlled and drive from the engine is through a three element hydraulic torque converter. The Type 37 transmission is a modified and stronger version of the Type 35. The six position selector lever in the car provides for selection of Park, Reverse, Neutral, Drive (D), 2nd gear (2) and 1st gear (1). In D the gears are all selected automatically, in 2 automatic selection is restricted to 1st and 2nd gears, and in 1, only 1st gear is engaged. A 'kick-down' facility is provided whereby maximum acceleration through the gears is possible by depressing the accelerator pedal fully to the floor.

Due to the complexity of the transmission, if performance is not up to standard, or overhaul is necessary, it is imperative that the unit is checked while still in the car by qualified personnel. Any work by the home mechanics should be limited to that described in this Chapter.

2   Fluid level – checking

1   Three different types of oil are contained in the automatic transmission casing – the engine oil, final drive oil, and automatic transmission fluid.

2   The engine and final drive oils can be drained and replenished but with automatic transmission fluid, although provided with a drain plug, draining is not specified as a routine operation.

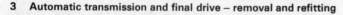

Fig. 7.4 Fluid level dipstick markings (Sec 2)

3   Regularly check the fluid level in the automatic transmission however, in the following way.

4   Run the engine at idling speed for a few minutes with the selector in P.

5   Switch off the engine and withdraw the transmission fluid dipstick. Wipe it clean on a piece of non-fluffy rag and re-insert it. Withdraw it for the second time when the oil level should be within the limits of the cut-out on the 'cold' edge of the dipstick if the engine and transmission are cold. Use the 'hot' edge of the dipstick if the engine and transmission are at normal operating temperature.

6   If necessary top up the fluid level through the dipstick/filler tube using only automatic transmission fluid.

3   Automatic transmission and final drive – removal and refitting

1   Remove the engine/transmission unit and separate the transmission from the engine as described in Chapter 1.

2   Refitting is also described in Chapter 1, but check the downshift cable adjustment as described in Section 5. Fill the transmission with fluid with reference to Section 2.

4   Selector cable – removal and adjustment

1   Jack up the front of the car and support on axle stands. Chock the rear wheels.

2   Unscrew the cable retaining bolt from the transmission and pull out the cable while moving the selector lever to position P.

3   Slide back the spring tensioned sleeve and unhook the cable end fitting.

4   Remove the selector housing using a special key to unscrew the nuts from inside the car (Fig. 7.6).

5   Extract the circlip from the end of the cable and note the position of the cable in the clamp.

6   Unscrew the clamp bolt and the outer cable nuts, and release the cable from the housing.

7   Lift the carpet inside the car and remove the heater duct, then withdraw the cable.

8   Fit the new cable using a reversal of the removal procedure, but before refitting the selector housing carry out the following adjustment.

9   With the clamp bolt loose pull out the cable end as far as possible then push it in two notches so that the transmission is in the neutral N mode. Now with the housing upright, move the selector lever to position N and tighten the clamp bolt.

10   Make sure that there is a good seal where the cable passes through the body, then refit the housing.

5   Downshift cable – renewal and adjustment

1   Disconnect the cable from the throttle and bracket.

2   Place a suitable container beneath the transmission then unscrew the drain plug and drain the fluid.

3   Unbolt the bottom cover from the front of the transmission beneath the primary gearcase, and remove the gasket. If necessary, jack up the front of the car and chock the rear wheels. Support the car with axle stands.

Fig. 7.5 Selector cable fitting to the transmission (Sec 4)

Fig. 7.6 Slotted key required to remove the selector housing (Sec 4)

Fig. 7.7 Loosening the cable clamp on the selector housing (Sec 4)

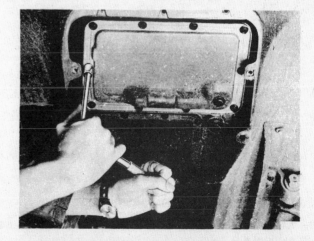

Fig. 7.8 Removing the primary gear case bottom cover (Sec 5)

7

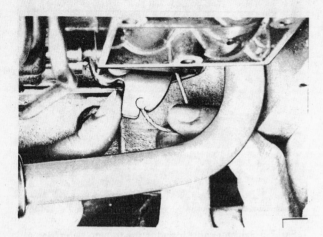

Fig. 7.9 Disconnecting the downshift cable from the control cam (Sec 5)

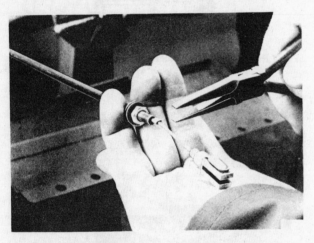

Fig. 7.10 Fixing the stop clip on the downshift cable (Sec 5)

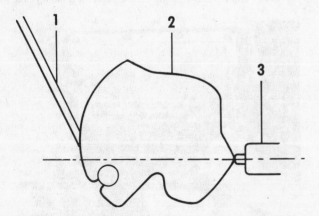

Fig. 7.11 Transmission control cam in 'kick-down' position (Sec 5)

1 Inner cable　　*2 Cam*　　*3 Valve*

4　Turn the control cam and disconnect the inner cable. If necessary first remove the strainer.

5　Unscrew the outer cable from the transmission casing, and withdraw the cable from the car.

6　Insert the new cable through the casing and tighten the outer cable.

7　Connect the inner cable to the control cam making sure that it is correctly located in the guide.

8　With the outer cable straight, pull the inner cable until the cam just starts to move, then use pliers to clamp the stop clip on the inner cable next to the threaded end of the outer cable.

9　Connect the cable to the throttle and bracket and adjust the outer cable until the highest point of the cam is in contact with the valve as shown in Fig. 7.11 with the accelerator pedal pressed against the floor. Have an assistant depress the pedal while making the adjustment.

10　Fit the bottom cover together with a new gasket and tighten the bolts.

11　Fill the transmission with fluid with reference to Section 2.

12　Final adjustment of the downshift cable must be made using a pressure gauge and if this is not available a Saab dealer should do the work.

13　If a pressure gauge is available remove the line pressure plug from the front right-hand side of the transmission and connect the gauge. Also connect a tachometer to the engine.

14　Fully apply the handbrake and chock the wheels.

15　Start the engine and check that the idling speed is as given in Chapter 3 with the selector lever in position P.

16　Select position D.

Type 35
17　Check that the line pressure is between 50 and 70 lbf/in^2 (3.5 and 4.9 bar) then increase the engine speed by 500 rpm and check that the pressure has increased by 10 to 20 lbf/in^2 (0.7 to 1.4 bar). If the pressure increase is too low adjust the cable to increase the idling pressure within the limit. If the pressure increase is excessive, reduce the idling pressure accordingly.

Type 37
18　Adjust the cable to give the lowest pressure on the gauge then adjust the cable to increase the pressure by 1.4 lbf/in^2 (0.1 bar).

19　Select P and check that the line pressure is now between 59.0 and 69.0 lbf/in^2 (4.2 and 4.9 bar).

20　Switch off the engine, remove the pressure gauge, and refit the plug.

6　Brake bands – adjustment

1　Adjustment of the brake bands will not normally be necessary unless the car has covered a high mileage or the transmission has been dismantled.

Rear brake band
2　The rear brake band adjustment is located on the left-hand side of the transmission.

3　Loosen the locknut then using a torque wrench tighten the adjusting screw to between 9.6 and 10.3 lbf ft (13 and 14 Nm).

4　Back off the screw 3/4 turn on a Type 35 transmission and 1-1/4 turn on a Type 37 transmission. Tighten the locknut.

Front brake band
5　Drain the fluid from the transmission then unbolt the bottom cover and remove the gasket.

6　Loosen the locknut on the adjusting screw on Type 37 transmissions. Type 35 transmissions have a self-adjusting spring and screw to retain it.

7　Position a spacer between the inner end of the screw and the boss on the piston. On Type 35 and 37 transmissions up to serial numbers 001-1700, 002-2800 the spacer must be 0.25 in (6.35 mm) thick. On Type 37 transmissions from serial numbers 001-1701, 002-2801 (except those ending in 008, 009, 010 or 011) the spacer must be 0.35 in (8.9 mm) thick. On those ending in 008, 009, 010 or 011, the spacer must be .31 in (7.8 mm) thick.

Fig. 7.12 Adjusting the rear brake band (Sec 6)

8 Using a torque wrench tighten the adjusting screw to 1.0 lbf ft (1.3 Nm).

9 On Type 35 transmissions check that the gap between the self-adjusting spring and the lever is $1\frac{1}{2}$ to 2 threads.

10 On type 37 transmissions up to serial numbers 001-1700, 002-2800 back off the adjusting screw one complete turn then tighten the locknut.

11 On Type 37 transmissions from serial numbers 001-1701, 002-2801 (including those ending in 008, 009, 010 or 011), DO NOT back off the adjusting screw, tighten the locknut.

12 On all types remove the spacer, fit the bottom cover with a new gasket and tighten the bolts.

13 Fill the transmission with fluid with reference to Section 2.

7 Inhibitor switch (Type 35) – adjustment

1 On early Type 35 transmissions the inhibitor switch is fitted to the right-hand side of the primary gear casing and its purpose is to prevent starting of the engine with the selector lever in positions other than N and P. On later models the switch is located in the selector lever housing and is not adjustable.

2 First disconnect the wires from the switch. The narrow terminals are for the starter motor and the wide ones for the reversing lights.

3 Select D then loosen the locknut and unscrew the switch.

4 Connect a test lamp and leads to the narrow terminals and check that the test lamp lights up. Now screw in the switch until the test lamp just goes out, and mark the switch and casing in relation to each other.

5 Unscrew the switch and connect the test lamp and leads to the wide terminals. Screw in the switch until the test lamp lights up and again mark the switch and casing in relation to each other.

6 Back off the switch until it is half way between the positions noted in paragraphs 4 and 5, then tighten the locknut. *Do not overtighten the locknut.*

8 Stall speed – checking

1 When the torque converter is functioning correctly it has the ability to multiply torque in a similar way to a set of gears except that the ratio is variable from between approximately 2.5 to 1 to 1 to 1. The unit can be tested by effectively locking the transmission and

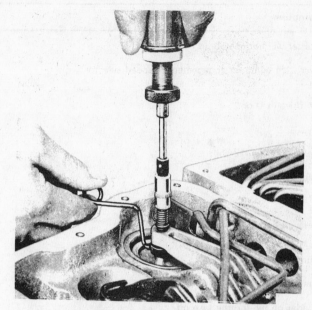

Fig. 7.13 Adjusting the front brake band on Type 35 transmission incorporating self-adjusting spring (Sec 6)

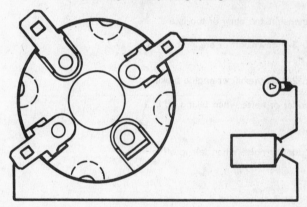

Fig. 7.14 Test lamp connected to starter terminals on the inhibitor switch (Sec 7)

determining the maximum engine speed which will be directly proportioned by the torque multiplication achieved.

2 Connect a tachometer to the engine.

3 Chock all wheels and fully apply the handbrake. *During the test the footbrake pedal must also be firmly applied.*

4 Start the engine and select D, 1 or R.

5 Fully depress the accelerator pedal for a maximum of 10 seconds and note the stall speed on the tachometer. As considerable heat will be generated in the torque converter, allow several minutes between tests for the fluid to cool.

6 Check the results with the stall speeds given in the Specifications. If the speed is up to 300 rpm below normal it is likely that the engine is not developing its normal power in which case the engine should be tuned or repaired. More than 800 rpm below normal indicates a faulty stator inside the torque converter in which case the unit should be renewed. A stall speed substantially *higher* than the normal speed indicates slip in the gearbox. In this case first check the fluid level. If the slip occurs only in position D the front clutch unit or one-way clutch is slipping. If the slip occurs only in position 1 the front clutch unit is slipping. If the slip occurs only in position R the rear clutch or rear brake band is slipping.

9   Fault diagnosis – automatic transmission and final drive

Symptom	Reason(s)
Starter will not operate in P or N	Inhibitor switch requires adjustment or faulty.
Excessive bump on engagement of speed selector	Idling speed too high Downshift cable out of adjustment
No drive in D or 2	Selector linkage out of adjustment Incorrect fluid level Downshift cable out of adjustment
Delayed or no 1-2 shift	Front band out of adjustment
Slip on 1-2 shift	Incorrect fluid level Downshift cable out of adjustment Front band out of adjustment
Delayed or no 2-3 shift	Downshift cable out of adjustment Front band out of adjustment
Bumpy shifts	Downshift cable out of adjustment
Drag on 2-3 shift	Front band out of adjustment
Judder on full-throttle take off	Selector linkage out of adjustment Incorrect fluid level Downshift cable out of adjustment
Downshift too early or too late	Downshift cable out of adjustment
No 3-2 downshift or engine braking	Speed selector linkage out of adjustment Front brake band out of adjustment
No 2-1 downshift or engine braking	Rear brake band out of adjustment
Judder or noise when taking off in 1	Speed selector linkage out of adjustment Incorrect fluid level Downshift cable out of adjustment
Judder or noise when taking off in R	Speed selector linkage out of adjustment Incorrect fluid level Downshift cable out of adjustment
Slip in R or no drive	Speed selector linkage out of adjustment Incorrect fluid level Downshift cable out of adjustment Rear band out of adjustment
Vehicle rolls in P	Incorrect linkage adjustment Worn or damaged internal parking pawl and linkage

The foregoing is limited to the faults which can be rectified by the home mechanic. Where the action indicated does not prove effective fault diagnosis and rectification should be undertaken by your dealer with the car under normal operating conditions.

Chapter 8 Driveshafts

For specifications applicable to later models, see Supplement at end of manual

Contents

Specifications

Type .... Solid driveshafts splined to needle roller type inner universal joints and constant velocity outer joints

Grease type .... Lithium lead base EP (Duckhams LB 10)

Spline lubricant type (when assembling) .... Molybdenum paste

Torque wrench settings

	lbf ft	Nm
Driveshaft nut	250 to 265	340 to 360
Differential bearing housing bolts	16 to 19	22 to 25

1 General description

The driveshafts are of solid type and are splined to needle roller type inner universal joints and constant velocity type outer joints. The inner shafts are splined to the transmission differential gears and supported in ball bearings located in the differential bearing housings. The outer shafts are splined to the front wheel hubs – on pre-1981 models the outer shafts are supported directly in double row ball bearings located in the steering knuckles, however on 1981 on models the hubs are supported in the bearings and the shafts in the hubs.

The inner joints incorporate three-arm spiders which are located in slotted cylindrical housings by needle roller bearing races. The outer joints incorporate a hub and six balls which move in slotted grooves designed to provide constant velocity rotation at different shaft angles.

No routine maintenance is required except to inspect the flexible bellows for damage or deterioration.

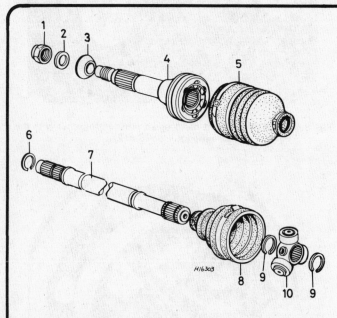

Fig. 8.1 Exploded diagram of the driveshaft fitted to pre-1981 models (Sec 1)

1	Nut	6	Circlip
2	Washer	7	Driveshaft
3	Cone ring	8	Bellows
4	Outer driveshaft and joint	9	Circlips
5	Bellows	10	Inner joint

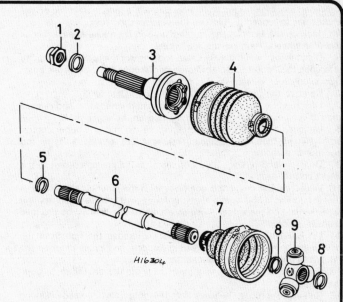

Fig. 8.2 Exploded diagram of the driveshaft fitted to 1981 on models (Sec 1)

1	Nut	5	Circlip
2	Washer	6	Driveshaft
3	Outer driveshaft and joint	7	Bellows
4	Bellows	8	Circlips
		9	Inner joint

8

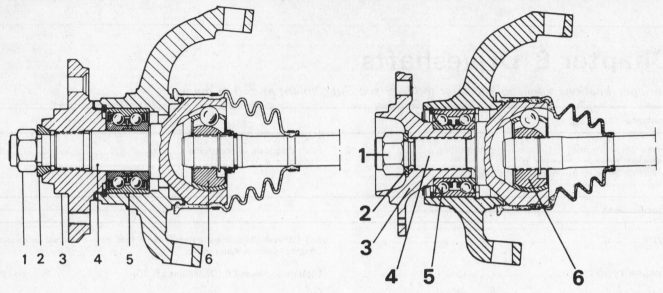

Fig. 8.3 Cross-section diagrams of the outer driveshafts and joints (Sec 2)

A Pre-1981 models   1 Nut   3 Hub   5 Wheel bearing
B 1981 on models   2 Cone ring/washer 4 Outer driveshaft 6 Outer joint

2 Driveshaft and outer joint – removal and refitting

1 Turn the steering on full lock, then with the full weight of the car on the suspension place a suitable block of hardwood or metal between the front suspension upper control arm and the body underframe. This is necessary to enable the lower control arm bolts to be removed without being under tension from the coil spring.
2 Prise the hub cap from the front wheel using a screwdriver.
3 With the handbrake applied, loosen the roadwheel nuts then unscrew and remove the driveshaft nut (photo). The driveshaft nut is tightened to a high torque so if necessary use a long metal tube on the socket bar to loosen it. Remove the washer/cone ring.
4 Jack up the front of the car and support it on axle stands. Chock the rear wheels. Remove the roadwheel.
5 Disconnect the handbrake cable and remove the brake caliper with reference to Chapter 9. Do not however disconnect the hydraulic hose. Use a length of wire to tie the caliper to one side.
6 Remove the brake disc with reference to Chapter 9.
7 Unscrew the large clip from the driveshaft inner joint, and release the rubber bellows (photo). Hang the clip on the inner shaft.
8 Unscrew the nuts from the steering tie-rod end and upper control arm balljoint, then use a balljoint separator tool to release the tie-rod and upper balljoint.
9 Unscrew and remove the bolts securing the lower balljoint to the lower control arm.
10 Withdraw the driveshaft complete with the steering knuckle from the car (photo). Make sure that the inner joint needle bearings and races remain on the spider – use an elastic band or plastic bag to hold them in place.
11 On pre-1981 models use a puller to remove the hub from the driveshaft, then support the steering knuckle and press or drive the driveshaft through the wheel bearing.
12 On 1981 on models use a puller to press the driveshaft through the hub.
13 Release the rubber bellows from the outer joint and slide it along the driveshaft.
14 Support the driveshaft with the outer joint downwards. Press down on the driveshaft then use circlip pliers to open the circlip inside the joint.
15 Withdraw the driveshaft from the outer joint and where applicable remove the special conical shaped washers. If fitted, these washers should be discarded as they have been discontinued.
16 Clean all the components and examine them for wear and damage. In particular check the joint balls and grooves. Renew the parts as necessary.

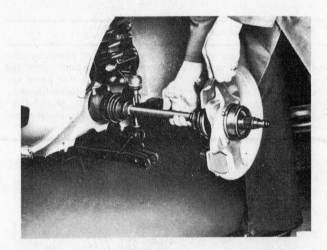

Fig. 8.4 Removing the left-hand side driveshaft together with the steering knuckle (Sec 2)

Fig. 8.5 Opening the circlip in the outer joint (Sec 2)

2.3 Driveshaft nut location

2.7 Driveshaft inner joint and rubber bellows

2.10 Removing the driveshaft

Fig. 8.6 Conical washers (1) and circlip (2) fitted to early models (Sec 2)

The conical washers should be discarded

17 Commence reassembly by packing the joint with the specified grease.

18 With the outer bellows on the driveshaft, insert the shaft into the outer joint until the circlip engages the groove.

19 On pre-1981 models support the joint housing then locate the steering knuckle on the end of the driveshaft and use a metal tube on the wheel bearing inner race to drive the assembly fully onto the driveshaft. Locate the hub on the driveshaft splines and tap it up to the bearing. Fit the conical washer and nut loosely.

20 On 1981 on models lubricate the driveshaft splines with a molybdenum based grease then insert the shaft into the splined hub and tap in fully. Fit the washer and nut loosely.

21 Pack the joint with more grease then fit the bellows to the joint housing and secure with a new clip.

22 Check that the inner joint housing is packed with grease and that the needle bearings are in position on the spider, then insert the driveshaft. Remove the elastic band or plastic bag as applicable.

23 Locate the lower balljoint in the lower control arm, insert the bolts (from the rear of the car) and tighten the nuts.

24 Fit the tie-rod end and upper control arm balljoints to the steering knuckle and tighten the nuts.

25 Locate the rubber bellows on the inner joint housing and secure with the large clip.

26 Refit the brake disc, brake caliper, and handbrake cable with reference to Chapter 9.

27 Refit the roadwheel and lower the car to the ground.

28 With the handbrake applied tighten the roadwheel nuts and the driveshaft nut to the specified torque. Lock the driveshaft nut by peening the flange into the groove in the driveshaft.

29 Refit the hub cap then remove the hardwood or metal from beneath the suspension upper control arm.

3 Driveshaft inner joint – removal and refitting

1 Remove the driveshaft complete with the steering knuckle as described in Section 2 paragraphs 1 to 10, however do not remove the driveshaft nut.

2 Place a suitable container beneath the rear of the transmission then unscrew the drain plug and drain the oil. Clean the drain plug then refit and tighten it.

3 Mark the differential bearing housing in relation to the transmission casing then unscrew and remove the bolts. Disconnect the speedometer cable where applicable.

8

Fig. 8.7 Peening the driveshaft nut flange into the groove (Sec 2)

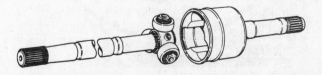

Fig. 8.8 Driveshaft inner joint components (Sec 3)

4   Tap the housing assembly from the casing with a wooden mallet. Keep the shims on the housing and recover the spring and plunger from the end of the inner driveshaft (photos). If the housing is tight use a slide hammer in the slots provided to remove it.

5   Extract the circlip from inside the housing, then support the housing and drive out the inner driveshaft using a soft metal drift (photo).

6   Extract the circlip and pull the joint spider from the end of the main driveshaft.

7   Clean all the components and examine them for wear and damage. In particular check the needle rollers, races, and spider. Renew the parts as necessary including the differential bearing housing oil seal (Chapter 6 or 7).

8   Commence reassembly by locating the joint spider on the main driveshaft and fitting the circlip.

9   Grease the spider trunnions and fit the needle rollers followed by the races. Fill the races with grease.

10 Stand the inner driveshaft upright on the bench and use a metal tube on the bearing inner race to drive the bearing housing fully onto the driveshaft (photos). Fit the circlip in the driveshaft groove.

11 Make sure that the spring and plunger are located in the end of the inner driveshaft, and the shims are in position on the differential bearing housing. Fit a new sealing ring to the housing.

12 Clean the mating faces then fit the housing and inner driveshaft to

3.4A Removing the differential bearing housing and inner driveshaft

3.4B Removing the plunger from the inner driveshaft

3.4C Removing the spring from the inner driveshaft

3.4D The bearing housing shims must be refitted in their original position

3.5 Extracting the inner driveshaft circlip

3.10A Locate the differential bearing housing on the inner driveshaft ...

3.10B ... and drive it on with a metal tube

the transmission casing using a wooden mallet to tap it fully into position. Coat the threads with sealing compound then insert them and tighten them evenly in diagonal sequence to the specified torque.
13 Reconnect the speedometer cable where applicable.
14 Fill the transmission/final drive with oil with reference to Chapter 6 or 7.
15 Refit the driveshaft and steering knuckle as described in Section 2 paragraphs 22 to 29. As the driveshaft nut has not been disturbed there is no need to check it for tightness.

4 Driveshaft bellows – renewal

1 Turn the steering on full lock, then with the full weight of the car on the suspension place a suitable block of hardwood or metal between the front suspension upper control arm and the body underframe. This is necessary to enable the lower control arm bolts to be removed without being under tension from the coil spring.
2 Prise the hub cap from the front wheel using a screwdriver, and loosen the nuts.
3 Jack up the front of the car and support it on axle stands. Chock the rear wheels. Remove the roadwheel.
4 Unscrew the large clip from the driveshaft inner joint, and release the rubber bellows. Hang the clip on the inner shaft.
5 Unscrew and remove the bolts securing the lower balljoint to the lower control arm, then pull out the steering knuckle and swivel it upwards. Support the knuckle on an axle stand. Do not lose any of the needle rollers from the inner joint spider.
6 Extract the circlip and remove the inner joint spider, then remove the inner circlip (only fitted to early models).

8

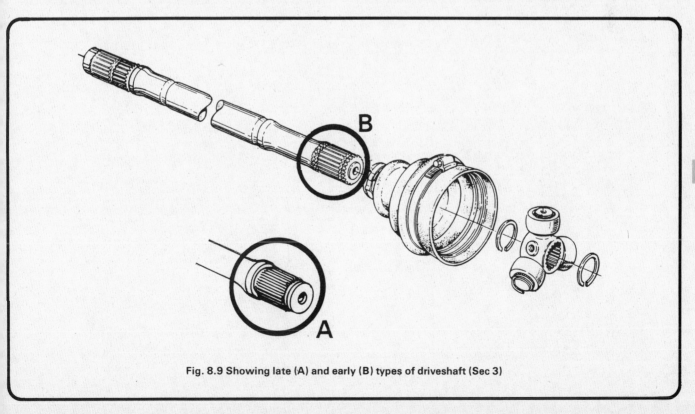

Fig. 8.9 Showing late (A) and early (B) types of driveshaft (Sec 3)

7   Release the clips and slide the bellows from the driveshaft as necessary.

8   Wipe clean the driveshaft and slide on the new bellows. Pack the outer joint with the specified grease if applicable.

9   Fit the inner joint spider and circlip(s).

10 Check that the needle rollers and races are in position on the inner joint spider then swivel the steering knuckle downwards and at the same time locate the spider and needle bearings in the inner joint

housing. Pack the inner joint with the specified grease.

11 Locate the lower balljoint in the lower control arm, insert the bolts (from the rear of the car) and tighten the nuts.

12 Locate the bellows on the joint housing(s) and secure with the clips.

13 Refit the roadwheel and lower the car to the ground.

14 Tighten the roadwheel nuts, refit the hub cap, and remove the hardwood or metal from beneath the suspension upper control arm.

5   Fault diagnosis – driveshafts

Symptom	Reason(s)
Vibration	Worn joints
	Worn wheel bearings or inner shaft bearings in differential bearing housing
Noise on taking up drive	Worn driveshaft splines
	Worn joints
	Loose driveshaft nut

Chapter 9 Braking system

For modifications, and information applicable to later models, see Supplement at end of manual

Contents

Specifications

System type	Discs all round with vacuum servo assistance, dual hydraulic circuit split diagonally. Self-adjusting cable operated handbrake on front wheels
Brake fluid type/specification	Hydraulic fluid to SAE J1703 or DOT 4 (Duckhams Universal Brake and Clutch Fluid)

Front discs
Thickness (new)	0.5 in (12.7 mm)
Minimum thickness after grinding	0.460 in (11.7 mm)
Maximum grinding each side	0.02 in (0.5 mm)
Maximum run-out:	
1979/1980 models	0.004 in (0.10 mm)
1981 on	0.003 in (0.08 mm)
Maximum thickness variation	0.0006 in (0.015 mm)
Minimum pad lining thickness	0.04 in (1.0 mm)

Rear discs
Thickness (new)	0.413 in (10.5 mm)
Minimum thickness after grinding	0.374 in (9.5 mm)
Maximum grinding each side	0.02 in (0.5 mm)
Minimum pad lining thickness	0.04 in (1.0 mm)

Vacuum servo
Type	Girling 9 in
Effort multiplication ratio	3.5 to 1 with 25 kgf pedal force

Torque wrench settings
	lbf ft	Nm
Brake disc (99 models)	22 tr 36	30 to 50
Front caliper yoke bolts	81 to 96	110 to 130
Rear caliper yoke bolts	52 to 66	70 to 90

1 General description

The braking system is of dual hydraulic circuit type with discs fitted to the front and rear wheels. The hydraulic circuit is split diagonally and each circuit is operated independently, so that, in the event of a failure in one circuit, one front and one rear brake still function.

The front calipers incorporate a cylinder housing with two pistons one of which operates directly on the inner brake pad and the other which operates on a sliding yoke which pulls the outer brake pad onto the disc. The cable operated handbrake incorporates a pushrod to

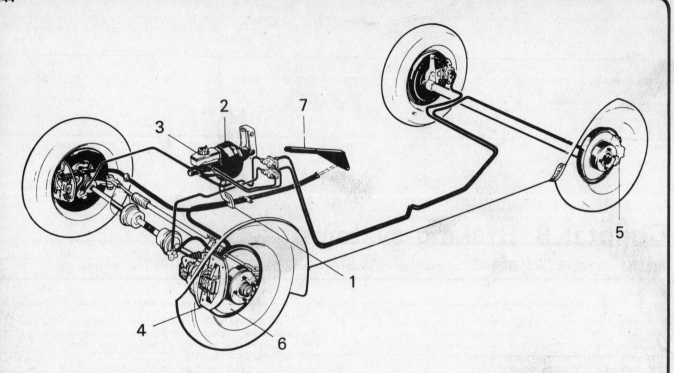

Fig. 9.1 Diagram of the braking system (Sec 1)

1 Footbrake pedal
2 Servo unit
3 Master cylinder
4 Front caliper
5 Rear caliper
6 Brake discs
7 Handbrake lever

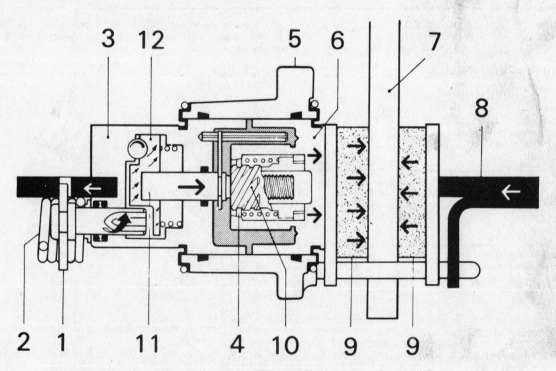

Fig. 9.2 Cross-section of front brake caliper showing handbrake mechanism (Sec 1)

1 Handbrake lever
2 Return spring
3 Brake piston
   (indirect)
4 Drive ring
5 Brake cylinder
   housing (caliper)
6 Brake piston
   (direct)
7 Brake disc
8 Yoke
9 Disc pad
10 Sleeve
11 Pushrod
12 Thrust plate

mechanically operate the caliper pistons, and the mechanism is automatically adjusted by hydraulic pressure when the footbrake pedal is depressed.

The rear calipers incorporate two cylinders and pistons, each mounted either side of the disc.

A vacuum servo is fitted to all models to provide assistance to the driver when the footbrake pedal is depressed.

2 Routine maintenance

1 Every 10 000 miles (15 000 km) on UK models or 7500 miles (12 000 km) on North American models check the level of hydraulic fluid in the reservoir and if necessary top it up. Note that the reservoir also supplies the clutch master cylinder.

2 At the same time check all the brake pads for wear and renew them if necessary. Lubricate the front caliper yoke guides and check that the handbrake operates correctly. Check the condition of the hydraulic hoses and rigid brake lines, and make sure that the union nuts are secure. Also check that the vacuum servo functions correctly.

3 Every 30 000 miles (45 000 km) or two years renew the hydraulic brake fluid.

3 Disc pads (front) — inspection and renewal

1 The front disc pad linings can be checked for wear by using a torch through one of the holes in the wheel rim (photo). However a more thorough check can be made by removing the wheel. If the lining thickness is less than the minimum amount given in the Specifications renew *all* the front disc pads.

2 Jack up the front of the car and support on axle stands. Chock the rear wheels and remove the front wheels.

3 Turn the brake disc so that one of the recesses on its edge is aligned with the disc pads.

4 Extract the spring clips from the ends of the pad retaining pin (photo).

5 Pull out the retaining pin and remove the damper spring plate (photo). Use a hammer to tap out the pin if it is tight.

6 Withdraw the disc pads from each side of the disc (photos). If they are tight tap them lightly with a hammer to release the accumulated dust and use grips on the backplates. Also press the two pads away from each other to return the pistons and give more room.

7 Brush the dust and dirt from the caliper, pads and disc *but do not inhale it as it is injurious to health.* Scrape any scale or rust from the disc (photo).

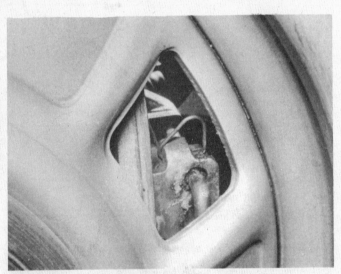

3.1 Checking front disc pad lining wear through the wheel rim

3.4 Showing spring clip location on front disc pad retaining pin

3.5 Removing the front disc pad retaining pin

3.6A Removing the outer front disc pad

9

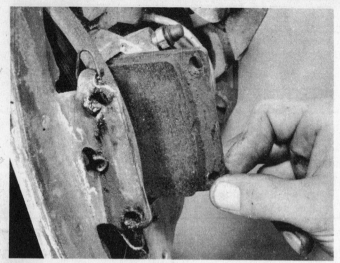

3.6B Removing the inner front disc pad

3.7 Showing the front brake caliper and piston

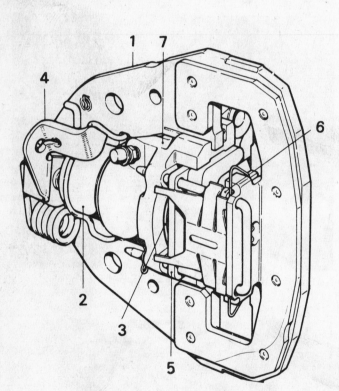

Fig. 9.3 Front brake caliper (Secs 3 and 5)

1 Yoke	5 Inner disc pad
2 Piston (indirect)	6 Outer disc pad
3 Piston (direct)	7 Cylinder housing
4 Handbrake lever	

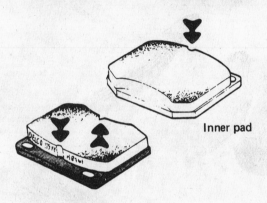

Fig. 9.4 Disc pad identification on pre-1983 models (Sec 3)

8   Apply a little brake grease to the sliding surfaces of the caliper yoke, at the same time moving the yoke in the groove.

9   Check the piston dust covers and retainers for condition and security.

10 Using circlip pliers or a purpose-made tool rotate (clockwise) the piston which contacts the inner disc pad while pressing the piston into the cylinder – this resets the self-adjusting handbrake mechanism (photos). Do not press the piston further than the face of the cylinder otherwise the internal seal may be damaged.

11 Insert the disc pads between the caliper and disc. Note on pre-1983 models the inner and outer pads are different – the inner pad has one groove on its outer edge but the outer pad also has a groove on its inner edge.

12 Position the damper spring plate on the pads then insert the retaining pin through the pads and fit the spring clips.

13 Using a feeler blade check that the clearance between the caliper handbrake lever and the yoke is no more than 0.019 in (0.5 mm). If necessary adjust the handbrake cable inside the car noting that, as the cables cross each other, the left-hand adjustment is for the right-hand cable and vice versa.

14 Depress the footbrake pedal several times, then pull up the handbrake lever five notches and depress the pedal several more times. This will set the handbrake mechanism. Check the adjustment by applying the handbrake two to four more notches and checking that the brake discs are held firmly.

15 Repeat the procedure given in paragraphs 3 to 14 on the remaining front brake, then refit the wheels and lower the car to the ground.

4   Disc pads (rear) – inspection and renewal

1   Apply the handbrake then jack up the rear of the car and support on axle stands. Remove the wheels.

2   Check the thickness of the disc pad linings and if less than the minimum amount given in the Specifications renew all the rear disc pads.

3   Using a soft metal drift tap out the lower retaining pin (photo).

4   Remove the damper spring plate then tap out the upper retaining pin (photo).

5   Withdraw the disc pads and backing plates from each side of the disc (photos). If they are tight tap them lightly with a hammer to

3.10A Using circlip pliers to reset the self-adjusting handbrake mechanism

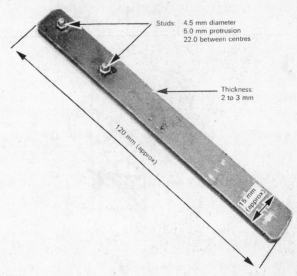

Studs: 4.5 mm diameter
5.0 mm protrusion
22.0 between centres

Thickness: 2 to 3 mm

120 mm (approx)

15 mm (approx)

3.10B Home made tool for resetting the self-adjusting handbrake mechanism

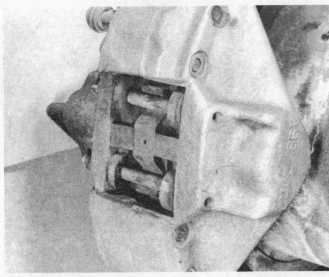

4.3 Rear brake caliper and disc pads

4.4 Removing the damper spring plate from the rear brake caliper

4.5A Removing the outer rear disc pad and backing plate

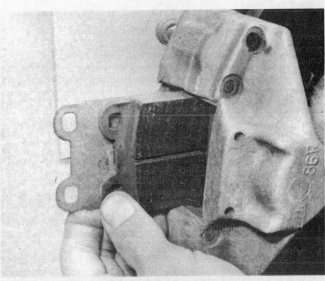

4.5B Removing the inner rear disc pad and backing plate

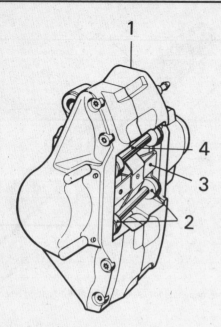

Fig. 9.5 Rear brake caliper (Secs 4 and 6)

1   Cylinder housing   3   Damper spring plate
2   Disc pad   4   Retaining pin

release the accumulated dust and use grips on the backplates. Also prise the two pads away from each other to return the pistons and give more room.

6   Brush the dust and dirt from the caliper, pads and disc *but do not inhale it as it is injurious to health.* Scrape any scale or rust from the disc.

7   Check the piston dust covers and retainers for condition and security.

8   Using a piece of wood, press the two pistons into their cylinders until flush with the inner faces of the caliper.

9   Insert the disc pads and backing plates each side of the disc. Note on early models the inner pad has one groove on its outer edge and the outer pad also has a groove on its inner edge. On later models both pads are interchangeable.

10   Insert the upper retaining pin through the pads and tap it firmly into the caliper.

11   Hook the damper spring under the upper retaining pin then depress the lower part of the spring and insert the lower retaining pin. Tap the pin firmly into the caliper.

12   Depress the footbrake pedal several times to set the pads in their normal position.

13   Repeat the procedure given in paragraphs 2 to 12 on the remaining rear brake, then refit the wheels and lower the car to the ground.

5   Disc caliper (front) – removal, overhaul and refitting

1   Remove the disc pads, as described in Section 3.

2   Disconnect the handbrake cable from the caliper.

3   Disconnect and plug the rigid hydraulic pipe from the flexible hose at the support bracket.

4   Unbolt and remove the caliper.

5   Clean the external surface of the caliper and mount it carefully in the jaws of a vice.

6   Release the return spring from the handbrake lever.

7   Remove the yoke from the caliper and withdraw the handbrake lever and return spring.

8   Remove the dust excluder and retaining ring from the indirect piston and then apply air pressure from a tyre pump at the fluid inlet port on the caliper and eject the indirect piston.

9   Now press the pushrod by hand and eject the direct piston from the cylinder.

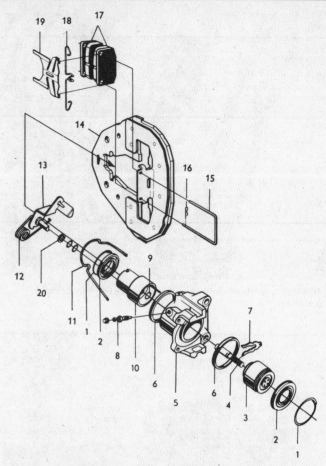

Fig. 9.6 Exploded view of the front disc caliper (Sec 5)

1   Dust cover holder   12   Spring (handbrake
2   Dust cover   lever)
3   Piston (direct)   13   Handbrake lever
4   Pushrod   14   Yoke
5   Brake housing   15   Pad retaining pin
6   Piston seal   16   Lock clip
7   Guide clip   17   Disc pad
8   Bleeder nipple   18   Spring
9   O-ring   19   Damper spring
10 Piston   20   Retainer (two
11 Yoke spring   O-rings)

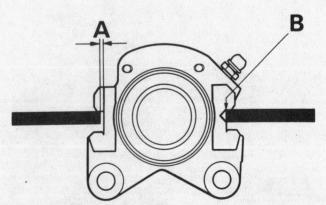

Fig. 9.7 Correct yoke clearances on the front brake cylinder housing (Sec 5)

A   0.006 to 0.012 in (0.15 to 0.30 mm)
B   Nil clearance

10 Extract the seals and O-rings from the pistons and cylinder bore, taking great care not to scratch the surfaces of these components. Also remove the two O-rings from the handbrake lever aperture.

11 Wash all components in clean hydraulic fluid or methylated spirit except the internal parts of the indirect piston otherwise the grease for the handbrake mechanism will be washed away.

12 Examine the surfaces of the pistons and cylinder bores for scoring or 'bright' wear areas. If these are evident, renew the caliper complete. Where such faults are not found, discard the old seals and obtain a repair kit.

13 Commence reassembly by fitting the pushrod and handbrake lever O-rings to the indirect piston. Secure the handbrake lever O-rings with the special retainer, and lubricate them with brake grease.

14 Lubricate the cylinder bore with brake fluid and fit the piston seals in their grooves.

15 Fit the anchor plate to the pushrod and then insert the pushrod into the hole in the indirect piston. Ensure that the recess in the anchor plate comes immediately over the tension pin in the piston.

16 Wipe the indirect piston with a clean lint-free rag, dip it in clean hydraulic fluid and insert it into the caliper so that the recess for the yoke is in direct alignment with the groove in the caliper body.

17 Dip the direct piston into clean hydraulic fluid and insert it into its cylinder, screwing together the piston and pushrod.

18 Screw and depress the two pistons until the edges of the dust excluder grooves are flush with the caliper body. Install the new dust excluders and their retaining rings.

19 Fit the spring and handbrake lever to the yoke, and lubricate the yoke sliding surfaces with grease.

20 Align the guide edges of the yoke with the grooves in the caliper body. Lift the handbrake lever and secure the end of its pivot pin in the hole in the indirect piston, making sure at the same time that the yoke engages in the recess in the indirect piston.

21 Install the handbrake lever return spring.

22 Check that the yoke to caliper clearances are as shown in the diagram (Fig. 9.7).

23 Refitting the caliper is a reversal of removal but the handbrake cables must be adjusted as described in Section 3, and the hydraulic

5.23 Front disc caliper mounting bolts

circuit bled, as described in Section 9. Use new locking plates on the caliper bolts and bend them over the bolt head flats after tightening the bolts (photo).

---

6 Disc caliper (rear) – removal, overhaul and refitting

---

1 Remove the disc pads as described in Section 4.

2 Disconnect the hydraulic brake pipe from the caliper and plug the pipe to prevent loss of fluid.

3 Unbolt (two bolts) the caliper unit from the rear axle.

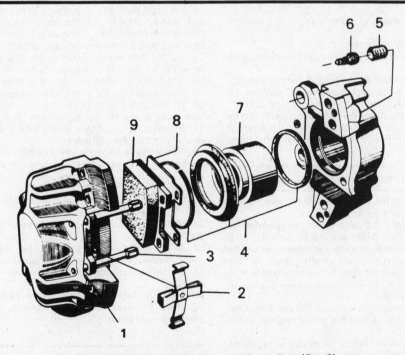

Fig. 9.8 Exploded view of the rear disc caliper (Sec 6)

1 Brake housing	4 Piston seal	7 Piston
2 Damper spring	5 Rubber cap	8 Twist stop
3 Lock pin	6 Bleeder nipple	9 Disc pad

Fig. 9.9 Using the special tool to position the cut-out in the rear caliper piston (Sec 6)

4 Clean the external surfaces of the caliper.

5 Prise off the dust covers.

6 Using a tyre pump in the hydraulic fluid aperture force both pistons from their cylinders. Take care not to damage the pistons or bores.

7 Prise the seals from the cylinder bores using a non-metallic instrument.

8 Wash all components in clean hydraulic fluid or methylated spirit. *Do not attempt to separate the two halves of the caliper.*

9 Examine the surfaces of the pistons and cylinder bore for scoring or 'bright' wear areas. If these are evident, renew the caliper complete. If the components are in good condition discard the old seals and obtain a repair kit.

10 Commence reassembly by applying brake fluid to the cylinder bores.

11 Fit the new seals to the cylinder bores.

12 Dip the inner surfaces of the pistons in brake fluid then insert them into their respective bores.

13 Fit the dust covers to the pistons and press the pistons in fully.

14 Using tool 89 95 342 or a piece of card cut to 20°, position the cut-outs on the piston facing the bottom of the caliper (Fig. 9.9).

15 Refitting is a reversal of removal, but the hydraulic circuit must be bled as described in Section 9. Use new locking plates on the caliper bolts and bend them over the bolt head flats after tightening the bolts.

7 Brake disc – examination, removal and refitting

1 To make an accurate check of the brake disc first remove the disc pads as described in Section 3 or 4 as applicable.

2 Rotate the disc and examine it for deep scoring or grooving on both the inner and outer surfaces. Light scoring is normal, but if excessive the disc should be removed and either renewed or ground by a suitable engineering works within the limits given in the Specifications. Alternatively on the front discs it may be possible for a Saab dealer to use special abrasive blocks which are fitted in place of the disc pads to remove light scoring.

3 Using a dial gauge or metal block and feeler gauges check that the disc endfloat and run-out does not exceed the amounts given in the Specifications.

4 To remove a front brake disc on pre-1982 99 models or pre-1981 900 models, temporarily refit the disc pads and have an assistant depress the footbrake pedal while the driveshaft nut is loosened and removed. Remove the disc pads, unscrew the caliper mounting bolts and suspend the caliper to one side taking care not to strain the hydraulic hose. Using a puller withdraw the hub from the driveshaft then unbolt the brake disc. Refitting is a reversal of removal, but refer to Chapter 8 when tightening the driveshaft nut.

5 To remove a front brake disc on 1982 on 99 models or 1981 on 900 models unscrew the caliper mounting bolts and suspend the caliper to one side taking care not to strain the hydraulic hose. Remove the cross-head screws and withdraw the brake disc from the hub. Refitting is a reversal of removal.

6 To remove a rear brake disc remove the rear disc caliper as described in Section 6, then remove the cross-head screws and withdraw the brake disc from the hub. Refitting is a reversal of removal.

8 Master cylinder – removal, overhaul and refitting

1 Open the bonnet and place cloth beneath and around the master cylinder to protect the bodywork from brake fluid which may be spilt. *Spilled fluid must be washed off the bodywork immediately with cold water otherwise the paintwork will be permanently damaged.*

2 Disconnect the wiring from the brake fluid reservoir filler cap.

3 Disconnect the clutch master cylinder hose from the reservoir and plug the outlet.

4 Unscrew the union nuts and disconnect the hydraulic pipes from the master cylinder. Plug the holes.

5 Unscrew the mounting nuts and withdraw the master cylinder from the servo unit.

6 Remove the filler cap and discard the brake fluid.

7 Wipe clean the exterior of the master cylinder then mount it in a vice.

8 Using a pin punch drive out the reservoir mounting pins.

9 Remove the reservoir and prise out the sealing rubbers.

10 Using a screwdriver push the primary piston into the cylinder and extract the secondary piston stop pin from the reservoir inlet.

11 Extract the circlip from the mouth of the cylinder and extract the primary piston.

12 Remove the cylinder from the vice and tap it on the bench or a piece of wood to extract the secondary piston.

13 Remove the sleeve and springs from the pistons, but keep the components identified for position. Also remove the seals from the pistons using a non-metallic instrument.

14 Clean all the components in methylated spirit and examine them for wear and damage. In particular check the surfaces of the pistons and cylinder bore for scoring and corrosion. If excessive renew the complete master cylinder otherwise obtain a repair kit. Check that the inlet and outlet ports are free and unobstructed.

15 Dip the new seals in clean brake fluid and fit them to the pistons using the fingers only to manipulate them into position. Make sure that they are fitted the right way round as shown in Figs. 9.11 and 9.12.

16 Mount the cylinder in the vice and apply brake fluid to the bore.

17 Fit the spring to the secondary piston then insert them into the bore using a twisting motion to avoid damage to the seals.

18 Depress the secondary piston with a screwdriver and insert the stop pin in the reservoir inlet.

19 Fit the sleeve and spring to the primary piston and insert them into the bore again using a twisting motion to avoid damage to the seals.

20 Depress the primary piston and fit the circlip in the mouth of the cylinder.

21 Locate the sealing rubbers in the cylinder, fit the reservoir, and drive in the mounting pins.

22 Fit the master cylinder to the servo unit and secure by tightening the nuts.

23 Fit the hydraulic pipes and tighten the union nuts, then fit the clutch master cylinder hose to the reservoir.

24 Connect the wiring to the filler cap, then top up the fluid and refit the cap.

25 Bleed the hydraulic system as described in Section 9.

26 Check the operation of the brake fluid level warning switch as described in Chapter 10.

9 Hydraulic system – bleeding

1 If any of the hydraulic components in the braking system have been removed or disconnected, or if the fluid level in the master cylinder has been allowed to fall appreciably, it is inevitable that air will have been introduced into the system. The removal of all this air from the hydraulic system is essential if the brakes are to function correctly, and the process of removing it is known as bleeding.

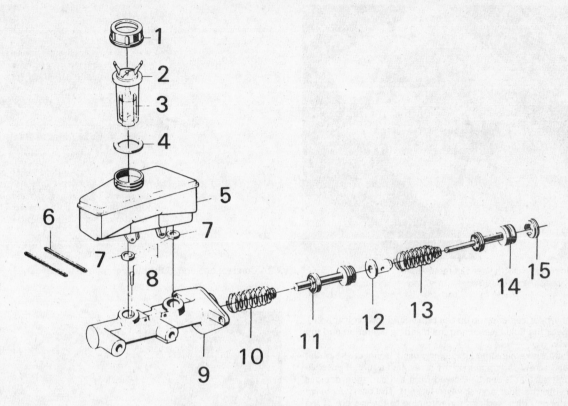

Fig. 9.10 Exploded view of the master cylinder (Sec 8)

1	Cap		reservoir
2	Fluid level contact	6	Pin
3	Float	7	Sealing ring
4	Sealing ring	8	Stop pin
5	Brake fluid	9	Cylinder housing

10	Spring, secondary piston	13	Spring, primary piston
11	Secondary piston	14	Primary piston
12	Sleeve	15	Lock ring

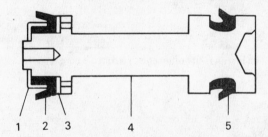

Fig. 9.11 Showing correct position of seals on primary piston (Sec 8)

1	Spring seat	4	Piston
2	Seal	5	Seal
3	Washer		

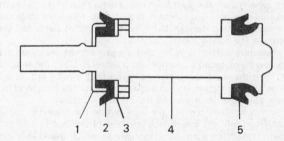

Fig. 9.12 Showing correct position of seals on secondary piston (Sec 8)

1	Spring seat	4	Piston
2	Seal	5	Seal
3	Washer		

2   There are a number of one-man, do-it-yourself, brake bleeding kits currently available from motor accessory shops. It is recommended that one of these kits should be used wherever possible as they greatly simplify the bleeding operation and also reduce the risk of expelled air and fluid being drawn back into the system.

3   If one of these kits is not available then it will be necessary to gather together a clean jar and a suitable length of clear plastic tubing which is a tight fit over the bleed screw, and also to engage the help of an assistant. Check the wheels and release the handbrake. Pump the brake pedal several times to dissipate the vacuum in the servo.

4   Before commencing the bleeding operation, check that all rigid pipes and flexible hoses are in good condition and that all hydraulic unions are tight. Take great care not to allow hydraulic fluid to come into contact with the vehicle paintwork, otherwise the finish will be seriously damaged. Wash off any spilled fluid immediately with cold water.

5   If hydraulic fluid has been lost from the master cylinder, due to a leak in the system, ensure that the cause is traced and rectified before proceeding further or a serious malfunction of the braking system may occur.

6   To bleed the system, clean the area around the bleed screw at the brake caliper to be bled. If the hydraulic system has only been partially disconnected and suitable precautions were taken to prevent further loss of fluid, it should only be necessary to bleed that part of the system. However, if the entire system is to be bled, start at the left rear wheel.

9

9.7 Brake fluid reservoir with filler cap removed

9.9A Connect one end of the bleeder tube to the caliper ...

7   Remove the filler cap and top up the brake fluid reservoir (photo). Periodically check the fluid level during the bleeding operation and top up as necessary.

8   If a one-man brake bleeding kit is being used, connect the outlet tube to the bleed screw and then open the screw half a turn. If possible position the unit so that it can be viewed from the car, then depress the brake pedal to the floor and slowly release it. The one-way valve in the kit will prevent dispelled air from returning to the system at the end of each stroke. Repeat this operation until clean hydraulic fluid, free from air bubbles, can be seen coming through the tube. Now tighten the bleed screw and remove the outlet tube.

9   If a one-man brake bleeding kit is not available, connect one end of the plastic tubing to the bleed screw and immerse the other end in the jar containing sufficient clean hydraulic fluid to keep the end of the tube submerged (photos). Open the bleed screw half a turn and have your assistant depress the brake pedal to the floor and then slowly release it. Tighten the bleed screw at the end of each downstroke to prevent expelled air and fluid from being drawn back into the system. Repeat this operation until clean hydraulic fluid, free from air bubbles, can be seen coming through the tube. Now tighten the bleed screw and remove the plastic tube.

10 If the entire system is being bled the procedures described above should now be repeated at the right front wheel to bleed the secondary circuit, then the right rear wheel followed by the left front wheel to bleed the primary circuit. Do not forget to recheck the fluid level in the reservoir at regular intervals and top up as necessary.

11 When completed, recheck the fluid level in the reservoir, top up if necessary and refit the cap. Check the 'feel' of the brake pedal which should be firm and free from any 'sponginess' which would indicate air still present in the system.

12 Discard any expelled hydraulic fluid as it is likely to be contaminated with moisture, air and dirt which makes it unsuitable for further use.

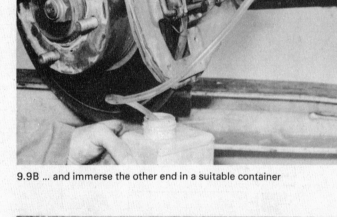

9.9B ... and immerse the other end in a suitable container

10 Hydraulic brake lines and hoses – removal and refitting

1   To remove a hydraulic brake line or hose, first clean the end fittings and the surrounding bodywork to prevent foreign matter from entering the hydraulic circuit (photo).

2   Where applicable fit a brake hose clamp to the nearest hose to isolate the section of the circuit. Alternatively remove the fluid reservoir filler cap and tighten it down onto a piece of polythene sheeting in order to reduce the loss of hydraulic fluid.

3   Unscrew the end fittings and remove the brake line/hose. Do not twist hoses as this may damage them, but instead first remove the rigid brake line union nut.

4   Refitting is a reversal of removal, but make sure that hoses are not twisted and that they do not touch surrounding components. Finally bleed the hydraulic system as described in Section 9.

10.1 Front brake hydraulic hose connection to the inner body panel

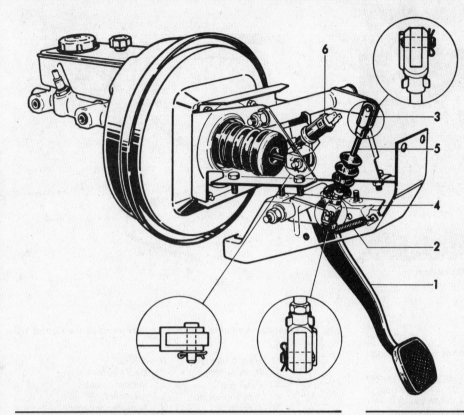

Fig. 9.13 Footbrake pedal components on left-hand drive 99 models (Sec 11)

1 Pedal
2 Return spring
3 Clevis
4 Locknut
5 Pullrod
6 Stop-light switch

11 Footbrake pedal – removal and refitting

1 Remove the lower facia panel (Chapter 12). Also remove the centre console where applicable (photo).
2 Extract the split pin and remove the washer and pivot pin securing the servo pushrod or linkage to the pedal. Note on right-hand drive models the pedal shaft is extended to the left-hand side of the car.
3 Unhook and remove the pedal return spring.
4 On right-hand drive models remove the circlip and washer from the left-hand end of the shaft, unscrew the right-hand bracket nuts, and withdraw the pedal and shaft.
5 On left-hand drive models unscrew the locknut, remove the pivot bolt, and withdraw the pedal.
6 Refitting is a reversal of removal, but where applicable adjust the length of the servo pushrod so that the brake pedal is the same height as the clutch pedal.

12 Handbrake cable – removal, refitting and adjustment

1 Remove the driver's seat as described in Chapter 12.
2 Remove the scuff plates and pull the carpet from the heater ducts.
3 Remove the screws and withdraw the gear lever cover taking care not to damage the ignition switch lamp.
4 Remove the air ducts then unscrew the adjustment nut from the handbrake lever. Note that the two cables cross each other in front of the lever.
5 Remove the clip securing the two cables to the floor.
6 Jack up the front of the car and support on axle stands. Chock the rear wheels and remove the relevant front wheel.
7 Remove the screws and withdraw the cable bush from the inner panel.
8 Unhook the inner cable from the lever on the caliper, pull out the outer cable, and remove the rubber dust cover (photo).

11.1 Showing footbrake pedal on right-hand drive 900 model

12.8 Handbrake cable connection to lever on front brake caliper

9

12.10 Cable adjustment nuts on rear of the handbrake lever

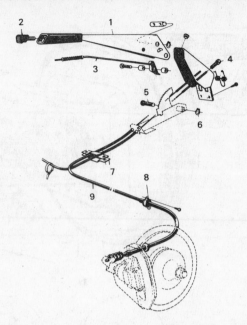

Fig. 9.14 Handbrake cable and lever components (Secs 12 and 13)

1 Handbrake lever	6 Circlip
2 Push button	7 Cable holder
3 Pawl rod	8 Wheel housing
4 Adjustment nut	grommet
5 Pivot bolt	9 Handbrake cable

9   Withdraw the handbrake cable from beneath the engine compartment.
10 Refitting is a reversal of removal, but finally adjust it as follows. Fully apply the handbrake lever several times then fully release it. Using a feeler gauge check that the clearance between the bottom of the lever on the caliper and the yoke is 0.19 in (0.5 mm) maximum. If not, turn the adjusting nut on the rear of the handbrake lever as necessary (photo). Check that the clearance is identical on the opposite front caliper, then refit the wheels and lower the car to the ground.

13 Handbrake lever – removal, refitting and adjustment

1   Remove the cover from the rear of the handbrake lever and unscrew the adjusting nuts.
2   Extract the circlip and pull out the pivot pin.
3   Withdraw the handbrake lever from the car. If required the pawl mechanism may be removed from the lever.
4   Refitting is a reversal of removal, but adjust the cables as described in Section 12. On pre-1983 models the distance from the end of the lever to the front of the pushbutton with the handbrake fully applied should be between 0.24 and 0.40 in (6.0 and 10.0 mm) – if necessary screw the pushbutton in or out as required. On 1983 on models, with the handbrake fully applied screw the pushbutton right in then back it off up to one turn. Check that the warning lamp comes on with the handbrake lever applied two or three notches, and if necessary adjust the position of the switch.

14 Vacuum servo unit – description, removal and refitting

1   The vacuum servo unit is fitted between the footbrake pedal and the master cylinder and provides assistance to the driver when the pedal is depressed. The unit operates by vacuum from the inlet manifold. With the footpedal released vacuum is channelled to both sides of the internal diaphragm, however when the pedal is depressed one side is opened to the atmosphere resulting in assistance to the pedal effort. Should the vacuum servo develop a fault the hydraulic system is not affected, however greater effort will be required at the pedal.
2   To remove the servo unit first remove the master cylinder as described in Section 8.
3   Remove the lower facia panel and where applicable the centre console.
4   Disconnect the vacuum hose from the servo.
5   Move the wiring harness from the servo unit.

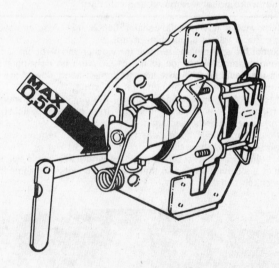

Fig. 9.15 Handbrake cable adjustment clearance on the caliper lever (Sec 12)

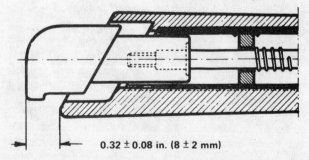

0.32 ± 0.08 in. (8 ± 2 mm)

Fig. 9.16 Handbrake lever pushbutton adjustment on pre-1983 models (Sec 13)

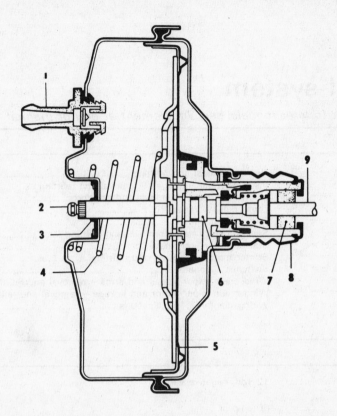

Fig. 9.17 Cross-section diagram of the vacuum servo (Sec 14)

1   Non-return valve
2   Pushrod (master cylinder)
3   Sealing ring
4   Return spring
5   Diaphragm
6   Valve piston
7   Filter
8   Dust cover
9   Pullrod (brake pedal)

6   On left-hand drive 99 models disconnect the pullrod from the intermediate lever and disconnect the wiring from the stop-light switch. Unscrew the mounting nuts and withdraw the servo together with the bracket. Unbolt the bracket from the servo unit.
7   On other models extract the circlip and remove the pivot pin from the servo pushrod. Unscrew the mounting nuts and withdraw the servo unit.
8   If the servo unit is to be refitted, the felt air filters should be renewed. To do this use a sharp knife to slit them before locating them over the pushrod.
9   Refitting is a reversal of removal with reference to Section 8 when refitting the master cylinder. To check the operation of the servo unit depress the footpedal whilst starting the engine. The footpedal should move towards the floor proving that the unit is providing assistance. To repeat the test the pedal must first be depressed several times with the engine switched off in order to dissipate the vacuum in the unit.

15 Fault diagnosis – braking system

Symptom	Reason(s)
Excessive pedal travel	Air in hydraulic system Failure of one hydraulic circuit
Uneven braking and pulling to one side	Contaminated disc pad linings Seized caliper Incorrect tyre pressures Faulty handbrake mechanism or incorrect adjustment
Brake judder	Worn or distorted discs Excessively worn disc pad linings Worn suspension balljoints
Brake pedal feels 'spongy'	Air in hydraulic system Worn master cylinder seals
Excessive effort to stop car	Servo unit faulty Excessively worn disc pad linings Seized caliper Contaminated disc pad linings Failure of one hydraulic circuit

9

Chapter 10 Electrical system

For modifications, and information applicable to later models, see Supplement at end of manual

Contents

Specifications

System type .... 12 volt, negative earth

Battery capacity .... 60 amp hr

Alternator
Type:

99 models .... Bosch 55 amp, 65 amp, 70 amp
SEV/Marchal 55 amp

900 models .... Bosch 55 amp, 65 amp, 70 amp
Motorola 70 amp

Brush protrusion (minimum):
Bosch and Motorola .... 0.20 in (5.0 mm)
SEV/Marchal .... 0.16 in (4.0 mm)

Starter motor
Type .... Bosch pre-engaged
Brush spring pressure .... 41 to 46 oz (11.3 to 12.8 N)
Pinion to ring gear clearance .... 0.098 to 0.118 in (2.5 to 3.0 mm)
Rotor endplay .... 0.002 to 0.012 in (0.05 to 0.30 mm)
Fuses .... 3 x 5 amp, 11 x 8 amp, 6 x 16 amp, 2 x 25 amp

Bulbs
Headlights   **Wattage**

Normal 40/45
Halogen .... 60/55 (UK), 65/55 (North America)
Front direction indicators 21/5
Rear direction indicators 21
Parking lights 21/5
Rear fog lights 21
Stop/tail lights 21/5
Reversing lights 21
Side markers 21
Number plate 5
Interior light 10
Rear view mirror 5
Glove compartment 5
Ignition switch 2
Instrument illumination 3
Ignition warning light 2
Facia and instrument panel lights 1.2

Torque wrench settings	lbf ft	Nm
Alternator pulley nut	26	35

1 General description

The electrical system is of 12 volt negative earth type. The battery is charged by a belt-driven alternator incorporating a voltage regulator. The starter motor is of pre-engaged type incorporating a solenoid which moves the drive pinion into engagement with the ring gear before the starter motor is energised.

Although repair procedures are given in this Chapter, it may well be more economical to renew worn components as complete units.

2 Battery – removal and refitting

1 The battery is located at the front on the right-hand side of the engine compartment (photo).
2 Disconnect the negative terminal first whenever removing the battery. **Never disconnect the battery when the engine is still running**.
3 Disconnect the positive terminal then unscrew the clamp nuts and lift the battery from the platform taking care not to spill any electrolyte on the bodywork. On Turbo models the pressure pipe from the exhaust manifold to the boost control must first be disconnected, and on APC models the hoses disconnected.
4 Refitting is a reversal of removal, however do not over-tighten the clamp nuts and terminal bolts.

3 Battery – maintenance

1 Every 10 000 miles (15 000 km) on UK models or 7500 miles (12 000 km) on North American models disconnect the leads from the battery and clean the terminals and lead ends. After refitting the leads smear the exposed metal with petroleum jelly.
2 Except on maintenance free batteries remove the cell covers and check that the electrolyte covers the tops of the plates by approximately 0.4 in (10.0 mm). Add distilled water if necessary (photo).
3 Check the battery platform for corrosion (white fluffy deposits on the metal which are brittle to touch). If any corrosion is found, clean off the deposits with ammonia and paint over the clean metal with an anti-rust/anti-acid paint.
4 At the same time inspect the battery case for cracks. If a crack is found, clean and plug it with one of the proprietary compounds marketed, for this purpose. If leakage through the crack has been excessive then it will be necessary to refill the appropriate cell with fresh electrolyte as detailed later. Cracks are frequently caused to the top of the battery case by pouring in distilled water in the middle of winter *after* instead of *before* a run. This gives the water no chance to mix with the electrolyte and so the former freezes and splits the battery case.
5 If topping-up the battery becomes excessive and the case has been inspected for cracks that could cause leakage, but none are found, the battery is being over-charged and the voltage regulator will have to be checked.
6 To test the battery disconnect the wiring from the coil positive terminal and spin the engine on the starter for 15 seconds, with a voltmeter connected across the battery terminals. If the voltage remains above 9.6 volt the battery is in good condition, but if it drops below this amount the battery should be charged as described in Section 5 and the test repeated.
7 On conventional batteries the state of charge can be checked using a hydrometer in each cell to record the specific gravity.

	Ambient temperature above 25°C (77°F)	Ambient temperature below 25°C (77°F)
Fully charged	1.210 to 1.230	1.270 to 1.290
70% charged	1.170 to 1.190	1.230 to 1.250
Fully discharged	1.050 to 1.070	1.110 to 1.130

Note that the specific gravity readings assume an electrolyte temperature of 15°C (60°F); for every 10°C (18°F) below 15°C (60°F) subtract 0.007. For every 10°C (18°F) above 15°C (60°F) add 0.007.
8 If the variation of specific gravity between any two cells exceeds 0.040 the battery internal plates are probably deteriorated or there has been a loss of electrolyte.

2.1 Battery showing terminals and retaining clamp position

3.2 Topping up the battery with distilled water

4 Battery – electrolyte replenishment

1 If the battery has been tested as described in Section 3 and additional electrolyte is required, the deficient cells must be topped up with a solution of 1 part sulphuric acid to 2.5 parts distilled water.
2 When mixing the sulphuric acid and water **never add water to sulphuric acid** – always pour the acid slowly onto the water in a glass container. **If water is added to sulphuric acid it will explode.**
3 Continue to top-up the cell with the freshly made electrolyte and then recharge the battery and check the hydrometer readings.

5 Battery – charging

1 In winter time when heavy demand is placed upon the battery, such as when starting from cold, and much electrical equipment is continually in use, it is a good idea to occasionally have the battery fully charged from an external source at the rate of 3.5 or 4 amps.
2 Continue to charge the battery at this rate until no further rise in specific gravity is noted over a four hour period.

10

3   Alternatively, a trickle charger charging at the rate of 1.5 amps can be safely used overnight.

4   Specially rapid 'boost' charges which are claimed to restore the power of the battery in 1 to 2 hours are most dangerous as they can cause serious damage to the battery plates.

6   Alternator – maintenance and special precautions

1   Periodically wipe away any dirt which has accumulated on the outside of the unit, and also check that the plug is pushed firmly on the terminals. At the same time check the tension of the drivebelt and adjust it if necessary as described in Section 7 (B engine) or Chapter 2 (H engine).

2   Take extreme care when making electrical circuit connections on the car, otherwise damage may occur to the alternator or other electrical components employing semi-conductors. Always make sure that the battery leads are connected to the correct terminals. Before using electric-arc welding equipment to repair any part of the car, disconnect the battery leads and the alternator multi-plug. Disconnect the battery leads before using a mains charger. Never run the alternator with the multi-plug or a battery lead disconnected.

7.3 Showing alternator wiring (Bosch)

7   Alternator – removal and refitting

1   On models equipped with power steering remove the power steering pump drivebelt with reference to Chapter 11.

2   Disconnect the battery negative lead.

3   Disconnect the wiring from the alternator (photo).

4   Loosen the mounting and adjustment bolts/nuts, swivel the alternator towards the engine, and remove the drivebelt from the pulleys (photo).

5   Remove the mounting and adjustment bolts and withdraw the alternator from the engine.

6   Refitting is a reversal of removal, but before fully tightening the mounting and adjustment bolts tension the drivebelt so that it can be depressed under firm thumb pressure 0.4 in (10.0 mm) midway between the alternator and crankshaft pulleys on type B engines, or 0.2 in (5.0 mm) midway between the alternator and water pump pulleys on type H engines. Lever the alternator on the drive end bracket and then tighten the bolts (photos). Tension the power steering pump drivebelt with reference to Chapter 11.

8   Alternator brushes – removal, inspection and refitting

1   Disconnect the battery negative lead.

7.4 Drivebelt adjustment nut on the alternator

7.6A Checking the alternator drivebelt tension

7.6B Showing the drivebelt and pulleys

8.2A Remove the screws ...

8.2B ... and remove the regulator and brush box from the alternator

8.2C The regulator and brush box

Bosch type

2   Remove the screws and withdraw the regulator and brush box from the rear of the alternator (photos).

3   If the length of either brush is less than the minimum given in the Specifications, unsolder the wiring and renew the brushes, then resolder the new wires in position.

Motorola type

4   Pull the multi-plug from the rear of the alternator.

5   Remove the screws and withdraw the regulator. Note the location of the wires then disconnect them and remove the regulator.

6   Remove the screws and carefully withdraw the brush box.

7   If the length of either brush is less than the minimum given in the Specifications, obtain a new brush box.

SEV/Marchal type

8   Remove the screws and withdraw the regulator and brush box from the rear of the alternator. Disconnect the wire from the terminal.

9   If the length of either brush is less than the minimum given in the Specifications, obtain a new regulator and brush box.

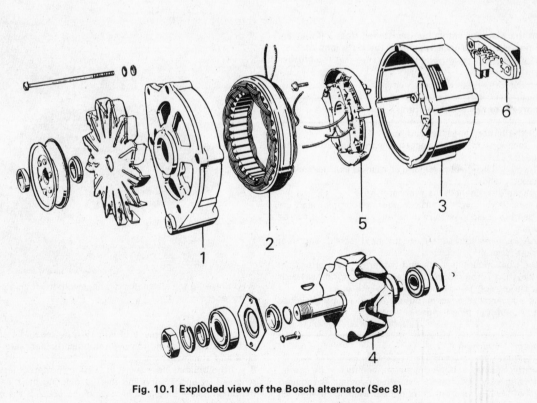

Fig. 10.1 Exploded view of the Bosch alternator (Sec 8)

1 Drive bearing assembly	3 Slip ring end bracket	5 Rectifier unit
2 Stator	4 Rotor	6 Voltage regulator and carbon brush holder

10

Fig. 10.2 Exploded view of the Motorola alternator (Sec 8)

1	Slip ring cap	6	V-belt pulley
2	Stator	7	Rectifier assembly
3	Rotor	8	Brush holder
4	Drive bearing cap	9	Voltage regulator
5	Cooling fan		

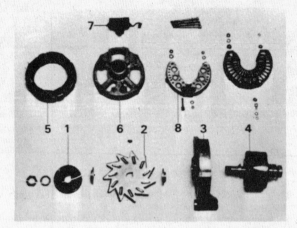

Fig. 10.3 Exploded view of the SEV alternator (Sec 8)

1	Belt pulley	6	Slip ring end cap
2	Fan	7	Charging regulator and
3	Drive bearing cap		brush holder
4	Rotor	8	Rectifier unit
5	Stator		

All types
10 Wipe clean the slip rings with a fuel-moistened cloth – if they are very dirty use fine glasspaper then wipe with the cloth (photo).
11 Refitting is a reversal of removal, but make sure that the brushes move freely in their holders.

---

9 Starter motor – removal and refitting

1 Disconnect the battery negative lead.
2 Note their locations then disconnect the wires from the starter motor (photo).
3 Remove the plastic flywheel cover, and on manual gearbox models only the gearbox dip stick.
4 Where applicable disconnect the preheater hose.
5 On Turbo models remove the turbocharger suction pipe and the stay from the gearbox. Disconnect the oil return pipe so that it can be bent to one side.
6 Unbolt and remove the starter motor heat shield and rear mounting bracket (photo).
7 Remove the front mounting bolts and withdraw the starter from the engine (photo). On Turbo models tilt the starter motor downwards then lift out while moving the oil return pipe to one side.
8 Refitting is a reversal of removal, but always fit a new gasket to the turbocharger oil return pipe flange.

---

10 Starter motor – overhaul

1 Renewal of the brushes and the drive components can be carried out in the following way but if more extensive overhaul is required such as renewal of the bearings, armature or field windings then it will probably be more economical to renew the complete unit for a new or factory reconditioned one.
2 Remove the starter from the car.
3 Disconnect the leads from the solenoid terminals and remove the solenoid securing screws (photo).
4 Lift the rear end of the solenoid slightly and unhook its front end from the engagement lever.
5 Remove the two screws which retain the armature shaft end cap and remove the cap, U-washer, spacers and gasket.
6 Remove the two tie-bolts and remove the commutator end cover.

8.10 Showing the alternator slip rings with the regulator/brush box removed

7 Using a hooked piece of wire, lift the brushes from their holders and then unscrew and remove the brush holder plate and extract the fibre and steel washers.
8 If the brushes have worn to 0.20 in (5 mm) or less, they must be renewed by unsoldering and then resoldering their leads from and to the brush holder plate and field windings. Localise the heat as much as possible from the field windings.
9 If the starter drive is to be renewed, pull off the drive housing, retaining the rubber and steel washers (photo).
10 Using a piece of tubing, drive the stop ring down towards the pinion gear to expose the snap-ring.
11 Extract the snap-ring.
12 Pull the stop ring and the pinion from the starter shaft.
13 Reassembly is a reversal of dismantling. The stop ring on the armature shaft can be pulled up to cover the snap-ring by using a two-legged puller.

9.2 Showing starter wiring

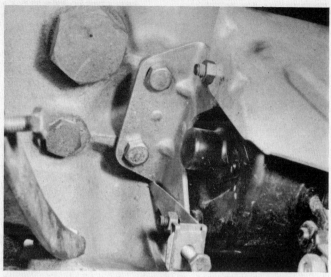
9.6 Starter motor rear mounting bracket

9.7 Starter motor front mounting bolts

10.3 Showing starter solenoid terminals

10.9 Starter pinion gear

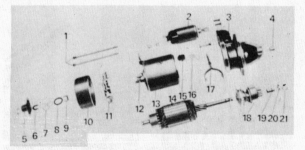

Fig. 10.4 Exploded view of the starter motor (Sec 10)

1 Screws, bearing housing	housing
2 Solenoid	11 Brush plate
3 Drive housing	12 Field winding
4 Bushing, drive side	13 Starter housing
5 Capsule bracket	14 Rotor
6 U-washer	15 Rubber washer
7 Shim	16 Steel washer
8 Rubber gasket	17 Engaging lever arm
9 Bushing, commutator side	18 Pinion
	19 Bushing, pinion
10 Commutator bearing	20 Stop ring
	21 Lock ring

11.1 Fusebox showing fuses and relays

11.2 Removing a relay

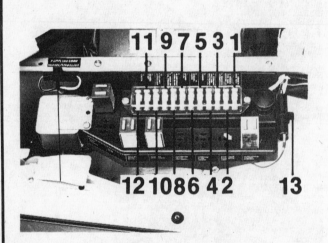

Fig. 10.5 Fuse box for 99 models (Sec 11)

Fig. 10.6 Fuse box for pre-1981 900 models (Sec 11)

Fig. 10.7 Fuse box for 1981 on 900 models (Sec 11)

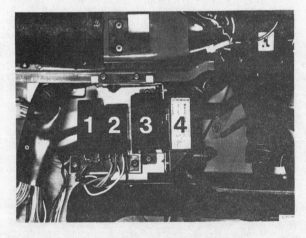

Fig. 10.8 Relays located beneath the facia on 900 models
(Sec 11)

1 Flasher unit	service counter (EXH)
2 Intermittent wiper unit	4 Speed transmitter, deceleration device (or fuel enrichment on 1979 Turbo models)
3 Exhaust emission control	

11 Fuses and relays – general

1   The fuses are located in the fuse box on the right-hand side of the engine compartment on 99 models or the left-hand side on 900 models (photo).

2   The fusebox also contains some relays, but certain relays are located beneath the facia and are accessible from inside the car (photo).

3   Always renew a fuse with one of identical rating and never renew it more than once without finding the source of the trouble (usually a short circuit). Always switch off the ignition before renewing a fuse or relay.

4   Access to the fuses and the relays in the fusebox is gained by removing the plastic cover. The fuses are retained by spring tensioned terminals, and the relays are a push fit.

5   Fuse and relay locations are shown on the fusebox cover and are numbered as follows.

Fuse Ratings (amps) Circuit

99 models

1	5	Left-hand rear tail and parking lights
2	5	Right-hand rear tail and town lights
3	8	Horn, reversing lights
4	8	Wiper washer, instruments (electric rear view mirror)
5	8 (to 1981) 16 (1982 on)	Electrically heated seat, town lights
6	16	Passenger compartment fan
7	16	Radiator fan (extra lights)
8	16	Heated rear window
9	8	Cigarette lighter, clock, interior lighting
10	16 (1979 and 1982) 8 (1980 and 1981)	Fuel pump
11	5 (to 1981) 8 (1982 on)	Direction indicators, hazard flashers
12	5 (to 1981) 8 (1982 on)	Brake lights
13	3	Headlight wipers (in-line)

900 models

1	8	Right-hand main beam
2	8	Left-hand main beam
3	8	Right-hand low beam
4	8	Left-hand low beam
5	16	Radiator fan
6	16	Heated rear window
7	5	Interior lighting
8	16	Fuel pump
9	8	Hazard warning lights
10	5	Brake lights
11	16 (to 1979) 8 (1980 on)	Air conditioning Rear fog lights
12	5	Right-hand parking lights
13	5	Left-hand parking lights
14	8	Horn
15	8	Headlight wipers
16	16	Electrically heated seat
17	25	Heater fan
18	8	Spare/air conditioning
19	8	Instrument panel lights
20	8	Direction indicators
21	8	Windscreen wipers
22	8	Day driving lights

Relay   Circuit

99 models

1	Headlight
2	Starter inhibitor (automatic models)
3	Safety relay (CI system)
4	Fuel pump (CI system)
5	Ignition switch

6	Radiator fan
7	Parking/town lights
8	Windscreen wiper delay
9	Lights
10	Heated rear window
11	Ignition system service outlet
12	Spare

900 models (to 1980)

A	Lights
B	Lights
C	Heated rear window
D	Lambda
E	Ignition switch
F	Reversing light
G	Fuel pump
H	Starter interlock
I	Air conditioning
J	Radiator fan

900 models (1981 on)

A	Lights
B	Lights
C	Heated rear window
D	Radiator fan
E	Ignition switch
F	Spare or governor on Turbo models
G	Fuel pump
H	Spare
I	Air conditioning
J	Horn
K	Cooling fan

12 Switches – general

Ignition switch

1   The ignition switch is located on the gear lever console and includes the security lock which locks the gear lever in the reverse gear position (photo).

Facia relays

2   The facia relays are located behind the lower facia panel on the left-hand side of the bulkhead (photo). They include the direction indicator flasher unit, the intermittent wiper unit, exhaust emission control reminder (North American models) and deceleration unit (Turbo models).

12.1 Ignition switch location

10

12.2 Removing a relay from under the facia panel

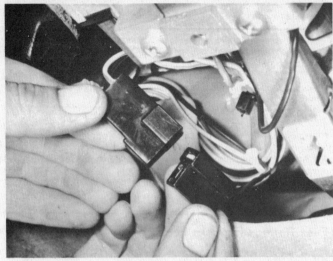

12.3 Disconnecting a wiring plug beneath the facia panel

Combination switches

3   The switches for the direction indicators, lights and windscreen wiper/washer are located on the steering column. They can be removed after removing the steering wheel (Chapter 11) and the lower facia panel (Chapter 12). Remove the lower shroud and disconnect the wiring plugs, then remove the screws and lower the switches (photo).

Stop light switch

4   On 99 models the stop-light switch is located in the engine compartment and is activated by the servo pushrod. On 900 models the switch is located inside the car and is activated by the footbrake pedal.

Brake warning switch

5   The brake fluid reservoir filler cap incorporates a warning switch which illuminates a warning light if the fluid drops to a dangerous level. To test the switch, depress the float extension in the centre of the filler cap and the warning light should come on.

Reversing light switch

6   On manual gearbox models the reversing light switch is located in the gearbox casing below the gear lever and is accessible after removing the centre console.

7   On some early automatic trasmission models the switch is located on the side of the transmission and access is from under the car. On later models it is operated by the gear lever and is accessible after removing the centre console.

12.10 Removing the hazard warning light switch

Luggage compartment light switch

8   On saloon models the luggage compartment light switch is located by the left-hand side hinge. On coupe models it is located below the rear door striker.

Seat belt warning switches

9   The seat belt warning light is switched on if the driver or passenger has not fastened the seat belt and the ignition is switched on. The circuit consists of the warning light on the facia, a switch in the seat belt latch buckle, and a pressure sensitive switch in the passenger seat cushion.

Facia switch

10   To remove a facia switch prise off the pushbutton and use long nose pliers to pull out the switch. Disconnect the wiring and remove the switch (photo).

Courtesy light switch

11   To remove a courtesy light switch, open the door and remove the switch retaining screw (photo). Withdraw the switch from the door

12.11 Front door courtesy light switch

12.12 Interior lighting switch location in central console

pillar and disconnect the wire – do not allow the wire to drop into the pillar.

Interior lighting switch

12 The interior lighting switch is located on the central console. To remove it prise it out with a screwdriver and disconnect the wiring (photo).

13 Instrument panel – removal and refitting

1 Disconnect the battery negative lead.

99 models

2 Remove the three screws under the instrument panel, then slide the safety padding from the clips on the facia.
3 Remove the retaining screws then withdraw the instrument panel so that the speedometer cable and wiring can be disconnected.
4 Withdraw the instrument panel from the facia.
5 Refitting is a reversal of removal.

900 models

6 Remove the steering wheel as described in Chapter 11.
7 Unscrew the four bolts from the bottom edge of the facia panel.

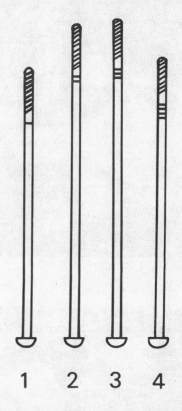

Fig. 10.9 Facia panel bolts on 900 models (Sec 13)

1	6.93 in (176.0 mm)	3	8.27 in (210.0 mm)
2	8.07 in (205.0 mm)	4	7.44 in (189.0 mm)

Identify each bolt for position as they are all of different lengths (photo).
8 Tilt the facia panel back to give sufficient room to remove the instrument panel. The facia panel need not be removed, but if it is the location of the wiring and vacuum hoses must be carefully noted (photos).
9 Prise out the defroster/speaker grille and disconnect the wiring multi-plugs and speedometer cable.
10 Remove the retaining screws and withdraw the instrument panel from the facia (photos).
11 Refitting is a reversal of removal.

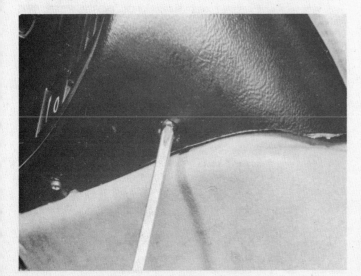

13.7 Removing a facia panel bolt on 900 models

13.8A Showing disconnected heater vacuum control plug

10

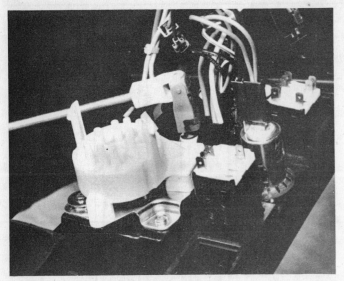

13.8B Rear view of the facia panel

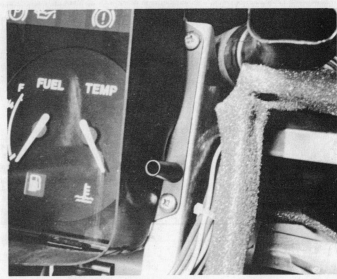

13.10A Instrument panel retaining screws location

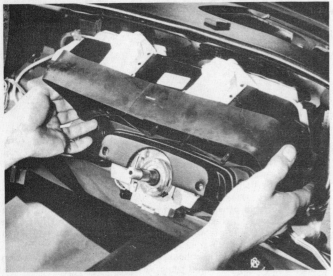

13.10B Removing the instrument panel

13.10C Front view of the instrument panel

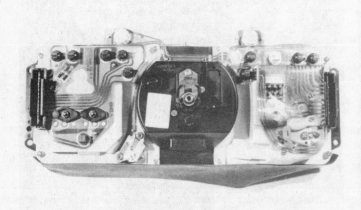

13.10D Rear view of the instrument panel

13.10E Facia with instrument panel removed

14 Instrument panel gauges – removal and refitting

1   Remove the instrument panel as described in Section 13 – the gauges and clock as applicable can then be removed by unscrewing the retaining screws.

2   Before disconnecting any wires identify them for position to ensure correct refitting.

15 Speedometer cable – removal and refitting

1   Jack up the front of the car and support on axle stands. Chock the rear wheels.

2   Unscrew the collar from the left-hand rear of the gearbox and disconnect the speedometer cable.

3   On 99 models remove the instrument panel as described in Section 13, then remove the grommet from the bulkhead and withdraw the speedometer cable.

4   On 900 models prise out the defroster/speaker grille, and bend back the cable entry spring at the bulkhead. Disconnect the cable from the instrument panel, release it from the grommet and withdraw it into the engine compartment (photos).

5   Refitting is a reversal of removal.

16 Headlamps and headlamp bulbs – removal and refitting

1   On UK models the headlamps incorporate separate bulbs, however on North American models sealed beam units are fitted.

2   To remove a headlamp bulb open the bonnet and remove the cap(s) from the rear of the headlamp. Pull the connector from the bulb, then depress the bulb retainer and turn it anti-clockwise, and withdraw the bulb (photos). Refitting is a reversal of removal, but make sure that the lugs on the bulb flange are correctly located in the headlamp.

3   To remove the headlamp on UK 900 models first remove the bulb then disconnect the battery negative lead and remove the direction indicator lamp. Lower the wiper blade then remove the screws and

15.4A Speedometer cable location on the instrument panel

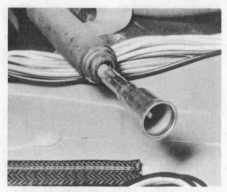
15.4B Instrument panel end of the speedometer cable

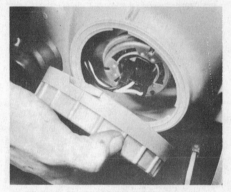
16.2A Remove the headlamp rear cap ...

16.2B ... pull off the connector ...

16.2C ... remove the bulb retainer ...

16.2D ... and remove the bulb

16.3A Disconnect the direction indicator plug ...

16.3B ... remove the front mounting screw ...

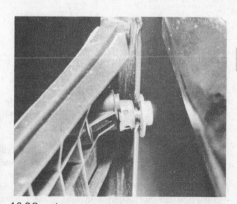
16.3C ... the rear mounting screw ...

10

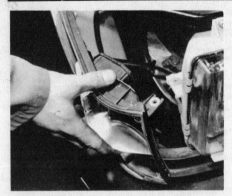

16.3D ... and remove the direction indicator lamp

16.3E Remove the headlamp lower mounting screw ...

16.3F ... the upper mounting screws ...

16.3G ... withdraw the connector through the hole in the headlamp ...

16.3H ... and remove the headlamp

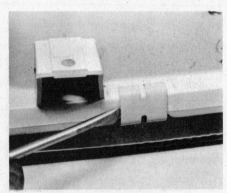

16.3I Removing the headlamp lens retaining clips

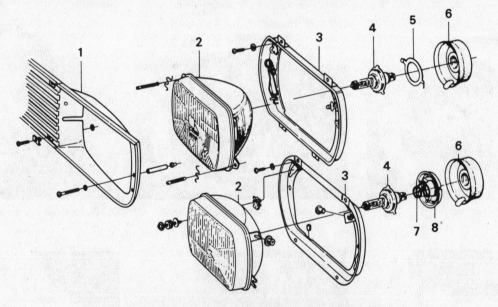

Fig. 10.10 Exploded view of the headlights on 99 models (Sec 16)

1	Grille	3	Frame	5	Retainer	7	Spring
2	Headlamp unit	4	Bulb	6	Cap	8	Retainer

withdraw the headlamp. If necessary prise off the clips and remove the lens. The reflector may also be removed. Refitting is a reversal of removal (photos).

4   To remove the headlamp on 99 models first remove the bulb then close the bonnet without locking it and remove the radiator grille (Chapter 12). Remove the screws and withdraw the headlamp from the frame. Release the adjusting screws and remove the frame from

the headlamp. Refitting is a reversal of removal.

5   To remove the sealed beam unit on North American models, remove the screw and withdraw the headlamp surround. Disconnect the plug from the rear of the unit. Remove the screws and withdraw the rim followed by the sealed beam unit. If necessary remove the retaining screws and withdraw the holder. Refitting is a reversal of removal.

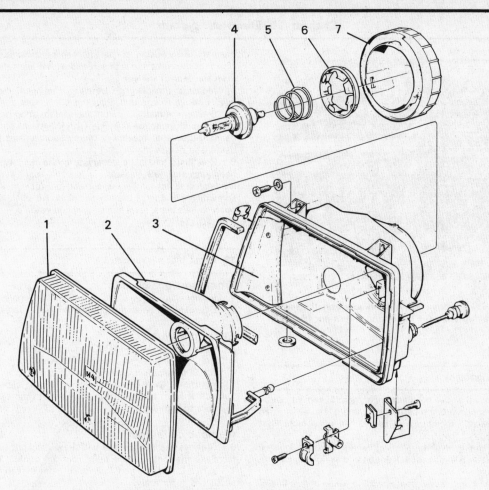

Fig. 10.11 Exploded view of the headlight on UK 900 models (Sec 16)

1	Lens	3	Frame	5	Spring	7	Cap
2	Reflector	4	Bulb	6	Retainer

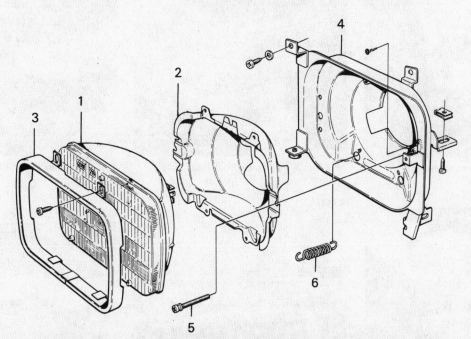

Fig. 10.12 Exploded view of the headlight on North American 900 models (Sec 16)

1	Sealed beam unit	3	Rim	5	Adjustment screw
2	Frame	4	Housing	6	Spring

10

Fig. 10.13 Using a screwdriver to hold the bonnet half open on 900 models while adjusting the headlamp alignment (Sec 17)

17 Headlamps – alignment

1   It is recommended that the headlamp alignment is carried out by a Saab dealer using modern beam setting equipment. However in an emergency the following procedure will provide an acceptable light pattern.
2   Position the car on a level surface with tyres correctly inflated approximately 16.5 feet (5.0 metres) in front of, and at right-angles to, a wall or garage door.
3   Draw a vertical line on the wall corresponding to the centre line of

the car. The position of the line can be ascertained by marking the centre of the front and rear screens with crayon then viewing the wall from the rear of the car.
4   Measure the distance between the headlamp centres and their height above the ground, then mark the positions on the wall.
5   Switch the headlamps on main beam and check that the areas of maximum illumination coincide with the marks on the wall. On dipped beam the area of maximum illumination should be 2.0 in (50 mm) below the centre marks.
6   If adjustment is necessary turn the adjustment screws on the headlamp rim (99 models) or on the rear of the headlamp (900 models) until the setting is correct (photo). On 900 models insert a screwdriver in one of the bonnet hinge holes to hold the bonnet half open so that the screws can be reached when adjusting the headlamps (Fig. 10.13).

18 Lamp bulbs – renewal

Front sidelight cluster

1   Remove the screws and withdraw the lens (photo).
2   Depress and twist the bulb to remove it (photo).

Rear light cluster

3   On all 99 models and 900 Coupe models remove the screws and withdraw the lens, then depress and twist the bulb to remove it.
4   On 900 saloon models remove the trim from inside the luggage compartment, then depress the two plastic clips and withdraw the bulbholder from the rear of the lamp unit (photo). Depress and twist the bulb to remove it.

Number plate light

5   Remove the screws and withdraw the light (photo).
6   Ease the festoon type bulb from the contact blades (photo).
7   When fitting the new bulb make sure that the contact blades are tensioned sufficiently.

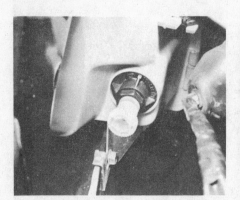

17.6 Headlamp alignment screw

18.1 Removing the front sidelight cluster lens

18.2 Removing a front sidelight cluster bulb

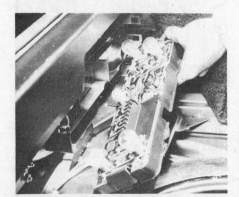

18.4 Removing the rear light cluster (900 models)

18.5 Remove the screws ...

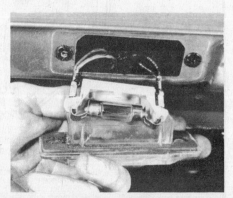

18.6 ... and withdraw the number plate light to remove the bulb

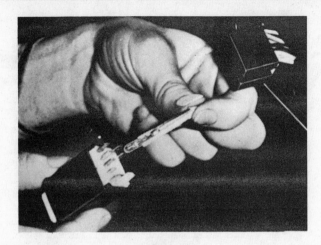

Fig. 10.14 Removing a bulb from a facia switch (Sec 18)

Interior dome light
8 Remove the screws and withdraw the light.
9 Ease the festoon type bulb from the contact blades.

Rear view mirror light
10 Prise off the lens.
11 Ease the festoon type bulb from the contact blades (photo).

Ignition switch light/gear lever light
12 Remove the screws from the centre console and lift the console

sufficient to insert a hand from the left-hand side and remove the bulbholder.
13 Remove the bulb from the bulbholder.

Luggage compartment light
14 Remove the two screws and withdraw the light. If there are no screws, prise out the left-hand edge with a screwdriver (photo).
15 Ease the festoon type bulb from the contact blades.

Facia lights (99 models)
16 To renew the heater control bulb open the glovebox, prise out the plastic cover, and remove the bulb.
17 To renew the control switch light bulb, remove the screen beneath the instrument panel.

Facia lights (900 models)
18 Prise the defroster/speaker grille from the top surface of the facia.
19 Reach down and remove the bulbholder from the rear of the instrument panel by twisting it through 90°, then pull the bulb from the holder. To renew the fuel warning light bulb the instrument panel must be completely removed (photos).
20 The facia switch bulbs may be renewed by prising off the pushbutton, pulling out the switch and disconnecting the multi-plug, then withdrawing the bulb and holder from the rear of the switch.
21 To renew other facia illumination bulbs, remove the lower facia panel with reference to Chapter 12.

Glovebox light
22 Open the glovebox and prise out the bulbholder (photo).
23 Ease the festoon type bulb from the contact blades.

19 Horn – removal and refitting

1 On 99 models the left-hand horn is located in the engine compartment next to the bumper bracket, and the right-hand horn is

18.11 Showing rear view mirror light bulb

18.14 Removing the luggage compartment light bulb

18.19A Removing a bulb from the instrument panel – type A ...

18.19B ... type B ...

18.19C ... type C

18.22 Removing the glovebox light bulb

10

19.1 Left-hand side horn location

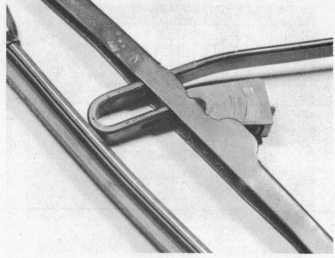

20.1 Removing a wiper blade from the arm

located outside beneath the bumper. On 900 models both horns are in the engine compartment (photo).
2   To remove a horn first disconnect the battery negative lead then disconnect the wiring from the horn.
3   Unscrew the bracket mounting bolt and withdraw the horn from the car.
4   Refitting is a reversal of removal.

20 Windscreen wiper blades and arms – removal and refitting

1   To remove a wiper blade lift the arm from the windscreen then depress the clip and separate the blade from the arm (photo). If necessary remove the rubber by sliding it out. Refitting is a reversal of removal.
2   To remove a wiper arm prise up the spindle cover, unscrew the nut and remove the arm from the spindle (photo). Early 99 models may have a different arrangement without a nut in which case simply prise off the arm. Remove the blade from the arm as described in paragraph 1. Refitting is a reversal of removal, however make sure that the motor is in its parked position before refitting the arm at the bottom of its stroke.

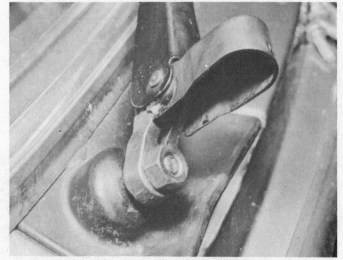

20.2 Wiper arm retaining nut on the spindle

21 Windscreen wiper motor and linkage – removal and refitting

1   Remove the wiper arms and blades as described in Section 20.
2   Disconnect the battery negative lead.

99 models
3   Working in the engine compartment unscrew the nut securing the steel tube to the wiper motor.
4   Unbolt the wiper motor strap, disconnect the wiring, and remove the motor, at the same time pulling the flexible cable from the steel tube.
5   Unscrew the bolts from the bottom of the spindle housings and detach the cable tubes.
6   Unscrew the spindle nuts and remove the housings noting the location of the washers and rubber spacers.
7   Refitting is a reversal of removal, but leave the housing bolts loose while inserting the cable.

900 models
8   Prise the rubber grommets from the spindles.
9   Unscrew the linkage mounting bolts and disconnect the wiring from the motor. There are two bolts by the spindles and two bolts on the bracket (photo).
10   Extract the circlip from the motor crank and disconnect the linkage rod, then unbolt the motor from the bracket.
11   Refitting is a reversal of removal.

21.9 Windscreen wiper motor (900 models)

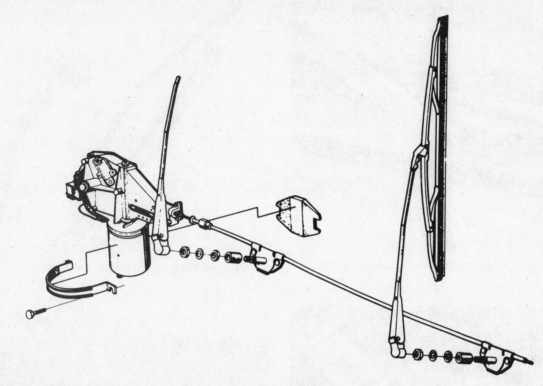

Fig. 10.15 Windscreen wiper motor and linkage on 99 models (Sec 21)

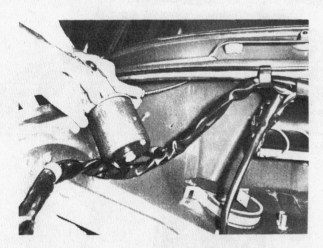

Fig. 10.16 Removing the windscreen wiper motor on 99 models
(Sec 21)

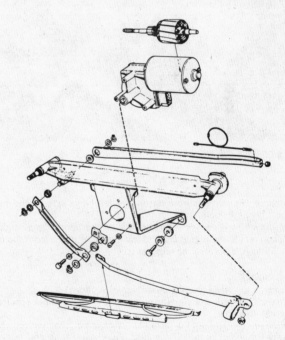

Fig. 10.17 Windscreen wiper motor and linkage on 900 models
(Sec 21)

22 Headlamp wiper motor/linkage – removal and refitting

1 Disconnect the battery negative lead.

99 models (except Turbo)

2 Remove the radiator grille (Chapter 12) and prise the linkage from the motor crank. Remove the crank.

3 Remove the battery (Section 2) and disconnect the wires from the wiper motor.

4 Unbolt the wiper motor from the fan cover and withdraw it from the car.

5 Unhook the spring securing the bushes to the front sheet, then unbolt the cover and linkage.

6 Refitting is a reversal of removal, but lubricate the recesses in the front sheet with grease, and apply locking fluid to the wiper motor crank securing screw. If necessary adjust the parked position of the wipers by altering the length of the linkage rod. Also check the tension of the cord and adjust if necessary.

99 models (Turbo)

7 Prise up the spindle cover, unscrew the nut, and remove the wiper arm from the spindle.

10

22.13A Removing the headlamp wiper (900 models)

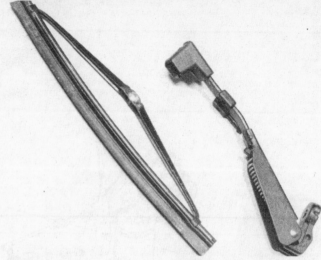

22.13B Headlamp wiper arm and blade (900 models)

22.14A Headlamp wiper motor (900 models)

22.14B Disconnecting the washer tube from the headlamp wiper

8　Remove the damper housing on the left-hand side or the heat shield on the right-hand side.
9　Unscrew the wiper mounting bolts from the headlamp surround.
10　Disconnect the wiring and withdraw the wiper motor from the car.
11　Refitting is a reversal of removal.

900 models

12　Remove the headlamp as described in Section 16.
13　Prise off the cap, unscrew the nut, and remove the wiper arm from the spindle (photos).
14　Remove the mounting screws, disconnect the wiring, and withdraw the wiper motor. Disconnect the washer tube and remove the wiper blade (photos).
15　Refitting is a reversal of removal.

23　Radio – installation

1　It is recommended that the radio is fitted by an automobile electrician, however the procedure is described in the following paragraphs for those who wish to do the work themselves. The radio is fitted in the accessory console on 99 models and in the central facia compartment on 900 models.
2　Fit the aerial to the rear panel, on the right-hand side for RHD

Fig. 10.18 Removing the headlamp wiper linkage on non-Turbo 99 models (Sec 22)

models and the left-hand side for LHD models, and feed the lead behind the trim panels to the radio position.

3   Fit the loudspeakers to the front door trim panels or rear parcel shelf on 99 models, or to the facia grilles on 900 models, and feed the wires to the radio position. 900 models from 1981 on may also have the loudspeakers fitted to the rear parcel shelf.

4   On 99 models fit the radio to the accessory console and connect the positive, negative and aerial leads – a connector plug is provided already connected to the main wiring harness.

5   On 900 models remove the facia compartment and fit the radio using the connector plug to connect the positive and negative wires to the wiring harness. Also connect the aerial lead.

6   For optimum performance the aerial must be well earthed to the body and the aerial lead should be routed away from the main wiring harness where possible. If four loudspeakers are fitted, a balance control must be fitted between the front and rear pairs to enable the front and rear volumes to be adjusted separately.

24 Wiring diagrams – applications

Owing to the many different Saab models available throughout the UK and USA, it has been necessary to restrict the number of wiring diagrams to a representative range. These cover all the major components in the electrical system of the vehicle concerned. Minor detail variations may occur between different territories, models and years.

24 Fault diagnosis – electrical system

Symptom	Reason(s)
Starter fails to turn engine	Battery discharged or defective
	Battery terminal and/or earth leads loose
	Starter motor connections loose
	Starter solenoid faulty
	Starter brushes worn or sticking
	Starter commutator dirty or worn
Starter turns engine very slowly	Battery discharged
	Starter motor connections loose
	Starter brushes worn or sticking
Starter noisy	Pinion or ring gear teeth badly worn
	Mounting bolts loose
Battery will not hold charge for more than a few days	Battery defective internally
	Electrolyte level too low
	Battery terminals loose
	Alternator drivebelt slipping
	Alternator or regulator faulty
	Short circuit
Ignition light stays on	Alternator fauly
	Alternator drivebelt broken
Ignition light fails to come on	Warning bulb blown or open circuit
	Alternator faulty
Instrument readings increase with engine speed	Voltage stabilizer faulty
Fuel or temperature gauge gives no reading	Wiring open circuit
	Sender unit faulty
	Gauge faulty
Fuel or temperature gauge gives maximum reading all the time	Wiring short circuit
	Gauge faulty
Lights inoperative	Bulb blown
	Fuse blown
	Battery discharged
	Switch faulty
	Wiring open circuit
	Bad connection due to corrosion
Failure of component motor	Commutator dirty or burnt
	Armature faulty
	Brushes sticking or worn
	Armature bearings seized
	Fuse blown
	Wiring loose or broken
	Field coils faulty

10

Key to Fig. 10.19

1 Battery (B2)
2 Alternator (B2)
4 Starter motor (B2)
5 Ignition coil (B5)
6 Ignition distributor (A5)
8 Lighting relay (D7)
10 Light switch (E8)
11 High beam (B1, E1)
12 Low beam (B1, E1)
13 Front parking light (A1, F1)
14 Tail light (A13, F13)
15 Number plate light (A12)
16 Instrument light rheostat (C10)
18 Instrument panel light (C10)
19 Light, glovebox (D11)
20 Ignition lock (B8)
21 Ignition relay (D5)
22 Fuse box (C4, D4)
24 Direction indicator switch (E10)
25 Warning flasher switch (E11)
27 Direction indicator lights, Left (F1, F13)
28 Direction indicator lights, Right (A1, A13)
29 Brake light contact (E12)
30 Brake lights (A13, F13)
31 Back-up lights contact (D8)
32 Back-up lights (A13, F13)
35 Fan switch (C12)
36 Fan motor (C12)
37 Cooling fan motor (D1)
38 Cooling fan relay (C5)
39 Cooling fan thermostat contact (D2)
40 Signal horn (B1, E1)
41 Signal contact (E8)
42 Brake warning contact (C3)
43 Handbrake contact (B12)
44 Oil warning contact (A7)
45 Temperature transmitter (A7)
46 Fuel level transmitter (B11)
47 Combination instrument (C10):
  A Fuel gauge (D10)
  B Fuel warning light (D10)
  C Temperature gauge (C10)
  D Oil warning light (C10)
  E Ignition light (C9)
  F Brake warning light (C10)
  G High beam indicator light C10)
  H Direction indicator repeater,

Left (D9)
I Direction indicator repeater, Right (D10)
J Electrically heated rear window, indicator light (C9)
K Extra (C10)
L Extra (C10)
M Handbrake indicator light (C10)
N Extra (C10)
O Choke indicator light (C9)
P Speed transmitter (D10)
48 Cigarette lighter (F10)
49 Clock (D10)
50 Dome light, interior centre (B10)
51 Dome light, interior front (B10)
52 Ignition lock light (B9)
53 Switch, interior light (B10)
54 Door contact, interior lighting (B7, B10, B11, B12)
55 Trunk light (B9)
56 Trunk light contact (B8)
57 3-pole connector (A11, B3, B6, B9, B11)
58 12-pole connector (B11, D8)
59 2-pole connector (A9, A10, A11 A12, D2, F8, F9)
60 1-pole connector (A4, A8, B4, B6, B7, B10, B12)
61 Switch, wiper system (E9)
62 2-speed windshield wiper motor (F4)
63 Washer motor (F3)
64 Electric pad with thermostat (A9)
70 Seat belt contact, "F" (B10)
72 Lamp, seat belt warning (B12)
73 Socket for ignition control (B7)
74 Resistance, fan low speed (C12)
79 Vacuum switch (A4)
80 Buzzer key and seat belt warning (B10)
82 Logic relay (B11)
83 Wiper washer interval relay (E9)
86 EGR contact (C11)
89 Start inhibitor relay (C6)
91 Gear position light (A8)
92 Temperature time switch (A2)
94 Starter valve (A4)
95 Make up air vent (A2)

96 Pilot pressure valve (A2)
102 Fuel pump relay (C6)
103 Fuel pump (A11)
107 Key contact (B8)
110 Tachometer (C9)
112 Electronic flasher unit (F10)
113 Relay, electrically heated rear window (D6)
115 Electrically heated rear window (B11)
116 Switch, electrically heated rear window (E11)
118 Cornering lamp (A1, F1)
119 Side back-up light (A1, F1)
121 Seat contact, electrical pad (A10)
123 4-pole connector (F7, F11)
124 Switch, electrical rear view mirror, Left (F8)
125 Switch, electrical rear view mirror, Right (F12)
126 Electrical rear view mirror, Left (F6)
127 Electrical rear view mirror, Right (F11)
135 Trigger unit Lambda (C1)
136 Sond (B2)
137 Valve switch (C1)
138 Relay (Lambda) (D5)
139 Timing valve (E2)
142 Solenoid valve (D2)
144 Pressure guard (B6)
146 Electronic unit, ignition system (A6)
147 Resistance (B5)
148 Light, ashtray (D12)
149 Main switch, fan (D12)
150 Switch, air conditioning (D12)
151 Speed transmitter, 18.5 mph (30 km/h) (F11)
152 29-pole connector (A-F7)
153 Light, cigarette lighter (E8)
154 Light, heating control (E9)
155 Socket for extra cooling fan relay (C5)
157 Spark plug (A4)
158 Distribution plinth - (C5)
159 Distribution plinth + (C6)
160 Contact, glove compartment Light (D11)

Colour code

BL	Blue	GN	Green	RD	Red	VL	Violet
BR	Brown	GR	Grey	SV	Black	VT	White
GL	Yellow	OR	Orange				

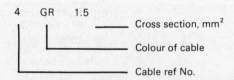

4   GR   1.5

————— Cross section, mm²

————— Colour of cable

————— Cable ref No.

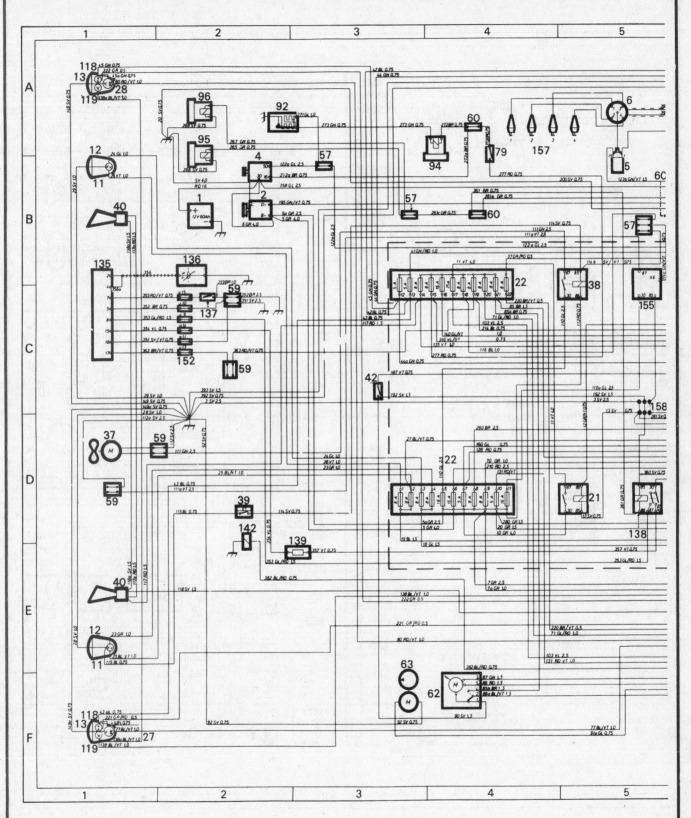

Fig. 10.19 Wiring diagram for 1979 (US) Turbo

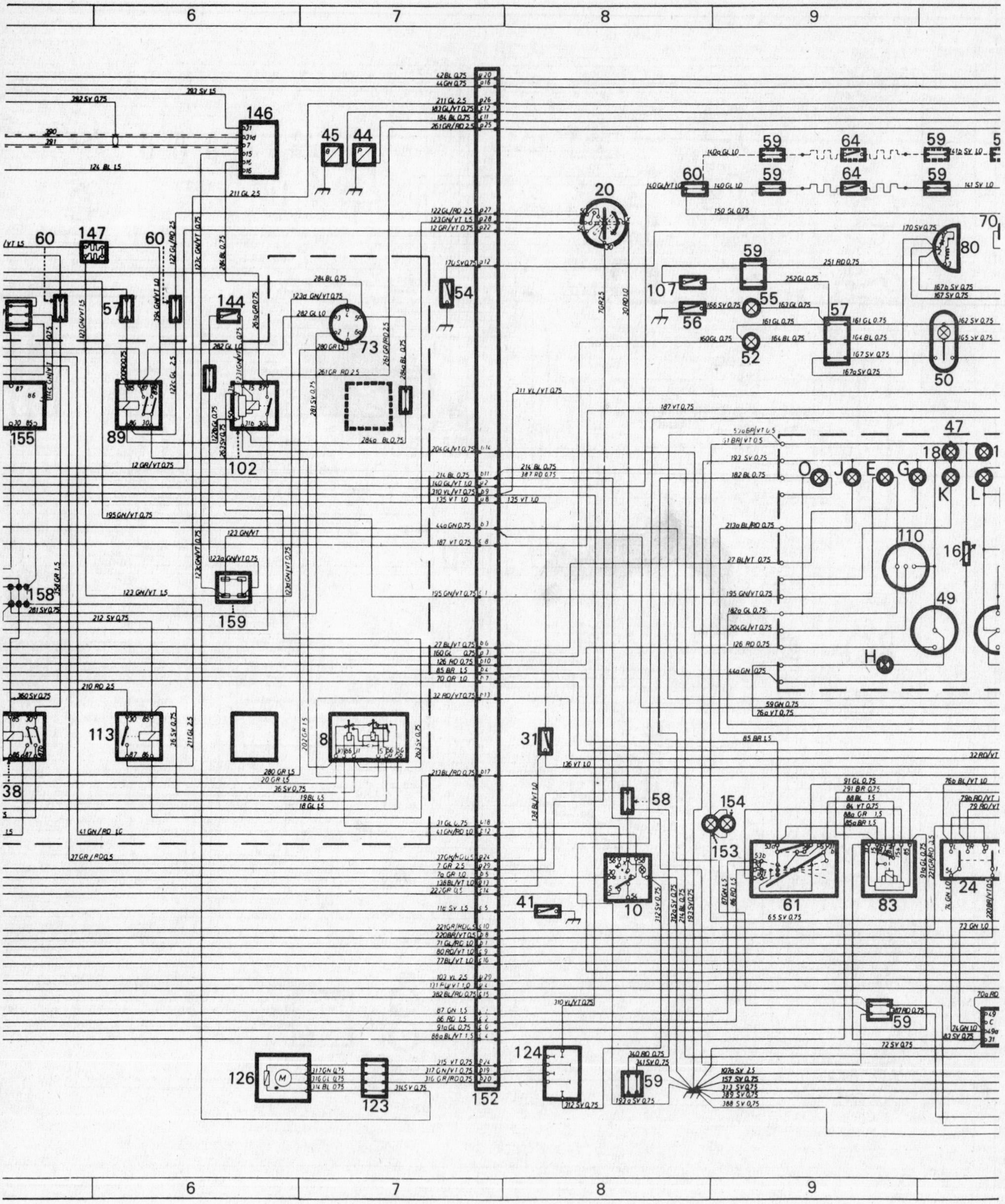

Fig. 10.19 Wiring diagram for 1979 (US) Turbo (continued)

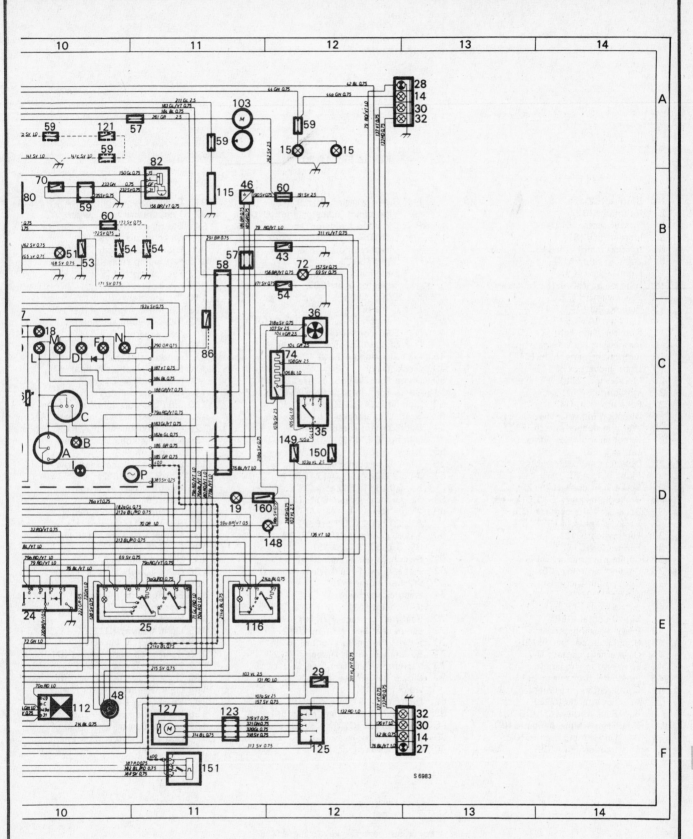

Fig. 10.19 Wiring diagram for 1979 (US) Turbo (continued)

Key to Fig. 10.20

1 Battery (B2)
2 Alternator (B2)
4 Starter motor (B2)
5 Ignition coil (B5)
6 Ignition distributor (A5)
8 Lighting relay (D7)
10 Light switch (E8)
11 High beam (B1, E1)
12 Low beam (B1, E1)
13 Parking light (A1, F1)
14 Tail light (A13,B13,E13,F13)
15 Number plate light (C13,D13)
16 Instrument light rheostat (C10)
18 Instrument panel light (C10)
19 Light, glove box (D11)
20 Ignition lock (B8)
21 Ignition relay (D5)
22 Fuse box (C4, D4)
24 Direction indicator switch (E10)
25 Warning flasher switch (E11)
27 Direction indicator lights
    Left (F1, F3)
28 Direction indicator lights
    Right (A1, A13)
29 Brake light contact (E12)
30 Brake lights (A13,B13,E13,F13)
31 Back-up lights contact (D8)
32 Back-up lights (A13, F13)
35 Fan switch (C12)
36 Fan motor (C12)
35 Cooling fan motor (D1)
38 Cooling fan relay (C5)
39 Cooling fan thermostat
    contact (D2)
40 Signal horn (B1, E1)
41 Signal contact (E8)
42 Brake warning contact (C3)
43 Handbrake contact (B12)
44 Oil warning contact (A7)
45 Temperature transmitter (A7)
46 Fuel level transmitter (B11)
47 Combination instrument (C10)
    A Fuel gauge (D19)
    B Fuel warning light (D10)
    C Temperature gauge (C10)
    D Oil warning light (C10)
    E Ignition light (C9)

F Brake warning light (C10)
G High beam indicator light (C10)
H Direction indicator repeater,
   Left (D9)
I Direction indicator repeater,
   Right (D10)
J Electrically heated rear window,
   indicator light (C9)
K Extra (C10)
L Extra (C10)
M Handbrake control light (C10)
N EGR control lamp (C10)
O Choke indicator light (C9)
48 Cigarette lighter (F10)
49 Clock (D10)
50 Dome light, interior centre (B10)
51 Dome light, interior front (B10)
52 Ignition lock light (B9)
53 Switch, interior light (B10)
54 Door contact, interior
    lighting (B7, B12)
55 Trunk light (B9)
56 Trunk light contact (B8)
57 3-pole connector (A12, B3,
    B5, B9, B11, B12)
58 12-pole connector (B11, D8)
59 2-pole connector (A9, A10, A11
    A12, D2, D11, D12, F8)
60 1-pole connector (A4, A5, A8
    B4, B5, B7, B12, E13)
61 Switch, wiper system (E9)
62 2-speed windshield wiper motor (F4)
63 Washer motor (F3)
64 Electrical pad with
    thermostat (A9)
70 Seat belt contact, F (B10)
72 Lamp, seat belt warning (B12)
73 Socket for ignition control (B7)
74 Resistance, fan low speed (C12)
79 Vacuum switch (A4)
80 Buzzer key and seat belt
    warning (B10)
82 Logic relay (B11)
83 Wiper washer interval relay (E9)
86 EGR contact (C11)
89 Start inhibitor relay (C6)
90 Start lock contact (A8)

91 Gear position light (A8)
92 Temperature time switch (A2)
94 Starter valve (A4)
95 Make-up air valve (A2)
96 Pilot pressure valve (A2)
102 Fuel pump relay (C6)
103 Fuel pump (A11)
107 Key contact (B8)
110 Tachometer (C9)
112 Electronic flasher unit (F10)
113 Relay, electrically heated
     rear window (D6)
115 Electrically heated rear
     window (B11)
116 Switch, electrically heated
     rear window (E11)
118 Cornering light (A1, F1)
119 Side back-up light (A1, F1)
121 Seat contact, electrical pad (A10)
123 4-pole connector (F7, F11)
124 Switch, electrical rear view
     mirror Left (F8)
125 Switch, electrical rear view
     mirror Right (F12)
126 Electrical rear view mirror
     Left (F6)
127 Electrical rear view mirror
     Right (F11)
135 Trigger unit Lambda (C1)
136 Sond (B2)
137 Valve switch (C2)
138 Relay (Lambda) (D5)
139 Timing valve (E2)
146 Electronic unit, ignition
     system (A6)
147 Resistance (B5)
148 Light, ashtray (D12)
149 Main switch, fan (D12)
150 Switch, air conditioning (D12)
152 29-pole connector (A-F7)
153 Light, cigarette lighter (E8)
154 Light, heating control (E9)
157 Spark plug (A4)
158 Distribution plinth - (C5)
159 Distribution plinth + (C6)
160 Contact, glove compartment
     light (D11)

For colour code see key to Fig. 10.19

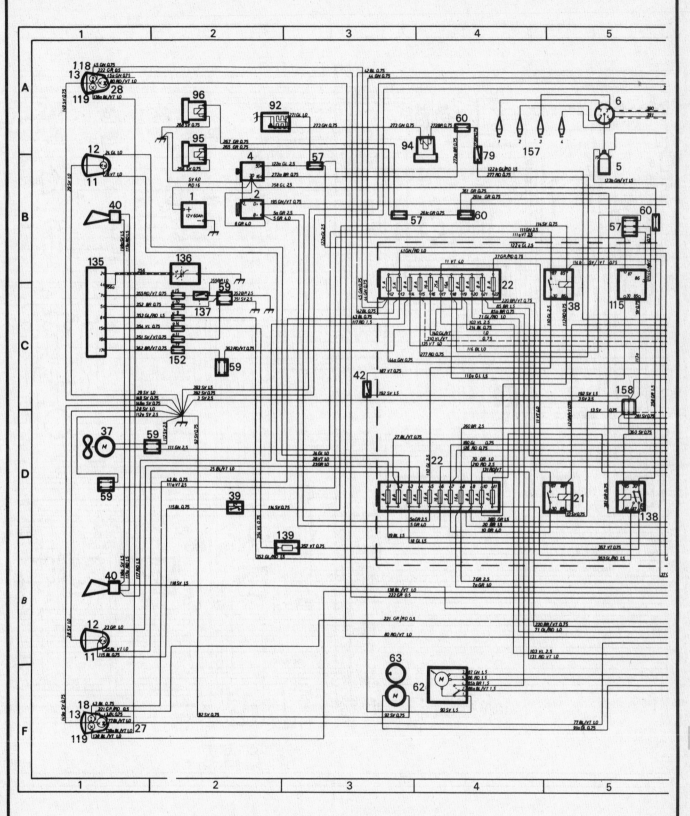

Fig. 10.20 Wiring diagram for 1980 (US) GL, GLE and EMS

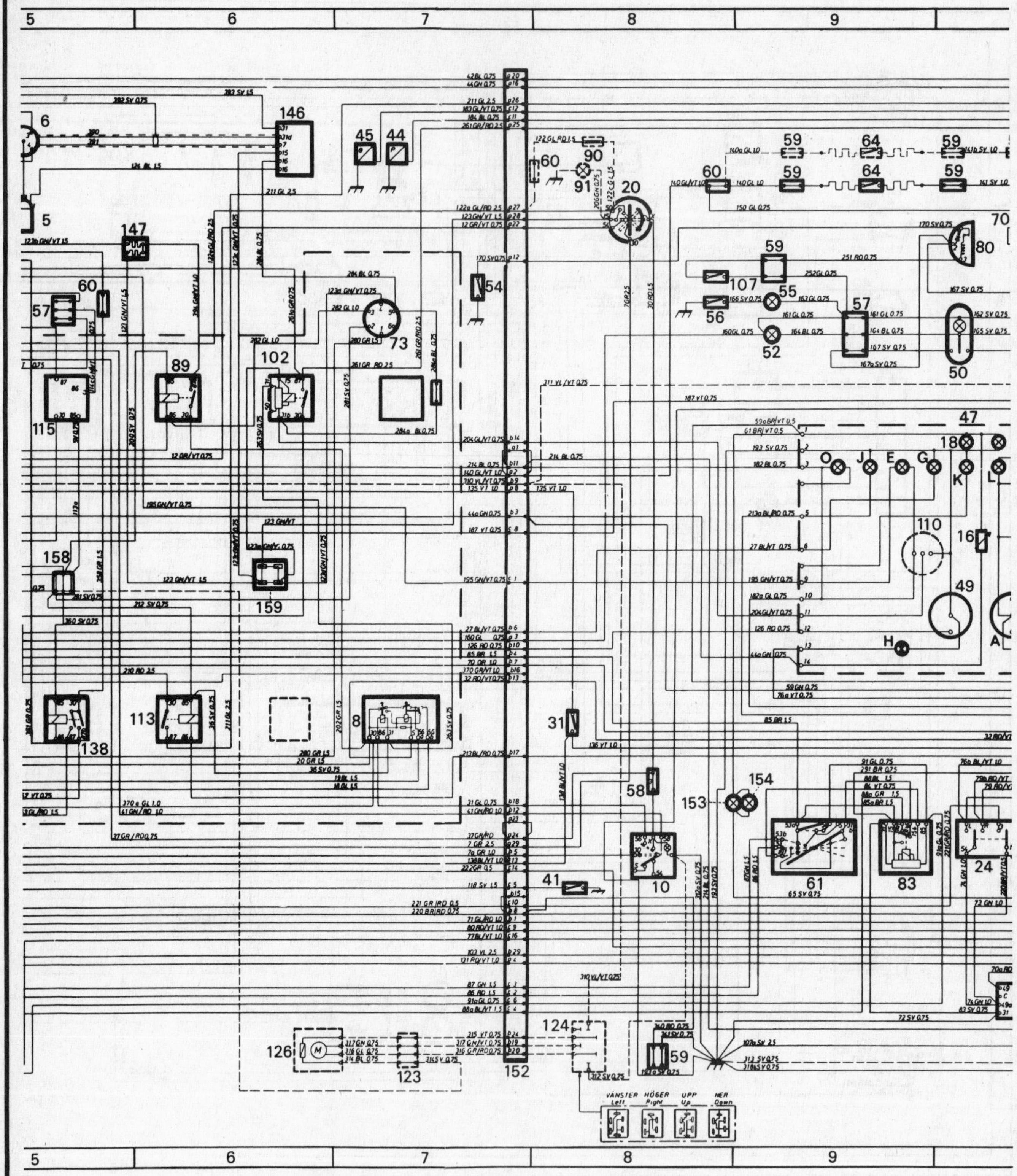

Fig. 10.20 Wiring diagram for 1980 (US) GL, GLE and EMS (continued)

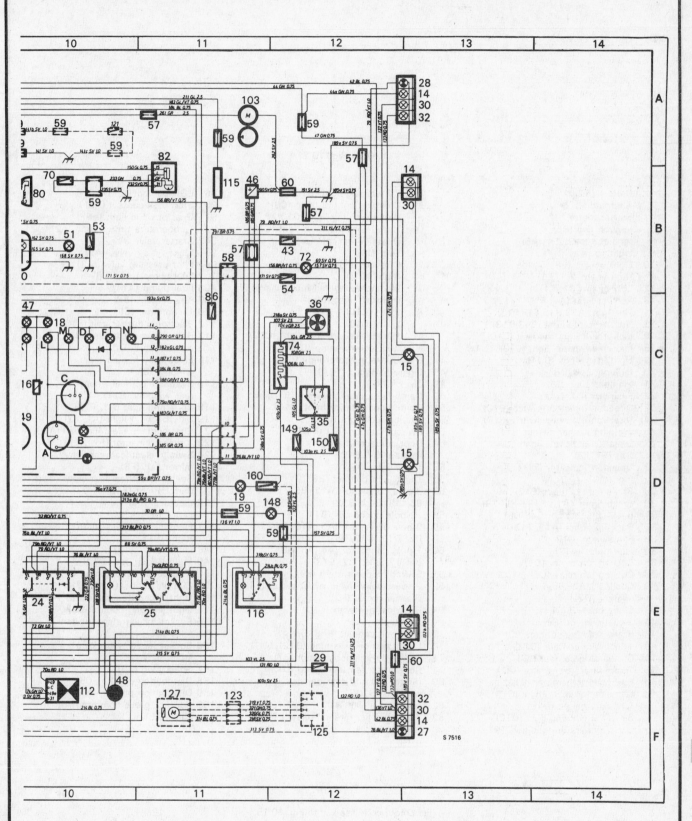

Fig. 10.20 Wiring diagram for 1980 (US) GL, GLE and EMS (continued)

Key to Fig. 10.21

1   Battery (B2)
2   Alternator (B2)
4   Starter motor (B2)
5   Ignition coil (B5)
6   Ignition distributor (A5)
8   Lighting relay (D7)
10 Light switch (E8)
11 High beam (B1, E1)
12 Low beam (B1, E1)
13 Parking light (A1, F1)
14 Tail light (A13,B13,E13,F13)
15 Number plate light (C13,D13)
16 Instrument light rheostat (C10)
18 Instrument panel light (C10)
19 Light, glove box (D11)
20 Ignition lock (B8)
21 Ignition relay (D5)
22 Fuse box (C4, D4)
23 Direction indicator switch (E10)
24 Direction indicator switch (E10)
25 Warning flasher switch (E11)
27 Direction indicator lights
    Left (F1, F3)
28 Direction indicator lights
    Right (A1, A13)
29 Brake light contact (E12)
30 Brake lights (A13,B13,E13,F13)
31 Back-up lights contact (D8)
32 Back-up lights (A13, F13)
35 Fan switch (C12)
36 Fan motor (C12)
35 Cooling fan motor (D1)
38 Cooling fan relay (C5)
39 Cooling fan thermostat
    contact (D2)
40 Signa horn (B1, E1)
41 Signal contact (E8)
42 Brake warning contact (C3)
43 Handbrake contact (B12)
44 Oil warning contact (A7)
45 Temperature transmitter (A7)
46 Fuel level transmitter (B11)
47 Combination instrument (C10)
    A   Fuel gauge (D19)
    B   Fuel warning light (D10)
    C   Temperature gauge (C10)

D   Oil warning light (C10)
E   Charging control lamp (C9)
F   Brake warning light (C10)
G   High beam indicator light (C10)
H   Direction indicator repeater,
    Left (D9)
I   Direction indicator repeater,
    Right (D10)
J   Electrically heated rear window,
    indicator light (C9)
K   Extra (C10)
L   Extra (C10)
M   Handbrake indicator light (C10)
N   EGR control lamp (C10)
O   Choke indicator light (C9)
48 Cigarette lighter (F10)
49 Clock (D10)
50 Dome light, interior centre (B10)
51 Dome light, interior front (B10)
52 Ignition lock light (B9)
53 Switch, interior light (B10)
54 Door contact, interior
    lighting (B7, B12)
55 Trunk light (B9)
56 Trunk light contact (B8)
57 3-pole conenctor (A12, B3,
    B5, B9, B11, B12)
58 12-pole connector (B11, D8)
59 2-pole connector (A9, A10, A11
    D2, D11, D12, F8)
60 1-pole connector (A4, A5, A8
    B4, B7, B12, C7, E13)
61 Switch, wiper system (E9)
62 2-speed windshield wiper motor (F4)
63 Washer motor (F3)
64 Electrical pad with
    thermostat (A9)
70 Seat belt contact, F (B10)
72 Lamp seat belt warning (B12)
73 Socket for ignition control (B7)
74 Resistance, fan low speed (C12)
80 Buzzer key and seat belt
    warning (B10)
82 Logic relay (B11)
83 Wiper washer interval relay (E9)

86 EGR contact (C11)
90 Start lock contact (A8)
91 Gear position light (A8)
92 Temperature time switch (A2)
94 Starter valve (A4)
95 Make-up air valve (A2)
96 Pilot pressure valve (A2)
102 Fuel pump relay (C6)
103 Fuel pump (A11)
107 Key contact (B8)
110 Tachometer (C9)
112 Electronic flasher unit (F10)
113 Relay, electrically heated
    rear window (D6)
115 Electrically heated rear
    window (B11)
116 Switch, electrically heated
    rear window (E11)
118 Cornering light (A1, F1)
119 Side back-up light (A1, F1)
121 Seat contact, electrical pad (A10)
123 4-pole connector (F7, F11)
124 Switch, electrical rear view
    mirror Left (F8)
125 Switch, electrical rear view
    mirror Right (F12)
126 Electrical rear view mirror
    Left (F6)
127 Electrical rear view mirror
    Right (F11)
148 Light, ashtray (D12)
149 Main switch, fan (D12)
150 Switch, air conditioning (D12)
152 29-pole connector (A-F7)
153 Light, cigarette lighter (E8)
154 Light, heating control (E9)
155 Socket for extra cooling fan
    relay (C5)
156 Socket for relay back-up
    lights (C7)
157 Spark plug (A4)
158 Distribution plinth - (C5)
159 Distribution plinth + (C6)
160 Contact, glove compartment
    light (D11)

For colour code see key to Fig. 10.19

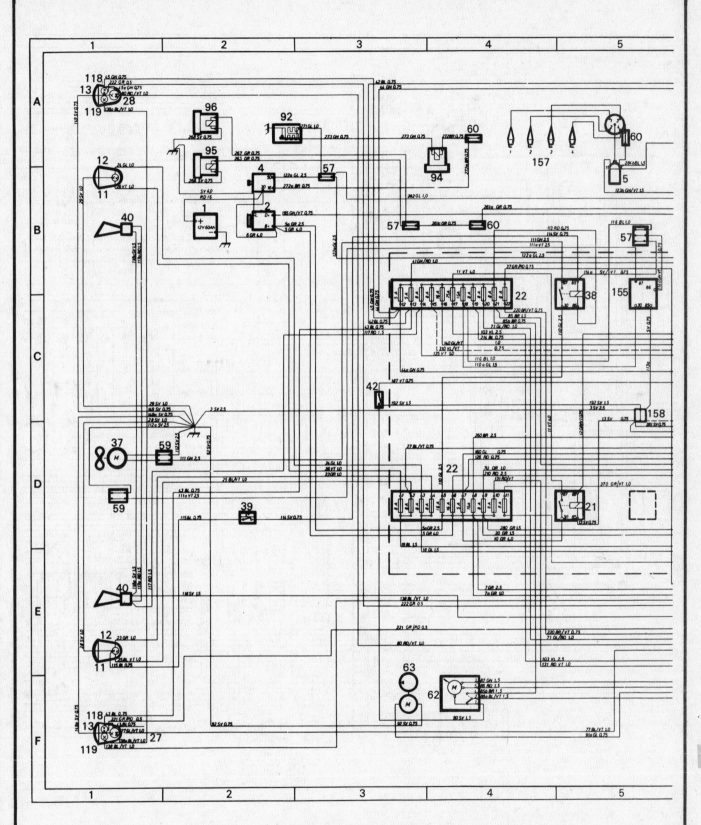

Fig. 10.21 Wiring diagram for 1980 (Canada) GL, GLE and EMS

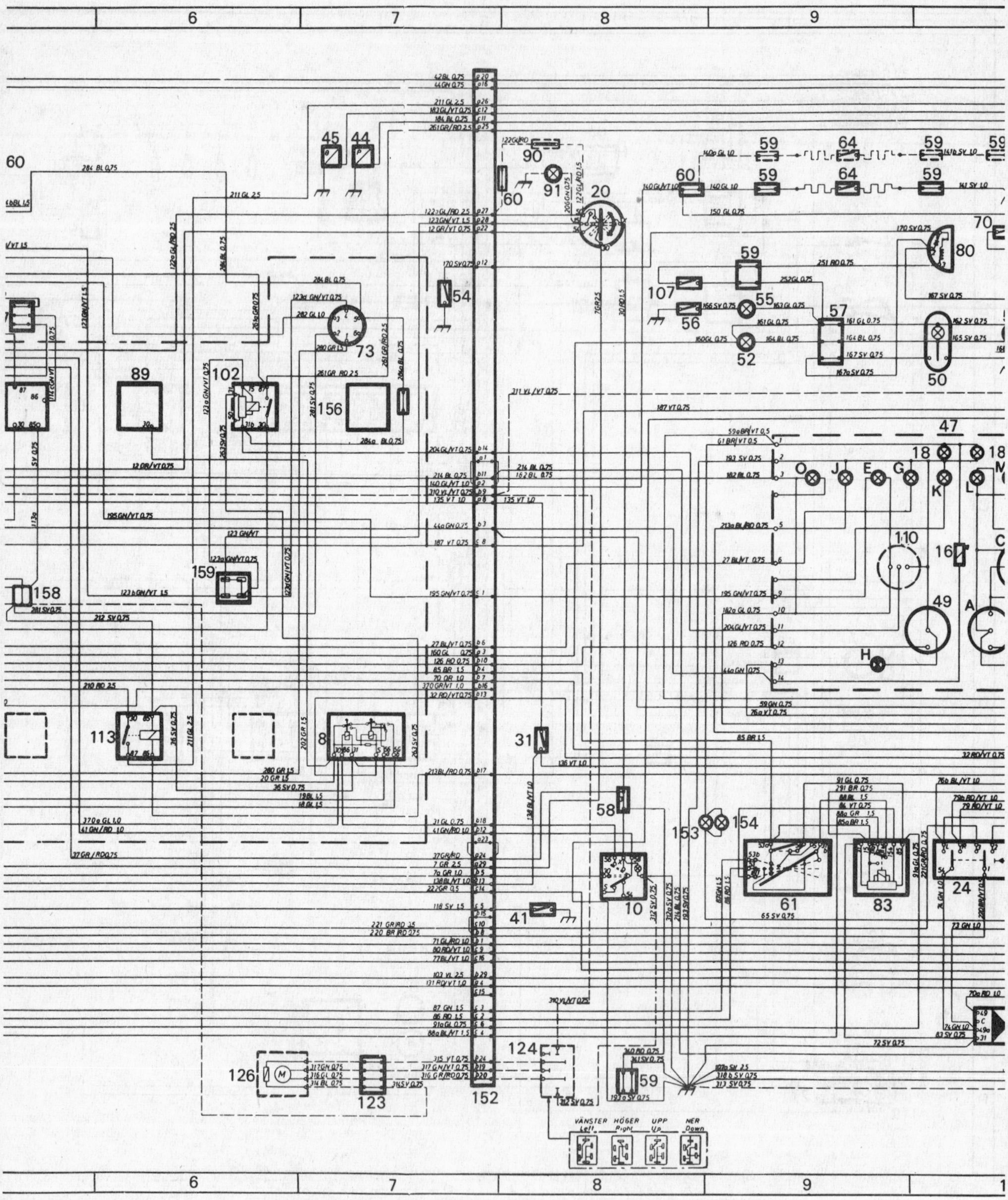

Fig. 10.21 Wiring diagram for 1980 (Canada) GL, GLE and EMS (continued)

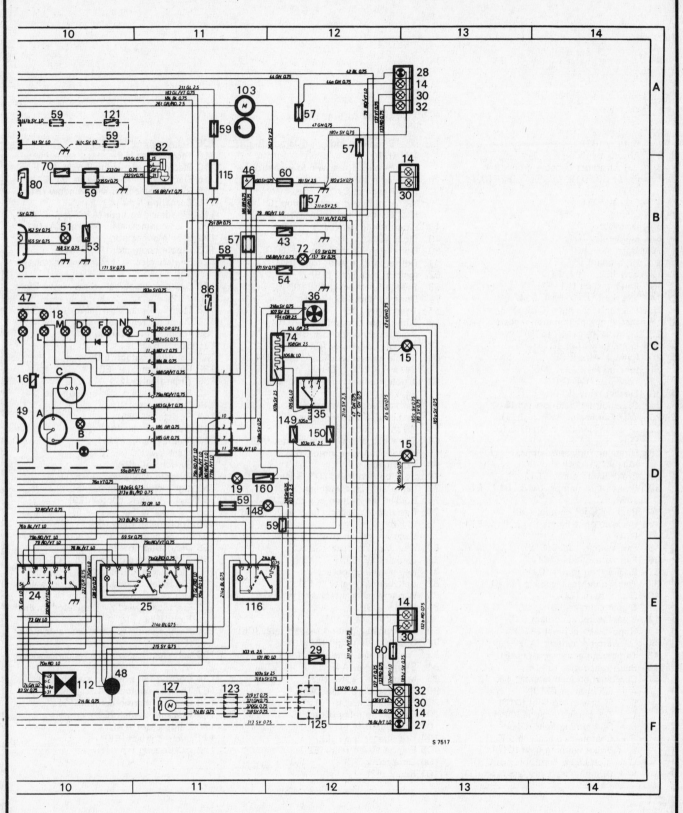

Fig. 10.21 Wiring diagram for 1980 (Canada) GL, GLE and EMS (continued)

Key to Fig. 10.22

1 Battery (B2)
2 Alternator (B2)
3 Instrument console ground tab (C11, D8, D12, E8, E11, F8, F10, F12)
4 Starter (B2)
5 Ignition coil (B5)
6 Distributor (A5)
8 Light relay (D7)
10 Light switch (E8)
11 High beam (B1, E1)
12 Low beam (B1, E1)
13 Parking light (A1, F1)
14 Tail light (A13, B14, E14)
15 Licence plate light (C13, D13)
16 Instrument illumination rheostat (C10)
18 Light, illumination (C10)
19 Light, glove box (D11)
20 Ignition lock (B8)
21 Ignition lock relay (D5)
22 Fuse box (C4, D4)
23 Flasher relay (E10)
24 Direction indicator switch (E10)
25 Warning flasher switch (E11)
27 Direction indicator lamps Left (E14, F1, F13)
28 Direction indicator lamps, Right (A1, A13, A14)
29 Brake light contact (E12)
30 Brake light lamps (A13, B14, E14, F13)
31 Back-up light contact (D8)
32 Back-up light lamps (A13, B14, E14, F13)
35 Fan switch, cabin (C12)
36 Fan motor, cabin (C12)
37 Cooling fan motor (D1)
39 Thermo contact, cooling fan (D2)
40 Signal horn (E1)
41 Signal contact (E8)
42 Brake warning contact (C3)
43 Hand brake contact (B12)
44 Oil warning contact (A6)
45 Temperature transmitter (A6)
46 Fuel transmitter (B11)
47 Combination instrument (C10):
　A　Fuel gauge (D10)
　B　Fuel warning light (D10)
　C　Temperature gauge (C10)
　D　Oil warning light (C10)
　E　Charging control lamp (C9)
　F　Brake warning light (C10)
　G　High beam control lamp (C10)
　H　Direction indicator lamp Left (D9)

I Direction indicator lamp, Right (D10)
J Electrical rear window control lamp (C9)
K Reserve (C10)
M Handbrake control lamp (C10)
N EGR control lamp (C10)
48 Cigarette lighter (F10)
49 Clock (D10)
50 Dome light, interior centre (B10)
51 Dome light, interior front (B10)
52 Ignition lock light (B9)
53 Switch, interior light (B10)
54 Door contact (B7, B12)
55 Trunk light (B9)
56 Trunk light contact (B8)
57 3-pole connector (B3, B9, B13, D11)
58 12-pole connector (B11, D8)
59 2-pole connector (A9, A10, A12, A13, B4, B9, C2, D1, D8)
60 1-pole connector (A4, A8, B6, D12, E4, E5)
61 Switch, wiper system (E9)
62 2-speed windshield wiper (F5)
63 Washer motor (B1)
64 Electrical pad with thermostat (A9)
66 Headlight wiper motor (B1)
68 Horn relay
70 Seat belt contact, "D" (B10)
72 Lamp seat belt warning (B12)
73 Socket for ignition control (C7)
74 Resistance, cabin fan, low speed, (C12)
79 Vacuum switch (A4)
80 Key warning buzzer (B10)
82 Logic relay (B11)
81 Key warning contact
82 Belt warning relay (B11)
83 Wiper washer interval relay (E9)
84 Diode (D9)
86 EGR contact (C11)
89 Electronical ignition system relay (C6)
91 Gear position light (A8)
92 Temperature time switch (A2)
94 Starter valve (A4)
95 Make-up air valve (A2)
96 Pilot pressure valve (A2)
97 Thermo-contract (F3)
102 Fuel pump relay (C6)
103 Fuel pump (A11)
104 Hot starter relay (E2)
105 Engine speed relay (E2)
106 Time relay (F3)
107 Relay (F2)

108 Relay central (E2-E3)
110 Tachometer (C9)
113 Electrical rear window relay (D6)
115 Electrical rear window (A12)
116 Switch, electrical rear window (E11)
118 Cornering light (A1, F1)
119 Side back-up light (A1, F1)
121 Seat contact, electrical pad (A10)
122 8-pole connector
123 4-pole connector (F7, F11)
124 Switch, electrical rear view mirror Left (F8)
125 Switch, electrical rear view Right (F12)
126 Electrical rear view mirror Left (F6)
127 Electrical rear view mirror Right (F11)
135 Trigger unit, Lambda (C1)
136 Sond (B2)
137 Throttle contact (E2)
138 Relay (Lambda) (E3)
139 Timing valve (E2)
142 Solenoid valve, idle speed raise (F4)
144 Pressure switch
147 Resistance (B5)
146 Electronic unit (A6)
148 Ashtray lamp (D11)
149 Main switch, fan (C12)
150 Switch, AC (B8)
152 29-pole connector (A7-F7)
153 Light, cigarette lighter (E8)
154 Light, heating control (E9)
155 AC cooling fan relay (C5)
156 Cooling fan relay (D5)
157 Spark plug (A4-A5)
158 Distribution plinth – (C5)
159 Distribution plinth + "15" (C6)
160 Glove compartment (D11)
162 Electrical window regulator switch Left (F8)
163 Electrical window regulator switch Right (F8)
164 Right electric window regulator motor (F9)
165 Left electrical window regulator motor (F7)
166 Cooling fan pressure switch (E4)
167 Throttle contact (F4)
168 Coolant thermo-contact (F3)
169 Pressure switch (E3)
170 Compressor (F4)
171 Cycle contact (B8)
172 AC Cooling fan (C1)

For colour code see key to Fig. 10.19

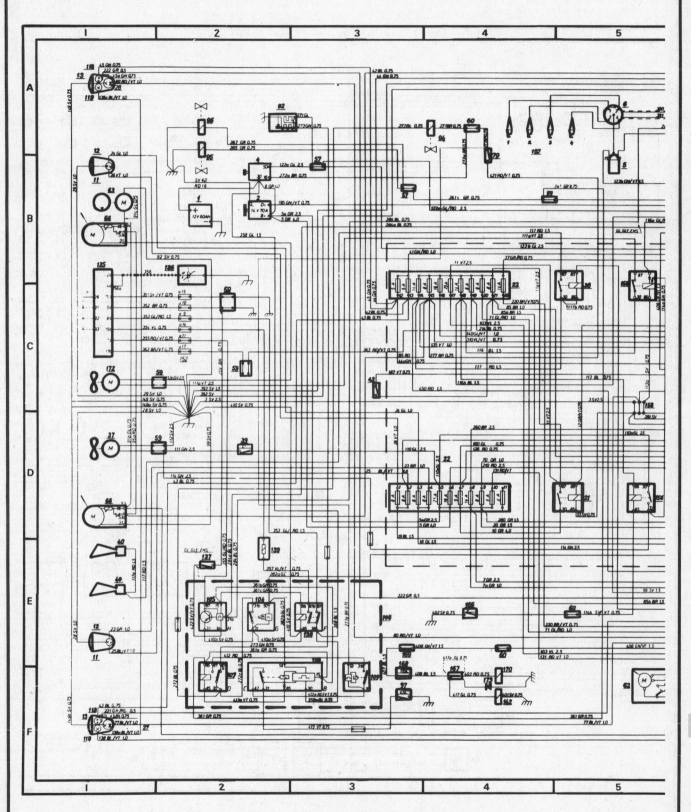

Fig. 10.22 Wiring diagram for 1981 (US and Canada) 900

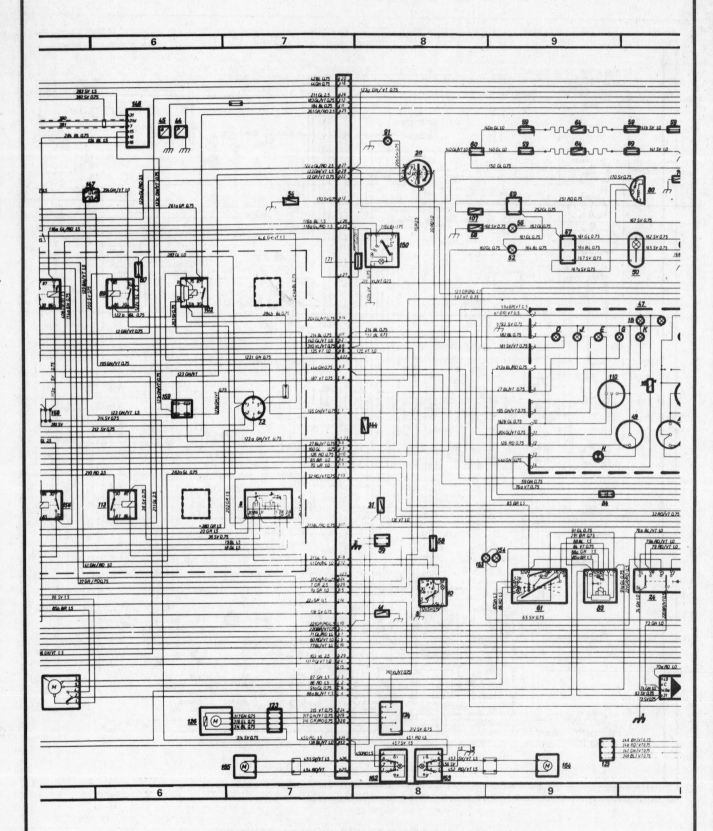

Fig. 10.22 Wiring diagram for 1981 (US and Canada) 900 (continued)

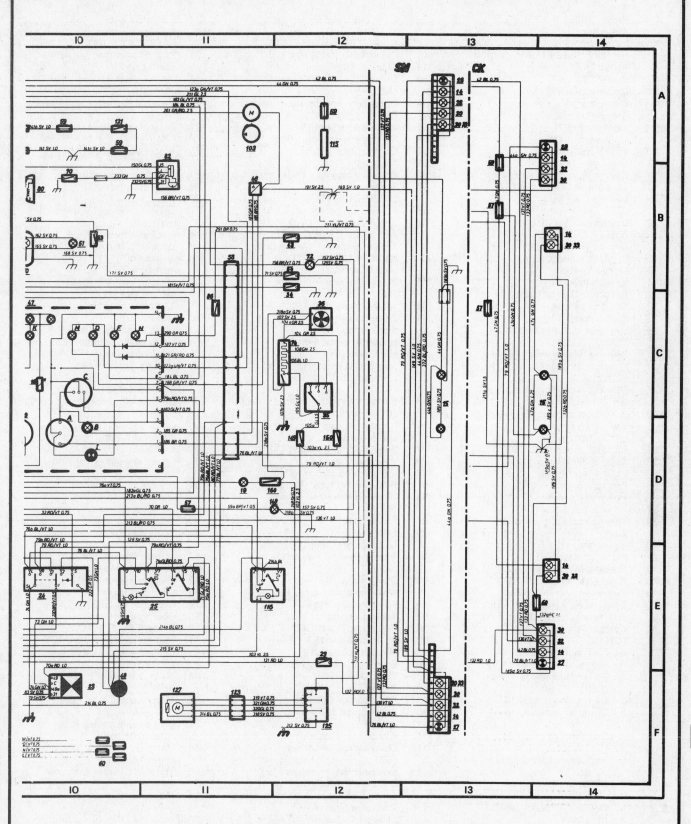

Fig. 10.22 Wiring diagram for 1981 (US and Canada) (continued)

Key to Fig. 10.23

1 Battery (B2)
2 Alternator (B2)
3 Instrument console ground
   tab (C11,D8,E8,E11,F8,
   F10,F12)
4 Starter (B2)
5 Ignition coil (B5)
6 Distributor (A5)
7 Ground tap (D2,F3)
8 Light relay (D7)
10 Light switch (E8)
11 High beam (B1,E1)
12 Low beam (B1,E1)
13 Parking light, front (A1,F1)
14 Tail light (A13,A14,E14,F13)
15 Licence plate light
   (C13,C14)
16 Instrument light rheostat
   (C10)
17 Electric switch, rheostat (B8)
18 Light, instrument (C10)
19 Light, glovebox (D11)
20 Ignition lock (B8)
21 Ignition lock relay (D5)
22 Fusebox (C4,D4)
23 Flasher relay (E10)
24 Direction indicator switch
   (E10)
25 Warning flasher switch (E11)
27 Direction indicator lamps, LH
   (E14,F1,F13)
28 Direction indicator lamps,
   RH (A1,A13,A14)
29 Brake light contact (E12)
30 Brake light lamps
   (A13,B14,E14,F13)
31 Back-up light contact (D8)
32 Back-up light lamps
   (A13,A14,E14,F13)
35 Fan switch, cabin (C12)
36 Fan motor, cabin (C12)
37 Cooling fan motor (D1)
39 Thermo contact, cooling fan
   (D2)
40 Signal horn (E1)
41 Signal contact (E8)
42 Brake warning contact (C3)
43 Hand brake contact (B12)
44 Oil warning contact (A6)
45 Temperature transmitter (A6)
46 Fuel transmitter (B11)
47 Combination instrument
   (C10):
   A Fuel gauge (D10)
   B Fuel warning light (D10)
   C Temperature gauge
      (C10)
   D Oil warning light (C10)
   E Charging control lamp
      (C9)
   F Brake warning light
      (C10)
   G High beam control lamp
      (C10)
   H Direction indicator lamp
      LH (D9)
   I Direction indicator lamp
      RH (D10)
   J Electrical rear window
      control lamp (C9)
   K Reserve (C10)

   M Hand brake control lamp
      (C10)
   N EGR control lamp (C10)
48 Cigarette lighter (F10)
49 Clock (D10)
50 Dome light, interior centre
   (B10)
51 Dome light, interior front
   (B10)
52 Ignition lock light (B9)
53 Switch, interior light (B10)
54 Door contact (B7,B12)
55 Trunk light (B9)
56 Trunk light contact (B8)
57 3-pole connector
   (B3,B9,B13,C13)
58 12-pole connector (B11,D8)
59 2-pole connector (A10,A12,
   A13,B8,C2,D2,D8,D12,F7)
60 1-pole connector (A4,A8,B8,
   B10,C7,E4,E5,E13,F11)
61 Switch, wiper system (E9)
62 2-speed windshield wiper
   (F5)
63 Washer motor (B1)
64 Electrical pad with
   thermostat (A9)
66 Headlight wiper motor (B1)
68 Horn relay (B5)
70 Seat belt contact, "D" (B10)
72 Lamp seat belt warning
   (B12)
73 Socket for ignition control
   (C7)
74 Resistance, cabin fan, low
   speed (C12)
77 Switch, starting ratchet (A8)
79 Vacuum switch (A4)
80 Key warning buzzer (B10)
82 Belt warning relay (B11)
83 Wiper washer interval relay
   (E9)
84 Diode (D10)
86 EGR contact (C11)
91 Gear position light (C8)
92 Temperature time switch
   (A2)
94 Starter valve (A4)
95 Make-up air valve (A2)
96 Pilot pressure valve (A2)
97 Thermo-contact (F3)
102 Fuel pump relay (C6)
103 Fuel pump (A11)
104 Hot starter relay (E2)
105 Engine speed relay (E2)
106 Time relay (F3)
107 Relay (F2)
108 Relay central (E2-E3)
109 Acceleration enrichment
    relay (F3)
110 Tachometer (C9)
113 Electrical rear window relay
    (D6)
115 Electrical rear window (A12)
116 Switch, electrical rear
    window (E11)
118 Cornering light (A1,F1)
119 Slide back-up light (A1,F1)
121 Seat contact, electrical pad
    (A10)

122 8-pole connector
123 4-pole connector (A8,A9,
    E2,E3,F2,F7,F10,F11)
124 Switch, electrical rear view
    mirror LH,(F8)
125 Switch, electrical rear view
    mirror RH (F12)
126 Electrical rear view mirror LH
    (F6)
127 Electrical rear view mirror RH
    (F11)
135 Trigger unit Lambda (C1)
136 Sond (B2)
137 Throttle contact (E2)
138 Relay (Lambda) (E3)
139 Timing valve (C2)
142 Solenoid valve, idle speed
    raise (F4)
144 Pressure switch (D8)
146 Electronic unit, ignition
    system (A6)
148 Ashtray lamp (D11)
149 Main switch, fan (C12)
150 Switch, AC (D12)
151 29-pole cannector
    (A7-F7,C2)
153 Light, cigarette lighter (E8)
154 Light, heating control (E9)
155 AC cooling fan relay (C5)
156 Cooling fan relay (D5)
157 Spark plug (A4-A5)
158 Distribution plinth – (C5)
159 Distribution plinth +
    "15"(C6)
160 Glove compartment (D11)
162 Electrical window regulator
    switch LH (F8)
163 Electrical window regulator
    switch RH (F8)
164 RH electrical window
    regulator motor (F9)
165 LH electrical window
    regulator motor (F7)
166 Cooling fan pressure switch
    (E4)
167 Throttle contact (F4)
168 Coolant thermo-contact (F3)
169 Pressure switch (B8)
170 Compressor (F4)
171 Cycle contact (B8)
172 Cooling fan (C1)
173 Diode (F4)
174 Thermo switch, coolant (E4)
183 Control unit, central lock,
    left, LHD
183 Motor, central lock, left,
    RHD (A7)
184 Motor, central lock, right,
    LHD (A8)
184 Control unit, central lock,
    right, RHD (A8)
185 Motor right, central lock, rear
    door (A8)
186 Motor left, central lock, rear
    door (A9)
188 Motor, cental lock, tail gate
    (A9)
190 Solenoid valve, fuel cut-off
    (E2)
191 Throttle contact (E4)

For colour code see key to Fig. 10.19

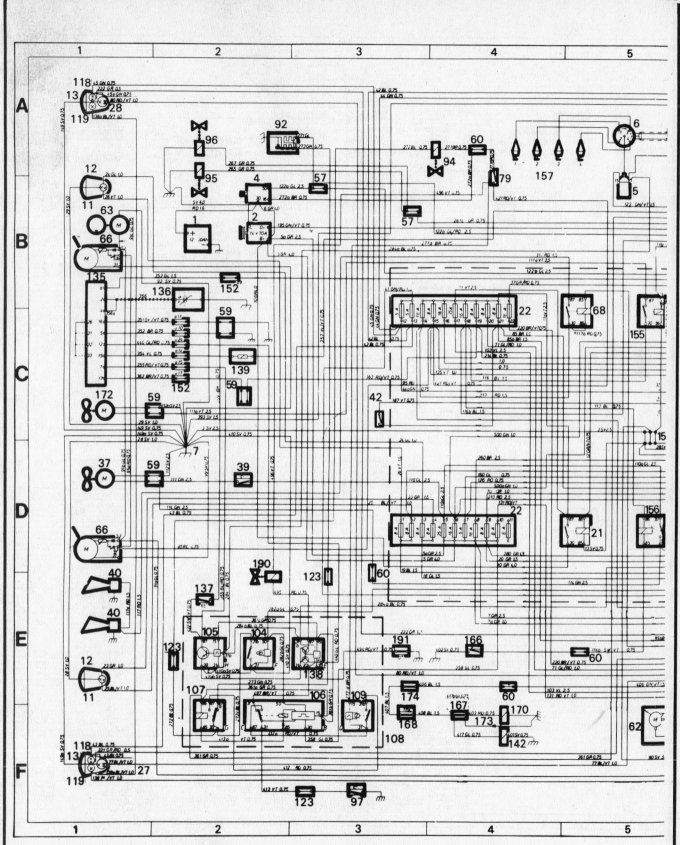

Fig. 10.23 Wiring diagram for 1982 (US) 900 and (Canada) Turbo

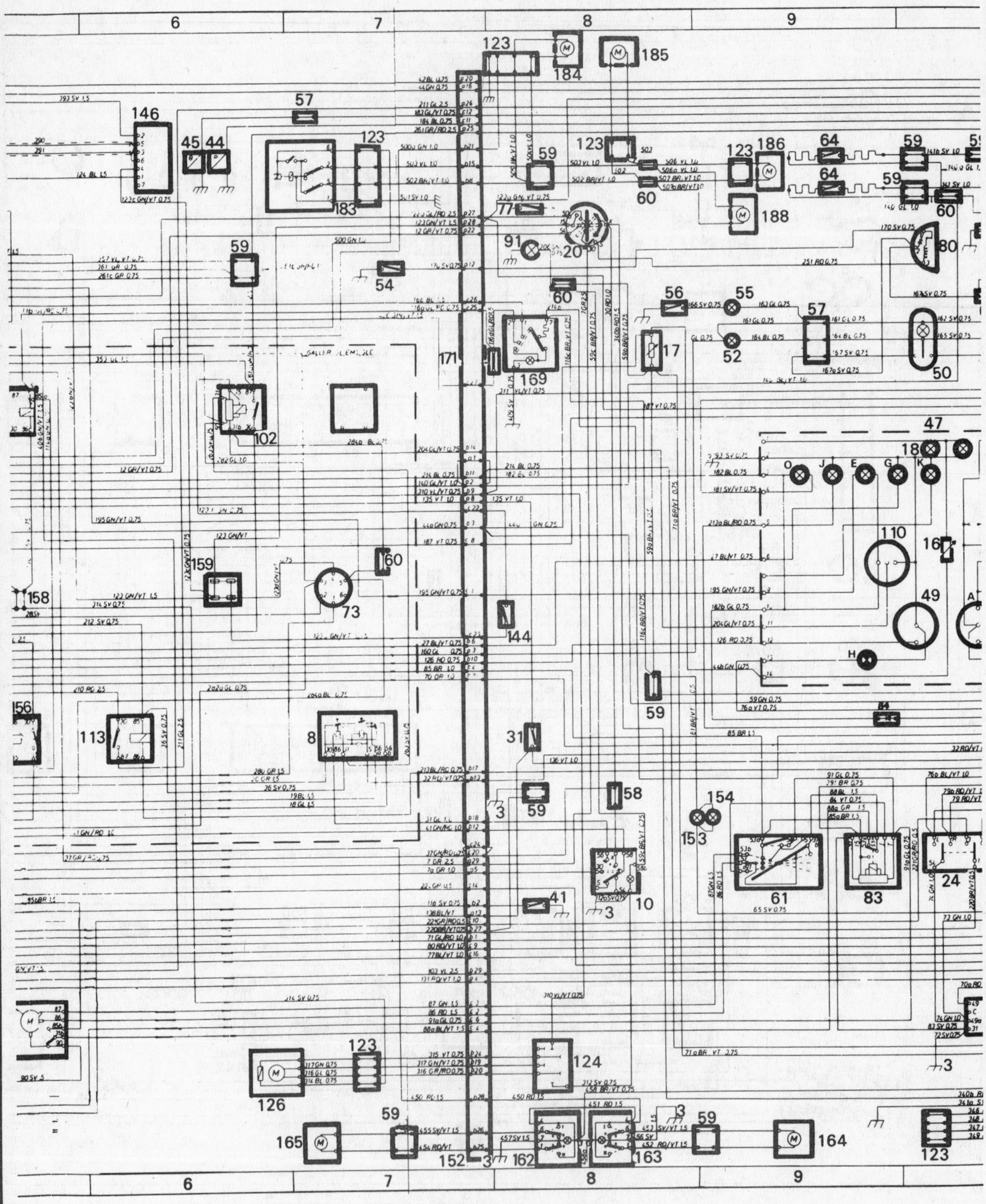

Fig. 10.23 Wiring diagram for 1982 (US) 900 and (Canada) Turbo (continued)

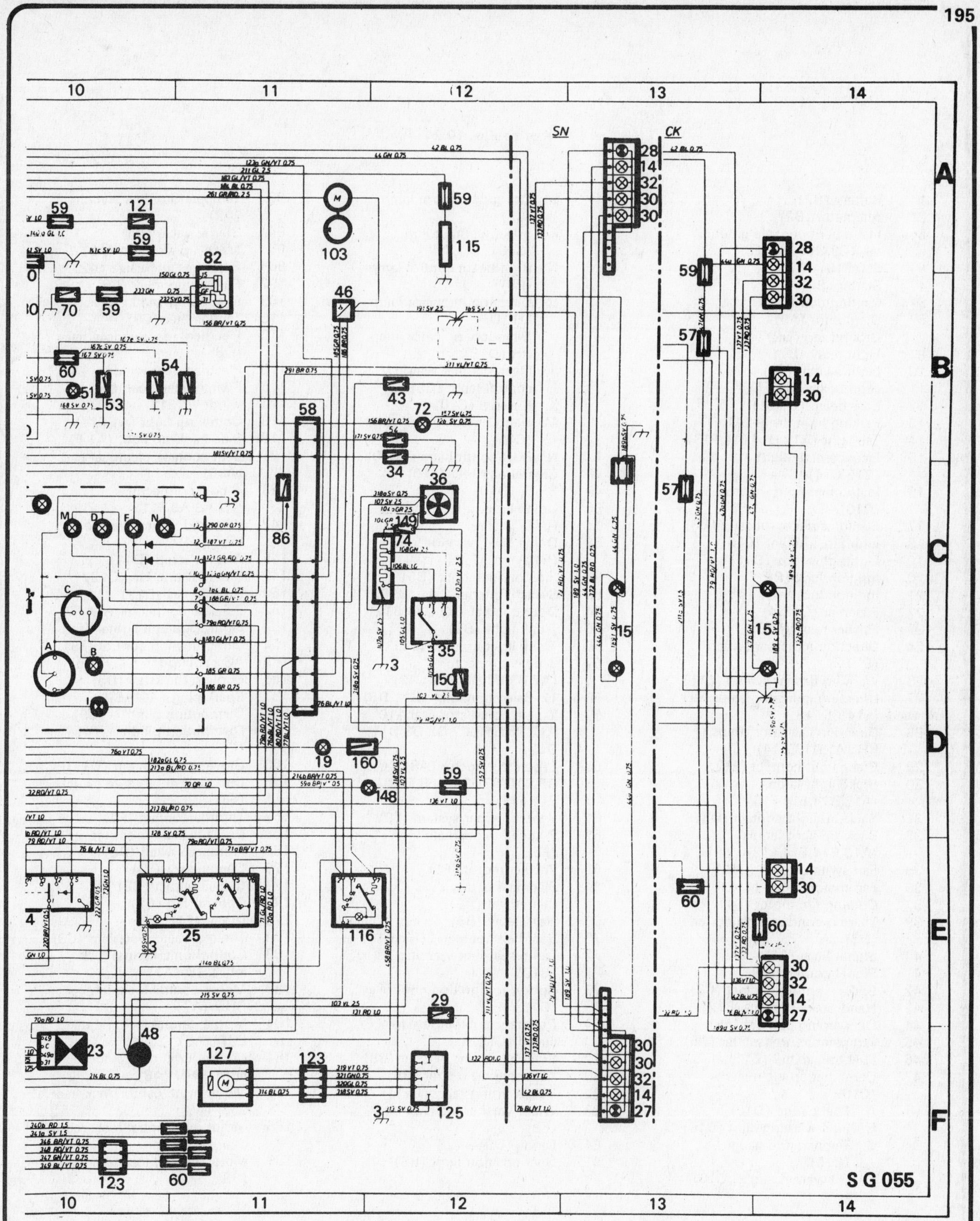

Fig. 10.23 Wiring diagram for 1982 (US) 900 and (Canada) Turbo (continued)

S G 055

Key to Fig. 10.24

1   Battery (B2)
2   Alternator (B2)
3   Instrument console ground tab (C9,C11,D12,E8, E10,F10)
4   Starter (B2)
5   Ignition coil (B5)
6   Distributor (A5)
7   Ground tap (D2)
8   Light relay (D7)
10   Light switch (E8)
11   High beam (B1,E1)
12   Low beam (B1,E1)
13   Parking light, front (A1,F1)
14   Tail light (A13,B14,E14,F13)
15   Licence plate light (C13,C14)
16   Instrument light rheostat (C10)
17   Electric switch, rheostat (B8)
18   Light, instrument (C10)
19   Light, glovebox (D11)
20   Ignition lock (B8)
21   Ignition lock relay (D5)
22   Fusebox (C4,D4)
23   Flasher relay (F10)
24   Direction indicator switch (E10)
25   Warning flasher switch (E11)
27   Direction indicator lamps, LH (E14,F1,F13)
28   Direction indicator lamps, RH (A1,A13,A14)
29   Brake light contact (E12)
30   Brake light lamps (A13,B14,E14,F13)
31   Back-up light contact (D8)
32   Back-up light lamps (A13,E14,E14,F13)
35   Fan switch, cabin (C12)
36   Fan motor, cabin (C12)
37   Cooling fan motor (D1)
39   Thermo contact, cooling fan (D2)
40   Signal horn (E1)
41   Signal contact (E8)
42   Brake warning contact (C3)
43   Hand brake contact (B12)
44   Oil warning contact (A6)
45   Temperature transmitter (A6)
46   Fuel transmitter (B11)
47   Combination instrument (C10):
   A   Fuel gauge (D10)
   B   Fuel warning light (D10)
   C   Temperature gauge (C10)
   D   Oil warning light (C10)

   E   Charging control lamp (C9)
   F   Brake warning light (C10)
   G   High beam control lamp (C9)
   H   Direction indicator lamp LH (D9)
   I   Direction indicator lamp RH (D10)
   J   Electrical rear window control lamp (C9)
   K   Reserve (C10)
   M   Hand brake control lamp (C10)
   N   EGR control lamp (C10)
48   Cigarette lighter (F10)
49   Clock (D10)
50   Dome light, interior centre (B10)
51   Dome light, interior front (B10)
52   Ignition lock light (B9)
53   Switch, interior light (B10)
54   Door contact (B7,B10,B12)
55   Trunk light (B9)
56   Trunk light contact (B8)
57   3-pole connector (A7,B3,B7,B9,B13,C13)
58   12-pole connector (B11,D8)
59   2-pole connector (A8,A10, A12,B6,B13,C2,D2,D8,D11, D12)
60   1-pole connector (A8,A10, B8,B10,C7,E3,E4,E5,E13, E14,F11)
61   Switch, wiper system (E9)
62   2-speed windshield wiper (F5)
63   Washer motor (F1)
64   Electrical pad with thermostat (A9)
68   Horn relay (B5)
70   Seat belt contact, "D" (B10)
72   Lamp seat belt warning (B12)
73   Socket for ignition control (C7)
74   Resistance, cabin fan, low speed (C12)
77   Switch, starting ratchet (B8)
80   Key warning buzzer (B9)
82   Belt warning relay (B11)
83   Wiper washer interval relay (E9)
84   Diode (D9)
91   Gear position light (B8)

92   Temperature time switch (A2)
94   Starter valve (A4)
95   Make-up air valve (A2)
96   Pilot pressure valve (A2)
102   Fuel pump relay (C6)
103   Fuel pump (A11)
110   Tachometer (C9)
113   Electrical rear window relay (D6)
115   Electrical rear window (A12)
116   Switch, electrical rear window (E11)
118   Cornering light (A1,F1)
119   Side back-up light (A1,F1)
121   Seat contact, electrical pad (A10)
123   4-pole connector (A7,A8,A9,F11)
142   Solenoid valve, idle speed raise (F4)
148   Ashtray lamp (D11)
149   Main switch, fan (C12)
150   Switch, AC (D12)
152   29-pole connector (A7-F7)
153   Light, cigarette lighter (E8)
154   Light, heating control (E9)
155   AC cooling fan relay (C5)
156   Cooling fan relay (D5)
157   Spark plug (A4-A5)
158   Distribution plinth – (C5)
159   Distribution plinth + "15" (C6)
160   Glove compartment (D11)
166   Cooling fan pressure switch (E4)
167   Throttle contact (F4)
168   Coolant thermo-contact (F3)
169   Pressure switch (B8)
170   Compressor (F4)
171   Cycle contact (B8)
172   Cooling fan (C1)
173   Diode (F4)
174   Thermo switch, coolant (C3)
183   Control unit, central lock, left, LHD (A7)
183   Motor, central lock, left, RHD (A7)
184   Motor, central lock, right, LHD (A8)
184   Control unit, central lock, right, RHD (A8).
185   Motor right, central lock, rear door (A8)
186   Motor left, central lock, rear door (A9)
188   Motor, central lock, tail gate (B9)

For colour code see key to Fig. 10.19

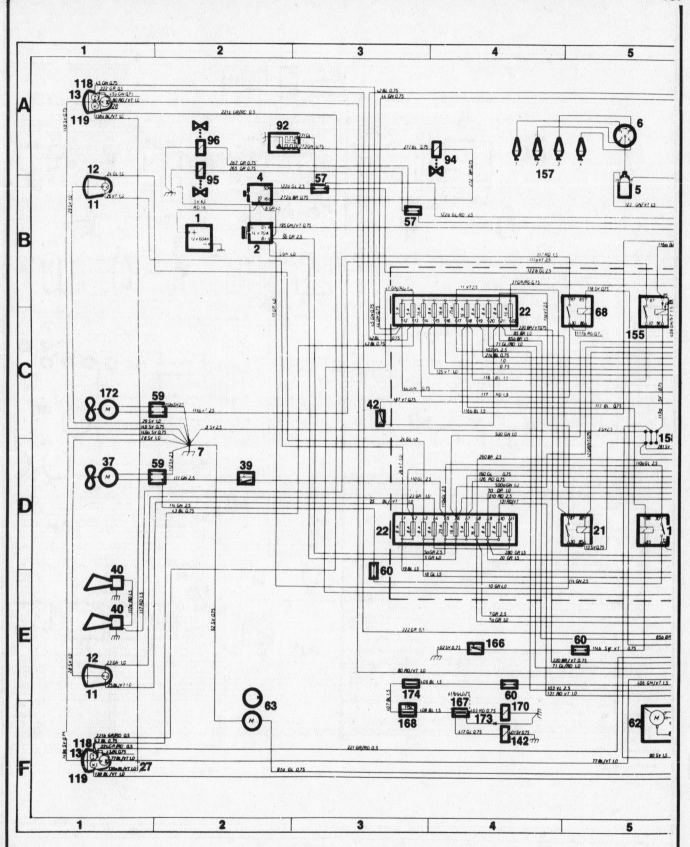

Fig. 10.24 Wiring diagram for 1982 (Canada) 900

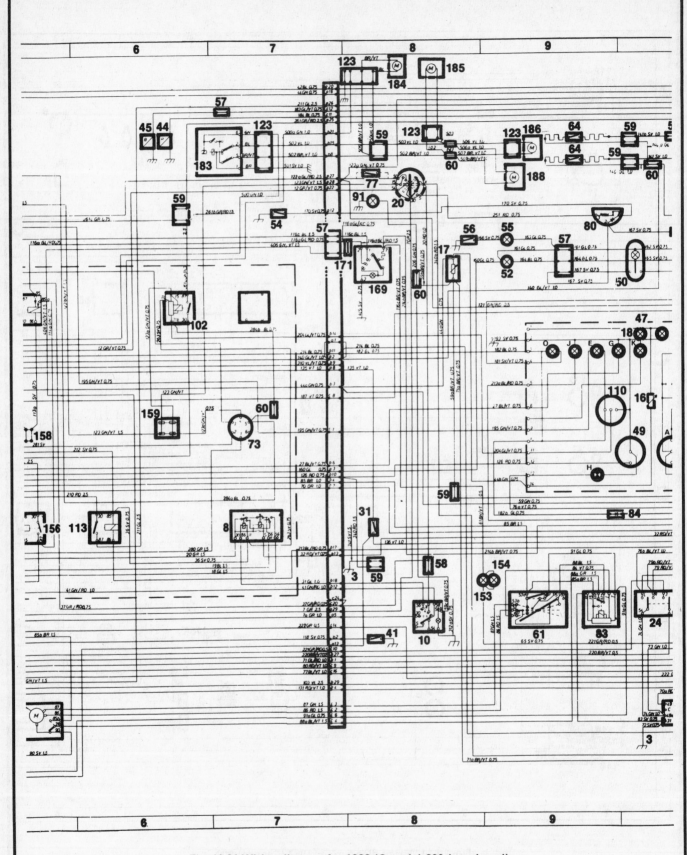

Fig. 10.24 Wiring diagram for 1982 (Canada) 900 (continued)

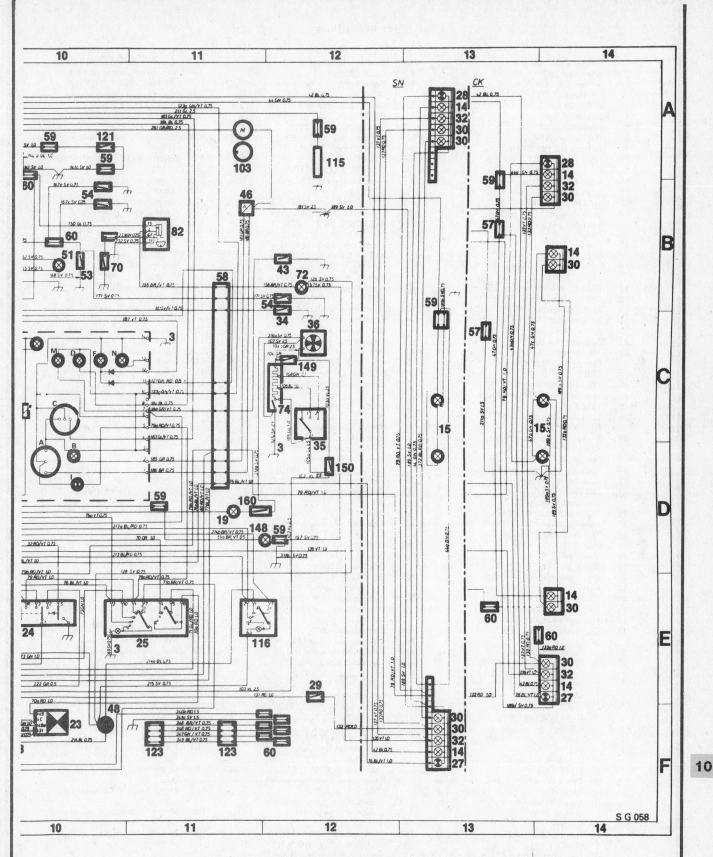

Fig. 10.24 Wiring diagram for 1982 (Canada) 900 (continued)

10

Key to Fig 10.25

1 Battery (B2)
2 Alternator (B2)
3 Instrument console ground tab (C8,C11,D12,E8,E11,F8, F10,F12)
4 Starter (B2)
5 Ignition coil (B5)
6 Distributor (A5)
7 Ground tap (B1,C7,D2,F1)
8 Light relay (D7)
9 Ground, trunk (B13)
10 Light switch (E8)
11 High beam (B1,E1)
12 Low beam (B1,E1)
13 Parking light, front (A1,F1)
14 Tail light (A13,A14,B14, E14,F13)
15 Licence plate light (C13,C14)
16 Instrument light rheostat (C10)
17 Electric switch, rheostat (B8)
18 Light, instrument (C10)
19 Light, glovebox (D11)
20 Ignition lock (B8)
21 Ignition lock relay (D5)
22 Fusebox (C4,D4)
23 Flasher relay (E10)
24 Direction indicator switch (E10)
25 Warning flasher switch (E11)
27 Direction indicator lamps, LH (E14,F1,F13)
28 Direction indicator lamps, RH (A1,A13,A14)
29 Brake light contact (E12)
30 Brake light lamps (A13,B14,E14,F13)
31 Back-up light contact (D8)
32 Back-up light lamps (A13,A14,E14,F13)
35 Fan switch, cabin (C12)
36 Fan motor, cabin (C12)
37 Cooling fan motor (D1)
39 Thermo contact, cooling fan (D2)
40 Signal horn (E1)
41 Signal contact (E8)
42 Brake warning contact (C3)
43 Hand brake contact (B12)
44 Oil warning contact (A6)
45 Temperature transmitter (A6)
46 Fuel transmitter (B11)
47 Combination instrument (C10):
  A Fuel gauge (D10)
  B Fuel warning light (D10)
  C Temperature gauge (C10)
  D Oil warning light (C10)
  E Charging control lamp (C9)
  F Brake warning light (C10)
  G High beam control lamp (C10)
  H Direction indicator lamp LH (D9)
  I Direction indicator lamp RH (D10)
  J Electrical rear window control lamp (C9)
  K Reserve (C10)
  M Hand brake control lamp (C10)
  N EGR control lamp (C10)

48 Cigarette lighter (F10)
49 Clock (D10)
50 Dome light, interior centre (B10)
51 Dome light, interior front (B10)
52 Ignition lock light (B9)
53 Switch, interiorlight (B10)
54 Door contact (B7,B10,B12)
55 Trunk light (B9)
56 Trunk light contact (B8)
57 3-pole connector (B3,B9, B13,C13)
58 12-pole connector (B11,D8)
59 2-pole connector (A10,A12, A13,C2,D2,D8,D12,F7, F9,F13)
60 1-pole connector (A4,B8, B10,C7,D8,E4,E5,E13, F9,F11)
61 Switch, wiper system (E9)
62 2-speed windshield wiper (F5)
63 Washer motor (B1)
64 Electrical pad with thermostat (A9)
65 Ground, handbrake (C10)
66 Headlight wiper motor (B1)
68 Horn relay (B5)
70 Seat belt contact, "F" (B10)
72 Lamp seat belt warning (B12)
73 Socket for ignition control (C7)
74 Resistance, cabin fan, low speed (C12)
77 Switch, starting ratchet (A8)
79 Vacuum switch (A4)
80 Key warning buzzer (B10)
82 Belt warning relay (B11)
83 Wiper washer interval relay (E9)
84 Diode (D10)
85 Extra foglight, mounting prepared (A1,E1)
86 EGR contact (C11)
87 Extra foglight relay, mounting prepared (E3)
88 Extra foglight – switch, mounting prepared (E8)
91 Gear position light (B8)
92 Temperature time swtich (A2)
94 Starter valve (A4)
95 Make-up air valve (A2)
96 Pilot pressure valve (A2)
97 Thermo-contact (F3)
102 Fuel pump relay (C6)
103 Fuel pump (A11)
104 Hot starter relay (E2)
105 Engine speed relay (E2)
106 Time relay (F3)
107 Relay (F2)
108 Relay central (E2-E3)
109 Acceleration enrichment relay (F3)
110 Tachometer (C9)
113 Electrical rear window relay (D6)
115 Electrical rear window (A12)
116 Switch, electrical rear window (E11)
118 Cornering light (A1,F1)
119 Side back-up light (A1,F1)
121 Seat contact, electrical pad (A10)

122 8-pole connector (B13,E13)
123 4-pole connector (A7,A8, A9,E2,E3,F2,F7,F10,F11)
124 Switch, electrical rear view mirror LH (F8)
125 Switch, electrical rear view mirror RH (F12)
126 Electrical rear view mirror LH (F6)
127 Electrical rear view mirror RH (F11)
135 Trigger unit Lambda (C1)
136 Sond (B2)
137 Throttle contact (E2)
139 Timing valve (C2)
142 Solenoid valve, idle speed raise (F4)
144 Pressure switch (D8)
146 Electronic unit, ignition system (A6)
148 Ashtray lamp (D11)
149 Main switch, fan (C12)
150 Switch, AC (D12)
152 29-pole connector (A7-F7,C2)
153 Light, cigarette lighter (E8)
154 Light, heating control (E9)
155 AC cooling fan relay (C5)
156 Cooling fan relay (D5)
157 Spark plug (A4-A5)
158 Distribution plinth – (C5)
159 Distribution plinth – "15" (C6)
160 Glove compartment (D11)
162 Electrical window regulator switch LH (F8)
163 Electrical window regulator switch RH (F8)
164 RH electrical window regulator motor (F9)
165 LH electrical window regulator motor (F7)
166 Cooling fan pressure switch (E4)
167 Throttle contact (F4)
168 Coolant thermo-contact (F3)
169 Pressure switch (B8)
170 Compressor (F4)
171 Cycle contact (B8)
172 Cooling fan (C1)
173 Diode (F4)
174 Thermo switch, coolant (E4)
177 Control unit APC (F6)
178 Sensor (F5)
179 Magnet valve (F4)
180 Pressure transmitter (F6)
181 Switch, sunroof (F9)
182 Motor, sunroof (F10)
183 Control unit, central lock, left, LHD (A7)
183 Motor, central lock, left, RHD (A7)
184 Motor, central lock, right, LHD (AB)
184 Control unit, central lock, right, RHD (A8)
185 Motor right, central lock, rear door (A8)
186 Motor left, central lock, rear door (A9)
188 Motor, central lock, tail gate (A9)
192 Branching connector (A8,F11,F12)

For colour code see key to Fig. 10.19

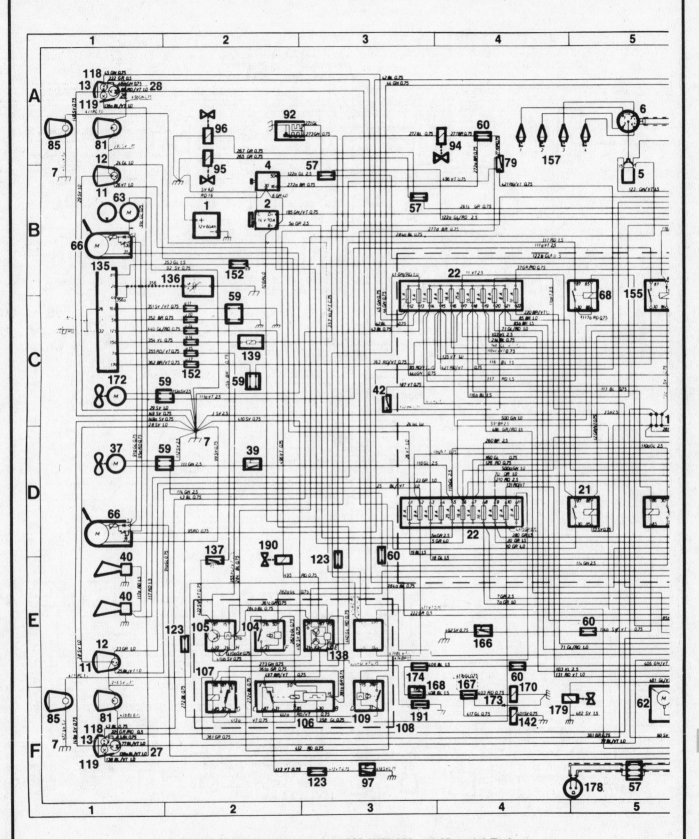

Fig. 10.25 Wiring diagram for 1983 (US) 900 and (Canada) Turbo

202

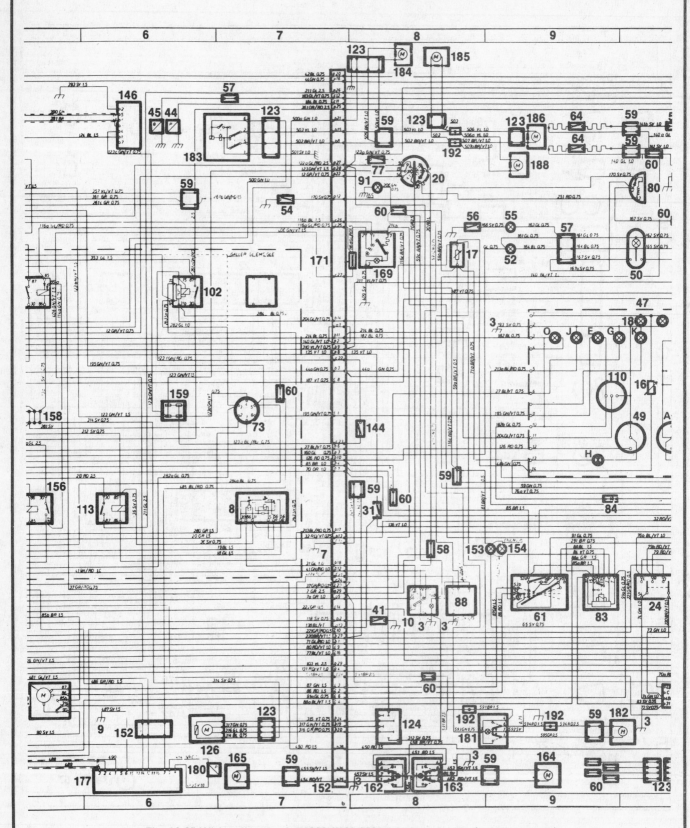

Fig. 10.25 Wiring diagram for 1983 (US) 900 and (Canada) Turbo (continued)

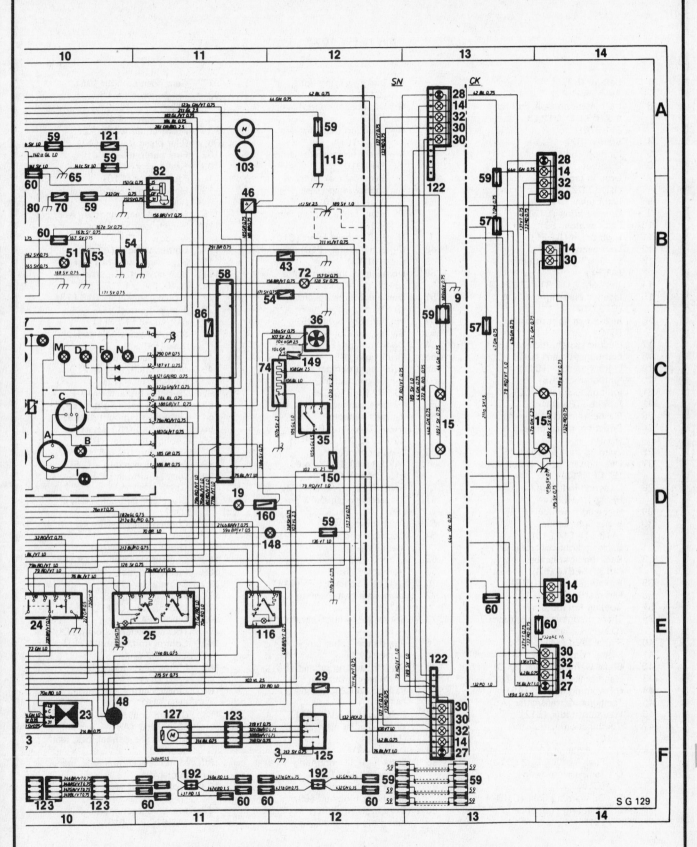

Fig. 10.25 Wiring diagram for 1983 (US) 900 and (Canada) Turbo (continued)

Key to Fig. 10.26

1 Battery (B2)
2 Alternator (B2)
3 Instrument console ground tab (C9,C11,D12,E8, E11,F10)
4 Starter (B2)
5 Ignition coil (B5)
6 Distributor (A5)
7 Ground tap (B1,B2,D2,D7,F1)
8 Light relay (D7)
9 Ground trunk (B13)
10 Light switch (E8)
11 High beam (B1,E1)
12 Low beam (A1,E1)
13 Parking light, front outer (A1,F1)
14 Tail light (A13,B14,E14,F13)
15 Licence plate light (C13,C14)
16 Instrument light rheostat (C10)
17 Electric switch, rheostat (B9)
18 Light, instrument (C10)
19 Light, glovebox (D11)
20 Ignition lock (B8)
21 Ignition lock relay (D5)
22 Fusebox (B4,D4)
23 Flasher relay (F11)
24 Direction indicator switch (E10)
25 Warning flasher switch (E11)
27 Direction indicator lamps, LH (E14,F1,F13)
28 Direction indicator lamps, RH (A1,A13,B14)
29 Brake light contact (E12)
30 Brake light lamps (A13,B14,E14,F13)
31 Back-up light contact (D8)
32 Back-up light lamps (A13,B14,E14,F13)
35 Fan switch, cabin (C12)
36 Fan motor, cabin (C12)
37 Cooling fan motor (D1)
39 Thermo contact, cooling fan (D2)
40 Signal horn (E1)
41 Signal contact (E8)
42 Brake warning contact (C3)
43 Hand brake contact (B12)
44 Oil warning contact (A6)
45 Temperature transmitter (A6)
46 Fuel transmitter (B12)
47 Combination instrument (C10):
   A Fuel gauge (D10)
   B Fuel warning light (D10)
   C Temperature gauge (C10)
   D Oil warning light (C10)
   E Charging control lamp (C10)

F Brake warning light (C11)
G High beam control lamp (C10)
H Direction indicator lamp LH (D10)
I Direction indicator lamp RH (D10)
J Electrical rear window control lamp (C9)
K Reserve (C10)
M Hand brake control lamp (C10)
N EGR control lamp (C10)
48 Cigarette lighter (F10)
49 Clock (D10)
50 Dome light, interior centre (B10)
51 Dome light, interior front (B10)
52 Ignition lock light (B9)
53 Switch, interior light (B10)
54 Door contact (B7,B11,B12)
55 Trunk light (B9)
56 Trunk light contact (B9)
57 3-pole connector (B3,B7,B9,B13,C13)
58 12-pole connector (B11,D8)
59 2-pole connector (A8,A10,A12,B6,B13, C2,D2,D11,D12,F13)
60 1-pole connector (A7,B8,B10,C7,E3,E4,E5, E13,E14,F10,F11,F12)
61 Switch, wiper system (E9)
62 2-speed windshield wiper (F5)
63 Washer motor (F2)
64 Electrical pad with thermostat (A10)
65 Ground, handbrake (A10)
68 Horn relay (B5)
70 Seat belt contact, "F" (B11)
72 Lamp seat belt warning (B12)
73 Socket for ignition control (C7)
76 Resistance, cabin fan, low speed (C12)
77 Switch, starting ratchet (B8)
80 Key warning buzzer (B9)
81 Parking light, front inner (A1,F1)
82 Belt warning relay (B11)
83 Wiper washer interval relay (E9)
84 Diode (D9)
85 Extra foglight, mounting prepared (A1,E1)
87 Extra foglight relay, mounting prepared (E3)
88 Extra foglight switch, mounting prepared (E8)

91 Gear position light (B8)
92 Temperature time switch (A2)
94 Starter valve (A4)
95 Make-up air valve (A2)
96 Pilot presure valve (A2)
102 Fuel pump relay (C6)
103 Fuel pump (A11)
110 Tachometer (C10)
113 Electrical rear window relay (D6)
115 Electrical rear window (A12)
116 Switch, electrical rear window (E12)
118 Cornering light (A1,F1)
119 Side back-up light (A1,F1)
121 Seat contact, electrical pad (A10)
122 8-pole connector (B13,E13)
123 4-pole connector (A7,A8,A9,F10,F11)
142 Solenoid valve, idle speed raise (F4)
148 Ashtray lamp (D11)
149 Main switch, fan (C12)
150 Switch, AC (D12)
152 29-pole connector (A7-F7)
153 Light, cigarette lighter (E9)
154 Light, heating control (E9)
155 AC cooling fan relay (C5)
156 Cooling fan relay (D5)
157 Spark plug (A4-A5)
158 Distribution plinth – (C5)
159 Distribution plinth + "15" (C6)
160 Glove compartment switch (D12)
166 Cooling fan pressure switch (E4)
167 Throttle contact (F4)
168 Coolant thermo-contact (F3)
169 Pressure switch (B8)
170 Compressor (F4)
171 Cycle contact (B8)
172 Cooling fan (C1)
173 Diode (F4)
174 Thermo switch, coolant (E3)
183 Control unit, central lock, left, LHD (A7)
183 Motor, central lock, left, RHD (A7)
184 Motor, central lock, right, LHD (A8)
184 Control unit, central lock, right, RHD (A8)
185 Motor right, central lock, rear door (A8)
186 Motor left, central lock, rear door (A9)
188 Motor, cental lock, tail gate (B9)
192 Branching connector, (A9,B10,F11,F12)

For colour code see key to Fig. 10.19

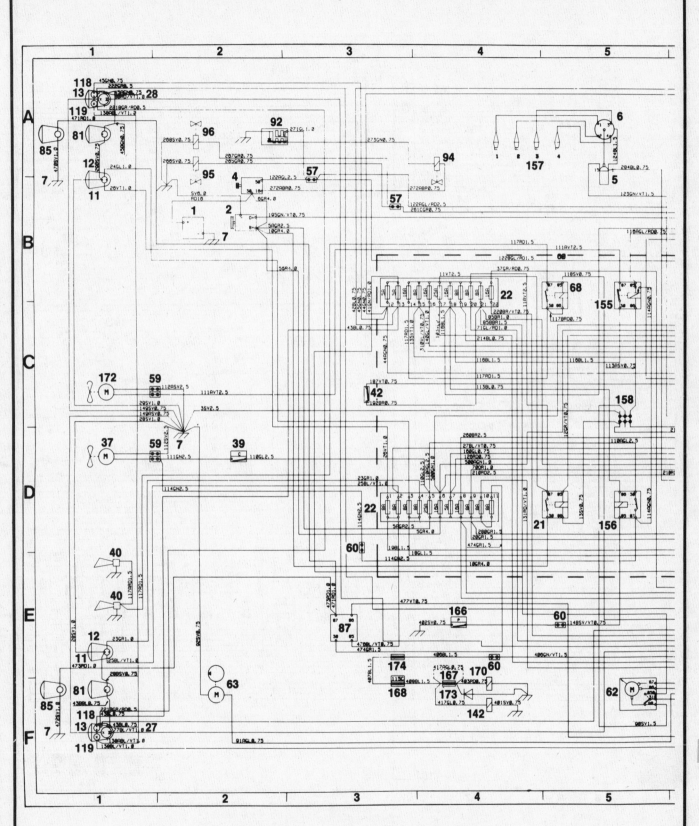

Fig. 10.26 Wiring diagram for 1983 (Canada) 900

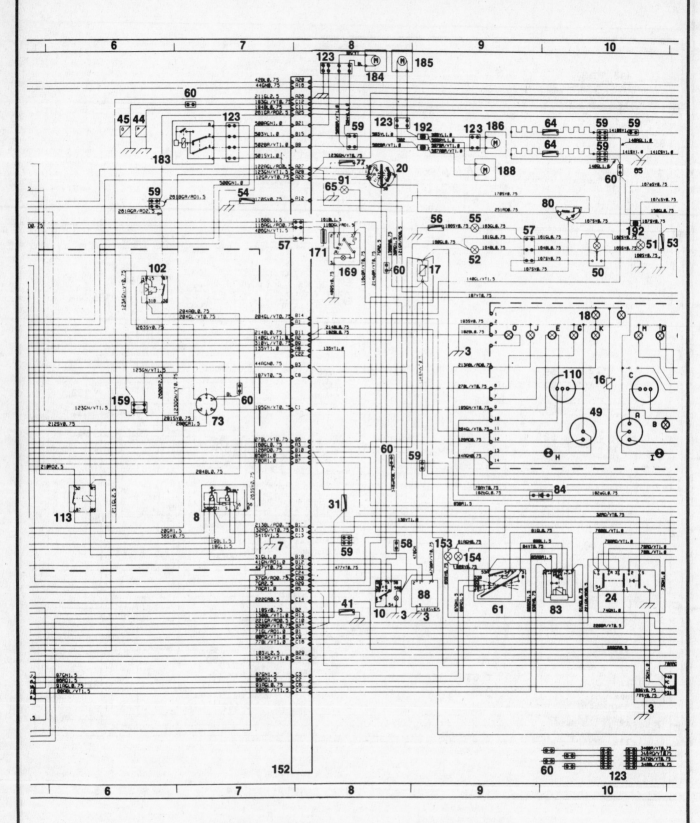

Fig. 10.26 Wiring diagram for 1983 (Canada) 900 (continued)

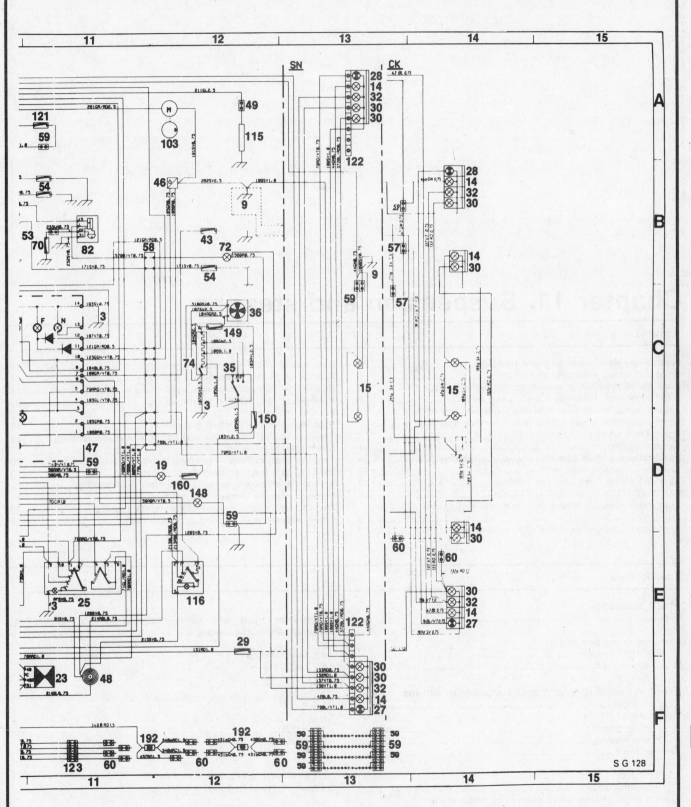

Fig. 10.26 Wiring diagram for 1982 (Canada) 900 (continued)

10

Chapter 11 Suspension and steering

Contents

Specifications

Front suspension

Type .... Independent, upper and lower control arms, coil springs, and telescopic shock absorbers

Front coil spring free length:
Pre-1981 models .... 14.6 in (370 mm)
1981 on models .... 14.7 in (373 mm)

Front wheel alignment and suspension angles

King pin inclination .... $11.5 \pm 1°$
Caster angle:
Manual steering .... $+1° \pm 0.5°$
Power steering .... $+2° \pm 0.5°$
Camber angle .... $+0.5° \pm 0.5°$
Toe-in:
99 models .... 0.04 in $\pm$ 0.04 in (1.0 mm $\pm$ 1.0 mm)
900 models .... 0.08 in $\pm$ 0.04 in (2.0 mm $\pm$ 1.0 mm)
Turning angle of inner wheel (with rotor wheel at 20°):
99 models .... $20.5° + 1°$
900 models .... $20.75° \pm 0.5°$

Rear suspension

Type .... Rigid rear axle on trailing links, coil springs, telescopic shock absorbers, transverse location bar (Panhard rod), and longitudinal torsion links

Rear coil spring free length
Colour code:

Green	15.08 in (383 mm) on 99 models
	12.13 in (308 mm) on 900 models
Yellow	12.95 in (329 mm)
White	12.40 in (315 mm)
Blue	12.76 in (324 mm)
Light blue	12.72 in (323 mm)
White/Light green/Black	12.24 in (311 mm)

Rear wheel alignment
Toe-in:

Total	0.08 in to 0.24 in (2.0 mm to 6.0 mm)
Each side	0.04 in to 0.12 in (1.0 mm to 3.0 mm)
Camber	-0.5° ± 0.25° (ie negative camber)

Steering

Type	Rack and pinion, collapsible (900 models only) steering column with intermediate shaft and universal joints, manual or power-assisted
Number of turns lock-to-lock:	
EMS models	3.5
Manual steering models	4.2
Power steering models	3.6
Manual steering gear plunger clearance	0.002 to 0.006 in (0.05 to 0.15 mm)
Manual steering gear pinion torque:	
99 models	10 to 18 lbf in (1.1 to 2.0 Nm)
900 models	7 to 15 lbf in (0.8 to 1.7 Nm)
Power steering fluid capacity	0.85 Imp qt; 0.79 US qt; 0.75 litre

Wheels

Type	Steel or light alloy (according to model)
Size	4½J x 15, 5J x 15, 5½J x 15, 135 TR x 390
Tyres	155 SR 15, 165 SR 15, 175/70 HR 15, 180/65 HR 390, 185/65 SR 15, 195/60 HR 15T

Tyre pressures lbf/in² (bar)

	Front	Rear
1 to 3 persons, to 100 mph	27 (1.9)	27 (1.9)
1 to 3 persons, over 100 mph	32 (2.2)	35 (2.4)
More than 3 persons	32 (2.2)	35 (2.4)

Torque wrench settings

	lbf ft	Nm
Front suspension		
Brake disc	22 to 36	30 to 50
Upper control arm brackets	54 to 66	75 to 90
Lower control arm brackets	70 to 77	100 to 120
Rear suspension		
Hub nuts (1982 on models only)	210	300
Steering		
Tie-rod end locknut	44 to 60	60 to 80
Tie-rod end to steering knuckle	35 to 44	50 to 60
Inner balljoint locknut	30 to 36	45 to 50
Cover screws	12 to 15	16 to 20
Steering gear	44 to 60	60 to 80
Intermediate shaft clamp screw	26 to 30	35 to 42
Steering wheel nut:		
Manual steering	22	30
Power steering	19	27
Power steering hydraulic unions	15 to 25	20 to 34
Tie-rod inner balljoint (enclosed)	80 to 94	110 to 130
Wheels		
Roadwheel nuts	65 to 80	88 to 108

1 General description

The front suspension is of independent type incorporating upper and lower control arms. The coil springs are located on top of the upper control arms, and the telescopic shock absorbers are attached to the lower control arms and bodyframe. The steering knuckle incorporates upper and lower balljoints. The suspension mounting points are rubber seated.

The rear suspension incorporates a rigid rear axle on trailing links. The telescopic shock absorbers and coil springs are located on top of the trailing links. Lateral movement of the axle is controlled by a transverse bar (Panhard rod), and braking torque is controlled by longitudinal torsion links located on the stub axle extensions and the bodyframe.

Rack and pinion steering is fitted which may be either manually operated or power assisted. On 900 models the steering column is of the safety type incorporating a collapsible outer column and telescopic

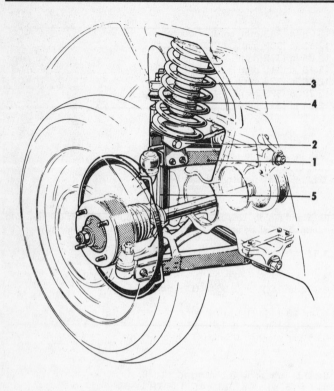

Fig. 11.1 Phantom view of the front suspension (Sec 1)

1   Upper control arm
2   Lower spring support
3   Coil spring
4   Rubber buffer
5   Shock absorber

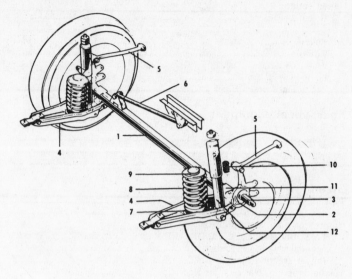

Fig. 11.2 View of the rear suspension (Sec 1)

1	Rear axle	7	Spring seat
2	End piece	8	Coil spring
3	Stub axle	9	Spring insulator
4	Spring links	10	Rubber buffer
5	Rear links	11	Stop
6	Panhard rod	12	Shock absorber

inner column (photo). The intermediate shaft incorporates two universal joints.

2   Routine maintenance

1   Every 10 000 miles (15 000 km) on UK models or 7500 miles (12 000 km) on North American models check the steering and suspension balljoints for wear. Also check the rubber bellows and dust covers on the tie-rods and driveshafts for damage.
2   At the same time check and if necessary top up the power steering fluid level, and also check and adjust the front wheel alignment.
3   Examine the tyres for damage and check the tread depth.
4   Check all the suspension and steering nuts and bolts for tightness.

3   Front shock absorber – removal, testing and refitting

1   Jack up the front of the car and support it on axle stands. Chock the rear wheels and remove the relevant front wheel.
2   Position a trolley jack beneath the outer end of the lower control arm and raise the suspension to relieve the pressure on the shock absorber mountings.
3   Unscrew the shock absorber mounting nuts and withdraw the unit from the car. On 99 models the upper mounting bolt is located in the wheel housing, but on 900 models it is located in the engine compartment (photos). Recover the washers and mounting rubbers as applicable.
4   Mount the shock absorber vertically in a vice and move the upper section through its full stroke. The resistance should be even throughout the stroke – if not, renew the shock absorber.
5   Refitting is a reversal of the removal procedure, however on the hydraulic type first bleed the air from the shock absorber by operating it through its full stroke several times while mounted vertically in a vice. Refer to Section 10 if disposing of the pneumatic (gas filled) shock absorber.

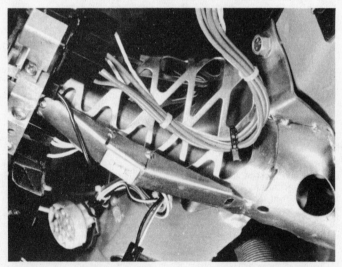

1.1 Showing collapsible outer steering column fitted to 900 models

4   Front wheel bearings – renewal

1   Remove the driveshaft as described in Chapter 8.
2   On 1981 on models use a metal tube to drive the hub from the wheel bearing. Note that this procedure renders the wheel bearing unserviceable so it must not be re-used. Use a puller to remove the inner race from the hub.
3   Extract the circlip(s) from the steering knuckle then drive out the wheel bearing using a metal tube or soft metal drift.
4   Clean the components with paraffin and wipe dry. Check that the

3.3A Front shock absorber upper mounting (900 models)

3.3B Front shock absorber lower mounting

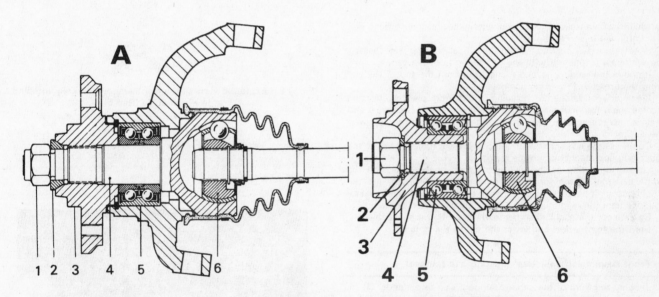

Fig. 11.3 Cross-section of the front wheel bearings on A pre-1981 models and B 1981 on models (Sec 49)

| 1 | Locknut | 3 | Hub | 5 | Wheel bearing |
| 2 | Washer | 4 | Driveshaft | 6 | CV joint |

bearing seating surfaces in the steering knuckle and on the driveshaft are not damaged.

5   Pack the new bearing with a molybdenum disulphide based grease and also smear some grease on the bearing recess surfaces.

6   On 1981 on models fit the circlip to the inner groove in the steering knuckle.

7   Support the steering knuckle then drive in the new wheel bearing using a metal tube on the outer race. Fit the outer circlip.

8   On 1981 on models support the bearing inner race then drive in the hub using a wooden mallet.

9   Refit the driveshaft as described in Chapter 8.

5   Front coil spring – removal and refitting

1   Jack up the front of the car and support it on axle stands. Chock the rear wheels and remove the relevant front wheel.

2   Using a proper spring compressor tool compress the coil spring to give approximately 1.5 in (38 mm) clearance at the top (photo). If necessary, extra clearance can be obtained by supporting the lower

Fig. 11.4 Using a spring compressor on the front coil spring
(Sec 5)

11

5.2 Front coil spring

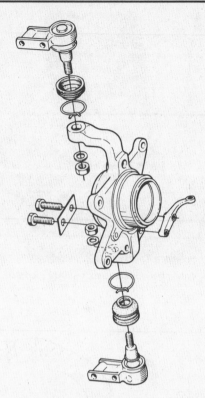

Fig. 11.5 Exploded view of the front suspension balljoints and
steering knuckle (Sec 6)

control arm with a trolley jack, disconnecting the shock absorber lower
mounting, then lowering the jack.
3   Prise the upper steel cone from the wheel housing if necessary,
then withdraw it together with the coil spring from the car.
4   Remove the steel cone and rubber ring from the top of the coil
spring then release the spring compressor tool.
5   Clean the components including the spring pivot plate, and
examine them for wear and damage. Renew them as necessary and
obtain a new rubber ring. The spring pivot plate bush can be renewed
if necessary.
6   Compress the coil spring with the compressor tool, and locate the
rubber ring and steel cone on the top.
7   Locate the spring on the pivot plate then gradually release the
compressor tool at the same time guiding the steel cone into the
wheel housing. If the pivot plate has been removed, the bolt should be
left loose until the compressor has been removed, then tightened.
8   Re-connect the shock absorber lower mounting if applicable.
9   Refit the front wheel and lower the car to the ground.

6   Front suspension balljoints – testing and renewal

1   Jack up the front of the car and support it on axle stands. Chock
the rear wheels and remove the front wheels.
2   Position a trolley jack under the outer end of the lower control arm
and raise the suspension until a hardwood or metal block can be
inserted beneath the upper control arm and the bodyframe (photo).
Lower the jack.
3   Using water pump pliers or a pair of grips, compress the upper and
lower balljoints in turn and check that the endfloat does not exceed
0.08 in (2.0 mm). Using a lever against the control arms check that the
side-to-side movement of the balljoint does not exceed 0.04 in (1.0
mm) (photos). If necessary renew the balljoints as follows.
4   Unscrew the shock absorber lower mounting nut and disconnect
the shock absorber.
5   Unscrew the balljoint nut and use a balljoint separator tool to
release the balljoint from the steering knuckle (photo). Support the
steering knuckle on an axle stand when removing the upper balljoint.
6   Unbolt the balljoint from the control arm noting which way round
the bolt heads are fitted.
7   Fit the new balljoint(s) using a reversal of the removal procedure,
but use new self-locking nuts on the control arm bolts. Tighten the
nuts to the specified torque.

7   Front suspension upper control arm – removal and refitting

1   If removing the left-hand side control arm, first remove the
engine/transmission unit as described in Chapter 1.

Fig. 11.6 Using a separator tool to release the upper balljoint from
the steering knuckle (Sec 6)

2   Remove the front coil spring as described in Section 5.
3   On 99 models remove the shock absorber with reference to
Section 3.
4   Support the lower control arm with a trolley jack, then unscrew
and remove the bolt securing the upper balljoint and spring seat to the
upper control arm. Note which way round the bolt heads are fitted.
5   Unscrew the bolts from the control arm inner bearing brackets,
then withdraw the control arm from the car (photo). Note the location
and number of spacers beneath the brackets.

6.2 Inserting a metal block beneath the front suspension upper control arm

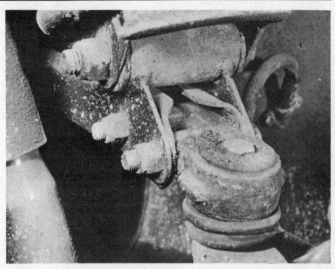

6.3A Front suspension upper balljoint

6.3B Front suspension lower balljoint

6.5 Showing front suspension lower balljoint nut

7.5 Front suspension upper control arm mountings

6   Mark the bearing brackets for position then unscrew the nuts and remove the washers and brackets.

7   Using a long bolt, metal tube, and washers press the rubber bushes from the brackets.

8   Clean all the components and check them for damage and distortion. Renew the parts as necessary. Obtain new rubber bushes.

9   Dip the new rubber bushes in soapy water then press them into the brackets using the method described in paragraph 7.

10 Fit the brackets to the control arm together with the washers and nuts. Position the brackets at an angle of 52° (99 models) or 62° (900 models) to the control arm then tighten the nuts to the specified torque. Note that the control arm is symmetrical so make sure that the brackets are fitted correctly.

11 Fit the control arm together with the spacers, and insert and tighten the bolts.

12 Locate the upper balljoint and spring seat on the control arm then insert and tighten the bolts.

13 On 99 models refit the shock absorber with reference to Section 3.

14 Refit the front coil spring as described in Section 5.

15 Refit the engine/transmission unit if applicable as described in Chapter 1.

16 Check and if necessary adjust the front wheel alignment.

11

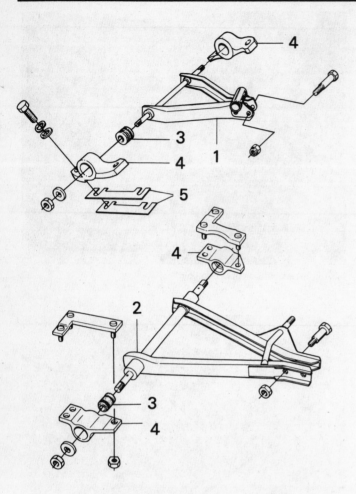

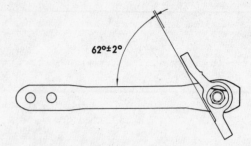

Fig. 11.8 Front suspension upper control arm bracket fitting angle
– 900 model shown (Sec 7)

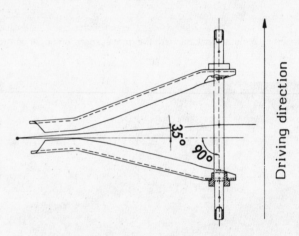

Fig. 11.9 Showing the asymmetrical design of the front
suspension upper control arm (Sec 7)

**Fig. 11.7 Exploded view of the front suspension control arms
(Secs 7 and 8)**

1	Upper control arm	4	Bearings
2	Lower control arm	5	Spacers
3	Rubber bushing		

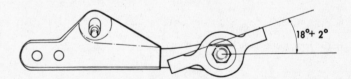

Fig. 11.10 Front suspension lower control arm bracket fitting
angle (Sec 8)

8 Front suspension lower control arm – removal and refitting

1   Jack up the front of the car and support it on axle stands. Chock
the rear wheels and remove the front wheel.
2   Position a trolley jack under the outer end of the lower control arm
and raise the suspension until a hardwood or metal block can be
inserted beneath the upper control arm and the bodyframe. Lower the
jack (photo).
3   Unscrew the shock absorber lower mounting nut and disconnect
the shock absorber.
4   Unscrew and remove the bolts securing the lower balljoint to the
lower control arm. Note which way round the bolt heads are fitted
(photo).
5   Unscrew the nuts from the control arm inner bearing brackets and
lower the control arm from the underframe (photo). If necessary
remove the upper brackets.
6   Mark the bearing brackets for position then unscrew the nuts and
remove the washer and brackets.
7   Using a long bolt, metal tube, and washers press the rubber
bushes from the brackets.
8   Clean all the components and check them for damage and
distortion. Renew the parts as necessary and obtain new rubber
bushes.
9   Dip the new rubber bushes in soapy water then press them into
the brackets using the method described in paragraph 7.
10   Fit the brackets to the control arm together with the washers and
nuts. Position the brackets at an angle of 18° to the control arm then
tighten the nuts to the specified torque.

11   Fit the control arm to the underframe then insert and tighten the
bolts.
12   Locate the balljoint in the lower control arm then insert and
tighten the bolts.
13   Re-connect the shock absorber then fit the washer and nut, and
tighten the nut.
14   Raise the front suspension with a trolley jack and remove the
hardwood or metal block.
15   Refit the front wheel and lower the car to the ground.
16   Check and if necessary adjust the front wheel alignment.

9 Rear shock absorber (hydraulic) – removal, testing and refitting

1   Jack up the rear of the car and support the bodyframe with axle
stands. Apply the handbrake and remove the rear wheel.
2   Position a trolley jack beneath the rear end of the trailing link, and
raise it slightly to relieve the tension on the shock absorber bolts.
3   Working in the rear luggage compartment, unscrew the nuts from

8.2 Front suspension lower control arm

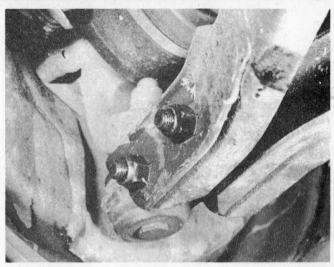

8.4 Lower balljoint to control arm bolts

8.5 Front suspension lower control arm inner bearing brackets

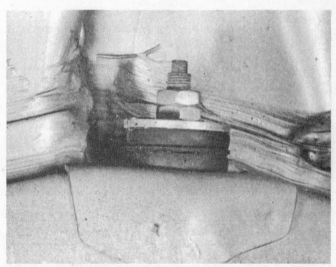

9.3 Rear shock absorber upper mounting

the top of the shock absorber and if necessary remove the upper mounting rubber and washer (photo).

4   Unscrew and remove the lower mounting bolt, and withdraw the shock absorber from the car.

5   Mount the shock absorber vertically in a vice and move the upper section through its full stroke. The resistance should be even throughout the stroke – if not, renew the shock absorber.

6   Refitting is a reversal of removal, however first bleed the air from the shock absorber by operating it through its full stroke several times while mounted vertically in a vice.

10 Rear shock absorber (pneumatic) – removal and refitting

1   Jack up the rear of the car and support the bodyframe with axle stands. Apply the handbrake and remove the rear wheel.

2   Place an additional axle stand under the rear axle near the shock absorber to be removed.

3   Position a trolley jack beneath the rear end of the trailing link, and raise it slightly to relieve the tension on the shock absorber bolts.

4   Working in the rear luggage compartment unscrew the nuts from the top of the shock absorber and if necessary remove the upper mounting rubber and washer.

11

Fig. 11.11 Removing the pneumatic rear shock absorber (Sec 10)

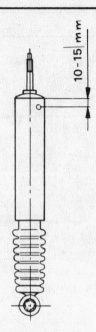

Fig. 11.12 Depressing hole location on pneumatic rear shock absorber with gas chamber at top (Sec 10)

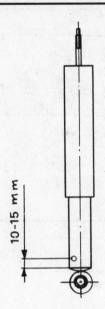

Fig. 11.13 Depressing hole location on pneumatic rear shock absorber with gas chamber at bottom (Sec 10)

5   Unscrew and remove the lower mounting bolt and also the bolt securing the trailing link to the rear axle.
6   Lower the trailing link and withdraw the shock absorber.
7   The pressure of the gas in the shock absorber is between 435 and 580 lbf/in² (30 and 40 bar) and therefore the unit should not be heated or damaged. To render the unit safe a 0.080 in (2.0 mm) hole should be drilled in the location shown in Fig. 11.12 or 11.13 but do this only in a well ventilated area and wear protective clothing and goggles.
8   Refitting is a reversal of removal.

11 Rear wheel hub and bearings – removal and refitting

1   Remove the rear brake disc as described in Chapter 9.
2   Prise off the hub grease cap then lever up the locking collar and unscrew the hub nut (photos). On 1982 on models the nut is tightened to a high torque and therefore a long socket extension will be required. Remove the washer.

3   Pull the hub from the stub axle using a puller if necessary.
4   Note that on 1981 on models the wheel bearings and oil seal form an integral part of the hub, therefore if the wheel bearings are worn on these models the complete hub must be renewed. However on pre-1982 models follow the procedure given in paragraphs 5 to 9.
5   Prise the oil seal from the hub and remove both bearing inner races.
6   Support the hub on a block of wood then use a soft metal drift through the special cut-outs to drive out the bearing outer races.
7   Clean the components in paraffin and wipe dry then check them for wear and damage. In particular check the surfaces of the tapered rollers and bearing races. Obtain a new oil seal and if necessary new bearings.
8   Drive the inner races into the hub using metal tubing then half fill the space between the races with a molybdenum disulphide based grease.
9   Fit the inner bearing inner race then smear a little grease on the outer periphery and lip of the oil seal and drive it into the hub until flush using a block of wood.

11.2A Rear wheel hub

11.2B Removing the rear wheel hub grease cap

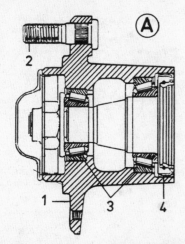
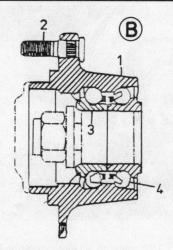

Fig. 11.14 Cross-section of the rear wheel hub and bearings on A pre-1982 models and B 1982 on models (Sec 11)

1	Hub	3	Bearings
2	Wheel stud	4	Oil seal

10 Clean the stub axle and smear a little grease on the sealing surface, then slide on the hub.

11 Fit the outer bearing inner race followed by the washer and nut.

12 On pre-1982 models tighten the nut to a torque of 36 lbf ft (49 Nm) then completely unscrew it and finally tighten it to 1.4 to 2.9 lbf ft (2 to 4 Nm). Lock the nut by peening the collar into the groove in the stub axle.

13 On 1982 on models tighten the nut to the specified torque, then lock it by peening the collar into the groove in the stub axle (photo).

14 Fill the grease cap with grease and tap it into the hub.

15 Refit the brake disc, caliper and wheel as described in Chapter 9.

12 Rear coil spring – removal and refitting

1 Jack up the rear of the car and support the bodyframe with axle stands. Apply the handbrake and remove the rear wheel (photo).

2 Position a trolley jack beneath the trailing link directly under the coil spring and raise it slightly.

3 Unscrew and remove the shock absorber lower mounting bolt and also unscrew the mounting brackets nuts from the front of the trailing link (photo).

4 Support the rear axle near the coil spring on an axle stand. This is necessary to prevent straining the hydraulic brake lines.

11.13 Tightening the rear wheel hub nut

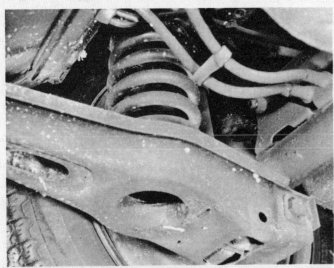

12.1 Rear coil spring location

12.3 Rear suspension trailing link front mounting

11

Fig. 11.15 Removing the rear coil spring (Sec 12)

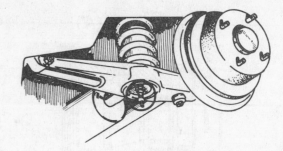

Fig. 11.16 Showing location of the auxiliary pneumatic spring air valve on the rear suspension (Sec 12)

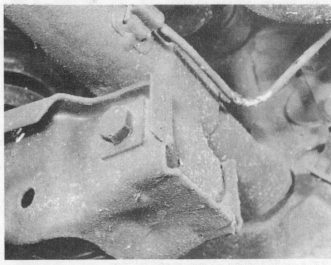

13.7 Rear suspension trailing link mounting on the rear axle

5   Lower the trailing link and withdraw the coil spring together with the upper and lower seats.
6   On models fitted with auxiliary pneumatic springs, release the air by unscrewing the valve then remove the unit from the trailing link.
7   Check the coil spring and seats for wear and damage, and check the free length with the dimension given in the Specifications. Renew the parts as necessary.
8   Refitting is a reversal of removal. Where applicable the auxiliary pneumatic springs should be inflated to a pressure of 28.5 lbf/in^2 (2.0 bar).

13 Rear axle – removal and refitting

1   Jack up the rear of the car and support the bodyframe with axle stands. Apply the handbrake and remove the rear wheels.
2   Unscrew the brake fluid reservoir filler cap and tighten it down onto a piece of polythene sheeting in order to reduce the loss of fluid in the subsequent procedure. Alternatively fit hose clamps to the two rear brake hoses.
3   Identify the brake hoses for position then unscrew the unions and disconnect them from the rear axle. Plug the hoses.
4   Working on each side in turn jack up the trailing link and unscrew and remove the shock absorber lower mounting bolt, then lower the jack and remove the spring.
5   Unscrew and remove the bolts securing the torsion links to the rear axle.
6   Unbolt the Panhard rod from the rear axle and bodyframe.
7   Unscrew and remove the bolts securing the trailing links to the rear axle, and withdraw the rear axle from under the car (photo).
8   If necessary the trailing link rubber bushes may be removed from the rear axle using a long bolt, metal tubing and washers. Dip the new bushes in soapy water before pressing them into the axle using the same method.
9   Refitting is a reversal of removal, but delay tightening the mounting bolts until the full weight of the car is on the suspension. The bolt securing the Panhard rod to the bodyframe should be inserted from the rear of the car. Finally bleed the brake hydraulic system as described in Chapter 9.

14 Rear trailing link – removal and refitting

1   Remove the rear coil spring as described in Section 12.
2   Unscrew and remove the bolts securing the trailing link to the rear axle and withdraw the link.
3   Check the rubber bushes on the rear axle and if necessary renew them with reference to Section 13.
4   Refitting is a reversal of removal, but delay tightening the rubber bush mounting bolts until the full weight of the car is on the suspension.

15 Rear torsion link – removal and refitting

1   Jack up the rear of the car and support the bodyframe with axle stands. Apply the handbrake and remove the relevant rear wheel.
2   Unscrew and remove the mounting bolts and remove the torsion link. Note which way round the bolts are fitted (photos).
3   If necessary renew the rubber bushes using a long bolt, metal tubing and washers. Dip the bushes in soapy water to facilitate fitting them.
4   Refitting is a reversal of removal, but delay tightening the mounting bolts until the full weight of the car is on the suspension.

16 Rear Panhard rod – removal and refitting

1   Jack up the rear of the car and support the bodyframe with axle stands. Apply the handbrake.
2   Unscrew and remove the mounting bolts and remove the Panhard rod.
3   If necessary renew the rubber bushes using a long bolt, metal tubing and washers. Dip the bushes in soapy water to facilitate fitting them.
4   Refitting is a reversal of removal, but delay tightening the mounting bolts until the full weight of the car is on the suspension.

17 Steering wheel – removal and refitting

1   Set the front wheels in the straight-ahead position.
2   Disconnect the battery negative lead.

15.2A Rear torsion link bearing on rear axle

15.2B Rear torsion link bearing on body

17.5 Removing the steering wheel retaining nut

3   On 99 models remove the screws and withdraw the steering column lower shroud.
4   Remove the centre pad from the steering wheel. To do this on the standard steering wheel remove the screws located behind the steering wheel, but on 1981 on models prise out the motif and on EMS models release the rubber flaps. Where applicable disconnect the wiring.
5   Hold the steering wheel stationary and unscrew the retaining nut (photo). Remove the washer.
6   Mark the steering wheel in relation to the inner column then pull off the steering wheel. Do not knock or jar the steering wheel particularly in a downward direction otherwise the collapsible outer column may be distorted – if possible use an extractor.

7   If necessary on 1981 on models prise out the direction indicator return actuator from the rear of the steering wheel.
8   Refit the direction indicator return actuator if applicable making sure that it is in its central position.
9   Refitting is a reversal of removal, but tighten the nut to the specified torque.

18 Steering column – removal and refitting

1   Remove the steering wheel as described in Section 17.
2   Working in the engine compartment mark the intermediate shaft

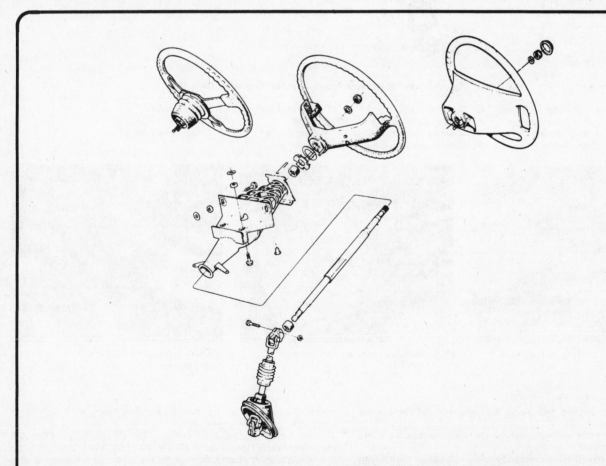

Fig. 11.17 Exploded view of the steering column for 900 models (Sec 18)

11

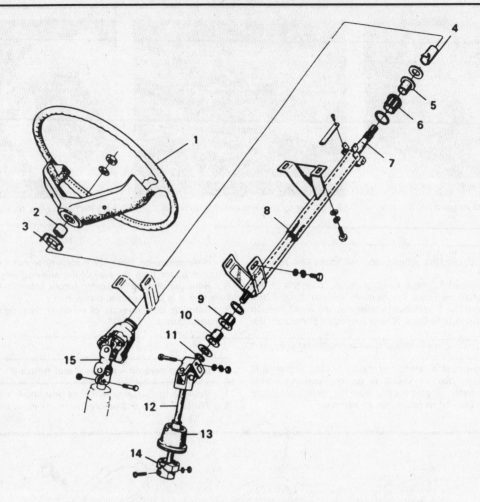

Fig. 11.18 Exploded view of the steering column for 99 models (Sec 18)

1	Steering wheel	5	Bushing	9	Rubber bushing	13	Rubber bellows
2	Plastic sleeve	6	Rubber bushing	10	Bushing	14	Universal joint half
3	Slip ring	7	Steering column	11	Rubber washer	15	Double universal joint
4	Driver	8	Steering column tube	12	Intermediate shaft		

18.2 Intermediate shaft to steering gear universal joint

18.4A Remove the cross-head screws ...

18.4B ... and withdraw the steering column lower shroud

in relation to the steering gear pinion then unscrew and remove the pinch-bolt (photo).

3   Unscrew the bolts and withdraw the column lower bearing cover and lower facia panel.

4   Remove the direction indicator and wiper combination switch with reference to Chapter 10 (photos).

5   Prise the rubber boot from the bulkhead.

6   Unscrew the mounting bracket bolts and withdraw the steering column from the car, at the same time disconnecting the intermediate shaft from the steering gear pinion.

7   Refitting is a reversal of removal, but do not fully tighten the mounting bracket bolts until all are inserted. Make sure that the intermediate shaft pinch-bolt engages the groove in the steering gear pinion. Suitable adhesive should be applied to the groove in the rubber boot before fitting it to the bulkhead. Seal the mounting holes in the bulkhead with sealing compound.

19.2 Intermediate shaft to steering column universal joint

Fig. 11.19 Special tool for fitting rubber bellows to the steering column intermediate shaft (Sec 19)

19 Steering column intermediate shaft – removal and refitting

1   Remove the steering column as described in Section 18.
2   Mark the intermediate shaft in relation to the inner column then unscrew and remove the pinch-bolt and slide off the intermediate shaft (photo).
3   To renew the rubber bellows prise it over the sealing ring and pull it off the universal joint. A tapered fork is now required in order to ease the new bellows over the universal joint – Saab tool 89 95 813 can be used or a home made tool from a suitable plastic bottle. Lubricate the tool with petroleum jelly to prevent damage to the bellows.
4   Refitting is a reversal of removal with reference to Section 18.

20 Steering gear (manual) – removal and refitting

1   Jack up the front of the car and support it on axle stands. Chock the rear wheels and remove the front wheels.
2   Working in the engine compartment mark the intermediate shaft in relation to the pinion then unscrew and remove the pinch-bolt.
3   Unscrew the tie-rod end nuts and use a separator tool to release the tie-rods from the steering arms.

99 models

4   Remove the lower facia panel and prise the intermediate shaft bellows from the body.
5   Unbolt the steering column from the bulkhead then pull the intermediate shaft from the pinion. Tie the column to one side taking care not to strain the wiring.

All models

6   Unscrew the clamp nuts and remove the washers and clamps.
7   Move the steering gear to the side (and disconnect the intermediate shaft on 900 models) then lower the unit between the bodyframe members.
8   Refitting is a reversal of removal, but tighten the nuts and bolts to the specified torque and finally check and adjust the front wheel alignment as described in Section 26.

21 Steering gear (manual) – overhaul

1   Loosen the locknuts and unscrew the tie-rod ends noting how many turns are required to remove them. Remove the locknuts.
2   Loosen the clips and remove the rubber bellows from the tie-rods.
3   To remove the *adjustable* balljoint use a 0.157 in (4.0 mm) drill to drill out the dowel pin which locks the balljoint to the rack. The pin is

0.370 in (9.4 mm) long and it is important not to drill further into the rack. Using grips and if available a notched key, unscrew and remove the balljoint bearing cup and locknut.
4   To remove the *enclosed* balljoint mount the toothed end of the rack in a soft jawed vice then use a 0.157 in (4.0 mm) drill to drill out the locking tab. Use grips or a suitable key to unscrew the balljoint.
5   Unscrew the bolts and remove the cap, shims, spring and plunger from the pinion end of the steering gear.
6   Unscrew the bolts and withdraw the pinion together with the bearing, cap, and sealing ring. Some early models may have a gasket and shims. Do not attempt to remove the bearing from the pinion as it is factory fitted and is supplied already fitted as a replacement.
7   Withdraw the rack from the housing.
8   Remove the pinion ball bearing or needle bearing as applicable.
9   Clean all the components and examine them for wear and damage. Renew them as necessary and obtain new rubber bellows for the tie-rods.
10 Commence assembly by filling the housing with 5 oz of the specified grease.
11 Fit the pinion ball bearing or needle bearing as applicable. Note that the extended inner races of the ball bearings on the pinion must face each other.
12 Fit the balljoint and tie-rod to the pinion end of the rack. To do this first mount the rack in a soft-jawed vice.
13 On the *adjustable* balljoint fit the locknut, then lubricate the balljoint with a molybdenum disulphide based grease and fit it to the rack. Early models incorporate a spring and washer but later models have a plastic cup. Tighten the balljoint cup until all looseness is eliminated but it is still possible to move the tie-rod in all directions – if available use a spring balance attached to the end of the tie-rod to check that the articulation force does not exceed 7.2 lb.f. Tighten the locknut then lock by drilling a new hole 0.157 in (4.0 mm) in diameter and 0.370 in (9.4 mm) deep and inserting a new dowel pin. Centre punch the hole to retain the pin.
14 On the *enclosed* balljoint screw the balljoint onto the rack and tighten it to the specified torque. Lock it by peening the balljoint shoulder into the groove in the rack. If the original balljoint is being refitted, the existing locking point must be displaced by 90° by fitting a spacer between the balljoint and rack.
15 Insert the rack into the housing.
16 Fit the pinion and bearing together with the cap and sealing ring then tighten the bolts. On early models with shims and a gasket check that all endplay of the pinion is eliminated, but make sure that the pinion can be rotated freely – adjust the shims if necessary. Note also that the threads of the bolt which protrudes into the inside of the housing should be sealed with sealing compound.
17 Insert the adjustment plunger without the spring and fit the cap without the gasket. Insert and tighten the bolts finger tight only. Using a feeler gauge check the clearance between the cap and housing then add 0.002 to 0.006 in (0.05 to 0.15 mm) to this amount to determine the total thickness of the gasket and shims.
18 Remove the cap and fit the spring. Fit the shims, gasket and cap then insert the bolts and tighten them.
19 Turn the pinion fully in each direction and check that there are no tight spots. If possible check that the turning torque of the pinion is between 7 and 15 lbf in (0.8 and 1.7 Nm).
20 Mount the free end of the rack in a soft-jawed vice and fit the balljoint and tie-rod with reference to paragraph 13 or 14.
21 Apply silicone grease to the contact surfaces of the rubber bellows and locate them on the tie-rods. Apply grease to the balljoints then fit the bellows on the housing and tie-rods, and tighten the clips. Fit the special caps to the ends of the clips.
22 Fit the tie-rod ends and locknuts.

11

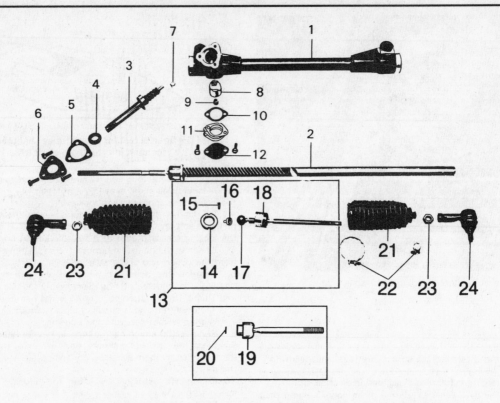

Fig. 11.20 Exploded view of the steering gear fitted to 900 models (Sec 21)

1	Steering gear housing assembly	6	Cap
2	Rack	7	Needle bearing
3	Pinion gear incorporating bearing	8	Needle bearing piston
4	Sealing ring	9	Spring
5	Gasket	10	Gasket
		11	Shims
		12	Cap

13	Adjustable balljoint	19	Fully enclosed balljoint
14	Lock nut	20	Shims
15	Locking pin	21	Bellows
16	Inner bearing cup	22	Clips
17	Tie-rod	23	Lock nut
18	Outer bearing cup	24	Tie-rod end

Fig. 11.21 Removing the tie-rod ends and balljoints (Sec 21)

Fig. 11.22 Using a feeler gauge to determine the shim thickness for the plunger cap (Sec 21)

22 Steering gear (power-assisted) – removal and refitting

1   Drain the fluid from the reservoir located in the engine compartment.

2   Unbolt the servo pump from its mounting.

3   Jack up the front of the car and support it on axle stands. Chock the rear wheels and remove the front wheels.

4   Support the engine/gearbox with a hoist or trolley jack then remove the left-hand side engine mounting.

5   Mark the intermediate shaft in relation to the pinion then unscrew

and remove the pinch-bolt.

6   Disconnect the pipe clips from the front suspension crossmember.

7   Unscrew the tie-rod end nuts and use a separator tool to release the tie-rods from the steering arms.

8   Remove the left-hand side handbrake cable from the yoke and wheel housing, and the right-hand handbrake cable clip from the steering gear.

9   Unbolt the steering gear from the bodyframe noting the location of the spacers and bracket.

10 Disconnect the hydraulic feed and return pipes from the servo valve on the steering gear. Plug the pipes and apertures to prevent the ingress of foreign matter.

11 Move the steering gear to the side and disconnect the intermediate shaft, then lower the unit between the bodyframe members.

12 Refitting is a reversal of removal, but make sure that no foreign matter enters the hydraulic lines and apertures. It may be advantageous to remove the tie-rod end from the pinion end tie-rod and move the rack in the opposite direction. Fit new seals to the hydraulic lines if necessary. Tighten all nuts and bolts to the specified torque and check and adjust the front wheel alignment as described in Section 26. Adjust the servo pump drivebelt as described in Section 24. Fill the reservoir with fluid then start the engine and top up the level to about 0.4 in (10.0 mm) above the bottom of the filter (photo). Turn the steering wheel from lock to lock several times in order to bleed any air from the system. Finally switch off the engine.

23 Steering gear (power-assisted) – overhaul

Overhaul of the power steering gear by the home mechanic is not recommended because several special tools are required. However an exploded diagram of the unit fitted to 900 models is shown in Fig. 11.23 which may be useful in diagnosing faults.

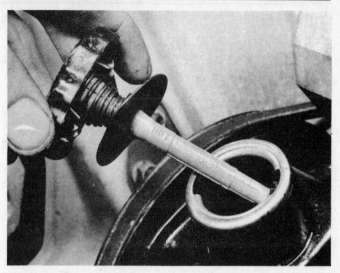

22.12 Checking power steering pump fluid reservoir level

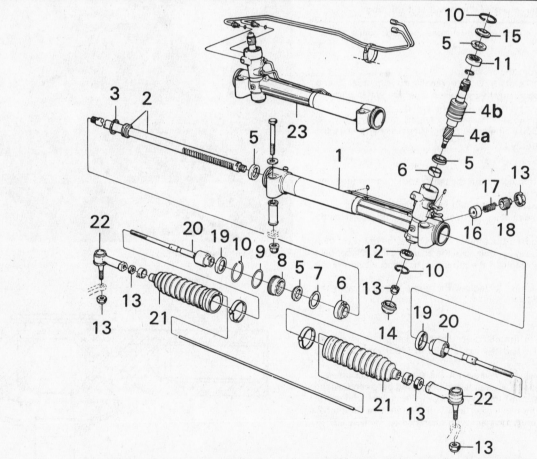

Fig. 11.23 Exploded view of the power-assisted steering gear fitted to 900 models (Sec 23)

1	Steering gear housing	7	Washer
2	Rack with piston	8	Sealing retainer
3	Piston ring	9	O-ring
4a	Pinion	10	Circlip
4b	Servo valve	11	Bearing holder with needle bearing
5	Hydraulic seal	12	Ball bearing
6	Bushing		

13	Lock nut
14	Cover
15	Dust cover
16	Radial bearing, piston
17	Spring
18	Adjustment screw
19	Damper ring (end stop

	position)
20	Inner balljoint with tie-rod
21	Rubber bellows
22	Tie-rod ends
23	RHD version

11

24.6 Pipe connections to the power steering pump

24.8 Power steering pump mounting bolt locations

24 Power steering servo pump – removal and refitting

1   Clean the servo pump particularly around the hose connections.

99 models
2   Siphon the fluid from the reservoir.
3   Drain the cooling system with reference to Chapter 2 and disconnect the hose between the expansion tank and water pump.
4   Disconnect the hydraulic lines from the pump.
5   Unbolt the pump from the bracket and engine mounting, release the drivebelt, and withdraw the servo pump. If necessary remove the pulley and pump mounting.

900 models
6   Disconnect the return hose from the pump and drain the fluid into a suitable container (photo).
7   Remove the alternator as described in Chapter 10.
8   Remove the adjusting links for the alternator and servo pump (photo).
9   On early models loosen the screws and remove the drivebelt then move the pump to one side and remove the adjusting link. Disconnect the pressure hose then remove the mounting bolt and withdraw the pump.
10 On later models simply withdraw the pump together with the adjustment link (photo).

99 models
11 Fit the mounting to the pump so that the clamp bolt is aligned with the delivery outlet and the lug is 1.93 in (49.0 mm) from the centre of the pulley.
12 Refit the pump using a reversal of the removal procedure and adjust the drivebelt tension so that it can be moved between 0.4 and 0.6 in (10.0 and 15.0 mm) midway between the pulleys under firm thumb pressure. Fill the cooling system with reference to Chapter 2. Fill and bleed the hydraulic system with reference to Section 22.

900 models
13 Refitting is a reversal of removal, but adjust the drivebe t tension so that it can be moved between 0.4 and 0.6 in (10.0 and 15.0 mm) midway between the pulleys under firm thumb pressure. Fill and bleed the hydraulic system with reference to Section 22. Refit the alternator with reference to Chapter 10.

25 Tie-rod end balljoint – removal and refitting

1   Wear in the tie-rod end balljoint can be checked by attempting to turn the roadwheel alternately on each lock while noting any play in

24.10 Power steering pump

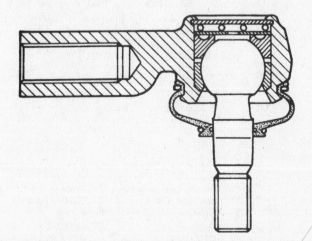

Fig. 11.24 Cross-section of a tie-rod end (Sec 25)

25.3 Using a separator tool to remove the tie-rod end balljoint

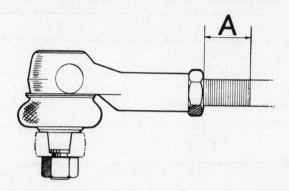

Fig. 11.25 The visible thread (A) on the tie-rods must be equal on each side (Sec 26)

the balljoint. Moderate wear is compensated for by a split bearing within the balljoint, so if any play is evident, the tie-rod end must be renewed.

2   Jack up the front of the car and support it on axle stands. Chock the rear wheels and remove the relevant front wheel.

3   Turn the steering wheel to give better access then unscrew the tie-rod end nut and use a separator tool to release the tie-rod from the steering arm (photo).

4   Loosen the locknut and unscrew the tie-rod end noting how many turns are required to remove it.

5   Screw the new tie-rod end onto the tie-rod to the previously noted position then fit it to the steering arm. Fit the nut and tighten it to the specified torque.

6   Fit the front wheel and lower the car to the ground.

7   Check and adjust the front wheel alignment as described in Section 26.

26 Wheel alignment – checking and adjustment

1   Accurate wheel alignment is essential for good steering and slow tyre wear. Before checking it, make sure that the car is only loaded to kerbside weight and the tyres are correctly inflated.

2   Position the car on level ground with the wheels straight-ahead, then roll the car backwards 12 ft (4 metre) and forwards again to settle the suspension.

3   Using a wheel alignment gauge, check that the front wheel toe-in dimension is as given in the Specifications.

4   If adjustment is necessary loosen the tie-rod end locknuts on both tie-rods and also the outer clips on the steering gear bellows. Turn each tie-rod by equal amounts until the alignment is correct then tighten the locknuts and bellows clips. Note that the visible length of thread on the tie-rods should be equal on each side and must not exceed 0.9 in (24.0 mm) on manual steering or 1.0 in (25.0 mm) on power steering on each side.

5   The camber angle can be adjusted by spacers under the upper control arm brackets, and the caster angle can be adjusted by changing the position of the same spacers between the front and rear brackets. However checking and adjustment of both angles is best left to a garage equipped with the special gauges.

27 Roadwheels and tyres – general

1   Clean the insides of the roadwheels whenever they are removed, and if necessary remove any rust and repaint them.

2   At the same time remove any flints or stones which may have become embedded in the tyres. Examine the tyres for damage and splits, and where the depth of tread is almost down to the legal minimum, renew them.

3   The wheels should be rebalanced half way through the life of the tyres to compensate for loss of rubber.

4   Check and adjust the tyre pressures regularly and make sure that the dust caps are correctly fitted. Remember also to check the spare tyre.

Fault diagnosis overleaf

11

28 Fault diagnosis – suspension and steering

Symptom	Reason(s)
Excessive play in steering	Worn rack and pinion or tie-rod inner balljoints Worn tie-rod end balljoints Worn control arm balljoints
Wanders or pulls to one side	Incorrect wheel alignment Worn tie-rod end balljoints Worn control arm balljoints Uneven tyre pressures
Heavy or stiff steering	Incorrect wheel alignment Low tyre pressures Incorrectly adjusted steering gear or lack of lubricant Seized control arm balljoint Faulty servo pump (power steering) or broken drivebelt or low fluid level
Wheel wobble and vibration	Wheels out of balance Wheels damaged Worn shock absorbers Worn wheel bearings Worn steering or suspension balljoints
Excessive tyre wear	Incorrect wheel alignment Worn shock absorbers Incorrect tyre pressures Wheels out of balance

Chapter 12 Bodywork and fittings

Contents

1 General description

The body and underframe are of all-steel welded construction incorporating heavy gauge pressed steel panels. Longitudinal and transverse beams are built into the floor, and the doors incorporate horizontal reinforcement beams for protection in the event of a side-on collision. Unlike the conventional design, the door panels extend downwards to cover the sill panels and are fitted with a rubber sealing strip along the bottom edge which abuts the sill panel when the doors are shut.

The body undergoes several rust inhibiting processes and is also fitted with sound insulating felt throughout.

The heater controls are vacuum operated from the inlet manifold (photos).

2 Maintenance – bodywork and underframe

1   The general condition of a vehicle's bodywork is the one thing that significantly affects its value. Maintenance is easy but needs to be regular. Neglect, particularly after minor damage, can lead quickly to

1.1A Heater control vacuum reservoir

1.1B Heater vacuum control unit

2.4A Clearing a sill drain hole

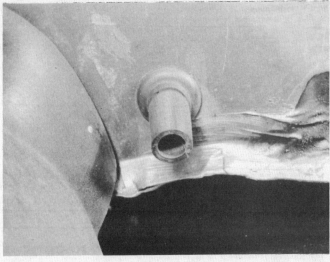

2.4B Sunroof drain tube

further deterioration and costly repair bills. It is important also to keep watch on those parts of the vehicle not immediately visible, for instance the underside, inside all the wheel arches and the lower part of the engine compartment.

2   The basic maintenance routine for the bodywork is washing – preferably with a lot of water, from a hose. This will remove all the loose solids which may have stuck to the vehicle. It is important to flush these off in such a way as to prevent grit from scratching the finish. The wheel arches and underframe need washing in the same way to remove any accumulated mud which will retain moisture and tend to encourage rust. Paradoxically enough, the best time to clean the underframe and wheel arches is in wet weather when the mud is thoroughly wet and soft. In very wet weather the underframe is usually cleaned of large accumulations automatically and this is a good time for inspection.

3   Periodically, it is a good idea to have the whole of the underframe of the vehicle steam cleaned, engine compartment included, so that a thorough inspection can be carried out to see what minor repairs and renovations are necessary. Steam cleaning is available at many garages and is necessary for removal of the accumulation of oily grime which sometimes is allowed to become thick in certain areas. If steam cleaning facilities are not available, there are one or two excellent grease solvents available which can be brush applied. The dirt can then be simply hosed off.

4   After washing paintwork, wipe off with a chamois leather to give an unspotted clear finish. A coat of clear protective wax polish will give added protection against chemical pollutants in the air. If the paintwork sheen has dulled or oxidised, use a cleaner/polisher combination to restore the brilliance of the shine. This requires a little effort, but such dulling is usually caused because regular washing has been neglected. Always check that the door and body drain holes and pipes are completely clear so that water can be drained out (photos). Bright work should be treated in the same way as paintwork. Windscreens and windows can be kept clear of the smeary film which often appears, by adding a little ammonia to the water. If they are scratched, a good rub with a proprietary metal polish will often clear them. Never use any form of wax or other body or chromium polish on glass.

3   Maintenance – upholstery and carpets

1   Mats and carpets should be brushed or vacuum cleaned regularly to keep them free of grit. If they are badly stained remove them from the vehicle for scrubbing or sponging and make quite sure they are dry before refitting. Seats and interior trim panels can be kept clean by wiping with a damp cloth. If they do become stained (which can be more apparent on light coloured upholstery) use a little liquid detergent and a soft nail brush to scour the grime out of the grain of the material. Do not forget to keep the headlining clean in the same way as the upholstery. When using liquid cleaners inside the vehicle do

2.4C Body drain tube

not over-wet the surface being cleaned. Excessive damp could get into seams and padded interior causing stains, offensive odours or even rot. If the inside of the vehicle gets wet accidentally it is worthwhile taking some trouble to dry it out properly, particularly where carpets are involved. *Do not leave oil or electric heaters inside the vehicle for this purpose.*

4   Minor body damage – repair

The photographic sequences on pages 230 and 231 illustrate the operations detailed in the following sub-sections.

Repair of minor scratches in bodywork

If the scratch is very superficial, and does not penetrate to the metal of the bodywork, repair is very simple. Lightly rub the area of the scratch with a paintwork renovator, or a very fine cutting paste, to remove loose paint from the scratch and to clear the surrounding bodywork of wax polish. Rinse the area with clean water.

Apply touch-up paint to the scratch using a fine paint brush; continue to apply fine layers of paint until the surface of the paint in the scratch is level with the surrounding paintwork. Allow the new paint at least two weeks to harden: then blend it into the surrounding paintwork by rubbing the scratch area with a paintwork renovator or a very fine cutting paste. Finally, apply wax polish.

Where the scratch has penetrated right through to the metal of the bodywork, causing the metal to rust, a different repair technique is required. Remove any loose rust from the bottom of the scratch with a penknife, then apply rust inhibiting paint to prevent the formation of rust in the future. Using a rubber or nylon applicator fill the scratch with bodystopper paste. If required, this paste can be mixed with cellulose thinners to provide a very thin paste which is ideal for filling narrow scratches. Before the stopper-paste in the scratch hardens, wrap a piece of smooth cotton rag around the top of a finger. Dip the finger in cellulose thinners and then quickly sweep it across the surface of the stopper-paste in the scratch; this will ensure that the surface of the stopper-paste is slightly hollowed. The scratch can now be painted over as described earlier in this Section.

Repair of dents in bodywork

When deep denting of the vehicle's bodywork has taken place, the first task is to pull the dent out, until the affected bodywork almost attains its original shape. There is little point in trying to restore the original shape completely, as the metal in the damaged area will have stretched on impact and cannot be reshaped fully to its original contour. It is better to bring the level of the dent up to a point which is about $\frac{1}{8}$ in (3 mm) below the level of the surrounding bodywork. In cases where the dent is very shallow anyway, it is not worth trying to pull it out at all. If the underside of the dent is accessible, it can be hammered out gently from behind, using a mallet with a wooden or plastic head. Whilst doing this, hold a suitable block of wood firmly against the outside of the panel to absorb the impact from the hammer blows and thus prevent a large area of the bodywork from being 'belled-out'.

Should the dent be in a section of the bodywork which has a double skin or some other factor making it inaccessible from behind, a different technique is called for. Drill several small holes through the metal inside the area – particularly in the deeper section. Then screw long self-tapping screws into the holes just sufficiently for them to gain a good purchase in the metal. Now the dent can be pulled out by pulling on the protruding heads of the screws with a pair of pliers.

The next stage of the repair is the removal of the paint from the damaged area, and from an inch or so of the surrounding 'sound' bodywork. This is accomplished most easily by using a wire brush or abrasive pad on a power drill, although it can be done just as effectively by hand using sheets of abrasive paper. To complete the preparation for filling, score the surface of the bare metal with a screwdriver or the tang of a file, or alternatively, drill small holes in the affected area. This will provide a really good 'key' for the filler paste.

To complete the repair see the Section on filling and re-spraying.

Repair of rust holes or gashes in bodywork

Remove all paint from the affected area and from an inch or so of the surrounding 'sound' bodywork, using an abrasive pad or a wire brush on a power drill. If these are not available a few sheets of abrasive paper will do the job just as effectively. With the paint removed you will be able to gauge the severity of the corrosion and therefore decide whether to renew the whole panel (if this is possible) or to repair the affected area. New body panels are not as expensive as most people think and it is often quicker and more satisfactory to fit a new panel than to attempt to repair large areas of corrosion.

Remove all fittings from the affected area except those which will act as a guide to the original shape of the damaged bodywork (eg headlamp shells etc). Then, using tin snips or a hacksaw blade, remove all loose metal and any other metal badly affected by corrosion. Hammer the edges of the hole inwards in order to create a slight depression for the filler paste.

Wire brush the affected area to remove the powdery rust from the surface of the remaining metal. Paint the affected area with rust inhibiting paint; if the back of the rusted area is accessible treat this also.

Before filling can take place it will be necessary to block the hole in some way. This can be achieved by the use of zinc gauze or aluminium tape.

Zinc gauze is probably the best material to use for a large hole. Cut a piece to the approximate size and shape of the hole to be filled, then position it in the hole so that its edges are below the level of the surrounding bodywork. It can be retained in position by several blobs of filler paste around its periphery.

Aluminium tape should be used for small or very narrow holes. Pull a piece off the roll and trim it to the approximate size and shape required, then pull off the backing paper (if used) and stick the tape over the hole; it can be overlapped if the thickness of one piece is insufficient. Burnish down the edges of the tape with the handle of a screwdriver or similar, to ensure that the tape is securely attached to the metal underneath.

Bodywork repairs – filling and re-spraying

Before using this Section, see the Sections on dent, deep scratch, rust holes and gash repairs.

Many types of bodyfiller are available, but generally speaking those proprietary kits which contain a tin of filler paste and a tube of resin hardener are best for this type of repair. A wide, flexible plastic or nylon applicator will be found invaluable for imparting a smooth and well contoured finish to the surface of the filler.

Mix up a little filler on a clean piece of card or board – measure the hardener carefully (follow the maker's instructions on the pack) otherwise the filler will set too rapidly or too slowly.

Using the applicator apply the filler paste to the prepared area; draw the applicator across the surface of the filler to achieve the correct contour and to level the filler surface. As soon as a contour that approximates to the correct one is achieved, stop working the paste – if you carry on too long the paste will become sticky and begin to 'pick up' on the applicator. Continue to add thin layers of filler paste at twenty-minute intervals until the level of the filler is just proud of the surrounding bodywork.

Once the filler has hardened, excess can be removed using a metal plane or file. From then on, progressively finer grades of abrasive paper should be used, starting with a 40 grade production paper and finishing with 400 grade wet-and-dry paper. Always wrap the abrasive paper around a flat rubber, cork, or wooden block – otherwise the surface of the filler will not be completely flat. During the smoothing of the filler surface the wet-and-dry paper should be periodically rinsed in water. This will ensure that a very smooth finish is imparted to the filler at the final stage.

At this stage the 'dent' should be surrounded by a ring of bare metal, which in turn should be encircled by the finely 'feathered' edge of the good paintwork. Rinse the repair area with clean water, until all of the dust produced by the rubbing-down operation has gone.

Spray the whole repair area with a light coat of primer – this will show up any imperfections in the surface of the filler. Repair these imperfections with fresh filler paste or bodystopper, and once more smooth the surface with abrasive paper. If bodystopper is used, it can be mixed with cellulose thinners to form a really thin paste which is ideal for filling small holes. Repeat this spray and repair procedure until you are satisfied that the surface of the filler, and the feathered edge of the paintwork are perfect. Clean the repair area with clean water and allow to dry fully.

The repair area is now ready for final spraying. Paint spraying must be carried out in a warm, dry, windless and dust free atmosphere. This condition can be created artificially if you have access to a large indoor working area, but if you are forced to work in the open, you will have to pick your day very carefully. If you are working indoors, dousing the floor in the work area with water will help to settle the dust which would otherwise be in the atmosphere. If the repair area is confined to one body panel, mask off the surrounding panels; this will help to minimise the effects of a slight mis-match in paint colours. Bodywork fittings (eg chrome strips, door handles etc) will also need to be masked off. Use genuine masking tape and several thicknesses of newspaper for the masking operations.

Before commencing to spray, agitate the aerosol can thoroughly, then spray a test area (an old tin, or similar) until the technique is mastered. Cover the repair area with a thick coat of primer; the thickness should be built up using several thin layers of paint rather than one thick one. Using 400 grade wet-and-dry paper, rub down the surface of the primer until it is really smooth. While doing this, the work area should be thoroughly doused with water, and the wet-and-dry paper periodically rinsed in water. Allow to dry before spraying on more paint.

Spray on the top coat, again building up the thickness by using several thin layers of paint. Start spraying in the centre of the repair area and then, using a circular motion, work outwards until the whole repair area and about 2 inches of the surrounding original paintwork is covered. Remove all masking material 10 to 15 minutes after spraying on the final coat of paint.

Allow the new paint at least two weeks to harden, then, using a paintwork renovator or a very fine cutting paste, blend the edges of the paint into the existing paintwork. Finally, apply wax polish.

12

These photos illustrate a method of repairing simple dents. They are intended to supplement *Body repair - minor damage* in this Chapter and should not be used as the sole instructions for body repair on these vehicles.

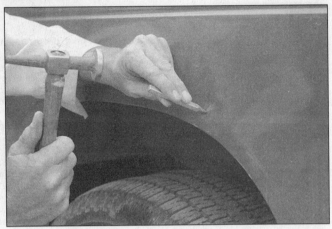

1   If you can't access the backside of the body panel to hammer out the dent, pull it out with a slide-hammer-type dent puller. In the deepest portion of the dent or along the crease line, drill or punch hole(s) at least one inch apart . . .

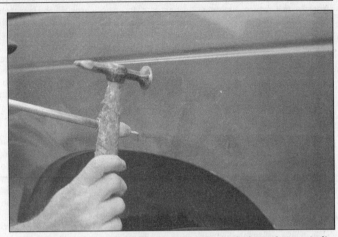

2   . . . then screw the slide-hammer into the hole and operate it. Tap with a hammer near the edge of the dent to help 'pop' the metal back to its original shape. When you're finished, the dent area should be close to its original contour and about 1/8-inch below the surface of the surrounding metal

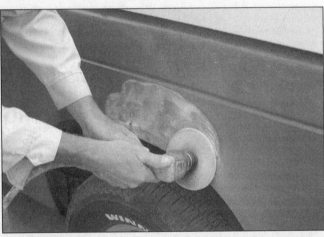

3   Using coarse-grit sandpaper, remove the paint down to the bare metal. Hand sanding works fine, but the disc sander shown here makes the job faster. Use finer (about 320-grit) sandpaper to feather-edge the paint at least one inch around the dent area

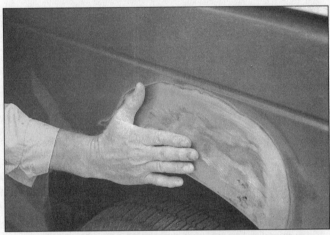

4   When the paint is removed, touch will probably be more helpful than sight for telling if the metal is straight. Hammer down the high spots or raise the low spots as necessary. Clean the repair area with wax/silicone remover

5   Following label instructions, mix up a batch of plastic filler and hardener. The ratio of filler to hardener is critical, and, if you mix it incorrectly, it will either not cure properly or cure too quickly (you won't have time to file and sand it into shape)

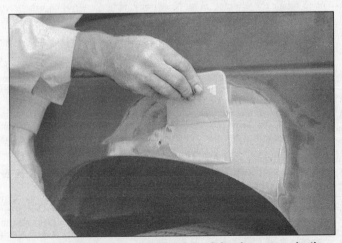

6   Working quickly so the filler doesn't harden, use a plastic applicator to press the body filler firmly into the metal, assuring it bonds completely. Work the filler until it matches the original contour and is slightly above the surrounding metal

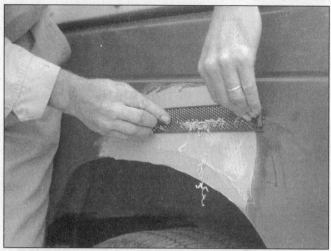

7   Let the filler harden until you can just dent it with your fingernail. Use a body file or Surform tool (shown here) to rough-shape the filler

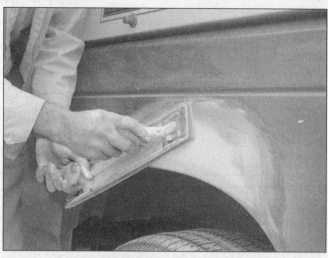

8   Use coarse-grit sandpaper and a sanding board or block to work the filler down until it's smooth and even. Work down to finer grits of sandpaper - always using a board or block - ending up with 360 or 400 grit

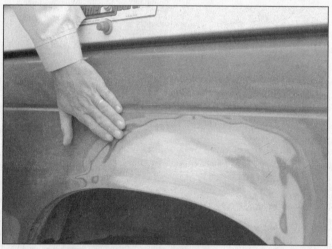

9   You shouldn't be able to feel any ridge at the transition from the filler to the bare metal or from the bare metal to the old paint. As soon as the repair is flat and uniform, remove the dust and mask off the adjacent panels or trim pieces

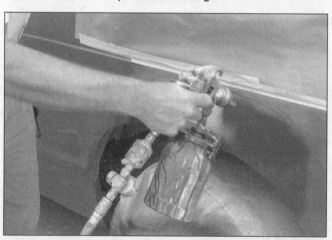

10   Apply several layers of primer to the area. Don't spray the primer on too heavy, so it sags or runs, and make sure each coat is dry before you spray on the next one. A professional-type spray gun is being used here, but aerosol spray primer is available inexpensively from auto parts stores

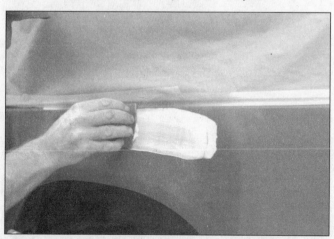

11   The primer will help reveal imperfections or scratches. Fill these with glazing compound. Follow the label instructions and sand it with 360 or 400-grit sandpaper until it's smooth. Repeat the glazing, sanding and respraying until the primer reveals a perfectly smooth surface

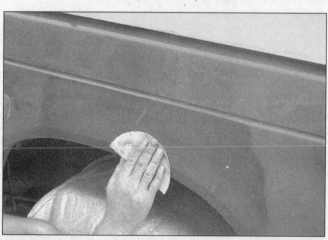

12   Finish sand the primer with very fine sandpaper (400 or 600-grit) to remove the primer overspray. Clean the area with water and allow it to dry. Use a tack rag to remove any dust, then apply the finish coat. Don't attempt to rub out or wax the repair area until the paint has dried completely (at least two weeks)

5 Major body damage – repair

Where serious damage has occurred or bodyframe panels require renewal the new sections must be welded into position professionally in order to ensure the overall rigidity of the body. If the damage is due to impact, the body must be checked for alignment using a special jig. A misaligned body is first of all dangerous as the car will not handle properly, and secondly uneven stresses will be imposed on the steering and suspension causing abnormal wear or complete failure. Tyre wear could also be excessive.

6 Maintenance – bodywork and fittings

1   Every 10 000 miles (15 000 km) on UK models or 7500 miles (12 000 km) on North American models lubricate the door, bonnet and bootlid hinges and locks with a little oil. Do not attempt to lubricate the ignition switch and gearchange lock.
2   At the same time check the underbody for damage and corrosion in particular the condition of the underseal. Apply new underseal and carry out repairs as necessary.
3   Every 20 000 miles (30 000 km) on UK models or 15 000 miles (24 000 km) on North American models renew the passenger compartment fresh air intake filter.

7 Bonnet – removal, refitting and adjustment

1   Pull the release handle located beneath the left-hand side of the facia panel, then pull out the safety catch and fully open the bonnet (photo).
2   Disconnect the windscreen washer hose and withdraw it from the retainers (photo).
3   On 99 models loosen the pivot bolts at the top of the hinges. On 900 models use a pencil to mark the position of the links then loosen the link retaining bolts on the hinge bar (photo).

Fig. 12.1 Removing the bonnet on a 99 models (Sec 7)

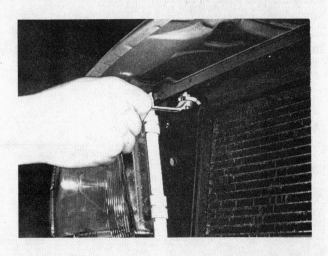

Fig. 12.2 Adjusting the bonnet on a 900 models (Sec 7)

7.1 Bonnet release handle .

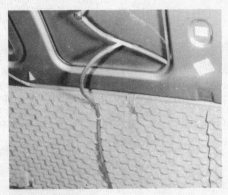

7.2 Windscreen washer hose location on the bonnet

7.3 Bonnet hinge

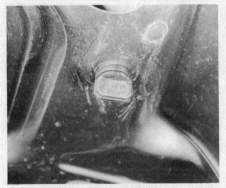

7.5A Bonnet support rubber stop

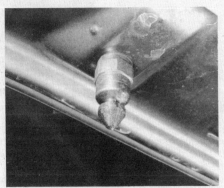

7.5B Bonnet front striker

7.5C Bonnet rear guide pin and roller

7.5D Bonnet rear roller guide

7.5E Bonnet front catch

8.1 Radiator grille mounting screw on 900 models

4   With the help of an assistant take the weight of the bonnet then remove the bolts and withdraw the bonnet from the car.

5   Refitting is a reversal of removal, but check that the bonnet aligns with the surrounding bodywork and that it locks correctly. If adjustment is required on 99 models loosen the lower hinge bolts and reposition the bonnet within the elongated slots. On 900 models remove the front radiator grille and loosen the hinge bolts on the cross-panel. The catch can be adjusted by means of shims (maximum thickness 0.2 in/5.0 mm), and the rubber stops on the front of the bonnet should be adjusted so that they support the bonnet in the closed position (photos).

8   Radiator grille – removal and refitting

1   To remove the radiator grille on 900 models remove the three screws from the cross-panel then lift the grille from the holes in the front valance (photo).

2   To remove the radiator grille on 99 models remove the seven screws (1 on top and 6 from the front) and withdraw the grille at the same time disconnecting the headlight washer tubes.

3   Refitting is a reversal of removal.

9   Front panel – removal and refitting

1   Disconnect the battery negative lead.

99 models

2   Remove the bonnet (Section 7) and the radiator grille (Section 8).

3   Remove the screws securing the headlights to the front panel and also the panel upper corner screws.

4   Unscrew the panel lower bolts from each side of the radiator, and also remove the radiator securing bolts.

5   Disconnect the bonnet release cable and release the headlight washer hoses.

6   Lift the front panel slightly and disconnect the wiper balljoint.

7   Withdraw the front panel from the car.

8   Refitting is a reversal of removal.

900 models

9   Remove the bonnet (Section 7) and drain the cooling system (Chapter 2).

10   Remove the sidelamp cluster (Chapter 10) and the bumper (Section 30).

11   Unscrew the headlight lower outer screws then unbolt and remove the spoiler.

12   Disconnect the wiring from the headlights, wiper motors, horns, fan motor and radiator thermal switch.

13   Disconnect the bonnet release mechanism and the washer tube.

14   Remove the top and bottom hoses from the radiator.

15   Unbolt and remove the front panel from the car complete with radiator and headlights.

16   Refitting is a reversal of removal. Refill the cooling system as described in Chapter 2.

Fig. 12.3 Removing the radiator grille on a 99 model (Sec 7)

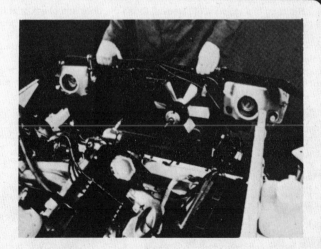

Fig. 12.4 Removing the complete front panel assembly (Sec 9)

12

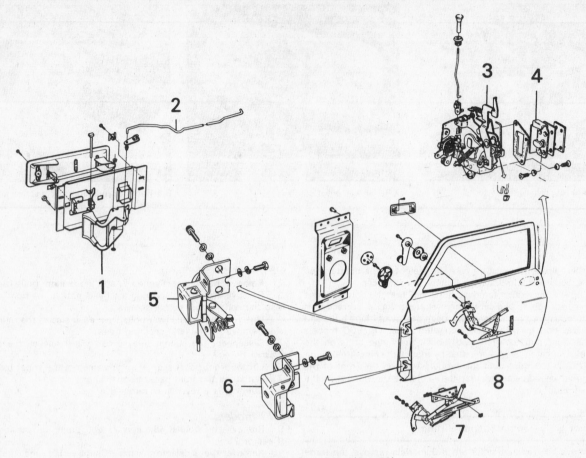

Fig. 12.5 Front door components (Sec 10)

1	Interior handle	3	Lock	5	Top hinge with door stop	7	Window regulator (early)
2	Link	4	Striker plate	6	Bottom hinge	8	Window regulator (late)

10 Doors – removal, refitting and adjustment

Front doors

1   Mark the position of the hinges on the front pillar with a pencil (photo).

2   Support the door on blocks of wood then unbolt the hinges and withdraw the door.

3   Refitting is a reversal of removal. Close the door and check that it is positioned correctly within its aperture and that it is flush with the surrounding bodywork. To adjust the door front edge in or out loosen the hinge bolts on the front pillar and move the door in the slotted holes, then tighten the bolts. To adjust the position of the door within its aperture first remove the trim panel (Section 27), then loosen the socket head screws through the access holes, move the door as

required and retighten the screws. Check that the door stopper supports and retains the door in the correct position – if necessary loosen the screws and reposition it.

Rear doors

4   Remove the trim from the lower section of the centre pillar.

5   Mark the position of the hinge through-bolts then unscrew the nuts and withdraw the door (photo).

6   Refitting is a reversal of removal. Close the door and check that it is positioned correctly within its aperture and that it is flush with the surrounding bodywork. To adjust the door loosen the hinge bolts on the door and reposition it as necessary. Some movement is also possible by loosening the through-bolt nuts. Check that the door striker supports and retains the door in the correct position – if necessary loosen the screws and reposition it (photo).

10.1 Front door hinge

10.5 Rear door hinge

10.6 Front door striker

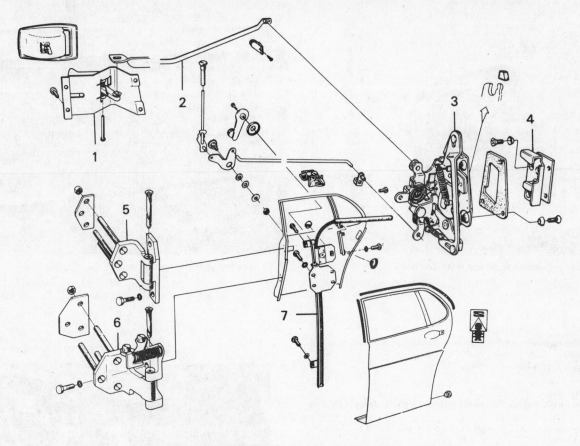

Fig. 12.6 Rear door components (Sec 10)

1	Interior handle	3	Lock	5	Top hinge
2	Link	4	Striker plate	6	Bottom hinge with door

stop

7 Window regulator

Fig. 12.7 Removing the electric motor from the window regulator (Sec 11)

Fig. 12.8 Removing the early type window regulator (Sec 12)

11 Window regulators (electric) – removal and refitting

1 Disconnect the battery negative lead.
2 Remove the door trim as described in Section 27.
3 Disconnect the wiring from the electric motor.
4 Remove the screw from the window channel and remove the window.
5 Unbolt the regulator and withdraw it through the aperture in the door.

6 Remove the protective foil from the electric motor then unbolt the motor from the regulator.
7 Refitting is a reversal of removal.

12 Window regulators (manual) – removal and refitting

Front door

1 Remove the door trim (Section 27) then remove the screw from the window channel and remove the window.

12

12.2A Window regulator spindle and mounting bolts

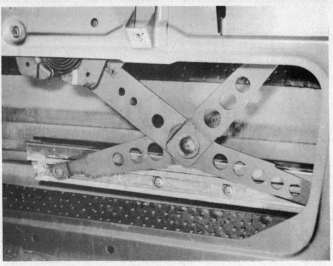

12.2B Window regulator control arms

2   Unbolt the regulator and withdraw it through the aperture in the door (photos).
3   Refitting is a reversal of removal.

Rear door
4   Fully open the window then remove the trim panel as described in Section 27.
5   Unscrew the regulator screws at the crank pivot and the bottom of the door frame.
6   Unbolt the window retainer, then withdraw the regulator through the aperture in the door taking care not to scratch the window.
7   Refitting is a reversal of removal.

13 Central door locking system – general

The central door locking system incorporates locks operated by electric motors – the driver's door lock automatically operates the other door locks and the luggage compartment lock, although each lock can be operated independently by key. In the event of electrical failure all locks can be operated manually.

14 Door locks – removal and refitting

Front door (two-door models)
1   Fully shut the window, then unscrew the locking knob and remove the door trim (Section 27).
2   Turn the lock to the closed position then remove the cross-head retaining screws.
3   On the link rod type disconnect the link from the lock cylinder and lock. On the crank rod type remove the clip and disconnect the link from the lock and crank rod.
4   Unscrew the outer door handle screws as necessary and withdraw the lock from the door. If necessary completely remove the outer door handle.
5   Refitting is a reversal of removal, but lubricate the moving parts with multi-purpose grease.

Front door (four-door models)
6   Fully shut the window, then remove the door trim as described in Section 27.
7   Turn the lock to the closed position then remove the cross-head retaining screws from the lock (photo).
8   Remove the screw from the bottom of the rear window channel.

Fig. 12.9 Removing the late type window regulator (Sec 12)

9   Disconnect the links from the interior handle, locking knob and lock cylinder (photo).
10 On models equipped with central locking disconnect the battery negative lead and remove the lock motor.
11 Withdraw the lock from the door. If necessary unbolt the outer door handle.
12 Refitting is a reversal of removal, but lubricate the moving parts with multi-purpose grease.

Rear door (four-door models)
13 Fully shut the window then remove the door trim as described in Section 27.
14 Turn the lock to the closed position then remove the cross-head retaining screws from the lock.
15 Disconnect the locking knob link.
16 Unscrew the outer door handle front screw and loosen the rear screw on the edge of the door.
17 Remove the screws from the interior door handle and disconnect the front end of the link.
18 Push the lock into the door, disconnect the link, then withdraw the lock.
19 If necessary remove the outer door handle and where applicable the central locking electric motor.

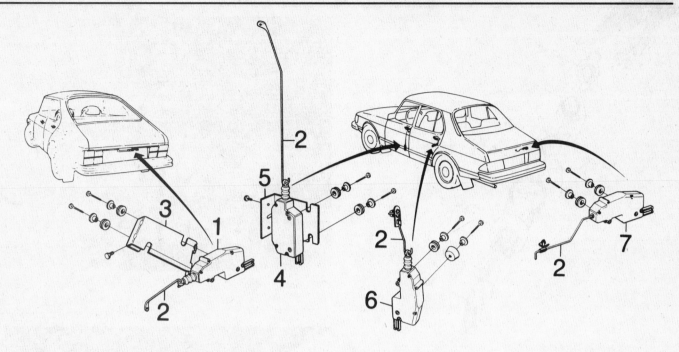

Fig. 12.10 Control door locking components (Sec 13)

1 Motor, luggage compartment   3 Attachment for motor,   4 Motor, front door lock   6 Motor, rear door lock
   lock Combi Coupé cars   luggage compartment lock,   5 Attachment for motor,   7 Motor, luggage compartment
2 Operating link   Combi Coupé cars   front door lock   lock, Sedan cars

14.7 Front door lock retaining screws

14.9 View of door lock from inside the car

20 Refitting is a reversal of removal, but lubricate the moving parts with multi-purpose grease.

15 Exterior door handle – removal and refitting

1 Remove the door trim panel as described in Section 27.
2 Remove the front screw and loosen the rear screw on the edge of the door.
3 Turn the handle and withdraw it diagonally upwards to the rear while disconnecting the lock lever.
4 Refitting is a reversal of removal.

16 Door lock cylinder – removal and refitting

1 Fully shut the window then remove the trim panel as described in Section 27.
2 Disconnect the link from the lock cylinder plastic arm.
3 Using a pair of grips extract the clip then withdraw the lock cylinder from the door.
4 Remove the circlip and prise off the lever ring followed by the plastic arm and spring.
5 With the key inserted withdraw the cylinder from the sleeve. Note that if the key is removed, the cylinder may fall apart.

12

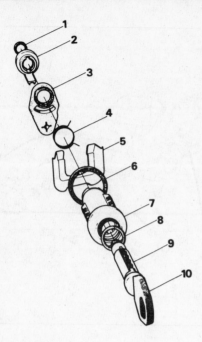

Fig. 12.11 Exploded view of the door lock cylinder (Sec 16)

1	Circlip	6	Gasket
2	Lever ring	7	Sleeve
3	Plastic arm	8	O-ring
4	Spring	9	Lock cylinder
5	Clip	10	Key

6   Remove the O-ring.
7   Refitting is a reversal of removal. Note that an identical lock can be obtained by quoting the key serial number when ordering the new lock.

17 Boot lid (Saloon models) – removal and refitting

1   Open the boot lid and mark the position of the hinges with a pencil.
2   With the help of an assistant unscrew the bolts/nuts and withdraw the boot lid from the car (photo). Disconnect the wiring where necessary.
3   Refitting is a reversal of removal, but make sure that the boot lid is central within its aperture. If necessary loosen the bolts and reposition the boot lid – the striker plate can also be adjusted in the same way (photo).

18 Boot lid lock and cylinder (99 Saloon models) – removal and refitting

1   With the boot lid open remove the two screws and withdraw the lock mechanism.
2   Remove the screws and withdraw the handle from the boot lid.
3   Prise off the plastic disc and remove the spring and push button.
4   Extract the circlip and remove the lever ring and torsion spring.
5   With the key inserted withdraw the cylinder from the sleeve.
6   Refitting is a reversal of removal.

19 Rear door (Coupe models) – removal and refitting

1   Open the door and disconnect the cable clip at the top of the aperture. Disconnect the battery negative lead.
2   Cut the cable between the body and door keeping all the wires identified, also disconnect the earth cable.

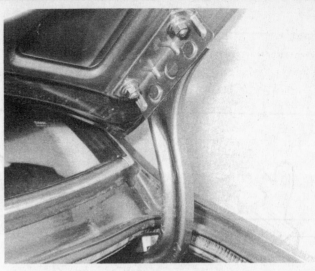

17.2 Boot lid hinge

17.3 Boot lid striker

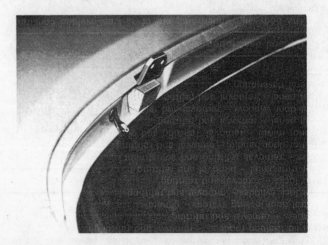

Fig. 12.12 Showing spacer fitted under hinge when refitting the rear door (Sec 19)

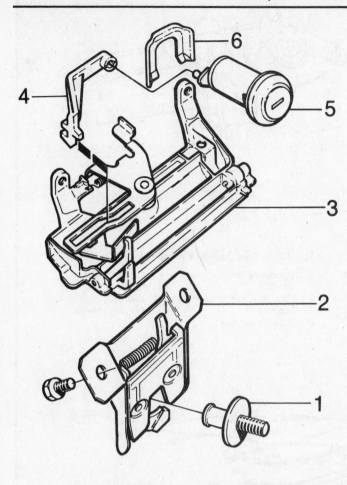

Fig. 12.13 Boot lid lock components (Sec 20)

1	Striker	4	Link
2	Lock	5	Lock cylinder
3	Handle	6	Clip

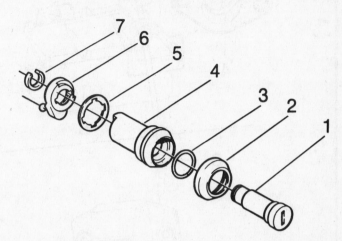

Fig. 12.14 Exploded view of the boot lid lock cylinder (Sec 20)

1	Lock cylinder	5	Spacer
2	Bezel	6	Lever ring
3	Seal	7	Circlip
4	Sleeve		

20.3 Boot lid lock

3   Mark the position of the hinges with a pencil then loosen the socket-head bolts.
4   Support the door then disconnect the two pneumatic springs.
5   With the help of an assistant remove the screws and withdraw the rear door from the car. Do not attempt to dismantle the pneumatic springs as the internal pressure of the gas is 850 lbf/in² (60 bar).
6   Refitting is a reversal of removal, but place spacers beneath the hinges temporarily. If necessary adjust the position of the door on the hinges before connecting the pneumatic springs. Reconnect the cable with proper connectors and cover with insulating tape if necessary.

20 Boot lid lock and cylinder (900 Saloon models) – removal and refitting

Conventional locking
1   Open the boot lid then pull the clip from the lock cylinder.
2   Prise the link from the cylinder lever and withdraw the cylinder.
3   Unscrew the bolts and withdraw the lock (photo).
4   Remove the handle from between the inner and outer panels.
5   Refitting is a reversal of removal.

Central locking
6   Disconnect the battery negative lead.
7   Open the boot lid and disconnect the wiring to the electric motor.
8   Unbolt and remove the electric motor.
9   Remove the lock and cylinder as described in paragraphs 1 to 5.

10 Disconnect the tie-rod from the link.
11 Refitting is a reversal of removal.

21 Rear door lock and cylinder (Coupe models) – removal and refitting

1   Open the rear door and remove the inner trim panel.
2   Disconnect the link rod and remove the screws then withdraw the cylinder from inside the door.
3   With the key inserted in the cylinder, prise off the lever and circlip and remove the control arm and spring.
4   Extract the cylinder from the sleeve.
5   Refitting is a reversal of removal, but do not remove the key from the cylinder until it is located in the sleeve otherwise the cylinder may fall apart.

12

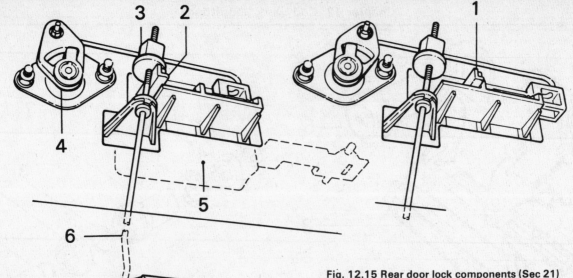

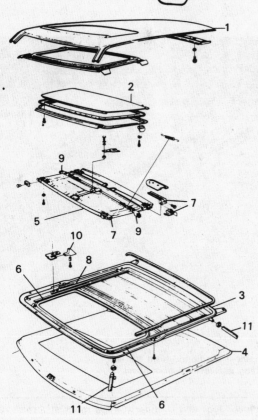

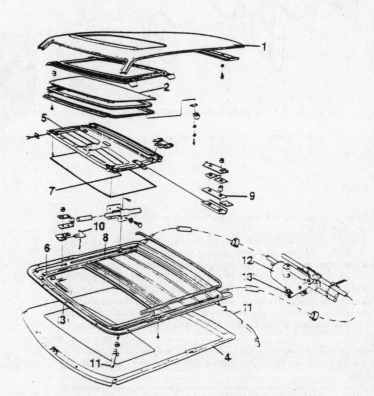

Fig. 12.15 Rear door lock components (Sec 21)

1 Operating link in locked position
2 Operating link in open position
3 Adjustment nut
4 Lock cylinder
5 Opening key
6 Pullrod
7 Locking device

Fig. 12.16 Manual sunroof components (Sec 22)

1 Roof plate
2 Sunroof plate
3 Mounting frame
4 Headlining
5 Panel
6 Runners
7 Guide clips with studs
8 Guide rails (toothed)
9 Catch
10 Wedges
11 Drainage hoses

Fig. 12.17 Electric sunroof components (Sec 22)

1 Roof panel
2 Sunroof top
3 Mounting frame
4 Headlining
5 Panel
6 Runners
7 Guide clips with studs
8 Cable, drive unit
9 Drive unit attachment
10 Rear guide shoe
11 Drainage hoses
12 Electric motor
13 Crank for manual operation

22 Sunroof lid – removal and refitting

1   Open the sunroof and remove the screws from the front edge of the lid.
2   Close the sunroof leaving a gap of approximately 0.75 in (2.0 cm).
3   From outside the car lift the front of the lid and pull it forwards and upwards until it can be removed from the car.
4   Unscrew the nuts and remove the front guide clips.
5   Flatten the locking plate and unscrew the catch nuts. Bend up the pull rods and disconnect the catches. Remove the springs, leaf springs, mountings, plastic bushes and sleeves.

6   Push the inner panel forwards and where applicable loosen the screws on the rear guide clips.
7   Lift the front of the inner panel and withdraw it from the car in a forwards direction.
8   Refitting is a reversal of removal, but lubricate the bearing surfaces with petroleum jelly. The front guide clips should be adjusted to give a clearance of between 0.008 and 0.020 in (0.2 and 0.5 mm). On the manually operated sunroof adjust the catches so that the clearance between the top of the teeth and the mounting is between 0.04 and 0.06 in (1.0 and 1.5 mm). With the sunroof shut, the adjustable guide shoe should overlap the fixed guide shoe by about 0.08 in (2.0 mm) – this will ensure that the rear edge of the sunroof starts to drop when the sunroof has been opened 0.08 in (2.0 mm) (photo). If the rear edge of the sunroof is not flush with the roof when shut, remove the lid and turn the adjusting screws beneath the guide shoes as necessary.

23 Windscreen, rear window and fixed side window – removal and refitting

Several special tools, adhesives and sealing compound are required in order to carry out this work, and it is therefore recommended that it is entrusted to a specialist.

24 Front door window – removal and refitting

1   Remove the door trim as described in Section 27.
2   Remove the inner weatherstrip from the bottom of the window opening.
3   Unscrew the regulator-to-window channel screws and rotate the window so that its front edge is downwards.
4   On early models prise off the plastic runner.
5   Withdraw the window from the outside of the door.
6   If necessary remove the channel and rubber pad from the window.
7   Refitting is a reversal of removal, but if the channel and rubber pad have been removed, fit them in the position shown in Fig. 12.20.

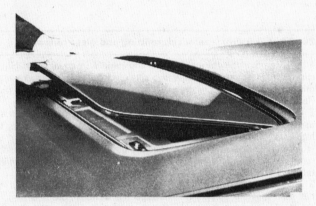

Fig. 12.18 Removing the sunroof lid (Sec 22)

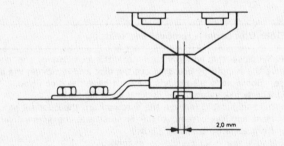

Fig. 12.19 Sunroof guide shoe adjustment (Sec 22)

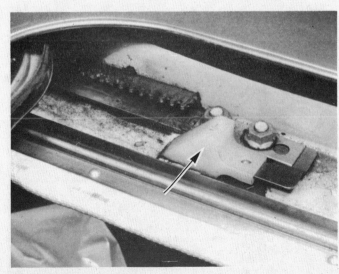

22.8 Sunroof guide shoe

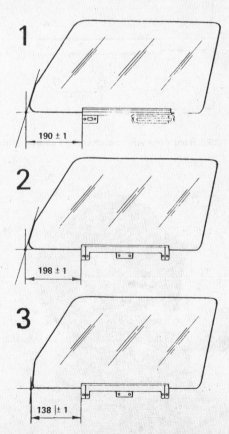

Fig. 12.20 Front door window channel position (Sec 24)

12

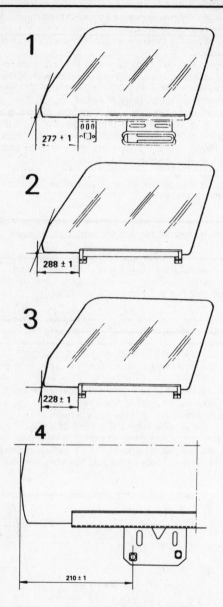

Fig. 12.21 Rear door window channel position (Sec 25)

25 Rear door window – removal and refitting

1   Remove the door trim as described in Section 27.
2   Remove the weatherstrip from the bottom of the window opening.
3   Push out the quarter-light window from the inside and remove the moulding.
4   Remove the regulator-to-window channel screws and lower the window.
5   Extract the rubber moulding from the rear channel then remove the channel screws. The bottom screw is reached by removing the rubber plug.
6   Move the channel to the rear then lift the window from the inside of the door.
7   If necessary remove the channel and rubber pad from the window.
8   Refitting is a reversal of removal, but if the channel and rubber pad have been removed, fit them in the position shown in Fig. 12.21.

26 Exterior mirror – removal, refitting and glass renewal

1   To remove the mirror, remove the handle (manual type) plastic clip, and bezel then unscrew the retaining bolts and withdraw the mirror from the door. On the electric type disconnect the wiring plug. Refitting is a reversal of removal.
2   To renew the glass on the manual type tilt the mirror down and use a wide blade screwdriver to prise out the mirror midway along the top edge. Slide the mirror up against the stop then press down the stop with a screwdriver and remove the glass. Refitting is a reversal of removal, but lubricate the joint with grease and press on the *middle* of the glass.
3   To renew the glass on the electric type first adjust it so that it is flat then insert a screwdriver through the bottom hole and turn the plastic ring two notches to the right to unlock the mirror. Tilt the glass and prise it out with a wide blade screwdriver. Remove the plastic ring. Refitting is a reversal of removal.

27 Door trim panel – removal and refitting

1   Fully close the window and note the position of the handle. Remove the handle by pressing out the disc and removing the screw (photo). Some early 99 models may not have the disc fitted.
2   Unscrew and remove the locking knob (photo).
3   Where applicable remove the screws from the door sill strip.
4   Where applicable remove the armrest and the screw from the lower front edge of the door (photo).
5   Remove the inner handle cover (photo).
6   On two-door models remove the special plastic retainers and washers by turning them through 90°.

27.1A Prise out the disc ...

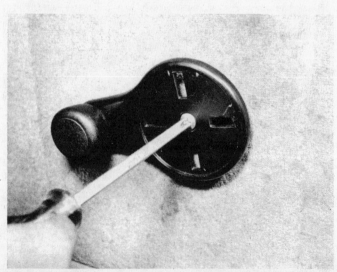

27.1B ... and remove the screw from the window regulator handle

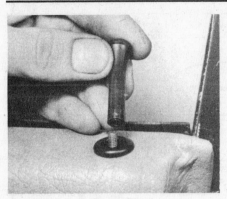
27.2 Removing the locking knob

27.4 Removing the armrest

27.5 Prising the cover from the inner door handle

27.8A View of front door with trim panel removed

27.8B Inner door lock

28.2 Front seat rear mounting

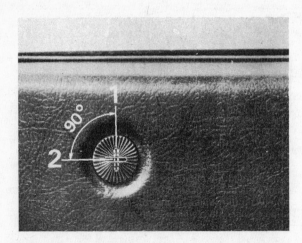

Fig. 12.22 Trim panel retainer on two-door model (Sec 27)

1   Locked position   2   Unlocked position

7   Prise the trim panel from the door using a wide blade screwdriver where necessary.
8   Remove the protective sheet if necessary (photos).
9   Refitting is a reversal of removal, but apply a liquid locking agent to the threads of the locking knob.

28 Seats – removal and refitting

Front driver's seat
1   On pre-1981 models set the seat to its middle height position then disconnect the wiring for the heating element and seat belt warning system. Push back the catches and raise the front of the seat until the rear brackets are disengaged. The seat can then be removed complete with the rails.
2   On 1981 on models slide the seat fully to the rear and remove the socket-head screws from the frame. Disconnect the wiring, tilt the seat back and remove the seat upwards (photo).

Front passenger seat
3   On pre-1981 models remove the socket-head screws and lift the seat from the rails.
4   On 1981 on models slide the seat fully to the rear, disconnect the wiring, and remove the screws from the frame. Slide the seat forwards and unscrew the nuts from the height adjusting mechanism then remove the seat.

Rear seats
5   The rear seats can be removed by unbolting the hinges from the body.

29 Facia panel – removal and refitting

Figs 12.23 and 12.24 show the individual components of the facia panel and removal is straightforward provided the following points are noted:

(a)   Disconnect the battery negative lead before commencing work
(b)   Remove the instrument panel as described in Chapter 10
(c)   The heater unit can be removed together with the facia panel in which case the cooling system must be drained as described in Chapter 2 and the hoses disconnected.

12

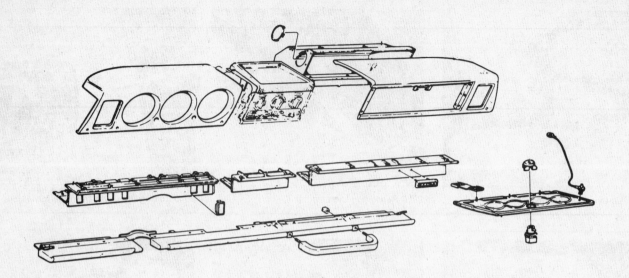

Fig. 12.23 Facia panel components on 99 models (Sec 29)

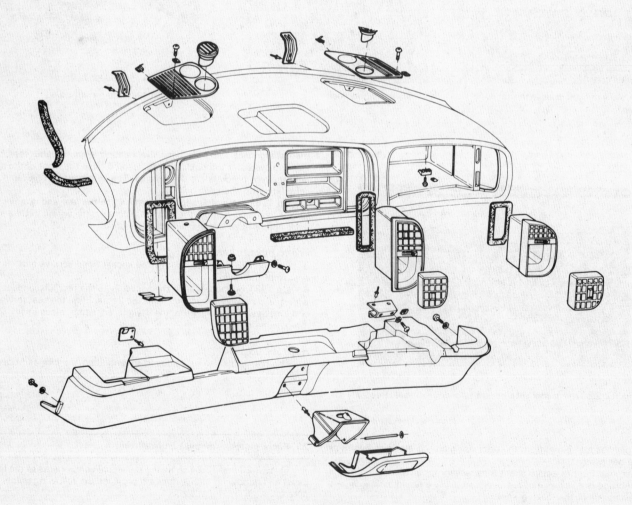

Fig. 12.24 Facia panel components on 900 models (Sec 29)

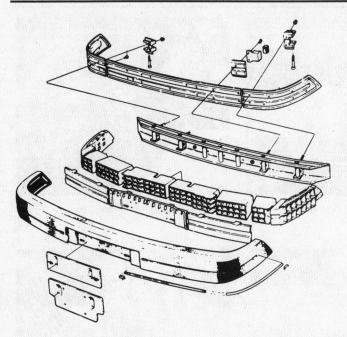

Fig. 12.25 Front bumper components (Sec 30)

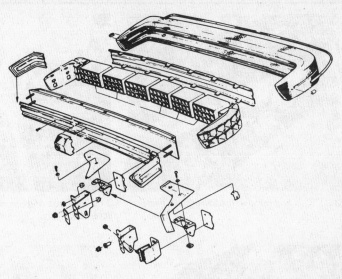

Fig. 12.26 Rear bumper components (Sec 30)

30 Bumpers – removal and refitting

Front bumper

1   On 99 models unscrew the bolts from the mounting brackets and withdraw the bumper.
2   On 900 models unscrew the two vertical socket-head bolts from beneath the mountings and withdraw the bumper.
3   Refitting is a reversal of removal.

Rear bumper

4   Unscrew the bolts/nuts from the mounting brackets or dampers and withdraw the bumper (photo).
5   Refitting is a reversal of removal.

31 Heater matrix – removal and refitting

99 models

1   Drain the cooling system as described in Chapter 2.
2   Remove the alternator as described in Chapter 10.
3   With the battery negative lead disconnected remove the radiator fan relay from the bulkhead.
4   Remove the screws and withdraw the fan casing panel, then remove the screws and withdraw the matrix retaining plate.

5   Remove the water valve cap and the control cable, then remove the valve screw.
6   Loosen the heater hose clips and disconnect the hoses.
7   Disconnect the thermostat coil from the matrix. Remove the water valve together with the coil.
8   Withdraw the matrix from the thermostat casing.
9   Refitting is a reversal of removal.

900 models

10 Disconnect the battery negative lead.
11 Working inside the car remove the steering column lower shroud.
12 Unscrew the nuts and bolts from the bulkhead and withdraw the lower facia panel (photos).
13 Remove the screws and withdraw the air duct (photos).
14 Prise out the left-hand side defroster/speaker grille, then slide the water valve control rod forwards so that it is released from the control knob. Then pull it from the water valve. Remove the heater control switches.
15 Remove the screws and withdraw the matrix lower covers (photo).
16 Drain the cooling system as described in Chapter 2.
17 Loosen the clips and disconnect the heater hoses from the engine compartment side of the bulkhead (photos). Plug the outlets.
18 Unhook the brake pedal return spring and hold the pedal down on left-hand drive models.
19 Separate the matrix and water valve from the heater housing and withdraw it from the car.
20 Where applicable remove the capillary tube from the matrix taking care not to damage it.
21 Unbolt the water valve and remove the gasket.
22 Refitting is a reversal of removal, but always fit a new gasket to the water valve. Fill the cooling system as described in Chapter 2.

30.4 Rear bumper mounting bracket

31.12A Remove the screw behind the ashtray ...

31.12B ... and the bolts from the bulkhead ...

12

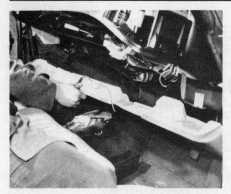
31.12C ... and remove the lower facia panel

31.13A Removing the air duct outer screws ...

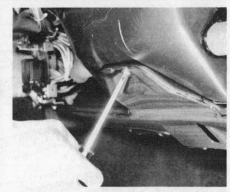
31.13B ... and central screw

31.15 Heater matrix lower cover and air tube

31.17A Loosen the clips ...

3.17B ... and disconnect the heater hoses

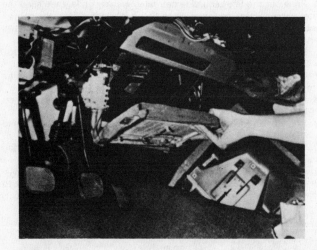
Fig. 12.27 Removing the heater matrix (Sec 31)

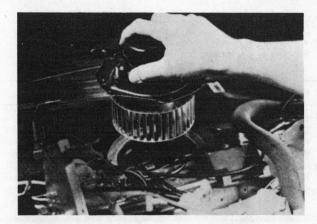
Fig. 12.28 Removing the heater fan motor on 900 models (Sec 32)

32 Heater fan motor – removal and refitting

99 models

1   Disconnect the battery negative lead.
2   Remove the wiper motor as described in Chapter 10.
3   Disconnect the fan motor wiring.
4   Unscrew the motor retaining screws and withdraw it slightly, then separate the motor from the fan and withdraw the motor followed by the fan.
5   If necessary remove the fan bearing and plate.
6   Refitting is a reversal of removal.

900 models

7   Disconnect the battery negative lead.
8   Remove the facia panel.
9   Disconnect the fan motor wiring (photo).
10 Remove the right-hand side defroster valve housing screws.
11 Remove the retaining screws and withdraw the fan motor.
12 Refitting is a reversal of removal.

33 Heater intake filter (900 models) – renewal

1   The heater intake filter is located on the right-hand side of the bulkhead in the engine compartment.

32.9 Heater fan motor and wiring

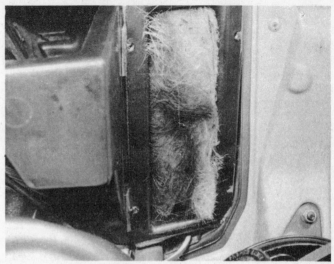

33.2 Heater intake filter

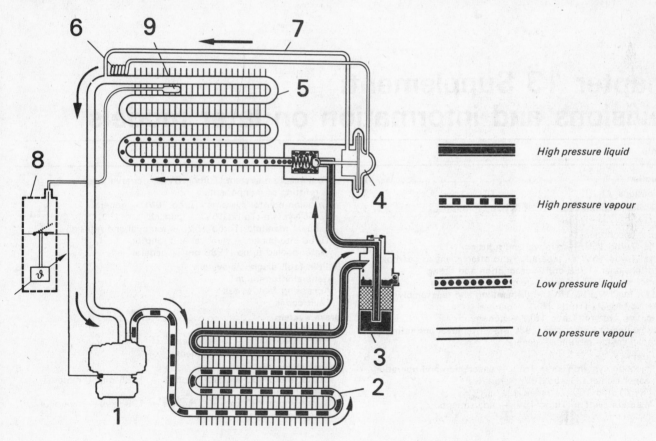

Fig. 12.29 Air conditioning system circulation diagram (Sec 34)

1 Compressor	4 Expansion valve	expansion valve body	9 Temperature-sensitive
2 Condenser	5 Evaporator	7 Compensating hose	anti-frost thermostat
3 Receiver shell	6 Temperature-sensitive	8 Anti-freezing thermostat	body

High pressure liquid

High pressure vapour

Low pressure liquid

Low pressure vapour

2 Remove the four screws and slide out the filter body (photo).
3 Insert the new filter and tighten the screws.

34 Air conditioning system – precautions and maintenance

Never disconnect any part of the air conditioning system unless it has previously been discharged by a qualified refrigeration engineer. Where the compressor, condenser or evaporator obstruct other mechanical operations such as engine removal, it is permissible to move them to the limit of their flexible hoses, but not to disconnect the hoses.

Regularly check the condenser for clogging with flies or leaves, and if necessary hose clean with water. Also check the tension of the compressor drivebelt. The belt deflection should be approximately 0.4 to 0.6 in (10.0 to 15.0 mm) at the centre point of its longest run. If adjustment is required loosen the pivot and adjustment bolts, move the compressor as necessary, then retighten the bolts.

12

Chapter 13 Supplement:
Revisions and information on later models

Contents

1 Introduction

Although a number of minor changes have been made to Saab 99 and 900 models, the most significant revisions occurred in 1984 with the introduction of the Saab 90 to replace the 99 model, and the introduction of the Saab 900 Turbo 16. In addition, some components from the 9000 model, such as the braking system, were incorporated on later models.

The Saab 90 is essentially a two-door model comprising the front half of a 99 and rear half of a 900, powered by a single carburettor version of the 1985cc engine. Apart from various minor modifications, the 90 should be regarded mechanically as a 99 with 900 rear suspension. Whilst few direct references are made to the 90 in this Supplement, the necessary technical information will readily be found in the manual.

The information in this supplement applies mainly to models manufactured from 1983 on; the remaining information for earlier models is to be found in Chapters 1 to 12. It is suggested that the Supplement is referred to before the main Chapters of the manual; this will ensure that any relevant information can be collected and accommodated into the earlier Chapters. Time and cost will therefore be saved, and the particular job completed correctly.

We are once again indebted to Saab (Great Britain) Limited and Saab-Scania of Sweden for the supply of technical information and certain illustrations used in this Supplement.

2   Specifications

The specifications listed here are revisions of, or supplementary to, the main specifications given at the beginning of each Chapter.

Type H (8V) engine — 1982 on

Compression ratio
North American models:

Turbo APC	8.5:1
Canada, excluding Turbo (1984 on)	9.25:1
Normally aspirated (1986 on)	10.1:1

Pistons (1986 on)
Normally aspirated engines:

Diameter of top depression	2.52 in (64 mm)
Top depression depth	0.39 in (1.00 mm)

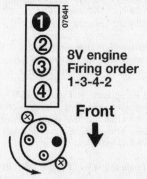

8V engine
Firing order
1-3-4-2

Front

Cylinder location and distributor rotation

Turbo 16V engine

General

Type	Four cylinder in-line, twin overhead camshaft, sixteen valve engine mounted with flywheel at front of car
Compression ratio	9.0:1

Camshaft

Bearing diameter	1.139 to 1.140 in (28.922 to 28.935 mm)
Endfloat	0.003 to 0.014 in (0.08 to 0.35 mm)

Pistons (1986 on)

Diameter of top depression	2.52 in (64 mm)
Top depression depth	0.152 in (3.85 mm)

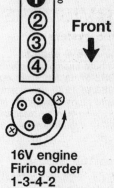

Front

Valve timing
To 1985:

Inlet opens	10° BTDC
Inlet closes	56° ABDC
Exhaust opens	56° BBDC
Exhaust closes	16° ATDC

Turbo 16V 1986 on:

Inlet opens	16° BTDC
Inlet closes	56° ABDC
Exhaust opens	61° BBDC
Exhaust closes	13° ATDC

Fuel injection 1986 on:

Inlet opens	16° BTDC
Inlet closes	44° ABDC
Exhaust opens	61° BBDC
Exhaust closes	13° ATDC

16V engine
Firing order
1-3-4-2

Cylinder location and distributor rotation

Valves
Valve seat width:

Inlet	0.039 to 0.059 in (1.0 to 1.5 mm)
Exhaust	0.049 to 0.068 in (1.25 to 1.75 mm)

Valve stem diameter:

Inlet	0.2742 to 0.2748 in (6.960 to 6.975 mm)
Exhaust	0.2740 to 0.2750 in (6.955 to 6.980 mm)
Maximum valve play in guide	0.020 in (0.5 mm)
Valve guide length	1.930 in (49.0 mm)
Valve spring free length	1.773 in (45.0 mm)
Valve clearance	Self-adjusting by hydraulic tappets

Torque wrench settings

	lbf ft	Nm
Camshaft bearing caps	11	15
Valve covers	11	15
Oil pump	6	7.8
Camshaft sprocket	46	62
Chain tensioner		
To 1987	46	62
1988 on	52	65
Cylinder head bolts (1988 on)		
Stage 1	44.5	60
Stage 2	59	80
Stage 3	Tighten an additional quarter turn (90°)	

13

Fuel system

Single carburettor engines

Type (1985 on) .... Zenith 175 CDSEVX
Fast idling speed (1983 on) .... 1350 rpm
CO content (with distributor vacuum and crankcase
   ventilation hoses disconnected):
   1979 to 1983 models .... 0.5 to 2.5% at 850 rpm
   1984 on .... 0.2 to 1.0% at 850 rpm

Twin carburettor engines

CO content (with distributor vacuum and crankcase
   ventilation hoses disconnected) — 1983 on .... 0.2 to 1.0% at 850 rpm

Fuel injection — Type H (8V) engines

CO content (at idling speed) — North American models:
   1982 USA models with catalyst .... Oxygen sensor pulse relation within 45 to 55% with warm engine
   1982 and 1983 Canada models.................... 0.5 to 1.5%
   1984 Canada models .... Oxygen sensor pulse relation within 45 to 55% with warm engine

Fuel injection — Turbo 16V engines

Type .... Bosch LH-Jetronic
Idling speed .... 850 ± 50 rpm

Fuel injection — all

Line pressure (at atmospheric in inlet manifold):
   1986 Turbo .... 36 psi (2.5 bar)
   1986 normally aspirated .... 43 psi (3.06 bar)
   1987 (all) .... 41 psi (2.8 bar)
Residual pressure, engine switched off:
   Turbo .... 33 psi (2.3 bar)
   Normally aspirated .... 39 psi (2.8 bar)
Idling control valve (1986 on) resistance .... 40 ± 4 ohm

Turbo system

Type H (8V) engines

Maximum charging pressure:
   1982 North American models .... 8.7 ± 0.7 lbf/in² (0.6 ± 0.05 bar)
   1983 to 1985 North American models .... 9.4 ± 0.7 lbf/in² (0.65 ± 0.05 bar)
   1986 North American models .... 10.3 ± 0.7 lbf/in² (0.72 ± 0.05 bar)
   1987 on North American models .... 9.7 ± 0.7 lbf/in² (0.67 ± 0.05 bar)
Pressure switch actuating pressure:
   North American models with APC .... 13.8 ± 0.7 lbf/in² (0.95 ± 0.05 bar)

Turbo 16V engines

Maximum charging pressure:
   UK models .... 12.3 ± 0.7 lbf/in² (0.85 ± 0.05 bar)
   North American models .... 10.8 ± 0.7 lbf/in² (0.75 ± 0.05 bar)
Pressure switch actuating pressure:
   UK models .... 15.9 ± 0/7 lbf/in² (1.10 ± 0.05 bar)
   North American models .... 13.8 ± 0.7 lbf/in² (0.95 ± 0.05 bar)

Ignition system

Ignition timing

Type H (8V) engines — Canada models:
   1981 to 1983............................... 18° BTDC at 2000 rpm with vacuum hose disconnected
   1984 on .... 20° BTDC at 2000 rpm with vacuum hose disconnected
Turbo 16V engines — all models .... 16° BTDC at 850 rpm with vacuum hose disconnected
Non-turbo 16V engines (1986 on) .... 14° BTDC at 850 rpm with vacuum hose disconnected

Spark plugs

Type — Turbo 16V engines .... Champion C7YG or C7GY
                                      NGK BCP 6ES or BCP 7ES
                                        Bosch F6DC or F7DC
Electrode gap .... 0.024 in (0.6 mm)

Driveshafts

Torque wrench settings	lbf ft	Nm
Driveshaft nut (1981 on)	214 to 228	290 to 310

Brake system

Front brakes — 1988 on

Make	Girling
Type	Ventilated disc with floating yoke
Outer diameter of disc	11 in (278 mm)
Thickness of new disc	0.87 in (23.5 mm)
Minimum thickness of disc after grinding	0.79 in (21.5 mm)
Maximum runout	0.003 in (0.08 mm)
Maximum thickness variation	0.0006 in (0.015 mm)
Lining thickness of new pad	0.434 in (11.0 mm)
Minimum lining thickness	0.04 in (1.0 mm)

Rear brakes — 1988 on

Make	ATE
Type	Disc with floating yoke
Outer diameter of disc	10.2 in (258 mm)
Thickness of new disc	0.35 in (9.0 mm)
Minimum thickness of disc after grinding	0.30 in (7.5 mm)
Maximum runout	0.003 in (0.08 mm)
Lining thickness of new pad	0.434 in (11.0 mm)
Minimum lining thickness	0.04 in (1.0 mm)

Torque wrench settings

	lbf ft	Nm
Front caliper guide pin	22 to 26	30 to 35
Rear caliper guide pin	18 to 22	25 to 30
Front brake yoke bolts	52 to 82	70 to 110
Rear brake yoke bolts	30 to 49	40 to 54

Electrical system

Alternator

Type	Bosch 55 amp, 65 amp, 70 amp or 80 amp/Motorola 70 amp
Brush protrusion (minimum)	0.20 in (5.0 mm)

Starter motor (90 and 900 models — 1985 on)

Type	Bosch pre-engaged with planetary reduction gear

Fuses

900 models — 1984 on	6 x 10 amp, 12 x 15 amp, 3 x 20 amp, 1 x 25 amp, 4 x 30 amp

3 Routine maintenance

The service and maintenance schedule and time intervals have been revised for 1985 on UK models and are as follows. The service requirements for North American models are essentially unchanged and are as given in Routine Maintenance at the beginning of this manual.

Further details of the operations described will be found in the appropriate Chapters indicated, where applicable.

Every 250 miles (400 km) or weekly – whichever comes first

Engine, cooling system and brakes (Chapters 1, 2 and 9)
Check the oil level and top up if necessary
Check the coolant level and top up if necessary
Check the brake fluid level in the master cylinder reservoir and top up if necessary

Lights and wipers (Chapter 10)
Check the operation of all interior and exterior lights, wipers and washers
Check and if necessary top up the washer reservoir

Tyres (Chapter 11)
Check the tyre pressures and adjust if necessary
Visually examine the tyres for wear or damage

Every 6000 miles (10 000) km) or 6 months – whichever comes first

Engine (Chapter 1)
Change the engine oil on Turbo models

Cooling system (Chapter 2)
Visually inspect the cooling system for signs of leaks
Check the coolant level and top up if necessary

Fuel and exhaust system (Chapters 3 and 13)
Check the condition and security of the fuel lines and connections in the engine compartment

Ignition system (Chapter 4)
Clean, check and adjust the spark plugs

Braking system (Chapter 9)
Check the disc pads for wear and renew if necessary
Check the brake fluid level in the master cylinder reservoir and top up if necessary

Suspension and steering (Chapter 11)
Check the power steering fluid level and top up if necessary
Visually examine the tyres for wear or damage
Check the tyre pressures and adjust if necessary

13

Every 12 000 miles (20 000 km) or 12 months – whichever comes first

Engine (Chapter 1)
Change the engine oil and filter on all models
Check and adjust the valve clearances on Turbo models (except Turbo 16V)
Check the condition and security of the crankcase ventilation hoses and connections
Visually check the engine for oil leaks and for the security and condition of all related components and attachments

Cooling system (Chapter 2)
Visually inspect the cooling system for signs of leaks or deterioration of the hoses or clips
Check the coolant level and top up if necessary

Fuel and exhaust system (Chapters 3 and 13)
Clean the air cleaner element on non-Turbo models
Renew the air cleaner element on Turbo models (except Turbo 16V)
Check the conditon and security of the fuel lines and connections in the engine compartment
Top up the damper oil level on carburettor engines
Adjust the idling speed and where applicable synchronise the twin carburettors
Check and if necessary adjust the CO content
Check and adjust the choke control and fast idling where applicable
Check the condition and security of the vacuum lines
Check the operation of the APC control unit and related components on Turbo models
Check Turbo charging pressure and operation
Check the exhaust system for leaks and security

Ignition system (Chapter 4)
Renew the spark plugs
Check the condition of the spark plug HT leads
Check and if necessary adjust the ignition timing
Check the function of the delay valve and renew if necessary

Transmission (Chapters 6 and 7)
Check the manual gearbox or automatic transmission oil/fluid level and top up if necessary
Check the differential oil level and top up if necessary (automatic transmission models only)

Braking system (Chapter 9)
Check the disc pads for wear and renew if necessary
Check the brake fluid level in the master cylinder and top up if necessary
Check and if necessary adjust the handbrake
Check the condition and security of the brake pipes and flexible hoses

Electrical system (Chapter 10)
Check all drivebelts for condition and tension
Check the battery terminals for cleanliness and security and top up the electrolyte level where applicable
Check and if necessary adjust the headlamp alignment
Check the operation of all electrical equipment

Suspension and steering (Chapter 11)
Check all rubber boots and gaiters for signs of damage or deterioration and renew as necessary
Check for excess wear or free play in all steering and suspension balljoints and pivot mountings
Check the shock absorbers for leaks and condition
Check the power steering fluid level and top up if necessary
Visually examine the tyres for wear or damage
Check the tyre pressures and adjust if necessary
Check the toe-in and adjust if necessary

Every 18 000 miles (30 000 km) or 18 months – whichever comes first

In addition to the items listed in the 6000 mile (10 000 km) service, carry out the following:

Body (Chapter 12)
Renew the heater intake filter on 900 models

Every 30 000 miles (50 000 km) or 30 months – whichever comes first

In addition to the item listed in the 6000 mile (10 000 km) service, carry out the following:

Engine (Chapter 1)
Check and adjust the valve clearances on non-Turbo models

Cooling system (Chapter 2)
Drain and flush the system and renew the antifreeze

Fuel and exhaust system (Chapters 3 and 13)
Renew the fuel filter (except Turbo 16V models)
Effective with the 1988 models, renew the fuel filter on all models

Braking system (Chapter 9)
Renew the brake fluid

Suspension and steering (Chapter 11)
Check the front suspension camber and castor angles

Every 54 000 miles (90 000 km) or 54 months – whichever comes first

In addition to the items listed in the 6000 mile (10 000 km) service, carry out the following:

Fuel and exhaust system (Chapters 3 and 13)
Renew the fuel filter on Turbo 16V engines

Every 60 000 miles (100 000 km)

In addition to the items listed in the 6000 mile (10 000 km) service, carry out the following:

Fuel and exhaust system (Chapters 3 and 13)
Effective with 1988 models, the heated oxygen sensor should be renewed on all models. Note that effective with 1988 models the service reminder lamp has been eliminated

4 Engine

General description
From approximately May 1984, Saab 900 Turbo models became available with a choice of two engines. The original engine continued virtually unchanged, but was redesignated Type H (8V). The new engine, designated Turbo 16V, is of the same capacity (displacement) as the previous unit and shares the cylinder block, crankcase and bottom end components of the Type H (8V) engine. The main differences occur in the cylinder head area which has new combustion chamber profiles and contains 4 valves per cylinder (2 inlet and 2 exhaust); giving 16 in all. The valves are operated by maintenance-free hydraulic tappets directly actuated by twin overhead camshafts, chain driven from the crankshaft.

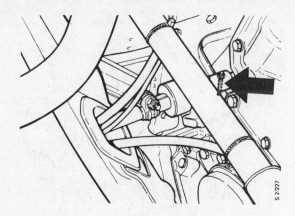

Fig. 13.1 Gearshift rod tapered pin location – arrowed
(Sec 4)

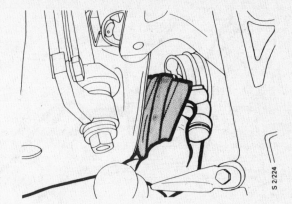

Fig. 13.2 Fold back the rubber bellows from the inner ends
of the driveshafts (Sec 4)

Apart from the operations described in the following sub-sections, the remainder of the repair and overhaul procedures are the same as for the Type H (8V) engine, described in Chapter 1.

Engine (Turbo 16V) – removal and refitting

1 Disconnect the battery negative terminal.
2 Drain the cooling system, as described in Chapter 2.
3 Remove the bonnet, as described in Chapter 12.
4 Jack up the front of the car and support it on axle stands. Chock the rear wheels and remove the right-hand front wheel.
5 Engage reverse gear then, from underneath the car, tap out the gearshift rod tapered retaining pin (Fig. 13.1).
6 Disconnect the speedometer cable from the rear of the gearbox.
7 Remove the exhaust pipe to transmission retaining bolt at the clamp bracket.
8 Loosen the clips and fold back the rubber bellows from the inner ends of the driveshafts.
9 Using a jack, raise the right-hand front suspension assembly slightly and place a metal or hardwood block between the upper control arm and the body. Lower the jack.
10 Unscrew and remove the bolts securing the right-hand lower control arm to the lower balljoint. Pull out the driveshaft until the inner

joint is free from the inner driveshaft.
11 Disconnect the battery positive terminal and release the lead from the retaining clips on the body.
12 Disconnect the earth braid from the transmission.
13 Make a note of their locations then disconnect the leads at the starter motor.
14 Undo the bolts securing the exhaust pipe to the manifold and separate the joint.
15 Disconnect the pressure pipe from the power steering pump and plug the pipe after removal. Take care not to allow fluid to drip on the engine mounting rubber block or rubber suspension bushes.
16 On models equipped with air conditioning, remove the compressor drivebelt, referring to Chapter 12 if necessary.
17 Disconnect the cooling system hoses at the thermostat housing, expansion tank, heat exchanger valve and at the radiator bottom outlet.
18 Disconnect the electrical wiring and cable harness connections at the following location (Fig. 13.3):

(A) At the air mass meter sensor
(B) At the throttle switch
(C) At the auxiliary air valve (or AIC actuators)
(D) At the fuel injection valves
(E) At the thermostatic switch (NTC transmitter)
(F) At the earthing point on the front engine lifting bracket

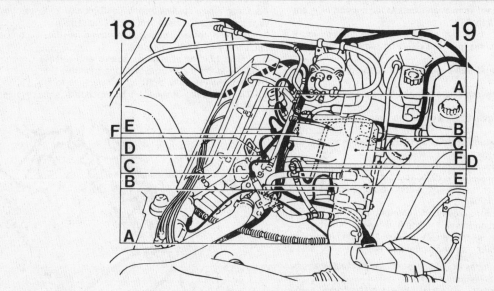

Fig. 13.3 Engine electrical wiring connections (Sec 4)

Left-hand side: Items described in paragraph 18   *Right-hand side: Items described in paragraph 19*

13

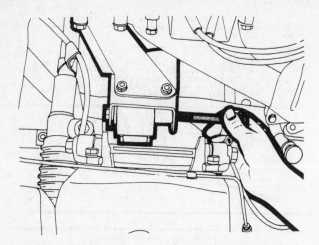

Fig. 13.4 Engine mounting bolt removal (Sec 4)

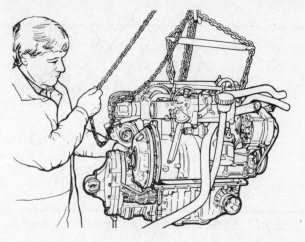

Fig. 13.5 Removing the engine and gearbox assembly (Sec 4)

19 Disconnect the remaining cable harness connections at the following locations (Fig. 13.3):

    (A) *Terminal block and connector at the air conditioning compressor (where fitted)*
    (B) *At the alternator*
    (C) *At the oil pressure switch*
    (D) *Black, yellow and red leads at the idling increase valve*
    (E) *At the temperature gauge transmitter*
    (F) *At the knock detector*

20 Release the clips securing the wiring harness in position, withdraw the loose cables and move the complete harness clear of the engine.
21 Remove the alternator, referring to Chapter 10 if necessary.
22 Disconnect the brake servo vacuum hose at the inlet manifold.
23 Disconnect the accelerator cable and sheath.
24 Undo the air conditioner bracket retaining bolts (where fitted) and move the compressor clear of the engine. **Do not** disconnect any of the air conditioning system pipes or hoses at the compressor.
25 Disconnect the fuel lines at the fuel pressure regulator and at the front of the fuel injection manifold.
26 Remove the ignition coil.
27 Disconnect the turbo pressure line at the turbo-compressor and at the intercooler/throttle housing.
28 Remove the air mass meter and suction pipe from the turbo unit.
29 Disconnect the crankcase ventilation hoses at the suction pipe and the hoses at the solenoid valve.
30 Disconnect the wiring at the Hall effect transmitter and coil in the distributor. Release the wiring from the retaining clips on the clutch cover.
31 Disconnect the solenoid valve hoses at the charging pressure regulator and turbo unit.
32 Disconnect the clutch hydraulic hose at the slave cylinder and plug the hose after removal.
33 Attach suitable lifting gear to the engine brackets and just take the weight of the power unit.
34 Remove the engine mounting bolts and raise the engine until the left-hand inner driveshaft joint can be released.
35 Raise the engine further until sufficient clearance exists to enable the air-cooled oil cooler hoses to be disconnected.
36 Disconnect the hose at the power steering pump and drain the remaining fluid into a container.
37 Continue lifting the engine slowly and carefully until it is clear of the engine compartment then lower it to the floor or onto the bench.
38 Refitting the engine is the direct reverse of the foregoing procedure, but note the following additional points:

    (a) *Ensure that the driveshaft inner joints are packed with the specified grease (see Chapter 8)*
    (b) *Tension the alternator, power steering and air conditioning drivebelts with reference to Chapter 10, 11 and 12 respectively*
    (c) *Fill and bleed the power steering system, as described in Chapter 11*

    (d) *Bleed the clutch hydraulic system, as described in Chapter 5*
    (e) *Fill the cooling system, as described in Chapter 2*

Engine (Turbo 16V) – separation and attachment to gearbox

39 With the power unit removed from the car, clean the engine and gearbox externally and wipe dry.
40 Drain the engine oil.
41 Remove the EGR pipe and the clutch cover.
42 Remove the oil dipstick pipe and oil return pipe from the turbo compressor. Remove the transmission stay plate.
43 The clutch shaft must now be removed. To do this use an 8 mm bolt to attach a suitable length of metal bar to the front of the shaft, then top the upper section of the bar until the shaft is released from the support bearing, clutch plate and primary gear.
44 Undo and remove the three socket-headed bolts from the clutch slave cylinder.
45 Undo all the bolts securing the engine to the gearbox and also release the oil filler pipe retaining clip on the inlet manifold.
46 Carefully lift the engine up and off the gearbox while at the same time remove the release bearing guide sleeve. Remove the gasket.
47 Before refitting the engine to the gearbox ensure that the mating faces are clean and check that the two guide dowels are in place in the gearbox mating face.
48 Place a new gasket on the gearbox and apply jointing compound to the cuttings in the gasket ends (Fig. 13.7).
49 Apply a thread sealing compound to the six tapped holes, as shown in Fig. 13.8.
50 While holding the guide sleeve and release bearing in position carefully lower the engine onto the gearbox.
51 Refit the retaining bolts, with reference to Fig. 13.7.
52 The remainder of the refitting procedure is the reverse sequence to removal.

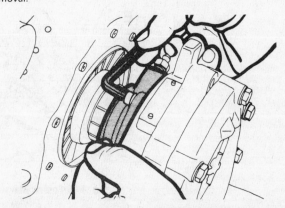

Fig. 13.6 Remove the three socket-headed bolts from the clutch slave cylinder (Sec 4)

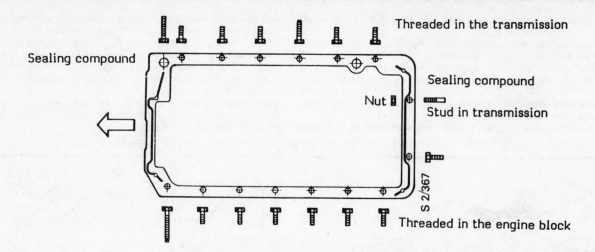

Threaded in the transmission

Sealing compound

Sealing compound

Nut

Stud in transmission

S 2/367

Threaded in the engine block

Long bolt for engine bracket (no washer)

Fig. 13.7 Engine to gearbox gasket and bolt layout (Sec 4)

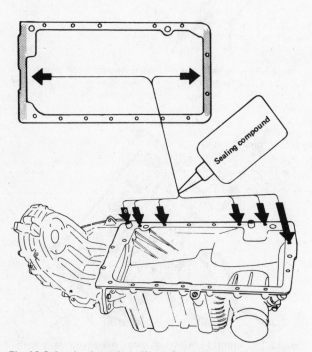

Sealing compound

Fig 13.8 Apply thread sealing compound to the gearbox threaded holes (Sec 4)

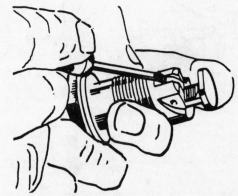

Fig. 13.9 To preset the chain tensioner, press down on the ratchet and push the tensioner in (Sec 4)

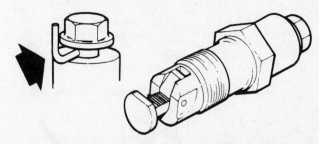

Fig. 13.10 Do not remove the safety pin (arrow) until the chain tensioner has been installed in the cylinder block (Sec 4)

Chain tensioner (1988 on) — description and fitting

53 A new chain tensioner with a tighter adjustment range is fitted to all 1988 US models, and should also be used as a replacement component for all earlier models.

54 To install the new tensioner, preset the unit by pressing down on the ratchet and pushing in the tensioner as shown in the accompanying illustration.

55 Fit the chain tensioner and new gasket into the cylinder block and tighten to the specified torque.

56 Withdraw the safety pin, which will allow the spring to push the tensioning arm out, thereby tensioning the chain. **Warning:** *Never remove the safety pin before the tensioner has been fitted to the engine.*

Cylinder head (Turbo 16V) — removal and refitting

Note: *If the engine has been removed from the car, ignore references to removal of wiring and services which will have been carried out during the engine removal procedure.*

57 Remove the bonnet as described in Chapter 12, and the battery as described in Chapter 10.

58 Drain the cooling system, as described in Chapter 2.

59 Refer to Section 5 of this Chapter and remove the exhaust manifold and turbo unit assembly.

60 On models equipped with air conditioning, remove the tensioning pulley and compressor drivebelt.

61 Slacken the power steering pump mounting bolts, remove the drivebelt and push the pump clear of the cylinder head.

62 Disconnect the radiator top hose at the thermostat housing.

63 Release the wiring harness and cable retaining clips on the cylinder head.

64 Remove the fuel pressure regulator.

65 Disconnect the earth leads for the fuel injection system.

66 Remove the auxiliary air valve.

13

67 On models equipped with air conditioning, remove the compressor bracket from the cylinder head.

68 Remove the inlet manifold with fuel injection manifold and fuel injection valves as a complete assembly.

69 Disconnect the lead at the water temperature transmitter.

70 Remove the two bolts securing the timing cover to the underside of the cylinder head.

71 Remove the right-hand engine mounting bolts and spacer sleeves which are secured to the cylinder head.

72 Remove the distributor cap, HT leads and valve cover lid, followed by the valve cover. Disconnect the crankcase ventilation hose and recover the two semi-circular rubber halves from the cylinder head.

73 Turn the engine over until the TDC 0° mark is aligned with the timing mark on the housing cover and with number 1 piston at TDC firing position. With the engine in this position the timing notch on each camshaft should be aligned with the mark on the respective bearing caps (Fig. 13.14).

74 Undo and remove the timing chain tensioner assembly from the side of the cylinder head. Take care not to lose the spring and plunger as the tensioner is withdrawn.

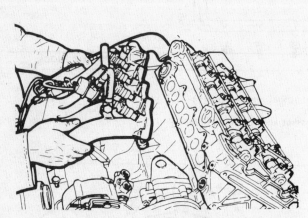

Fig. 13.11   Remove the inlet manifold and fuel injection manifold as a complete assembly (Sec 4)

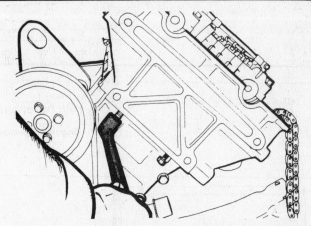

Fig. 13.12   Remove the two bolts securing the timing cover to the cylinder head (Sec 4)

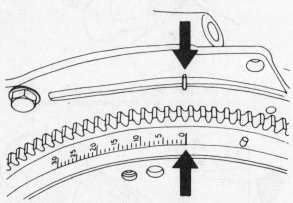

Fig. 13.13   Flywheel positioned at TDC (Sec 4)

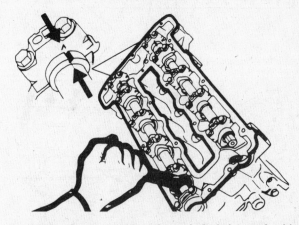

Fig. 13.14   Correct position of camshaft timing mark with No 1 piston at TDC firing position (Sec 4)

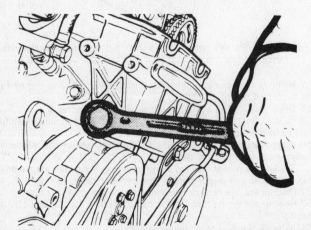

Fig. 13.15   Timing chain tensioner removal (Sec 4)

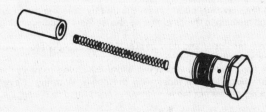

Fig. 13.16   Timing chain tensioner components (Sec 4)

75 Using a spanner on the flats of each camshaft to prevent rotation, undo and remove the camshaft sprocket retaining bolts.
76 Withdraw each sprocket from its respective camshaft and disengage it from the timing chain.
77 Using a syringe or old rags, remove as much oil as possible from around the camshafts and in the cylinder head recesses.
78 Raise the engine slightly as necessary so that there is clearance between the cylinder head and the right-hand engine mounting.
79 Using a suitable Torx type socket bit adaptor, undo the cylinder head retaining bolts in the reverse order to that shown in Fig. 13.21.
80 Carefully lift the cylinder head up and off the engine, taking care not to damage the timing chain guides. Lay the chain over the guide after the head has been removed. Remove the cylinder head gasket.
81 After removal of the cylinder head do not lay it directly on the bench as this may damage the slightly protruding valves. Use blocks of wood at each end to prevent valve-to-bench contact.
82 Before refitting the cylinder head, ensure that the block and head mating faces are clean and dry.
83 Make sure that the crankshaft and camshafts are still at the TDC position as described in paragraph 73 and reposition them if necessary.
84 Locate a new cylinder head gasket over the dowels on the block

mating face. **Do not** use any joining compound on the gasket.
85 To facilitate refitting of the cylinder head, make up a guide pin by sawing the head off an old cylinder head bolt, chamfering its end, then fitting it to the end bolt hole, as shown in Fig. 13.20.
86 Locate the cylinder head over the guide pin, then, using this pin as a pivot, twist the cylinder head to clear the pivoting timing chain guide. Now lower the head fully into place and remove the guide pin.
87 Fit the cylinder head bolts and tighten them in the sequence shown in Fig. 13.21 to the torque settings given at the beginning of Chapter 1. Refit the two additional bolts securing the cylinder head to the timing cover.
88 With the chain in place over the exhaust valve camshaft sprocket, hold the chain taut and fit the sprocket to the camshaft.
89 Keep the chain between the sprockets taut and slip the inlet valve camshaft sprocket into position under the chain and onto the camshaft. Fit the sprocket retaining bolts, but only lightly tighten them at this stage.
90 Set the timing chain tensioner by pressing the plunger in against spring tension, then turning it until it locks in place. Check that the copper sealing washer is sound, then fit the tensioner to the cylinder head.

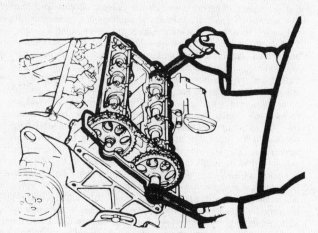
Fig. 13.17 Removing the camshaft sprocket retaining bolts (Sec 4)

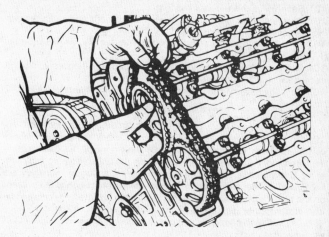
Fig. 13.18 Removing the camshaft sprockets (Sec 4)

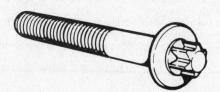
Fig. 13.19 Torx type cylinder head retaining bolts (Sec 4)

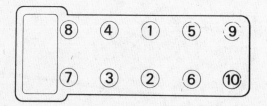
Fig. 13.21 Cylinder head bolt tightening sequence (Sec 4)

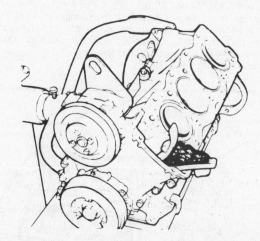
Fig. 13.20 Guide pin in position prior to refitting cylinder head (Sec 4)

13

91 Release the tensioner by pushing the chain guide against it using a stout screwdriver. Now push the pivoting chain guide against the chain to induce a basic tension in the cabin. Check that when the pivoting guide is pushed against the tensioner it returns under spring pressure.

92 Turn the crankshaft two complete turns clockwise, as viewed from the transmission end, then return the crankshaft to the TDC position. Check that the timing marks for both camshafts are realigned with the marks on the bearing caps.

93 If the timing marks are still correct, remove the sprocket retaining bolts, apply thread locking compound to their threads and refit them. Hold the camshaft as was done for removal and tighten the bolts to the specified torque. Make sure that the camshafts and sprockets do not move during tightening.

94 With a new gasket and semi-circular rubber plug halves in position, refit the valve cover.

95 Refit the right-hand engine mounting bolts and spacer sleeves.

96 Refit the distributor cap, HT leads and valve cover lid.

97 Refit the water temperature transmitter lead.

98 Refit the inlet manifold and injection manifold assembly.

99 Refit the auxiliary air valve and fuel pressure regulator.

100 Refit the air conditioning compressor, refit the air conditioning compressor and power steering pump drivebelts and tension the belts.

101 Reconnect the radiator top hose.

102 Reconnect the fuel injection system earth leads and reclip the wiring harness to the cylinder head.

103 Refit the exhaust manifold and turbo assembly, as described in Section 5.

104 Refill the cooling system as described in Chapter 2 and, if necessary, top up the engine oil.

105 Refit the battery and bonnet, as described in Chapters 10 and 12 respectively.

Cylinder head (Turbo 16V) — dismantling and reassembly

106 With the cylinder head on the bench, mark the position of the distributor body using a dab of paint, then remove the distributor.

107 Remove the oil feed pipe, then undo the bolts securing the camshaft bearing caps. Lift off the bearing caps, ensuring that they are kept in strict order and position. If no identification markings are present on the bearing caps, suitably identify each cap for fitted direction, location and whether it is fitted to the inlet or exhaust camshaft.

108 Lift out each camshaft and mark or identify them inlet or exhaust as applicable.

109 Withdraw the hydraulic tappets and place them in a suitably marked partitioned box or similar in such a way that they will not be interchanged.

110 To remove the valves, a special valve spring compressor is needed (Saab tools 83 93 761 and 83 93 779) due to the recessed location of the springs. Also, the surface around the springs is the sealing surface for the hydraulic tappets and great care must be taken not to nick or scratch this surface with the spring compressor. A plastic protector sleeve is available for this purpose and should be used during the valve removal and refitting operation.

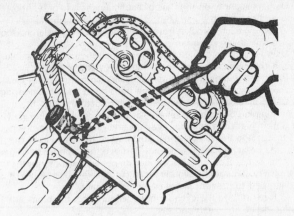

Fig. 13.22   Releasing the timing chain tensioner using a stout screwdriver (Sec 2)

111 With the special tools to hand, compress the valve springs, hook out the split collets and remove the valves, springs and caps. Store the valves in holes in two sheets of cardboard, one for the inlet valves marked 1 to 8 and one for the exhaust valves also marked 1 to 8.

112 With the cylinder head now dismantled, the valve components, camshafts and cylinder head can be inspected and renovated where necessary using the procedures described in Chapter 1.

113 Begin reassembly of the cylinder head by refitting the valves and springs using the same procedure as for removal. Use new valve stem oil seals, liberally lubricate the stems and ensure each valve is fitted to its original position. If any of the valves have been renewed, had the seats recut or their faces ground, then their static fitted height must be checked. The valve stems must protrude by a predetermined amount, measured from the base of the camshaft bearing journals in order for the hydraulic tappets to operate correctly. If this height is not correct a small amount of metal must be ground off the valve stem, or the valve seat must be recut as required to alter the valve height. A special measuring tool is used to check the height and this can only be done by a Saab dealer who will also be able to take any corrective action that may be necessary. If, therefore, any work has been done to the valve assemblies, the cylinder head should be taken to a suitably equipped dealer at this stage for checking before proceeding with the reassembly.

114 Assuming the cylinder head has been checked and attended to as necessary, liberally lubricate the hydraulic tappets and insert them into their respective bores.

115 Lubricate the camshaft bearing journals and lay the two camshafts in position.

116 Fit the bearing caps and retaining bolts, then progressively tighten the bolts to the specified torque.

117 Finally, refit the oil feed pipe and the distributor.

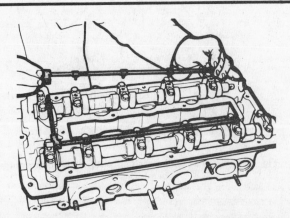

Fig. 13.23   Removing the cylinder head oil feed pipe (Sec 4)

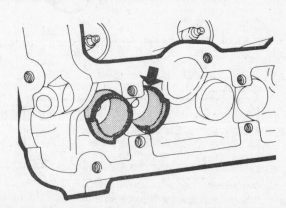

Fig. 13.24   Plastic protector sleeves in place prior to valve removal (Sec 4)

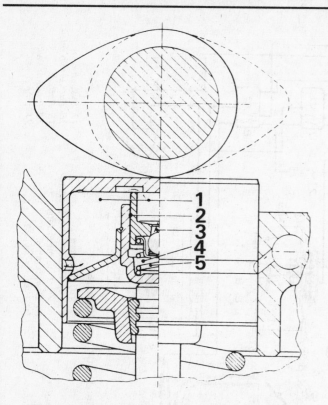

Fig. 13.25 Sectional view of a hydraulic tappet (Sec 4)

1 Storage chamber   4 High pressure chamber
2 Leakage passage   5 Spring
3 Check valve

Hydraulic tappets (Turbo 16V) — general

118 The Turbo 16V engine is fitted with hydraulic tappets which automatically maintain the valve clearances within a predetermined working range and eliminate the need for periodic adjustment.
119 Each tappet is a sealed unit and cannot be dismantled for inspection or repair. In the event of failure or damage the tappet must be renewed as an assembly.
120 The tappets are normally silent in operation but some noise, identifiable as a rattling or tapping sound from one or more tappets, may be experienced under certain conditions, such as after an oil change, on starting a cold engine, after any work that has involved cranking the engine on the starter motor, or after engine overhaul or renewal of a tappet. Any noise which does occur should disappear within a few minutes or at worst approximately 15 minutes. If persistent noise is noticeable, the advice of a dealer should be sought.

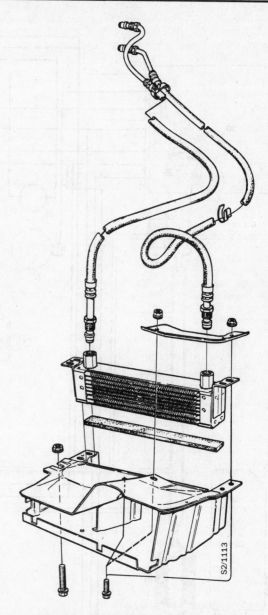

Fig.   13.26 The later model air-cooled oil radiator is located below the left headlight cluster (Sec 4)

Lubrication system (Turbo 16V) — general

121 The Turbo 16V engine incorporates a forced feed lubrication system with flow and pressure generated by a crankshaft driven gear and eccentric ring oil pump.
122 The oil level dipstick has marks for minimum and maximum oil level in the sump with 1.76 Imp pt (1.0 litre, 2.1 US pt) difference between the markings.
123 The engine oil level should be checked with the car on level ground and 2 to 5 minutes after switching off a warm engine. Oil should only be added if the level is lower than midway between the two marks on the dipstick. If topping-up is necessary, oil is added through the dipstick tube.

Air-cooled engine oil cooler (1986 on) — removal and refitting

124 Remove the left-hand light cluster.
125 Remove the baffle plate and the left-hand headlight.
126 Remove the nut from the bolt in the radiator member as shown in Fig. 13.27, then remove the bolt from underneath.
127 Remove the six bolts securing the shroud and cooler to the body, lower the cooler and disconnect the oil lines.
128 Installation is the reverse of the removal procedure.

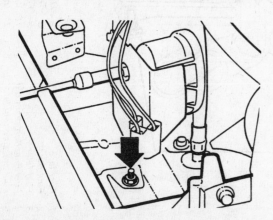

Fig. 13.27   Remove the nut (arrow) from the top of the radiator support member (Sec 4)

13

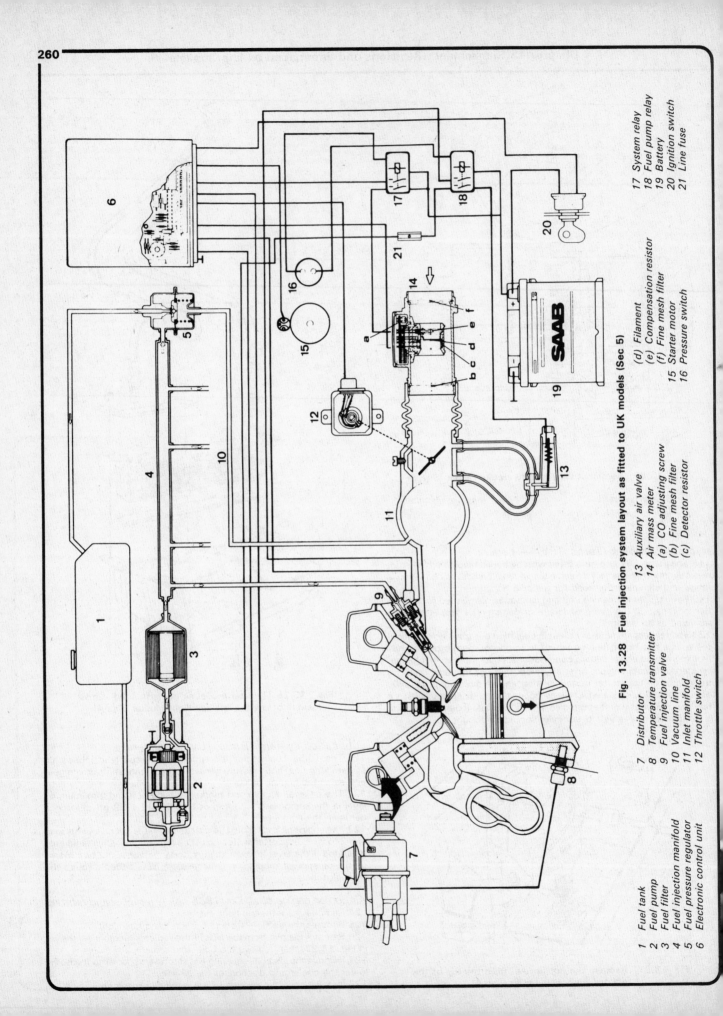

Fig. 13.28 Fuel injection system layout as fitted to UK models (Sec 5)

1   Fuel tank
2   Fuel pump
3   Fuel filter
4   Fuel injection manifold
5   Fuel pressure regulator
6   Electronic control unit

7   Distributor
8   Temperature transmitter
9   Fuel injection valve
10 Vacuum line
11 Inlet manifold
12 Throttle switch

13 Auxiliary air valve
14 Air mass meter
(a) CO adjusting screw
(b) Fine mesh filter
(c) Detector resistor

(d) Filament
(e) Compensation resistor
(f) Fine mesh filter
15 Starter motor
16 Pressure switch

17 System relay
18 Fuel pump relay
19 Battery
20 Ignition switch
21 Line fuse

Hydraulic engine mounts — general

129 On later 1985 Turbo 16 models fitted with a manual gearbox, hydraulic engine mounts are fitted at the two rear mounting points.

130 On 1986 and later models all vehicles equipped with manual gearboxes have hydraulic engine mounts fitted front and rear, and models fitted with an automatic transmission have hydraulic mounts fitted at the rear only.

131 The removal and installation procedure for the hydraulic engine mounts remains essentially unchanged from that for the rubber mounts.

5 Fuel system

Fuel injection system (Turbo 16V) — description and operation

Saab 900 models powered by the Turbo 16V engine are equipped with a turbocharger with intercooler and Bosch LH Jetronic microprocessor-controlled fuel injection system. This new system incorporates the best features of previous systems with the capability to measure air mass and hence the density of the induction air rather than just its volume as in previous fuel injection systems. In addition the LH-Jetronic system utilizes a microprocessor which receives information from various sensors to accurately determine fuel injector opening duration.

The component parts of the system and their operation are as follows.

Fuel pump: The fuel pump is an electrically driven rotary unit located in and totally surrounded by fuel in the fuel tank. On North American models the pump is located inside a container within the fuel tank. The container is pressurised by an additional feed pump enabling the main pump to draw pressurised fuel, thus eliminating the formation of vapour bubbles. The pumps are fitted with a non-return valve in the pressure line to prevent the fuel pressure dropping after the pump stops running.

Fuel filter: The filter consists of a nylon filter and paper element located in an aluminium housing. This assembly is connected in the pressure line between fuel pump and pressure regulator and is mounted on the left-hand inner wheel arch. On 1986 and later models the filter is mounted to the right-hand side of the chassis forward of the fuel tank.

Fuel pressure regulator: The fuel pressure regulator is mounted on a bracket attached to the cylinder head and inlet manifold, immediately adjacent to the fuel injection manifold. The regulator maintains fuel pressure in the pressure line at a set value above the pressure in the inlet manifold. Excess fuel is returned to the fuel tank via the fuel return line.

Fuel injection valves: The fuel injection valves are operated by solenoids according to impulses received from the microprocessor in the electronic control unit. The valves open and close simultaneously, once for each engine revolution during normal running and twice when cold starting.

Fuel injection manifold: Each of the fuel injection valves is connected to the fuel injection manifold which supplies fuel to each valve from the fuel pressure line, controlled by the fuel pressure regulator.

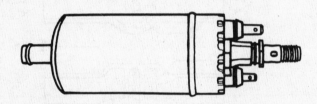

Fig. 13.29 Fuel pump as used on UK models (Sec 5)

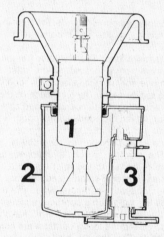

Fig. 13.30 Fuel pump as used on North American models (Sec 5)

1 Main pump   3 Feed pump
2 Container

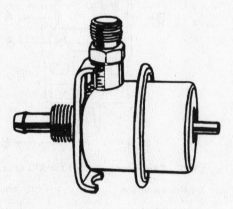

Fig. 13.31 Fuel pressure regulator (Sec 5)

Fig. 13.32 Fuel injection valve (Sec 5)

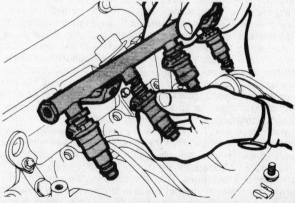

Fig. 13.33 Fuel injection manifold (Sec 5)

13

Fig. 13.34   NTC temperature transmitter (Sec 5)

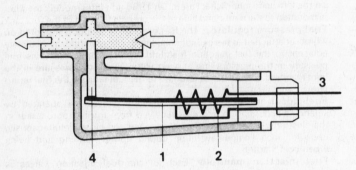

Fig. 13.36   Component parts of the auxiliary air valve (Sec 5)

1 Bi-metal strip   3 Terminal
2 Coil   4 Valve disc

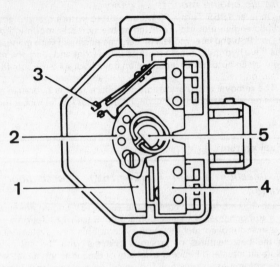

Fig. 13.35   Throttle switch internal components (Sec 5)

1 Throttle shaft arm   4 Idling contacts
2 Throttle switch cam   5 Throttle shaft
3 Full throttle contacts

Inlet manifold: The inlet manifold houses the fuel injection valves and the NTC temperature transmitter and is bolted to the left-hand side of the cylinder head.

NTC temperature transmitter: The Negative Temperature Coefficient temperature transmitter is located in the inlet manifold and provides the microprocessor in the electronic control unit with information on engine temperature. The resistance of the NTC resistor within the unit alters according to temperature and this is interpreted by the microprocessor which responds with longer injection valve duration (cold engine – richer mixture) or shorter injection valve duration (warm engine – weaker mixture) accordingly.

Throttle switch: The throttle switch is attached to the throttle housing which is in turn bolted to the inlet manifold. The switch is connected to the throttle butterfly spindle and consists internally of a cam plate and two sets of switch contacts. When the throttle is open the cam plate actuates the full throttle contacts, a signal is sent to the microprocessor and the engine is provided with full throttle enrichment. With the throttle closed the idling contacts are actuated and the engine is provided with fuel for the idle mode.

Auxiliary air valve: On UK models an auxiliary air valve located on the thermostat housing, is used to allow air to bypass the throttle butterfly during cold starting. The unit contains a heating coil and bi-metal strip connected to a valve disc. During cold starting the heating coil is energised, causing the bi-metal strip to deform thus opening the valve. Air now bypasses the throttle butterfly by passing through the valve via hoses connected to the throttle housing. After starting the heating coil is de-energised and the valve slowly shuts.

AIC actuator: On North American models an Automatic idling Control actuator is used to provide a stabilised idling speed under all conditions. The AIC actuator consists of a small electric motor with a valve attached to its spindle and enclosed within a housing. The unit is connected via hoses to the throttle housing and acts as an air bypass during idling. According to information received from the various sensors, the microprocessor in the electronic control unit actuates the AIC motor accordingly which in turn opens or closes the valve to control the bypass airflow. Thus the idling speed can be maintained at a stable speed despite any change in engine load which would otherwise cause a corresponding change in engine idling speed.

Electronic control unit: The unit contains the systems microprocessor, the main function of which is to calculate and control the injection valve opening duration according to information received from the various engine and fuel system sensors.

Air mass meter: The air mass meter is located between the air cleaner and inlet manifold and comprises an aluminium housing with integral

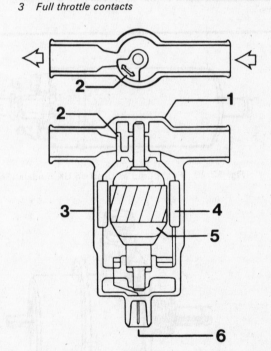

Fig. 13.37   Component parts of the AIC actuator (Sec 5)

1 Valve housing   4 Solenoid
2 Valve   5 Motor armature
3 Housing   6 Wiring connector

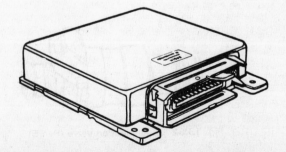

Fig. 13.38   Electronic control unit (Sec 5)

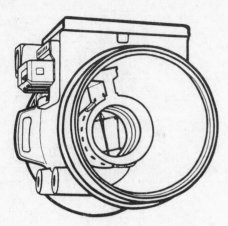

Fig. 13.39 Air mass meter (Sec 5)

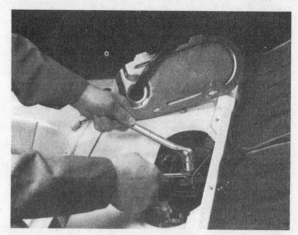

Fig. 13.40 Fuel pump removal — North American models (Sec 5)

air duct and a tube in the centre of the duct which contains a platinum wire filament. The filament is electrically heated and its temperature maintained at a constant 100 °C (approximately) above the temperature of the inlet airflow. As the intake air passes the filament the wire will cool which in turn alters its resistance. This information is analysed by the microprocessor which can then determine rate of flow and mass of air according to the changing properties of the filament.

Air cleaner element (Turbo 16V) – renewal
1 Release the turbo toggle clips securing the air mass meter to the air cleaner lid and the clips securing the lid to the air cleaner body.
2 Separate the air mass meter and lid, remove the lid from the body and lift out the element.
3 Clean the element using compressed air or renew it if at the end of its service life. Also wipe clean the inside of the air cleaner body and lid.
4 Fit the element then secure the lid and air mass meter.

Fuel filter (Turbo 16V) – renewal
5 Clean the area around the fuel line connections on the filter then undo the union bolts. Use a second spanner on the filter body hexagons to prevent the filter from twisting. Lift away the fuel lines and remove the filter.
6 Fit the new filter with the arrow pointing in the direction of fuel flow and reconnect the fuel lines. Wipe up any spilled fuel from around the filter.

Fuel injection system (Turbo 16V) — adjustments
7 Due to the complexity of the system, and the operation of the electronic control unit, the only adjustment possible without the use of special tools and equipment is the idling speed setting on UK models. All other adjustments entail the use of special electronic diagnostic equipment, a sequential setting-up procedure, and specialist knowledge which is considerably beyond the scope of this manual. In the event of a fault in the system, loss of performance, or if for any reason the function of the system does not appear satisfactory, the advice of a Saab dealer should be sought.
8 To adjust the idling speed on UK models, connect a tachometer to the engine according to the manufacturer's instructions then start the engine and allow it to reach normal operating temperature.
9 Turn the adjusting screw in the bypass passage of the throttle housing as necessary until the specified idling speed is obtained.
10 After adjustment switch off the engine and disconnect the instruments.

Fuel injection system (Turbo 16V) — removal and refitting of components
 The removal and refitting of the following components can be carried out without too much difficulty and without the use of special equipment for setting-up or adjustment after refitting. Any operations involving components not listed in this sub-section should be entrusted to a Saab dealer.

Fuel pump:
11 The procedure for fuel pump removal on UK models is the same as described in Chapter 3, Section 17 for 1980 on models. On vehicles for North America proceed as follows.
12 Disconnect the battery negative terminal, raise the luggage compartment floor hatch then remove the hatch after undoing the two retaining screws.
13 Release the two bayonet catches and lift off the fuel pump access cover.
14 Disconnect the fuel pump, feed pump and fuel flow transmitter electrical leads then remove the access cover.
15 Undo the fuel line banjo union taking care not to lose the washers.
16 Using a jointed screwdriver, release the pump sealing collar clamp then lift out the pump and container.
17 Disconnect the fuel return hose from the pump and release the feed pump wiring from the gland in the tank. Withdraw the pump assembly and remove it from the car.
18 Refitting is the reverse sequence to removal.
Electronic control unit
19 At the right-hand side of the car interior, remove the sill scuff plate then release the lower leading edge of the door weatherstrip seal.
20 Remove the carpet-to-wheel arch retaining plate and fold back the carpet.
21 Disconnect the wiring plug at the control unit by releasing the fastener then withdrawing the plug diagonally upwards and outwards.
22 Undo the retaining screws and remove the control unit from the car.
23 Refitting is the reverse sequence to removal.
NTC temperature transmitter
24 Refer to Chapter 2 and drain approximately 7 Imp pt (4.2 US qt, 4 litre) of coolant from the system.
25 Disconnect the crankcase ventilation hose from the valve cover.
26 Remove the fuel pressure regulator complete with mounting bracket from the cylinder head.
27 Disconnect the wiring connector then undo the transmitter using a deep socket.
28 Refitting is the reverse sequence to removal, but use a new copper washer if necessary. Refill the cooling system, as described in Chapter 2 after refitting.
Fuel injection manifold and injection valves
29 Thoroughly clean the manifold and injection valves externally and dry with compressed air or lint-free rags.
30 Disconnect the crankcase ventilation hose from the valve cover and the electrical connections at each injection valve. Release the cable harness clip at the fuel injection manifold to inlet manifold joint.
31 Disconnect the fuel hose banjo unions at each end of the fuel injection manifold. Wipe up any spilled fuel immediately.
32 Undo the bolts securing the fuel injection manifold to the inlet manifold and lift off the injection manifold complete with injection valves.
33 Slide off the retaining clips and remove the injection valves using a twisting action.
34 Refitting is the reverse sequence to removal, but renew any O-rings

13

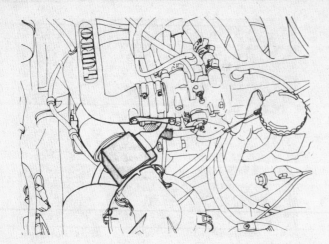

Fig. 13.41 Air mass meter (shaded) location and attachments (Sec 5)

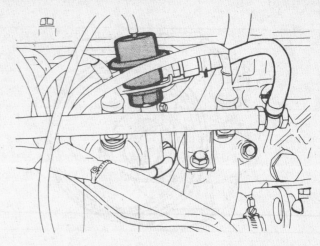

Fig. 13.42 Fuel pressure regulator (shaded) location and attachments (Sec 5)

that are in any way damaged or deformed. To facilitate refitting, smear the O-rings lightly with petroleum jelly.

Air mass meter

35 Slacken the air mass meter gaiter retaining clip and disconnect the electrical wiring plug.

36 Release the two toggle clips and withdraw the air mass meter from the gaiter and air cleaner cover.

37 Refitting is the reverse sequence to removal.

Fuel pressure regulator

38 Disconnect the hose from the fuel injection manifold and the hose from the inlet manifold at the fuel pressure regulator. Wipe up any spilled fuel immediately.

39 Remove the regulator, complete with bracket, from the cylinder head and disconnect the fuel return hose.

40 Remove the fuel pressure regulator from the bracket

41 Refitting is the reverse sequence to removal.

Auxiliary air valve (UK models)

42 Disconnect the hoses and electrical connections at the air valve then undo the screws and remove the unit from its location.

43 Refitting is the reverse sequence to removal.

Emission control systems (Turbo 16V) – general

44 The emission control systems fitted to the Turbo 16V engine vary considerably according to operating territory, but the principles of their operation are essentially the same as described in Chapter 3.

45 The complexities of the system are such that repair, adjustment or component replacement should be carried out by a suitably equipped Saab dealer.

Turbo system (Turbo 16V) – general

46 The turbo system used on Turbo 16V engines is the same as used on 1981 on models and details will be found in Chapter 3, Section 27. Removal of the turbocharger complete with exhaust manifold is described in the following sub-section.

Exhaust manifold (Turbo 16V) – removal and refitting

47 Refer to Chapter 10 and remove the battery.

48 Refer to Chapter 4 and remove the distributor.

49 Disconnect the pressure pipe, suction pipe and oil pipe at the turbo compressor and also disconnect the oil pipe at its cylinder block attachment.

50 Disconnect the solenoid at the turbo compressor and at the charging pressure regulator.

51 Disconnect the EGR pipe at the EGR valve and at the exhaust manifold.

52 Detach the turbo unit stay plate at the transmission casing.

53 Disconnect the oil return pipe at the turbo compressor.

54 Remove the oil dipstick pipe.

55 Detach the exhaust pipe at the turbo unit flange.

56 Undo and remove the nuts, washers and spacers securing the exhaust manifold in position.

57 Ease the manifold off its mounting studs then remove it, complete with turbo unit, from the engine.

58 Detach the turbo unit from the exhaust manifold.

59 Refitting is the reverse sequence to removal using new gaskets on all mating flanges and new manifold retaining nuts.

Turbo intercooler – removal and refitting

60 Remove the mounting plate between the radiator member and the intercooler.

61 On 1986 and later models, remove the plastic shroud between the radiator member and intercooler.

62 Remove the single bolt securing the intercooler to the radiator member.

63 Remove both turbo pressure pipes and lift out the intercooler.

64 Installation is the reverse of the removal procedure.

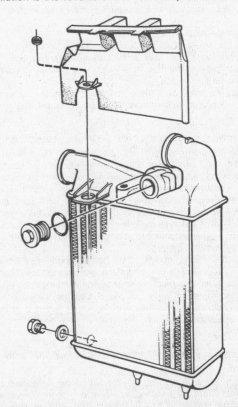

Fig. 13.43 Turbocharger intercooler radiator — exploded view (Sec 5)

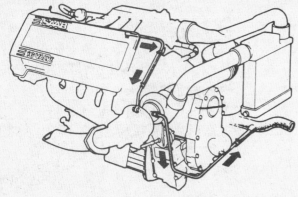

Fig. 13.44 On later models a water cooling system has been incorporated on the turbocharger to extend bearing life (Sec 5)

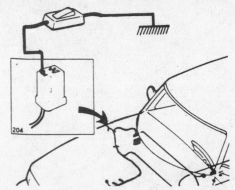

Fig. 13.45 Connect a jumper wire with an On-Off switch between the No. 3 pin in the test socket and a good ground (Sec 6)

Water-cooled turbo (1988 on) — general

65 To increase turbo bearing cooling, a water cooling system has been incorporated effective with the 1988 models.

66 With the exception of disconnecting and reconnecting the cooling water lines shown in the accompanying illustration, the turbo removal and installation procedure remains essentially unchanged.

6 Built-in fault diagnosis system

General information

The 1988 and later Model 900S (US only) is equipped with a memory facility for storing detected faults for later diagnosis. This memory facility can store up to three faults at a time, and is accessed through the "Check Engine" light on the instrument panel.

Accessing fault codes

1 A jumper wire with an on-off switch is needed to access the fault codes. The jumper is connected to the number 3 pin in the three-pin test socket on the right side of the engine compartment as shown in Fig. 13.45.

2 With the switch in the jumper wire set to *Off* (no ground circuit), turn the ignition switch to the "Run" position. The "Check Engine" light should now come on.

3 Set the jumper wire switch to *On* (completed circuit to ground). The "Check Engine" light should go off, then, in approximately 2.5 seconds, flash briefly. As soon as the light flashes turn the jumper wire switch to *Off*.

4 The first fault code will now be displayed as a series of flashes of the "Check Engine" light. There will be a single long flash to indicate the start of the process, then a series of short flashes in groups of one to four flashes, totaling five numbers. A sample fault code is shown in Fig. 13.46. In this case a fault code of 12112 is shown.

5 To display the second stored fault code, set the jumper wire switch to *On*. After a single short flash of the "Check Engine" light, set the jumper wire switch to *Off* and the next code will be displayed.

6 The third fault code (if stored) can be displayed by repeating the procedure in Step 5.

7 If no second or third fault codes have been stored, the "Check Engine" light will flash either a continuous series of long flashes or code 12444.

8 To erase the stored fault codes, set the jumper wire switch to *On*, and after three short flashes of the "Check Engine" light, turn the switch to *Off*.

Fault codes	Diagnosis
12221	Air mass meter signal faulty. Engine is in "limp-home" mode
12225	Oxygen sensor signal faulty
12223	Air leak, mixture lean
12224	Mixture excessively rich
12214	Temperature sensor faulty
12211	Incorrect battery voltage with engine running
12232	Break in circuit to ECU pin 4
12212	Throttle position sensor idle contacts faulty
12213	Throttle position sensor full-throttle contacts faulty
12222	ECU defective
12111	Air-fuel mixture fault, vehicle running
12112	Air-fuel mixture fault, engine idling
12113	Air-fuel mixture pulse ratio low
12114	Air-fuel mixture regulation faulty

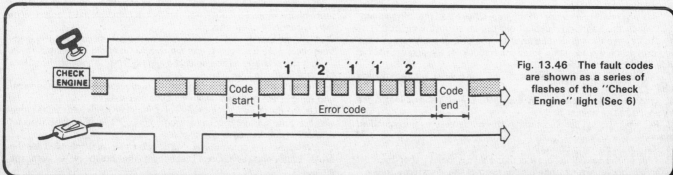

Fig. 13.46 The fault codes are shown as a series of flashes of the "Check Engine" light (Sec 6)

13

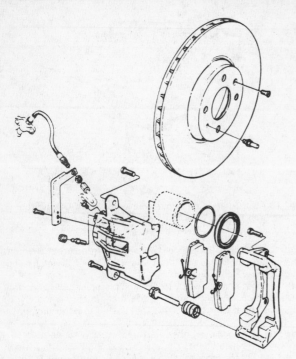

Fig. 13.47   1988 and later model front brakes feature Girling calipers and a vented disc (Sec 7)

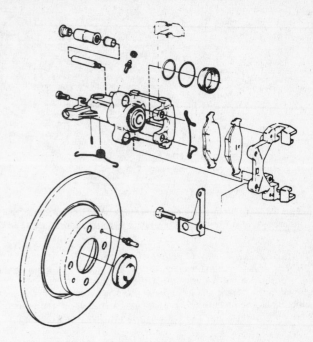

Fig. 13.48   1988 and later model rear brakes use an ATE caliper with an automatic adjustment mechanism for the handbrake (Sec 7)

7 Brake system

General information

Beginning in 1988, all models are equipped with the four-wheel disc brake system previously used on the 9000 Series, featuring Girling brake calipers and vented discs at the front and ATE calipers at the rear.

The handbrake has been relocated from the front wheels to the rear, and an automatic adjustment mechanism has been included.

Front brake pads — replacement

1   Raise the front of the vehicle, support it securely on jackstands, and remove the front wheels.
2   Simultaneously push in on the brake piston and outwards on the caliper to release the pads from the disc.
3   Remove the caliper guide pin at the top of the caliper and swivel the caliper forwards and down on the lower guide pin.
4   Remove the pads from the caliper support.
5   Fit the new pads into the carrier, rotate the caliper back into position and install the guide pin, tightening it to the specified torque.
6   The remainder of the installation is the reverse of the removal procedure. Be sure to pump the brake pedal several times to bring the new pads into contact with the disc before attempting to drive the vehicle.

Rear brake pads — replacement

7   Raise the rear of the vehicle, support it securely on jackstands and remove the rear wheels.
8   Use a screwdriver to pry off the outer brake pad retaining spring.
9   Detach the handbrake cable from the lever on the caliper.
10 Just above the handbrake lever on the caliper body remove the plug protecting the adjusting screw, then back off the screw until the pads are free of the disc.
11 Remove the caliper guide pins, lift off the caliper and remove the pads.
12 Press the caliper piston fully back into the caliper and install the new pads in the caliper body.
13 Reinstall the caliper and tighten the guide pins to the specified torque.
14 Refit the retaining spring.
15 Tighten the adjusting screw until the disc is locked, then back off the screw one-quarter to one-half turn, until the disc turns freely.

16 Reconnect the handbrake cable to the lever and check to make sure the clearance between the lever and stop is between 0.5 and 1.5 mm, adjusting as necessary.
17 The remainder of the installation is the reverse of the removal procedure. Be sure to pump the brake pedal several times to bring the new pads into contact with the disc before attempting to drive the vehicle.

8 Electrical system

Starter motor (90 and 900 models – 1985 on) – removal and refitting

1   The starter motor fitted to later 90 and 900 models is of a more powerful type and incorporates a planetary reduction gear. The unit is mounted on the inlet manifold side of the engine and removal and refitting is as follows.
2   Disconnect the battery negative terminal.
3   Disconnect the electrical connections at the solenoid.
4   Undo the two retaining bolts, move the unit back and remove it from the engine.
5   Refitting is the reverse sequence to removal.

Starter motor (90 and 900 models – 1985 on) – overhaul

6   Renewal of the brushes and the drive components can be carried out in the following way, but if more extensive overhaul is required such as renewal of the bearings, armature or field windings then it will probably be more economical to renew the complete unit for a new or factory reconditioned one.
7   With the starter motor removed from the car, disconnect the leads from the solenoid terminals and remove the solenoid retaining screws.
8   Lift the rear end of the solenoid slightly and unhook its front end from the actuator fork.
9   Remove the two screws which retain the armature shaft end cap and remove the end cap, washer, shims and seal.
10 Undo the two commutator end bracket retaining bolts then withdraw the starter body, commutator end bracket and armature as an assembly from the drive end bracket.
11 Withdraw the commutator end bracket and seal followed by the brush plate and armature. Disconnect the brush plate from the armature.

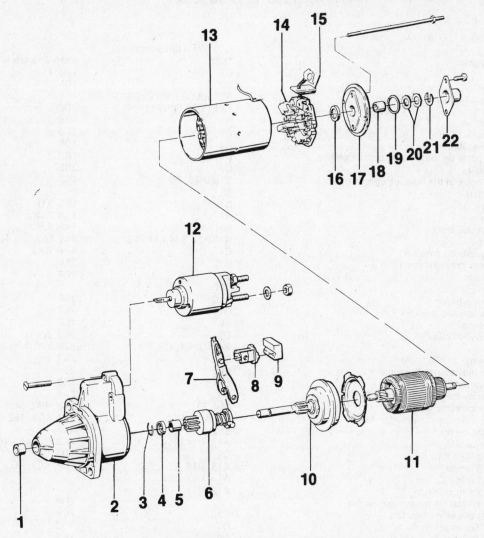

Fig. 13.49 Exploded view of the reduction gear type starter motor (Sec 6)

1 Support bush	7 Actuating fork	13 Starter body	18 Commutator end bush
2 Drive end bracket	8 Bearing bracket	14 Brush plate	19 Seal
3 Circlip	9 Bearing bracket seal	15 Seal	20 Shims
4 Stop ring	10 Planetary gear	16 Seal	21 Spring washer
5 Pinion bush	11 Armature	17 Commutator end bracket	22 End cap
6 Pinion	12 Solenoid		

12 Remove the bearing bracket seal.

13 Withdraw the planetary gear, pinion and actuating fork from the drive end bracket then remove the planetary gear cover.

14 Using a suitable tube, drive the stop ring down the armature to expose the pinion retaining circlip.

15 Extract the circlip then withdraw the pinion from the armature.

16 Extract the planetary gear retaining circlip and washer then remove the gear.

17 Inspect the dismantled components for signs of wear or damage and renew any that are suspect.

18 Reassembly is the reverse of the dismantling sequence, but lubricate the pinion spiral splines and engaging ring with silicone grease.

Fuses and relays – general

19 From 1984 on additional fuses are used to protect the electrical circuits of the vehicle, all of which are now protected except the headlights and ignition system.

20 The fuses are also a different type, known as a blade fuse, which gives greater resistance to corrosion and causes a lower voltage drop than the earlier type of fuse.

21 The blade fuses are colour-coded according to their rating as follows:

Red 10 amp
Blue 15 amp
Yellow 20 amp
Clear 25 amp
Green 30 amp

22 The fuses can be removed by simply withdrawing them from their push-fit locations. Once a fuse is removed, visual inspection will indicate whether the fuse wire has melted.

23 The fuse locations and the circuits they protect are shown on a plate adjacent to the fuse box.

13

Key to Figs. 13.50, 13.51 and 13.52

No	Component	Location 1984	1985 and later
		1984	**1985 and later**
1	Battery	B2	1C6
2	Alternator	B2	1D5
3	Earthing point, instrument panel	A12,B8,C8,C9,C11,D12, E8,E11,E12,F9,F12	2D8
4	Starter motor	B2	1D5
5	Ignition coil	A5	1C6
6	Ignition distributor	A5	1D6
7	Earthing point on the radiator cross-member	D2, E9	1A6
8	Lighting relay	D7	3B5
9	Earthing point in the luggage compartment	B12, B13, F6	4C3
10	Light switch	E8	
11	Full beam	B1, E1	1B8, 1E8
12	Dipped beam	B1, E1	1B8, 1E8
13	Parking lights, front	A1, F1	1A8, 1F8
14	Rear lights	A13,A14,B14,E14,F13	4A3,4B2,4B4,4C2,4D2,4E2
15	Number plate illumination	C13, C14	4A4, 4B3
16	Instrument lighting rheostat	C10	2E4
17	Light switch	B8	2C7
	Rheostat	C10	
18	Instrument lighting	C10	2F4
19	Glove compartment lamp	D11	2B2
20	Ignition switch	B8	4E8
21	Ignition switch relay	D5	3B8
22	Fusebox	B4, C3, C4, D3, D4	332-3D8
23	Flasher relay	E11	2C7
24	Direction indicator stalk switch	E10	2B6
25	Hazard warning light switch	E11	2B3
26	Timing delay for the AC radiator fan	D2	1A6
27	Direction indicator lamps, left-hand	E14, F1, F13	1A8, 4B2, 4C2
28	Direction indicator lamps, right-hand	A1, A13, A14	1F8, 4D2, 4E2
29	Brake light switch	E12	4C8
30	Brake lamps	A13, B14, E14, F13	4A3,4B2,4B4,4C2,4D2,4E2
31	Reversing light switch	D8	4D7
32	Reversing lamps	A13, B14, E14, F13	4B2, 4C2, 4D2, 4E2
33	Rear foglights	A13, F13	
34	Choke control contacts	B12	
35	Selector switch for the ventilation fan		2D4
36	Motor for the ventilation fan	C12	2E4
37	Radiator fan motor	D1	1D8
38	Recirculation valve	A4	1B3
39	Temperature switch, radiator fan	D2, E3	1B7, 1B2
40	Horn	D1, E1	1B8, 1D8
41	Horn contacts	E8	2C5
42	Brake warning switch	C3	1C3
43	Handbrake switch	B12	4B6
44	Oil pressure transmitter	A6	1C5
45	Coolant temperature transmitter	A6	1C5
46	Fuel level transmitter	B12	4E4
47	Combined instrument	C11	2E5
A	Fuel gauge	D10	2E6
B	Fuel reserve warning lamp	D10	2E6
C	Coolant temperature gauge	D10	2E6
D	Oil pressure warning lamp	D10	2E6
E	Charging warning lamp	C9	2E5
F	Brake system warning lamp	C10	2E5
G	Full beam warning lamp	C10	2E5
H	Direction indicator warning lamp, left-hand	D9	2E4
I	Direction indicator warning lamp, right-hand	D10	2E5
J	Indicating lamp for the rear windoow heater element	C9	2E5
K	Spare		
L	Spare		
M	Handbrake warning lamp	C10	2E5
N	EGR indicating lamp	C11	2E5
O	Choke warning lamp	C9	2E5

Key to Figs. 13.50, 13.51 and 13.52 (continued)

No	Component	Location 1984	1985 and later
48	Cigarette lighter	E11	2B2
49	Clock	D10	2E4
50	Roof lamp, centre	B10	4B4
51	Roof lamp, front	B10	4C3
52	Ignition switch illumination	B9	4D8
53	Interior lighting switch	B10	4D7
54	Door switch, courtesy lights	B7, B10, B12	2C2, 3C3, 4C7, 4E7
55	Luggage compartment lamp	B9	4D3
56	Luggage compartment light switch	B9	4E3
57	Three-pole connector		
58	Twelve-pole connector	B11, D8, E8	2A7
59	Two-pole connector		
60	Single-pole connector		
61	Windscreen wiper stalk switch	E9	2C4
62	Windscreen wiper motor	F5	1E3
63	Washer motor	B1	1E8
64	Heating pad with thermostat	A11	4A8, 4B8
65	Earthing point at the handbrake	A11, B8, B11, E9, F11	4B7, 4B8
66	Headlamp wiper motor	B1, D1	1C8, 1D8
67	Six-pole connector	B2, C1, C2, E2	1C5, 1E3
68	Horn relay	B5	3B8
69	Co-driver's seat switch for seat-belt warning lamp	B11	
70	Seat-belt switch, driver's side	B11	
71	Seat-belt switch, co-driver's side	B11	
72	Seat-belt warning lamp	B12	2B3
73	Socket for checking the timing sequence	C7	3B3
74	Resistor for reduced ventilation fan speed	C12	2D3
75	Distribution block, positive	B8	1D5
76	Switch for raising the engine idling speed	B8	4D7
77	Starting interlock contacts	B8	4D7
78	Spare		
79	Vacuum switch	E2	1A6
80	Ignition key warning buzzer	B10	
81	Parking lights	A1, F1	1A8
82	Seat belt/ignition switch warning relay	A11	4B8
83	Relay for intermittent operation of the windscreen wipers	E10	2C7
84	Diode	C10	2D5
85	Extra foglamps	A1, F1	1A8, 1F8
86	EGR selector switch		2B6
87	Spare		
88	Extra foglamp switch	E9	2E7
89	Spare		
90	Spare		
91	Selector lever position light	B8	4B8
92	Thermal time-delay switch	A2	1D5
93	Spare		
94	Starting valve	A4	
95	Auxiliary air valve	A2	1C5
96	Control pressure valve	A2	1C5
97	Temperature switch	A3	1D5
98	Spare		
99	Spare		
100	Spare		
101	Fuel feed pump	A12	4F4
102	Fuel pump relay	B6	2B7, 3B5
103	Fuel pump	A12	4E4
104	Hot-starting relay	B6	1A4
105	Engine speed relay	E2	1A4
106	Time-delay relay	F2	1A4
107	Relay for extra foglamps	F3	1A3, 3B5
108	Relay box, Lambda system	F2	
109	Spare	F2, 3	
110	Tachometer	C9	2E5
111	Spare		

13

Key to Figs. 13.50, 13.51 and 13.52 (continued)

No	Component	Location 1984	1985 and later
112	Spare		
113	Relay for the electrically heated rear window	D6	3B6
114	Spare		
115	Electric heater for the rear window	A12	4A4, 4B4
116	Switch for the electrically heated rear window	E12	2B4
117	Spare		
118	Driving lights	A1, F1	1A8, 1F8
119	Side reversing lights	A1, F1	1A8, 1F8
120	Spare		
121	Seat switch for the heating pad	A11	4B8
122	Eight-pole connector	B13, E13	
123	Four-pole connector	A8,A9,A12,F7,F9,F13,F14	2C2,3C3,4A6,4C4,4C8,4F6
124	Switch for the left-hand electrically operated rear-view mirror	F8	2E7
125	Switch for the right-hand electrically operated rear-view mirror	A12	2E4
126	Motor for the left-hand electrically operated rear-view mirror	F6	3B3
127	Motor for the right-hand electrically operated rear-view mirror	A11, 12	2B2
128	Cruise Control relay	F9	
129	Buzzer for coolant temperature	E8	
130	Coolant temperature switch	E9	
131	Electronic control unit for Cruise Control	F8	2E7
132	Sensor for the speed transmitter	F8	2E7
133	Clutch switch for Cruise Control	F8	2B5
134	Brake switch for Cruise Control	F8	2B5
135	Control unit for Lambda system	B1	1E6
136	Lambda probe	B1	1E6, 1F3
137	Throttle contacts	C2	1F5
138	Engine speed relay	E3	1A4
139	Timing valve	C1	1A6
140	Fuel shut-off valve	B5	
141	Selector for Cruise Control	F10	2B5
142	Solenoid valve for raising the engine idling speed (AC)	A4, F3	1D2
143	Recirculation switch	B8	2E6
144	Pressure switch, Turbo	D8	2C6
145	Spare		
146	Electronic unit for ignition system	A6	1D6
147	Spare		
148	Ashtray illumination	D12	2B4
149	Main switch for the fan	C12	2D4
150	Switch for air conditioner	D12	2E3
151	Time-delay relay for the interior lighting	A10	4C4
152	29-pole connector	A7-F7, F6	1E1, 3E1, 3F6
153	Lighting for the cigarette lighter	E9	2B3
154	Lighting for heater controls	E9	2B3
155	Relay for the AC radiator fan	B5	3B7
156	Relay for the AC radiator fan	D5	3B7
157	Spark plug	A4, 5	1D6
158	Negative distribution terminal	C5	3B4
159	Distribution terminal, +15	C6	3B4
160	Switch for glove compartment illumination	2B2	
161	Switch for the rear foglights	E12	
162	Switch for left-hand front electric window regulator	F10	
163	Switch for right-hand front electric window regulator	F10	4D6
164	Motor for left-hand front electric window regulator	F7	3B3
165	Motor for right-hand front electric window regulator	F9	4F8
166	Pressure switch for the AC radiator fan	E4	1B3
167	Throttle contacts for AC cut-out	F3	1E3
169	AC selector switch	B8	2E6
170	Compressor for the AC	F4	1D3, 1F3
171	Cycling clutch contact	B8	2D2
172	Radiator fan	C1	1C8
173	Diode	F4	1D3
174	Temperature switch for refrigerant	E3	
175	Electronic unit for the central locking system	A10	4D8

Key to Figs. 13.50, 13.51 and 13.52 (continued)

No	Component	Location 1984	1985 and later
176	Spare		
177	Control unit for the APC system	F6	4E5
178	Knocking sensor	F4	4F5
179	Solenoid valve	F4	1E8
180	Pressure transmitter	F6	4F4
181	Switch for the electrically operated sunroof	E9	4C7
182	Motor for the electrically operated sunroof	E10	4E4
183	Control unit for the master lock on the driver's side	A7	3B2
184	Motor for the lock on the co-driver's side	A10	3C2, 4F8
185	Motor for the right-hand rear door lock	A10	4F5
186	Motor for the left-hand rear door lock	A8	4A5
187	Vacuum pump for Cruise Control	B9	1B5
188	Motor for the tailgate lock	B9	4E3
189	Switch for the rear-door electric window regulators	F11	4D6
190	Switch for left-hand rear electric window regulator	F11, 12	4A6, 4B5
191	Switch for right-hand rear electric window regulator	F11, 12	4D5, 4F6
192	Distribution block		
193	Window regulator motor for the left-hand rear door	F12	4A5
194	Window regulator motor for the right-hand rear door	F12	4F5
195	Solenoid valve for fuel shut-off	E2	1C8
196	Throttle switch	F3	1C6
197	Temperature switch, shift-up indicator		1C4
198	Vacuum switch, gear indication		1A5
199	Switch, fifth gear		1E5
201	Relay for electric aerial		4C3
202	Loudspeaker		4D4
204	Connections for radio		2F3, 4C8
206	AC connection		
207	Test outlet, LH injection system		1D5
209	Idling speed raising valve		
210	Electronic unit for LH injection		2D2
212	Jumper unit, 2-pole		
213	Air mass meter		1E5
214	Throttle angle transmitter		1D5
215	Injection valve		1F5
216	Engine temperature transmitter		1E5
217	Main relay		2C8
218	Relay, gear indication		3B5
219	Preheater, Lambda		1F3
220	Earthing point, engine cylinder head		1C3
221	Automatic idling speed adjustment		1F3
222	Vacuum switch, Cruise Control		

Not all items are fitted to all models

The first number in the 1985 and later location codes indicates the relevant diagram (part 1, part 2 etc.)

Colour Code

BL	Blue	GN	Green	RD	Red	VL	Violet
BR	Brown	GR	Grey	SV	Black	VT	White
GL	Yellow	OR	Orange				

13

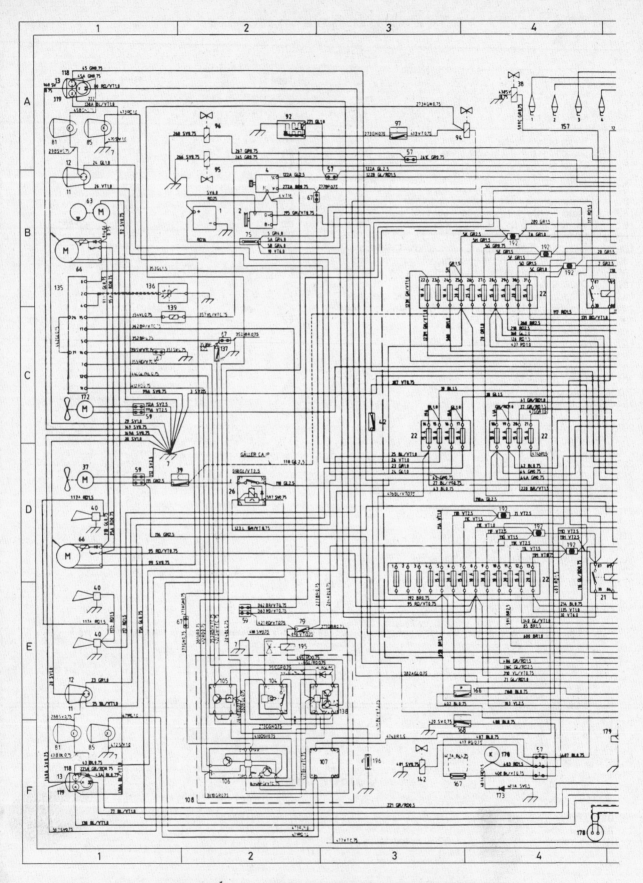

Fig. 13.50 Wiring diagram for 1984 (US and Canada) 900

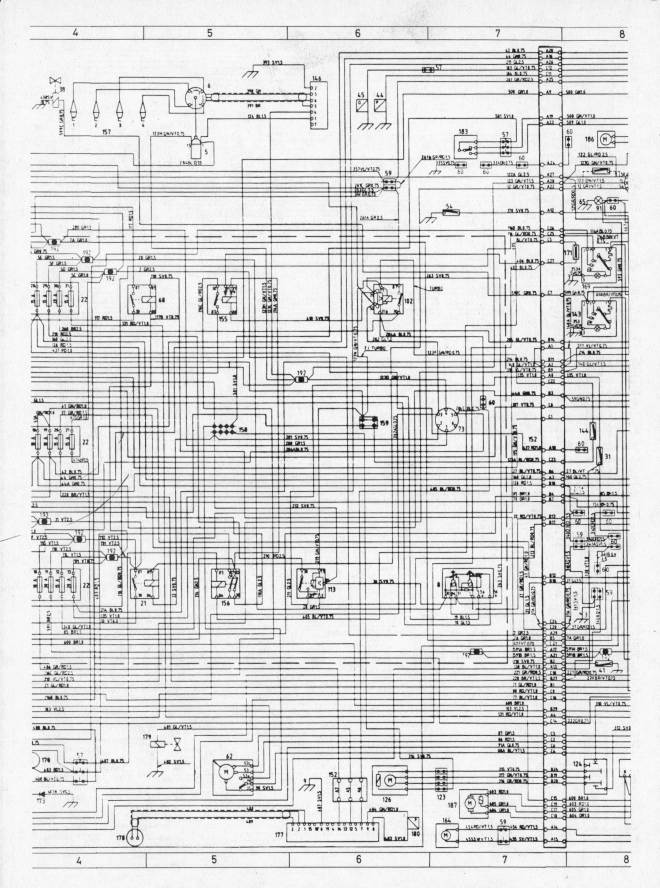

Fig. 13.50 Wiring diagram for 1984 (US and Canada) 900 (continued)

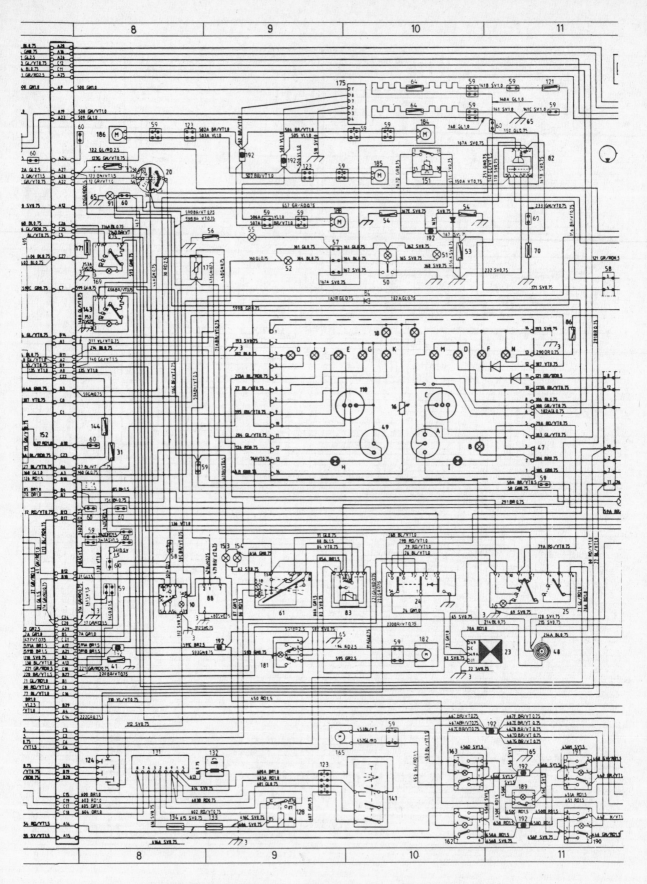

Fig. 13.50 Wiring diagram for 1984 (US and Canada) 900 (continued)

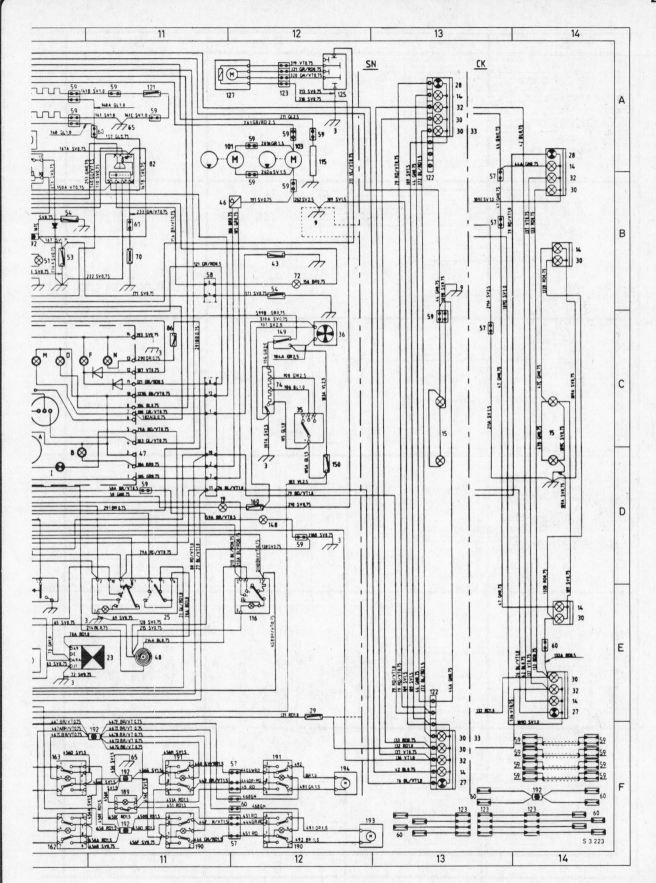

Fig. 13.50 Wiring diagram for 1984 (US and Canada) 900 (continued)

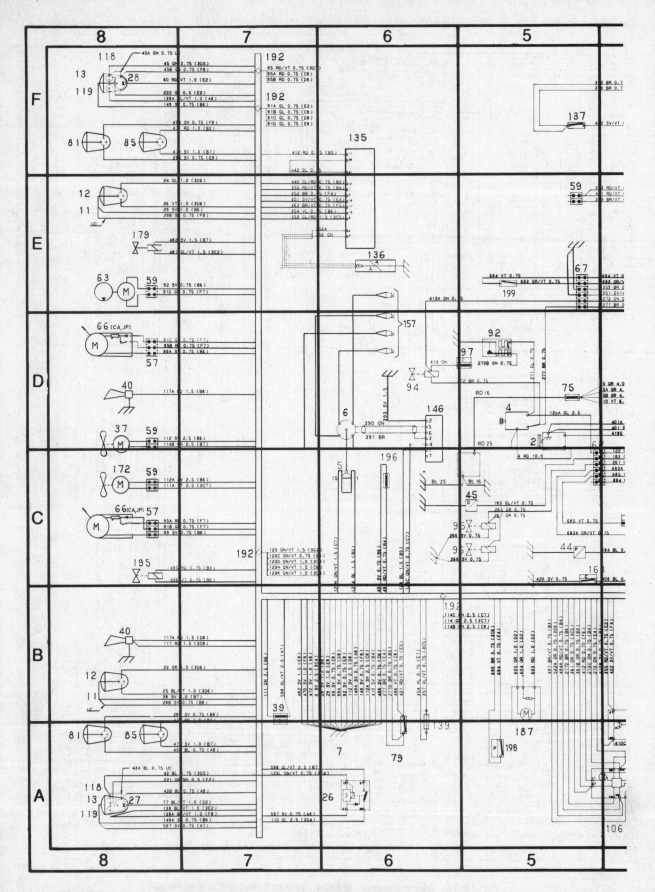

Fig. 13.51 Wiring diagram for 1985 and later (US and Canada) 8-valve 900 — part 1 engine compartment

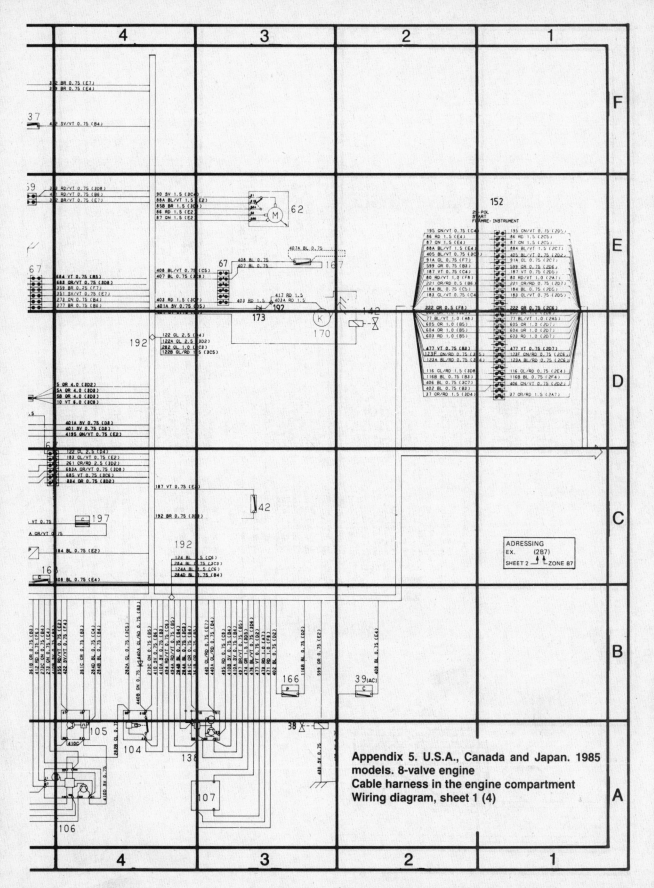

Fig. 13.51   Wiring diagram for 1985 and later (US and Canada) 8-valve 900 — part 1 engine compartment (continued)

Appendix 5. U.S.A., Canada and Japan. 1985 models. 8-valve engine
Cable harness in the engine compartment
Wiring diagram, sheet 1 (4)

ADRESSING
EX.   (2B7)
SHEET 2 ⌐ ⌐ ZONE B7

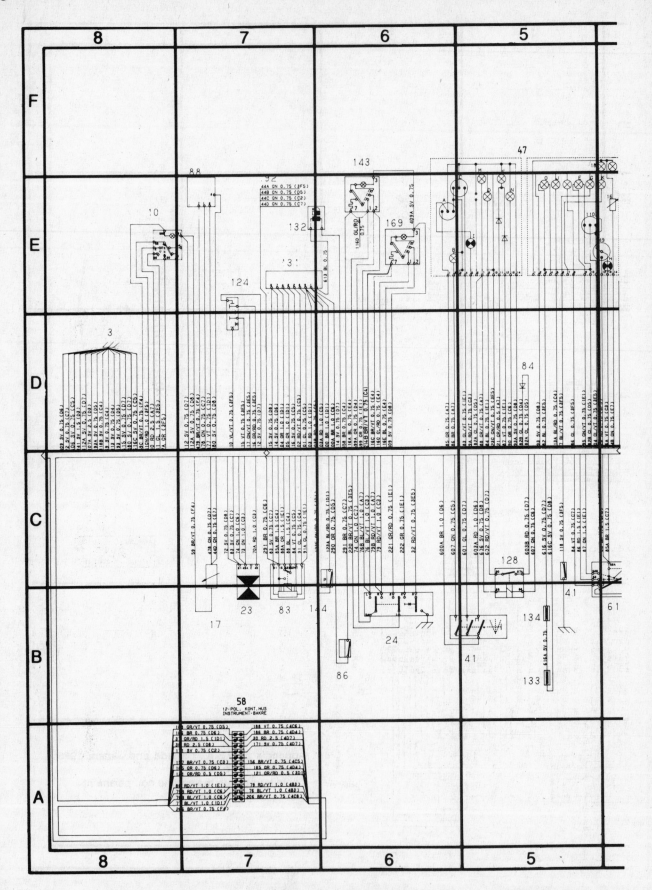

Fig. 13.51 Wiring diagram for 1985 and later (US and Canada) 8-valve 900 — part 2 instrument panel

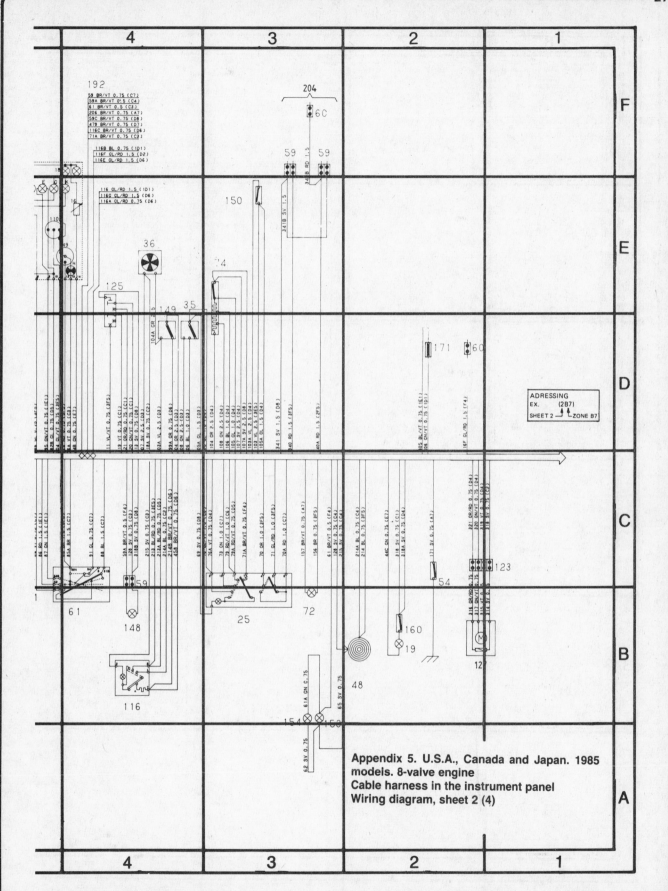

Appendix 5. U.S.A., Canada and Japan. 1985 models. 8-valve engine
Cable harness in the instrument panel
Wiring diagram, sheet 2 (4)

Fig. 13.51 Wiring diagram for 1985 and later (US and Canada) 8-valve 900 — part 2 instrument panel (continued)

13

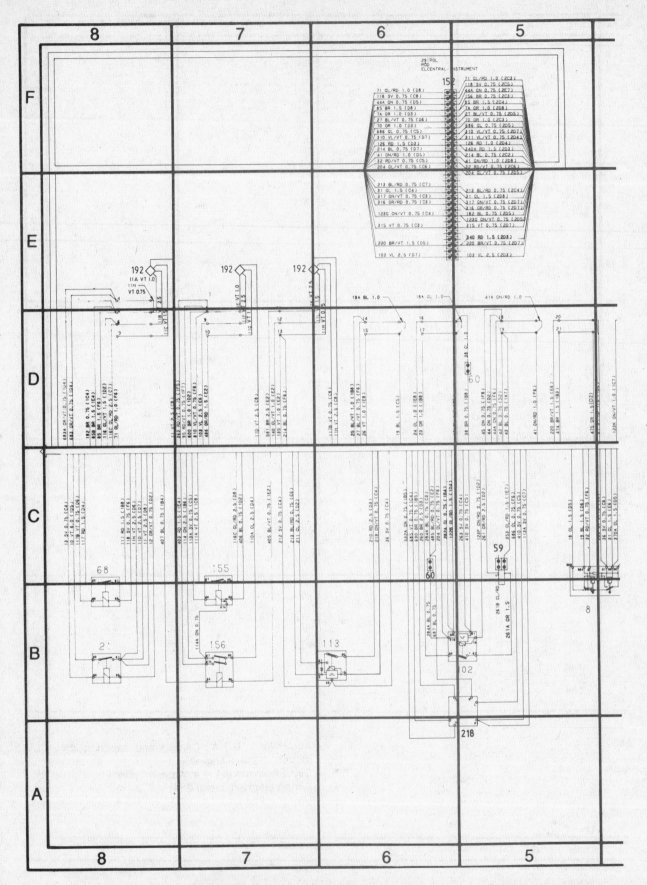

Fig. 13.51   Wiring diagram for 1985 and later (US and Canada) 8-valve 900 — part 3 electrical distribution box

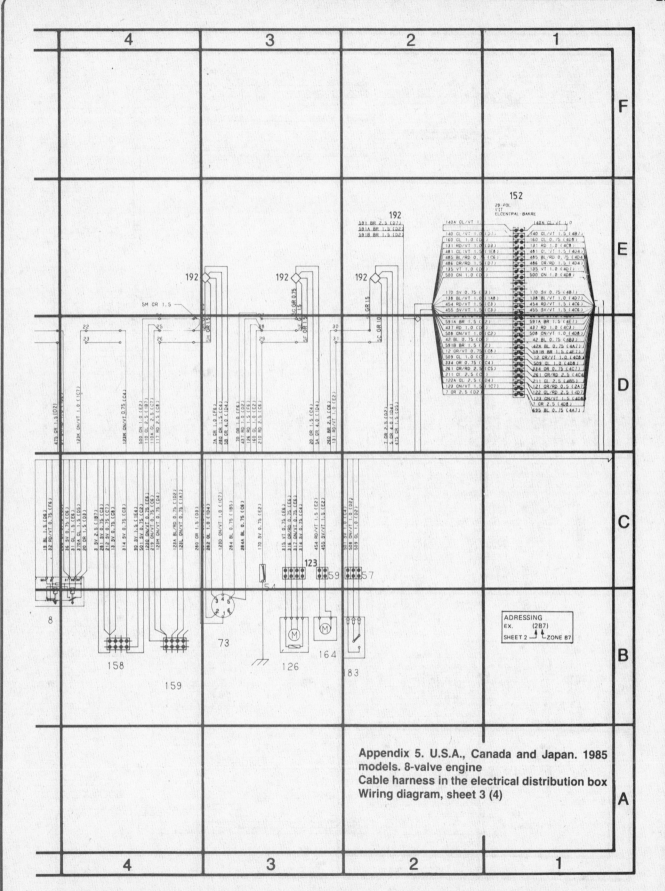

Appendix 5. U.S.A., Canada and Japan. 1985 models. 8-valve engine
Cable harness in the electrical distribution box
Wiring diagram, sheet 3 (4)

Fig. 13.51 Wiring diagram for 1985 and later (US and Canada) 8-valve 900 — part 3 electrical distribution box (continued)

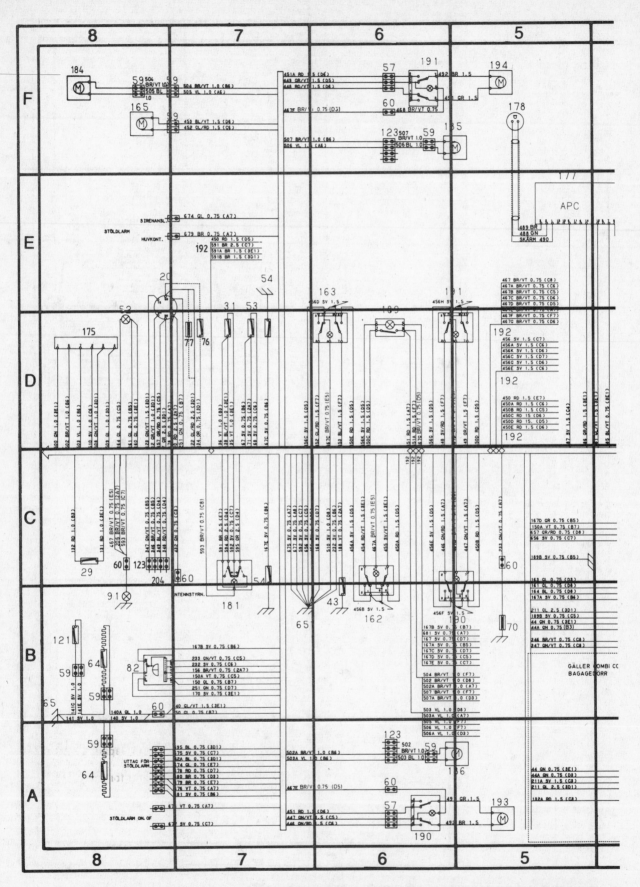

Fig. 13.51 Wiring diagram for 1985 and later (US and Canada) 8-valve 900 — part 4 interior and rear lighting

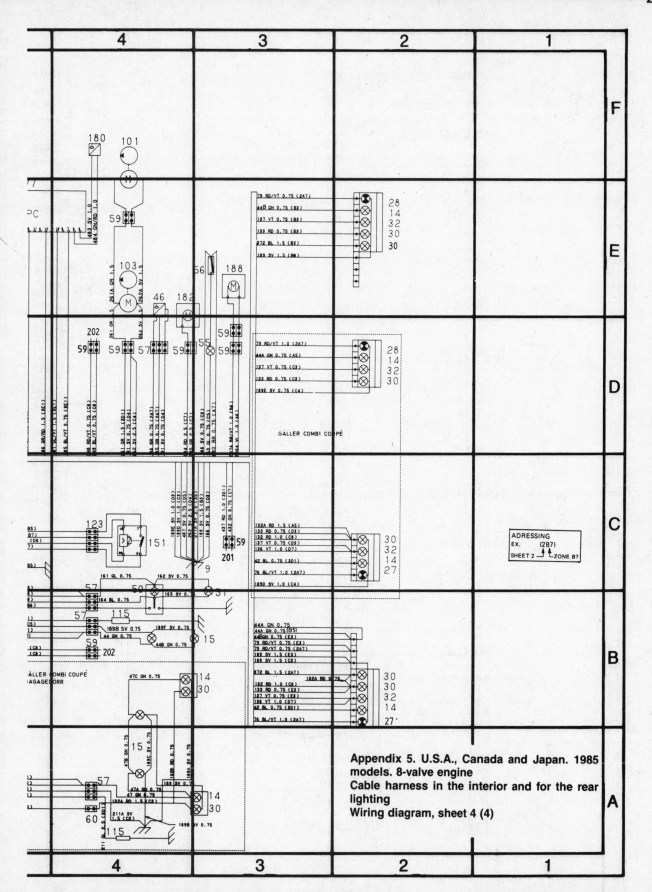

Appendix 5. U.S.A., Canada and Japan. 1985 models. 8-valve engine
Cable harness in the interior and for the rear lighting
Wiring diagram, sheet 4 (4)

ADRESSING
EX. (2B7)
SHEET 2 ←→ ZONE B7

GÄLLER COMBI COUPÉ

GÄLLER COMBI COUPÉ
BAGAGEDÖRR

13

Fig. 13.51 Wiring diagram for 1985 and later (US and Canada) 8-valve 900 — part 4 interior and rear lighting (continued)

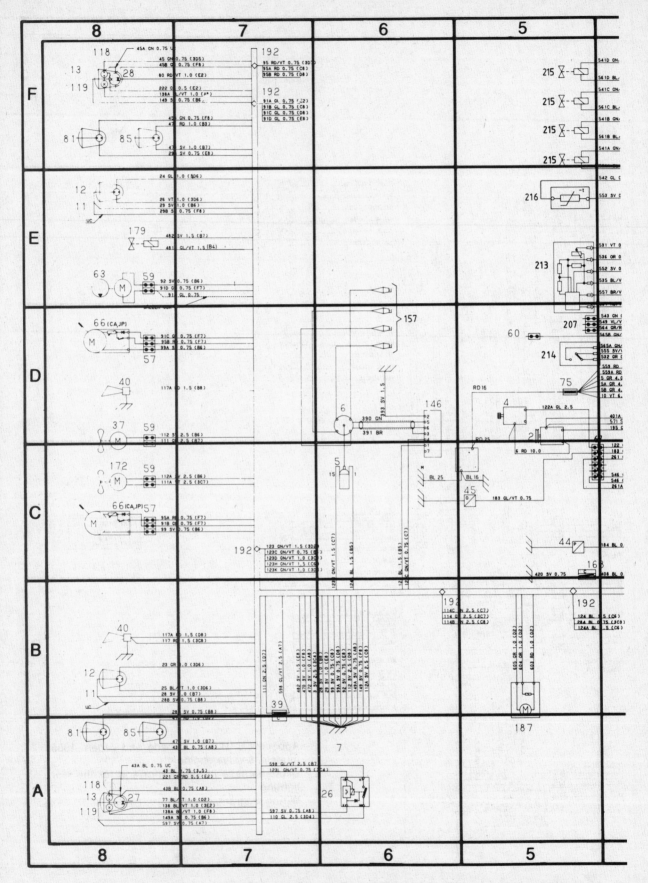

Fig. 13.52 Wiring diagram for 1985 and later (US and Canada) 16-valve 900 — part 1 engine compartment

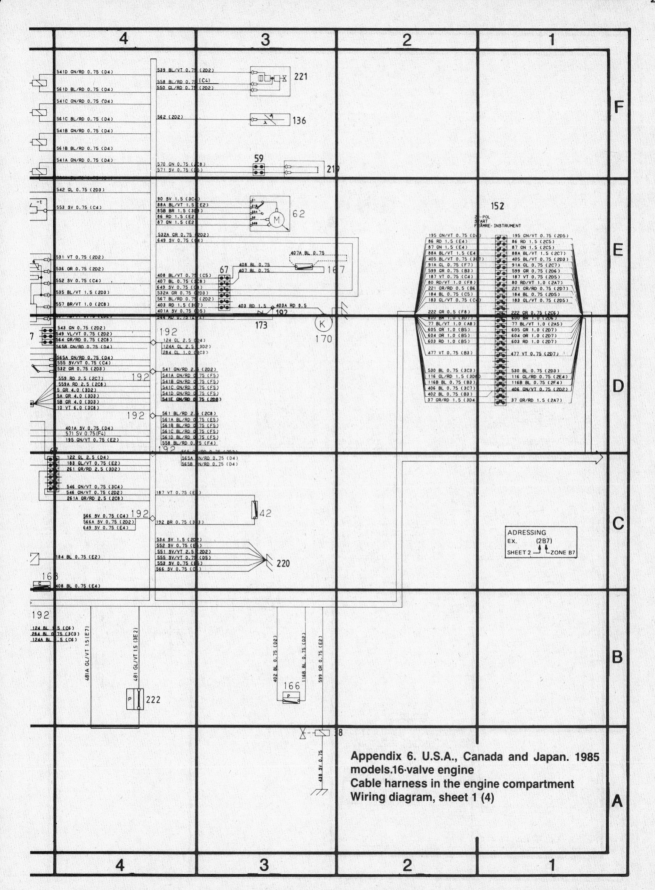

Fig. 13.52 Wiring diagram for 1985 and later (US and Canada) 16-valve 900 –- part 1 engine compartment (continued)

286

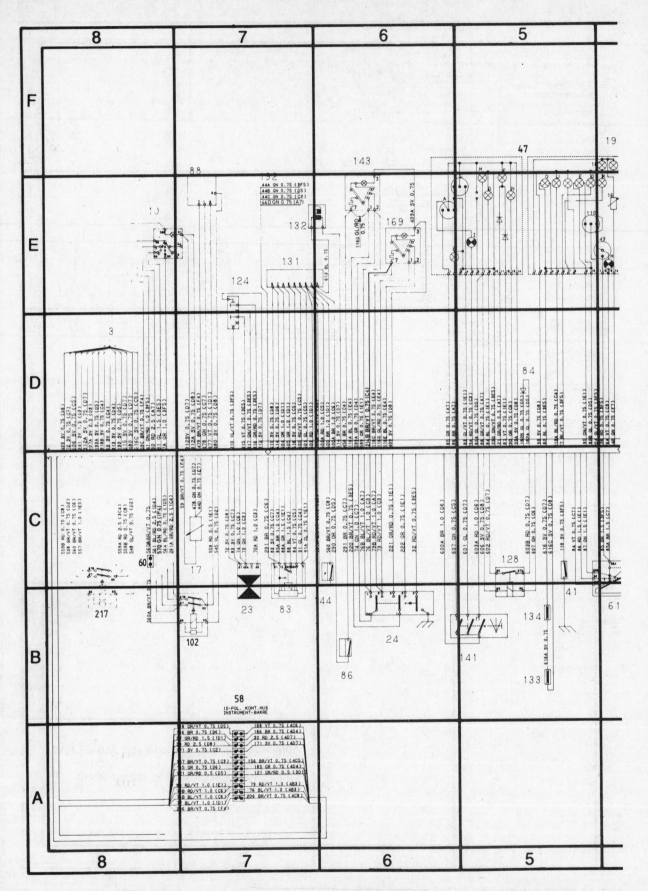

Fig. 13.52 Wiring diagram for 1985 and later (US and Canada) 16-valve 900 — part 2 instrument panel

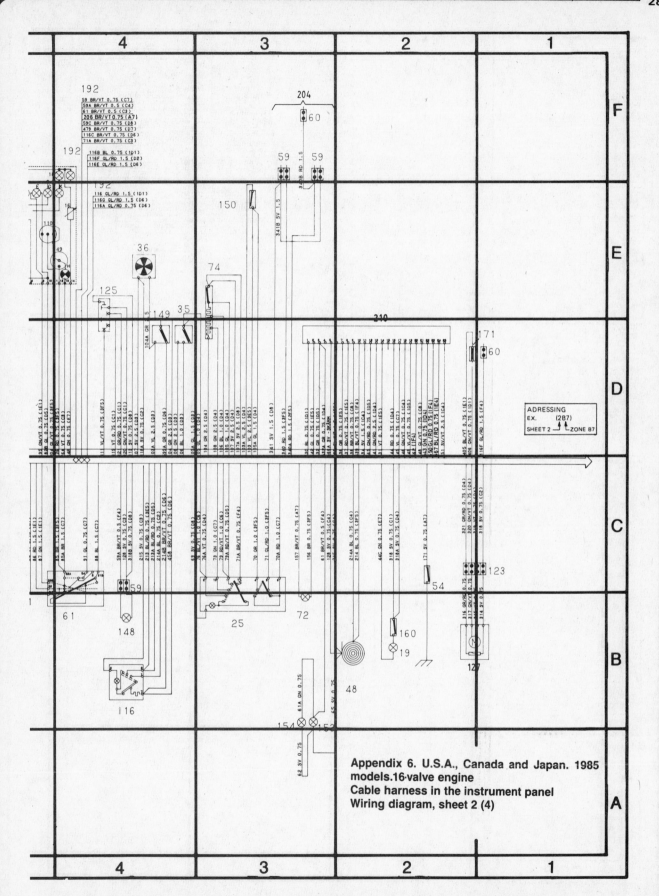

Fig. 13.52 Wiring diagram for 1985 and later (US and Canada) 16-valve 900 — part 2 instrument panel (continued)

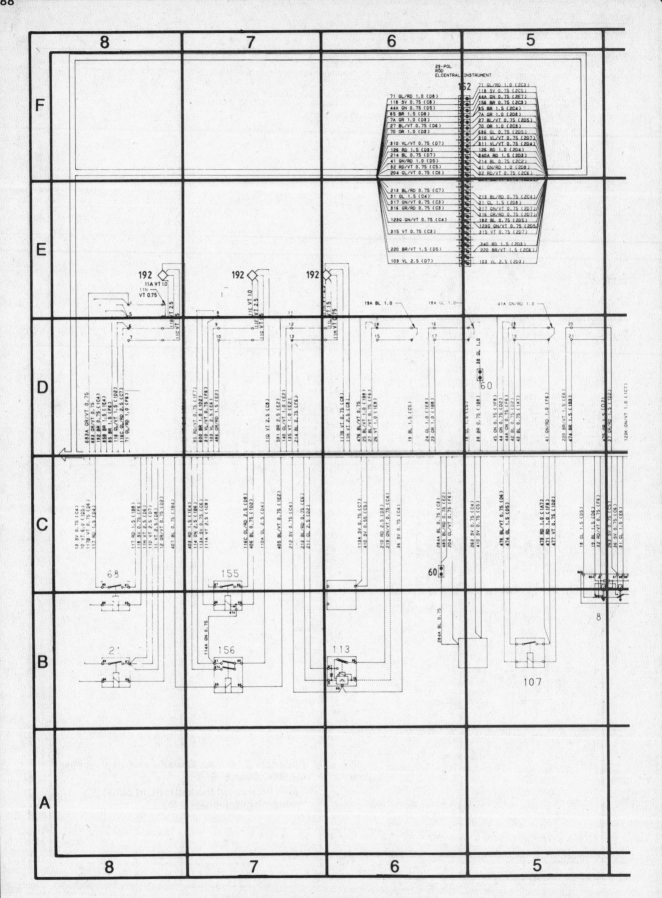

Fig. 13.52 Wiring diagram for 1985 and later (US and Canada) 16-valve 900 — part 3 electrical distribution box

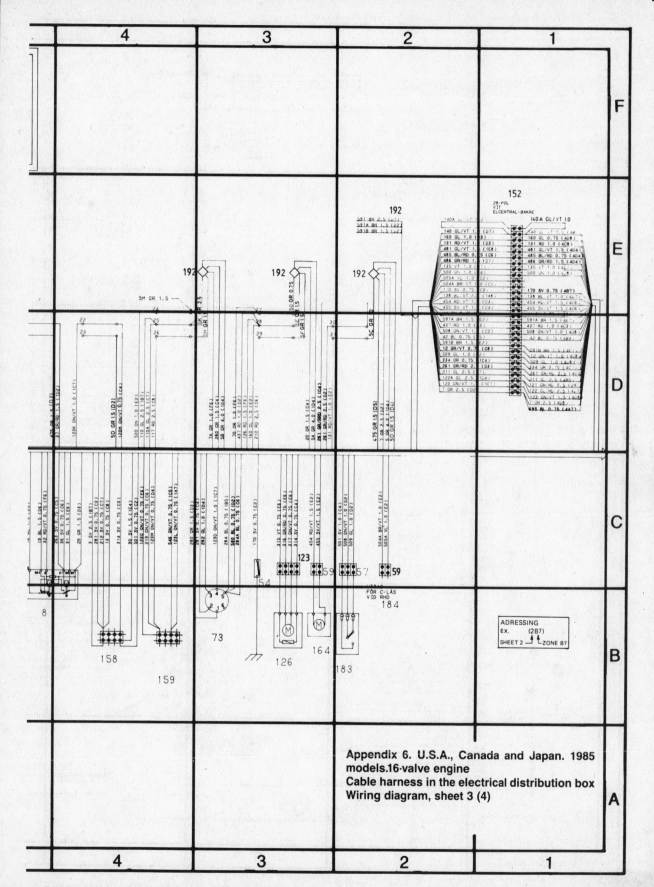

Appendix 6. U.S.A., Canada and Japan. 1985 models.16-valve engine
Cable harness in the electrical distribution box
Wiring diagram, sheet 3 (4)

Fig. 13.52 Wiring diagram for 1985 and later (US and Canada) 16-valve 900 — part 3 electrical distribution box (continued)

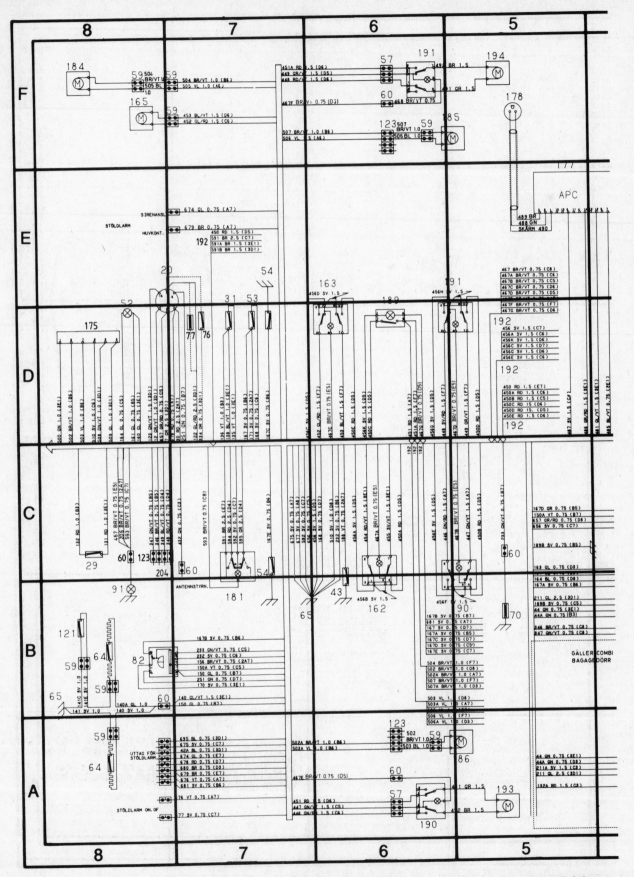

Fig. 13.52 **Wiring diagram for 1985 and later (US and Canada) 16-valve 900 — part 4 interior and rear lighting**

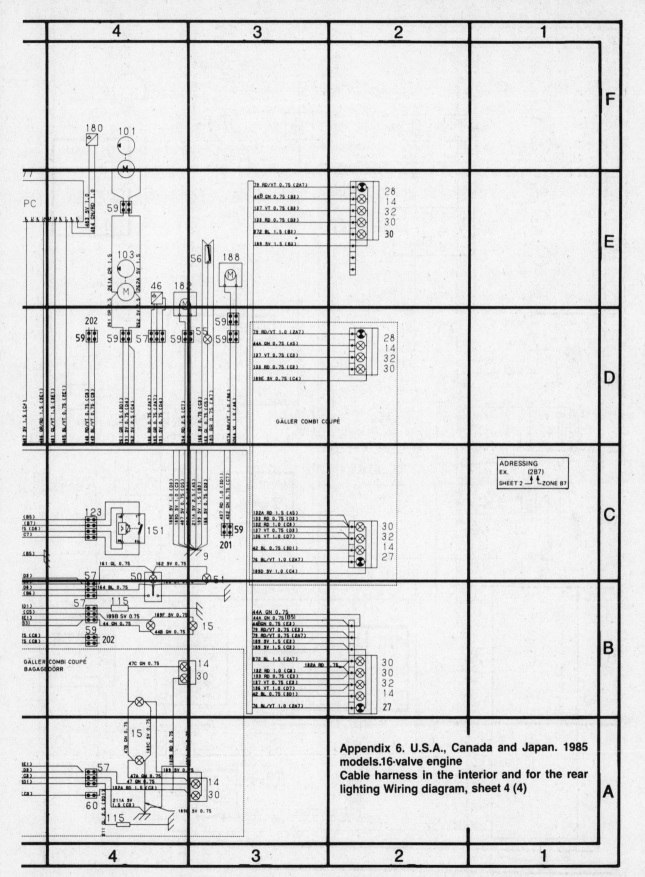

Appendix 6. U.S.A., Canada and Japan. 1985 models.16-valve engine
Cable harness in the interior and for the rear lighting Wiring diagram, sheet 4 (4)

13

Fig. 13.52 Wiring diagram for 1985 and later (US and Canada) 16-valve 900 — part 4 interior and rear lighting (continued)

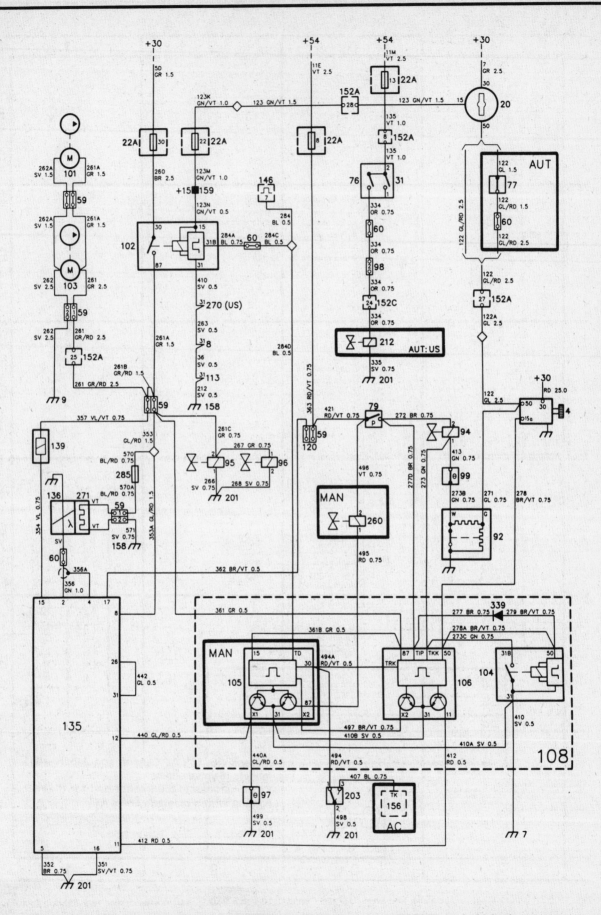

Fig. 13.53 Changes to wiring diagrams for 1988 and later models — part 2 900 Turbo fuel injection system

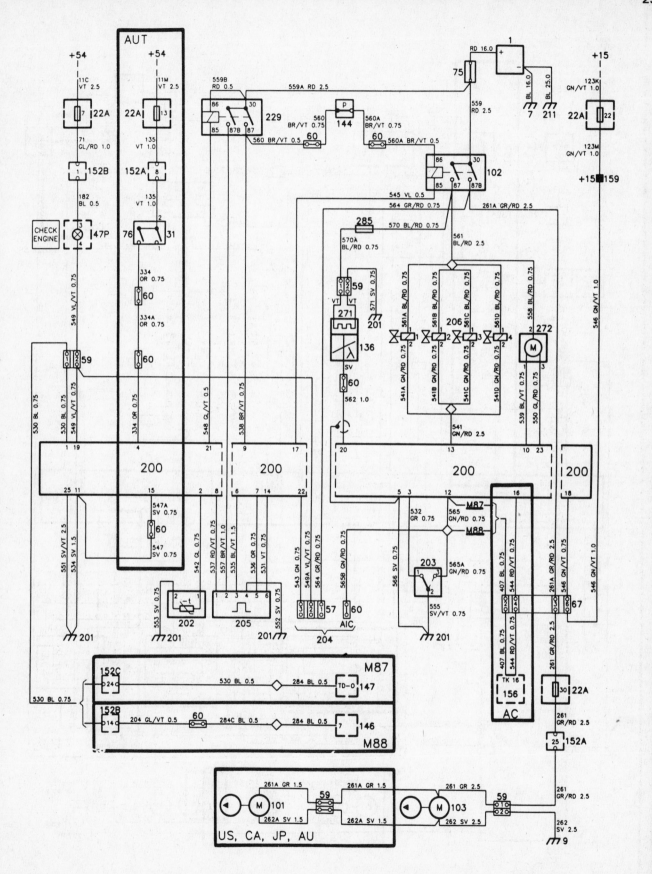

Fig. 13.53 Changes to wiring diagrams for 1988 and later models — part 1 8V fuel injection system

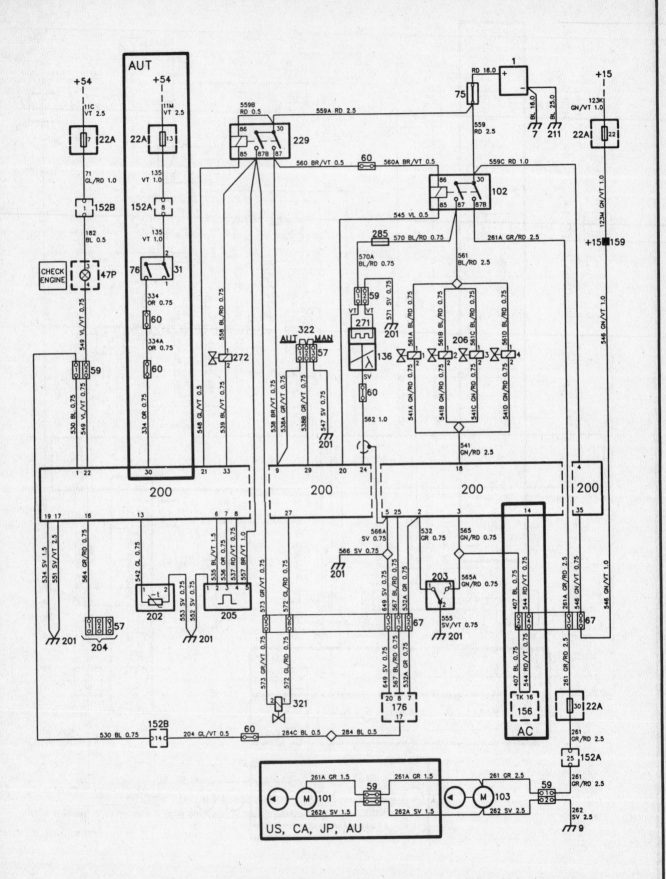

Fig. 13.53 Changes to wiring diagrams for 1988 and later models — part 3 900S fuel injection system

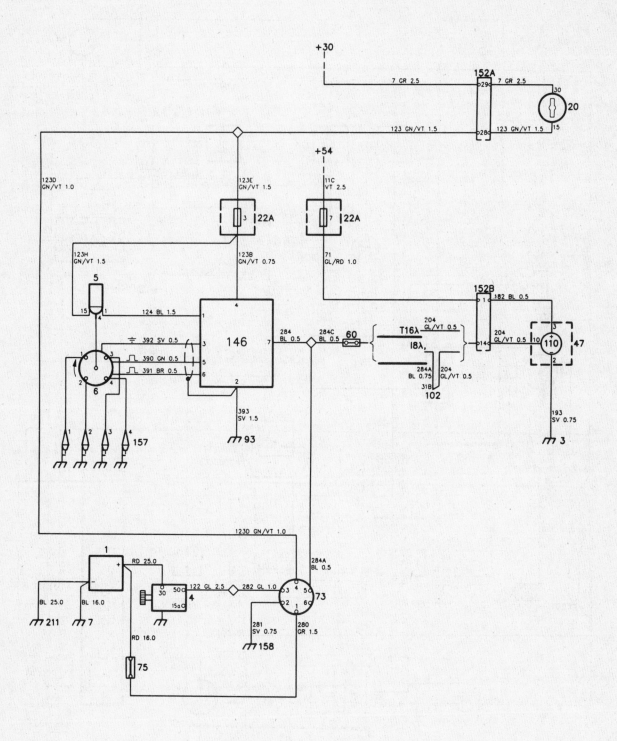

Fig. 13.53 Changes to wiring diagrams for 1988 and later models — part 4 900 and 900 Turbo ignition system with TSI socket and tachometer

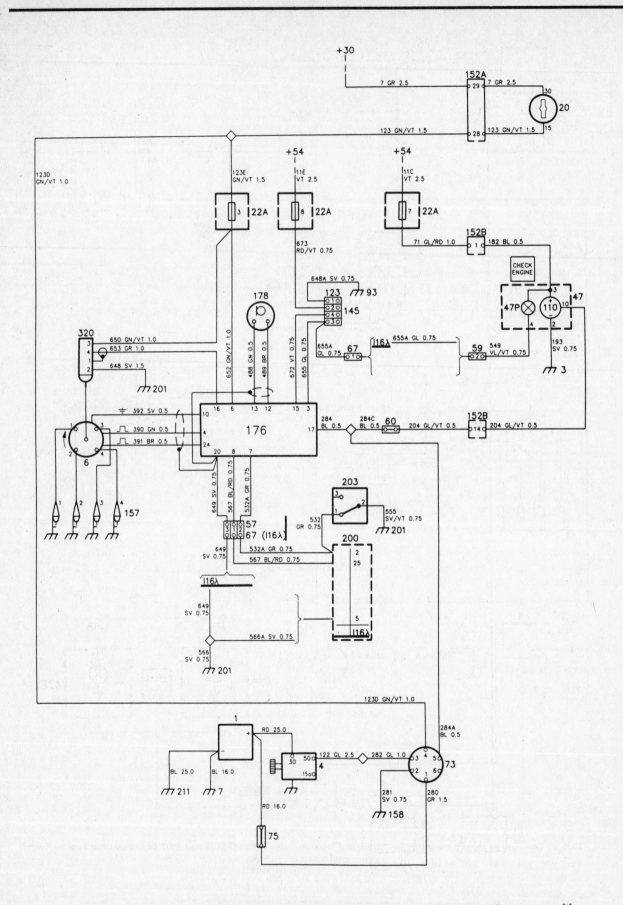

Fig. 13.53 Changes to wiring diagrams for 1988 and later models — part 5 900S ignition system with TSI socket and tachometer

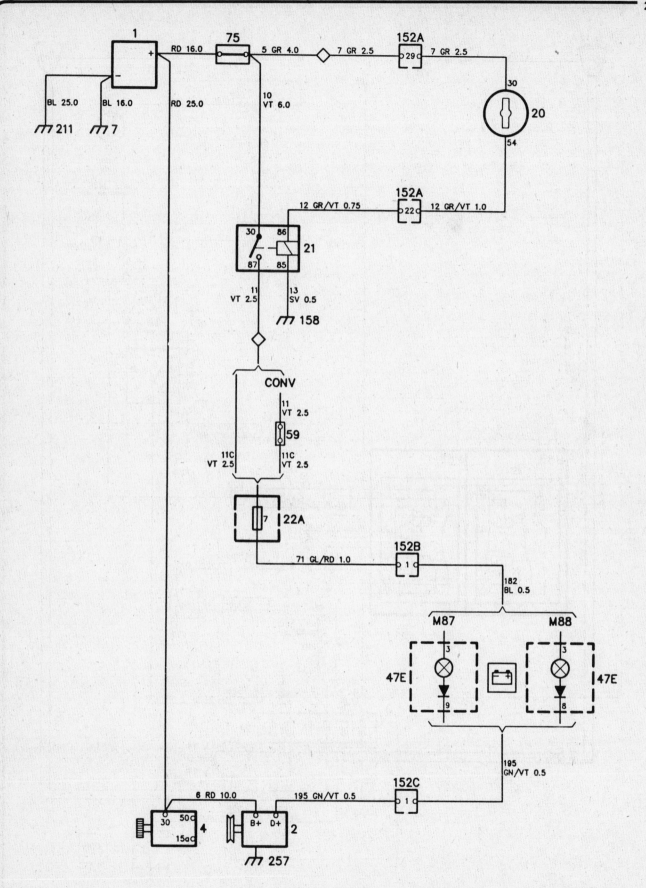

Fig. 13.53 Changes to wiring diagrams for 1988 and later models — part 6 battery charging system

13

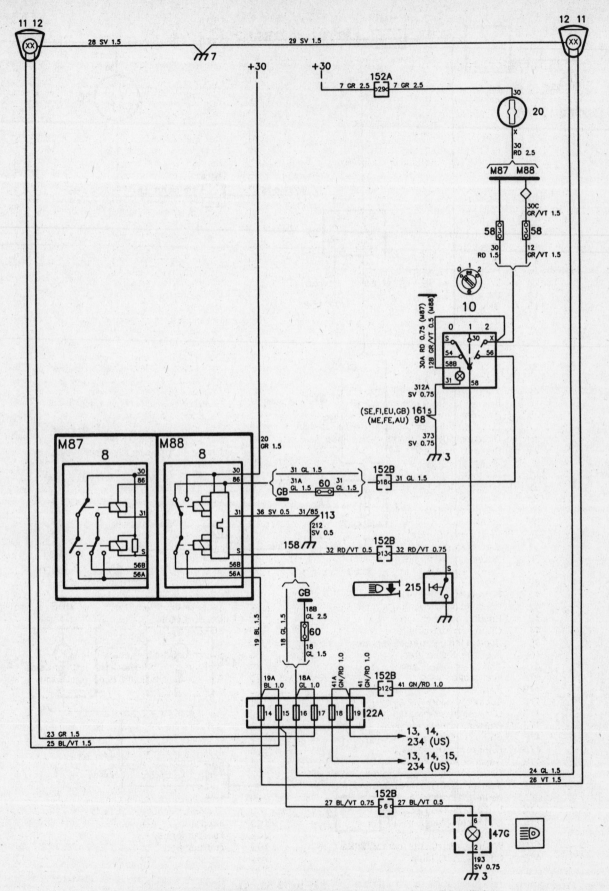

Fig. 13.53 Changes to wiring diagrams for 1988 and later models — part 7 headlights

List of components

Numerical index

1	Battery
2	Alternator
3	Ground point, facia
4	Starter motor
5	Ignition coil
6	Ignition distributor
7	Ground point, radiator cross-member
8	Lighting relay
9	Ground point, luggage compartment
10	Light switch
11	Full beam filament
12	Dipped beam filament
13	Parking lights
14	Rear lights
15	Number plate illumination
16	Instrument lighting rheostat
17	Extra rheostat, lighting for controls
18	Instrument lighting
19	Glove compartment lamp
20	Ignition switch
21	Ignition switch relay
22	Electrical distribution box
22A	Fuse board
22B	Relay board
23	Flasher relay
24	Direction indicator stalk switch
25	Switch for hazard warning lights
26	Time delay relay for the radiator fan
27	Direction indicator lamps, left-hand side
28	Direction indicator lamps, right-hand side
29	Brake lamp switch
30	Brake lamps
31	Reversing light switch
32	Reversing lights
33	Rear fog lights
34	Choke control switch
35	Selector switch for the ventilation fan
36	Ventilation fan motor
37	Radiator fan motor
38	Recirculation damper motor, AC
39	Temperature switch for the radiator fan
40	Horns
41	Horn switch
42	Brake fluid level warning switch
43	Handbrake switch
44	Oil pressure transmitter
45	Coolant temperature transmitter
46	Fuel level transmitter
47	Combined instrument
47A	Fuel gauge
47B	Fuel reserve warning lamp
47C	Coolant temperature gauge
47D	Oil pressure warning lamp
47E	Charging warning lamp
47F	Brake fluid level warning lamp
47G	Full-beam warning lamp
47H	Direction indicator warning lamp, left-hand
47I	Direction indicator warning lamp, right-hand
47J	Indicating lamp for the rear-window electric heater
47K	Lamp for shift-up indication
47L	EXH warning lamp
47M	Handbrake warning lamp
47N	Warning lamp for the rear fog lights
47O	Choke warning lamp
47P	CHECK ENGINE warning lamp
47Q	-
47R	-
47S	Warning lamp for passive seat belts
48	Cigarette lighter
49	Clock
50	Roof lamp, centre
51	Interior lighting lamp, front
52	Ignition switch illumination
53	Switch, interior lighting
54	Door switch for the interior lighting
55	Luggage compartment light fitting
56	Luggage compartment light switch
57	Three-pole connector
58	Twelve-pole connector
59	Two-pole connector
60	Single-pole connector
61	Windscreen wiper stalk switch
62	Windscreen wiper motor
63	Washer motor
64	Heating pad
65	Ground point, back seat
66	Headlamp wiper motor
67	Six-pole connector
68	Horn relay
69	Seat switch for the co-driver's seat-belt warning lamp
70	Seat-belt switch for the driver
71	Seat-belt switch for the co-driver
72	Seat-belt warning lamp
73	Timing service instrument (TSI) socket
74	Resistor for ventilation fan
75	Distribution block, positive supplies from battery
76	Switch for raising the engine idling speed, automatic transmission
77	Starting interlock contacts, automatic transmission
78	Relay, dim dipped beams
79	Vacuum switch
80	Resistor, dim dipped beams
81	-
82	Seat belt/ignition switch warning relay
83	Relay for intermittent operation of the wipers
84	Diode for brake lamp test
85	Extra fog lights
86	EGR switch
87	-
88	Switch for extra fog lights
89	Side direction indicator lamp, left-hand side
90	Side direction indicator lamp, right-hand side
91	Selector lever lamp
92	Temperature time switch
93	Ground point, left-hand wing
94	Starting valve
95	Auxiliary air valve
96	Control-pressure valve
97	Temperature switch I, Lambda
98	Ten-pole connector
99	Temperature switch II, Lambda
100	Ci diode, Lambda
101	Feed pump
102	Fuel pump relay
103	Fuel pump
104	Hot start relay

Key to 13.53

13

105	Engine speed relay	166	Pressure switch for the AC radiator fan
106	Time-delay relay	167	Spare
107	Relay for the extra fog lights	168	Coolant temperature switch, AC
108	Relay panel, Lambda	169	Switch for the AC
109	High-level brake light	170	Compressor for the AC
110	Tachometer	171	Anti-freeze thermostat (cycling clutch switch), AC
111	-	172	Radiator fan for the AC
112	-	173	Diode for the AC compressor
113	Relay/time-delay relay for the electric heater for the rear window	174	Refrigerant temperature switch
114	Float chamber valve, carburetor	175	Electronic unit for the central locking system
115	Electric heater for the rear window	176	Control unit, EZK ignition system
116	Switch for the rear window heating	177	Control unit for the APC system
117	Ground point for the handbrake	178	Knock sensor for the APC/EZK system
118	Corner lights	179	Solenoid valve, APC
119	Side reversing lights	180	Pressure transmitter, APC
120	Test socket, Lambda	181	Switch for the electrically operated sunroof
121	Seat switch for the heating pad	182	Motor for the electrically operated sunroof
122	Eight-pole connector	183	Control unit for central locking system, driver's door
123	Four-pole connector	184	Motor for central locking system, co-driver's door
124	Switch for the rear-view mirror, left-hand side	185	Motor for the central locking system, right-hand rear door
125	Switch for the rear-view mirror, right-hand side	186	Motor for the central locking system, left-hand rear door
126	Motor for the left-hand rear-view mirror	187	Vacuum pump for Cruise Control
127	Motor for the right-hand rear-view mirror	188	Motor for the central locking system, luggage compartment lid
128	Relay for Cruise Control	189	Interlock switch for the rear-door electric window regulators
129	Buzzer for engine coolant temperature	190	Switch for the left-hand rear electric window regulator
130	Temperature switch for engine coolant	190A	Switch for the left-hand rear electric window regulator
131	Electronic unit for the Cruise Control	191	Switch for the right-hand rear electric window regulator
132	Sensor for the speed transmitter	191A	Switch for the right-hand rear electric window regulator
133	Clutch switch for the Cruise Control	192	Distribution block
134	Brake switch for the Cruise Control	193	Motor for the electric window regulator, left-hand rear door
135	Control unit, Lambda	194	Motor for the electric window regulator, right-hand rear door
136	Lambda sensor	195	-
137	Throttle switch, full load, Lambda	196	Throttle switch, zero position, Lambda
138	Engine speed relay, manual, Turbo	197	-
139	Timing valve, Lambda	198	-
140	Fuel shut-off valve, carburetor	199	-
141	Selector for Cruise Control	200	Control unit for the LH fuel injection system
142	Solenoid valve for increasing the idling speed, AC	201	Engine ground point
143	Recirculation switch for the AC	202	Engine temperature transmitter, LH fuel injection system
144	Pressure switch, Turbo	203	Throttle angle transmitter, LH fuel injection system
145	Test tapping, EZK	204	Test connector, LH fuel injection system
146	Ignition amplifier	205	Air mass meter, LH fuel injection system
147	Ignition pulse amplifier	206	Fuel injection valves, LH fuel injection system
148	Ashtray illumination	207	Heating element for the rear-view mirrors
149	Main switch for the fan	208A	Door lock, reed switch, driver's door
150	Air distribution switch, AC	208B	Door lock, reed switch, co-driver's door
151	Time-delay relay for the interior lighting	209	-
152A	29-pole connector, white	210	-
152B	29-pole connector, red	211	Ground point, gearbox
152C	29-pole connector, black	212	Valve for increasing idling speed, automatic transmission
153	Cigarette lighter illumination	213	-
154	Lighting for the heater controls	213A	-
155	Relay for the AC radiator fan		
156	Relay for the AC compressor		
157	Spark plugs		
158	Negative distribution terminal		
159	Distribution terminal +15		
160	Switch for glove compartment illumination		
161	Switch for the rear fog lights		
162	Switch for the electric window regulator, driver's door		
163	Switch for the electric window regulator, co-driver's door		
164	Motor for the electric window regulator, left-hand front door		
165	Motor for the electric window regulator, right-hand front door		

Key to 13.53 (continued)

213B	-	274	
213C	-	275	Connector for horn, burglar alarm
213D	-	276	Connector for main switch, burglar alarm
213E	-	277	-
213F	-	278	-
213G	-	279	-
213H	-	280	-
214	Seat belt warning lamp (ME)	281	-
215	Dip switch	282	-
216	-	283	-
217	-	284	-
218	-	285	Lambda sensor fuse
219	-	286	-
220	-	287	Relay, automatic window regulator controls
221	-	288	Connector for ON/OFF switch, burglar alarm
222	-	289	Connector for burglar alarm control unit
223	-	290	-
224	-	291	-
225	Reading lamp	292	-
226	-	293	-
227	-	294	-
228	-	295	-
229	Main relay, LH fuel injection system	296	-
230	-	297	-
231	-	298	-
232	-	299	-
233	Vacuum switch, Cruise Control/APC	300	-
234	Side marker lights	301	-
235	-	302	-
236	-	303	-
237	-	304	Motion detector, burglar alarm
238	-	305	LED, burglar alarm
239	Selector lever switch (automatic transmission)	306	Control unit for passive seat belts
240	-	307A	Belt reel, driver's side, passive seat belts
241	-	307B	Belt reel, co-driver's side, passive seat belts
242	-	308A	Motor with limit switch, passive seat belts, driver's side
243	-		
244	-	308B	Motor with limit switch, passive seat belts, co-driver's side
245	-		
246	-	309	G sensor, passive seat belts
247	-	310	Fuses for passive seat belts
248	-	311D	Relay, motor drive, passive seat belts, driver's side
249	-		
250	Multi-lead connector, 6 circuits	311P	Relay, motor drive, passive seat belts, co-driver's side
251	Multi-lead connector, 3+3 circuits		
252	Rheostat for the heating pad, driver's seat	312D	Relay, motor drive, passive seat belts, driver's side
253	-		
254	Thermostat for the heating pad, driver's seat	312P	Relay, motor drive, passive seat belts, co-driver's side
255	-	313	Relay, burglar alarm
256	-	314	Seat switch, burglar alarm, driver's side
257	Ground point, alternator bracket	315	Seat switch, burglar alarm, co-driver's side
258	-	316	Diode, burglar alarm
259	Relay, reverse current protection	317	Spare
260	Solenoid valve, fuel shut-off, Lambda	318	Spare
261	Throttle switch, zero position, shift-up indication	319	Spare
262	Temperature switch, shift-up indication	320	Ignition coil with integrated amplifier
263	Vacuum switch, shift-up indication	321	Valve for charcoal canister
264	Switch, fifth gear, shift-up indication	322	Connector, Auto/Man, LH 2.4
265	Electric antenna	324	Spare
266	Speakers	325	Spare
267	Connectors for radio	326	Spare
268	AC connector at the back seat	327	Spare
269	Multi-lead connector, two-pole	328	Spare
270	Shift-up indication relay	329	Spare
271	Lambda sensor preheater	339	Ci diode
272	Engine idling speed adjustment, LH fuel injection system	348	Contact box without amplifier, for radio
		349	Contact box with amplifier, for radio
273	-	350	Contact box for CD player/equalizer
		351	13-pole connector

Key to 13.53 (continued)

Conversion factors

Length (distance)
Inches (in)	X	25.4	= Millimetres (mm)	X 0.0394	= Inches (in)
Feet (ft)	X	0.305	= Metres (m)	X 3.281	= Feet (ft)
Miles	X	1.609	= Kilometres (km)	X 0.621	= Miles

Volume (capacity)
Cubic inches (cu in; in³)	X	16.387	= Cubic centimetres (cc; cm³)	X 0.061	= Cubic inches (cu in; in³)
Imperial pints (Imp pt)	X	0.568	= Litres (l)	X 1.76	= Imperial pints (Imp pt)
Imperial quarts (Imp qt)	X	1.137	= Litres (l)	X 0.88	= Imperial quarts (Imp qt)
Imperial quarts (Imp qt)	X	1.201	= US quarts (US qt)	X 0.833	= Imperial quarts (Imp qt)
US quarts (US qt)	X	0.946	= Litres (l)	X 1.057	= US quarts (US qt)
Imperial gallons (Imp gal)	X	4.546	= Litres (l)	X 0.22	= Imperial gallons (Imp gal)
Imperial gallons (Imp gal)	X	1.201	= US gallons (US gal)	X 0.833	= Imperial gallons (Imp gal)
US gallons (US gal)	X	3.785	= Litres (l)	X 0.264	= US gallons (US gal)

Mass (weight)
Ounces (oz)	X	28.35	= Grams (g)	X 0.035	= Ounces (oz)
Pounds (lb)	X	0.454	= Kilograms (kg)	X 2.205	= Pounds (lb)

Force
Ounces-force (ozf; oz)	X	0.278	= Newtons (N)	X 3.6	= Ounces-force (ozf; oz)
Pounds-force (lbf; lb)	X	4.448	= Newtons (N)	X 0.225	= Pounds-force (lbf; lb)
Newtons (N)	X	0.1	= Kilograms-force (kgf; kg)	X 9.81	= Newtons (N)

Pressure
Pounds-force per square inch (psi; lbf/in²; lb/in²)	X	0.070	= Kilograms-force per square centimetre (kgf/cm²; kg/cm²)	X 14.223	= Pounds-force per square inch (psi; lbf/in²; lb/in²)
Pounds-force per square inch (psi; lbf/in²; lb/in²)	X	0.068	= Atmospheres (atm)	X 14.696	= Pounds-force per square inch (psi; lbf/in²; lb/in²)
Pounds-force per square inch (psi; lbf/in²; lb/in²)	X	0.069	= Bars	X 14.5	= Pounds-force per square inch (psi; lbf/in²; lb/in²)
Pounds-force per square inch (psi; lbf/in²; lb/in²)	X	6.895	= Kilopascals (kPa)	X 0.145	= Pounds-force per square inch (psi; lbf/in²; lb/in²)
Kilopascals (kPa)	X	0.01	= Kilograms-force per square centimetre (kgf/cm²; kg/cm²)	X 98.1	= Kilopascals (kPa)
Millibar (mbar)	X	100	= Pascals (Pa)	X 0.01	= Millibar (mbar)
Millibar (mbar)	X	0.0145	= Pounds-force per square inch (psi; lbf/in²; lb/in²)	X 68.947	= Millibar (mbar)
Millibar (mbar)	X	0.75	= Millimetres of mercury (mmHg)	X 1.333	= Millibar (mbar)
Millibar (mbar)	X	0.401	= Inches of water (inH₂O)	X 2.491	= Millibar (mbar)
Millimetres of mercury (mmHg)	X	0.535	= Inches of water (inH₂O)	X 1.868	= Millimetres of mercury (mmHg)
Inches of water (inH₂O)	X	0.036	= Pounds-force per square inch (psi; lbf/in²; lb/in²)	X 27.68	= Inches of water (inH₂O)

Torque (moment of force)
Pounds-force inches (lbf in; lb in)	X	1.152	= Kilograms-force centimetre (kgf cm; kg cm)	X 0.868	= Pounds-force inches (lbf in; lb in)
Pounds-force inches (lbf in; lb in)	X	0.113	= Newton metres (Nm)	X 8.85	= Pounds-force inches (lbf in; lb in)
Pounds-force inches (lbf in; lb in)	X	0.083	= Pounds-force feet (lbf ft; lb ft)	X 12	= Pounds-force inches (lbf in; lb in)
Pounds-force feet (lbf ft; lb ft)	X	0.138	= Kilograms-force metres (kgf m; kg m)	X 7.233	= Pounds-force feet (lbf ft; lb ft)
Pounds-force feet (lbf ft; lb ft)	X	1.356	= Newton metres (Nm)	X 0.738	= Pounds-force feet (lbf ft; lb ft)
Newton metres (Nm)	X	0.102	= Kilograms-force metres (kgf m; kg m)	X 9.804	= Newton metres (Nm)

Power
Horsepower (hp)	X	745.7	= Watts (W)	X 0.0013	= Horsepower (hp)

Velocity (speed)
Miles per hour (miles/hr; mph)	X	1.609	= Kilometres per hour (km/hr; kph)	X 0.621	= Miles per hour (miles/hr; mph)

Fuel consumption*
Miles per gallon, Imperial (mpg)	X	0.354	= Kilometres per litre (km/l)	X 2.825	= Miles per gallon, Imperial (mpg)
Miles per gallon, US (mpg)	X	0.425	= Kilometres per litre (km/l)	X 2.352	= Miles per gallon, US (mpg)

Temperature

Degrees Fahrenheit = ($°C \times 1.8$) + 32   Degrees Celsius (Degrees Centigrade; °C) = ($°F - 32$) x 0.56

*It is common practice to convert from miles per gallon (mpg) to litres/100 kilometres (l/100km), where mpg (Imperial) x l/100 km = 282 and mpg (US) x l/100 km = 235

Index

Haynes Automotive Manuals

NOTE: New manuals are added to this list on a periodic basis. If you do not see a listing for your vehicle, consult your local Haynes dealer for the latest product information.

ACURA
*12020 Integra '86 thru '89 & Legend '86 thru '90

AMC
Jeep CJ - see JEEP (50020)
14020 Concord/Hornet/Gremlin/Spirit '70 thru '83
14025 (Renault) Alliance & Encore '83 thru '87

AUDI
15020 4000 all models '80 thru '87
15025 5000 all models '77 thru '83
15026 5000 all models '84 thru '88

AUSTIN
Healey Sprite - see MG Midget (66015)

BMW
*18020 3/5 Series '82 thru '92
*18021 3 Series except 325iX models '92 thru '97
18025 320i all 4 cyl models '75 thru '83
18035 528i & 530i all models '75 thru '80
18050 1500 thru 2002 except Turbo '59 thru '77

BUICK
Century (FWD) - see GM (38005)
*19020 Buick, Oldsmobile & Pontiac Full-size
(Front wheel drive) '85 thru '98
Buick Electra, LeSabre and Park Avenue;
Oldsmobile Delta 88 Royale, Ninety Eight
and Regency; Pontiac Bonneville
19025 Buick Oldsmobile & Pontiac Full-size
(Rear wheel drive)
Buick Estate '70 thru '90, Electra'70 thru '84,
LeSabre '70 thru '85, Limited '74 thru '79
Oldsmobile Custom Cruiser '70 thru '90,
Delta 88 '70 thru '85,Ninety-eight '70 thru '84
Pontiac Bonneville '70 thru '81,
Catalina '70 thru '81, Grandville '70 thru '75,
Parisienne '83 thru '86
19030 Mid-size Regal & Century '74 thru '87
Regal - see GENERAL MOTORS (38010)
Skyhawk - see GM (38030)
Skylark - see GM (38020, 38025)
Somerset - see GENERAL MOTORS (38025)

CADILLAC
*21030 Cadillac Rear Wheel Drive '70 thru '93
Cimarron, Eldorado & Seville - see
GM (38015, 38030)

CHEVROLET
10305 Chevrolet Engine Overhaul Manual
24010 Astro & GMC Safari Mini-vans '85 thru '93
24015 Camaro V8 all models '70 thru '81
24016 Camaro all models '82 thru '92
Cavalier - see GM (38015)
Celebrity - see GM (38005)
24017 Camaro & Firebird '93 thru '97
24020 Chevelle, Malibu, El Camino '69 thru '87
24024 Chevette & Pontiac T1000 '76 thru '87
Citation - see GENERAL MOTORS (38020)
*24032 Corsica/Beretta all models '87 thru '96
24040 Corvette all V8 models '68 thru '82
*24041 Corvette all models '84 thru '96
24045 Full-size Sedans Caprice, Impala,
Biscayne, Bel Air & Wagons '69 thru '90
24046 Impala SS & Caprice and
Buick Roadmaster '91 thru '96
24048 Lumina '90 thru '94 - see GM (38010)
24048 Lumina & Monte Carlo '95 thru '98
Lumina APV - see GM (38035)
24050 Luv Pick-up all 2WD & 4WD '72 thru '82
24055 Monte Carlo all models '70 thru '88
Monte Carlo '95 thru '98 - see LUMINA
24059 Nova all V8 models '69 thru '79
*24060 Nova/Geo Prizm '85 thru '92
24064 Pick-ups '67 thru '87 - Chevrolet & GMC,
all V8 & in-line 6 cyl, 2WD & 4WD '67 thru '87;
Suburbans, Blazers & Jimmys '67 thru '91
*24065 Pick-ups '88 thru '98 - Chevrolet & GMC,
all full-size models '88 thru '98; Blazer &
Jimmy '92 thru '94; Suburban '92 thru '98;
Tahoe & Yukon '95 thru '98
*24070 S-10 & GMC S-15 Pick-ups '82 thru '93
*24071 S-10, Gmc S-15 & Jimmy '94 thru '96
*24075 Sprint & Geo Metro '85 thru '94
*24080 Vans - Chevrolet & GMC '68 thru '96

CHRYSLER
10310 Chrysler Engine Overhaul Manual
*25015 Chrysler Cirrus, Dodge Stratus,
Plymouth Breeze, '95 thru '98
*25020 Full-size Front-Wheel Drive '88 thru '93
K-Cars - see DODGE Aries (30008)
Laser - see DODGE Daytona (30030)
25025 Chrysler LHS, Concorde & New Yorker,
Dodge Intrepid, Eagle Vision, '93 thru '97
*25030 Chrysler/Plym. Mid-size '82 thru '95
Rear-wheel Drive - see DODGE (30050)

DATSUN
28005 200SX all models '80 thru '83
28007 B-210 all models '73 thru '78
28009 210 all models '78 thru '82
28012 240Z, 260Z & 280Z Coupe '70 thru '78
28014 280ZX Coupe & 2+2 '79 thru '83
300ZX - see NISSAN (72010)
28016 310 all models '78 thru '82
28018 510 & PL521 Pick-up '68 thru '73
28020 510 all models '78 thru '81
28022 620 Series Pick-up all models '73 thru '79
720 Series Pick-up - NISSAN (72030)
28025 810/Maxima all gas models, '77 thru '84

DODGE
400 & 600 - see CHRYSLER (25030)
*30008 Aries & Plymouth Reliant '81 thru '89
30010 Caravan & Ply. Voyager '84 thru '95
*30011 Caravan & Ply. Voyager '96 thru '98
30012 Challenger/Plymouth Saporro '78 thru '83
Challenger '67-'76 - see DART (30025)
30016 Colt/Plymouth Champ '78 thru '87
*30020 Dakota Pick-ups all models '87 thru '96
30025 Dart, Challenger/Plymouth Barracuda
& Valiant 6 cyl models '67 thru '76
*30030 Daytona & Chrysler Laser '84 thru '89
Intrepid - see Chrysler (25025)
*30034 Dodge & Plymouth Neon '95 thru '97
30035 Omni & Plymouth Horizon '78 thru '90
30040 Pick-ups all full-size models '74 thru '93
30041 Pick-ups all full-size models '94 thru '96
*30045 Ram 50/D50 Pick-ups & Raider and
Plymouth Arrow Pick-ups '79 thru '93
30050 Dodge/Ply./Chrysler RWD '71 thru '89
30055 Shadow/Plymouth Sundance '87 thru '94
*30060 Spirit & Plymouth Acclaim '89 thru '95
*30065 Vans - Dodge & Plymouth '71 thru '96

EAGLE
Talon - see MITSUBISHI Eclipse (68030)
Vision - see CHRYSLER (25025)

FIAT
34010 124 Sport Coupe & Spider '68 thru '78
34025 X1/9 all models '74 thru '80

FORD
10355 Ford Automatic Transmission Overhaul
10320 Ford Engine Overhaul Manual
*36004 Aerostar Mini-vans '86 thru '96
Aspire - see FORD Festiva (36030)
*36006 Contour/Mercury Mystique '95 thru '98
36008 Courier Pick-up all models '72 thru '82
36012 Crown Victoria & Mercury
Grand Marquis '88 thru '96
36016 Escort/Mercury Lynx '81 thru '90
*36020 Escort/Mercury Tracer '91 thru '96
Expedition - see FORD Pick-up (36059)
*36024 Explorer & Mazda Navajo '91 thru '95
36028 Fairmont & Mercury Zephyr '78 thru '83
36030 Festiva & Aspire '88 thru '97
36032 Fiesta all models '77 thru '80
36036 Ford & Mercury Full-size,
Ford LTD & Mercury Marquis ('75 thru '82);
Ford Custom 500,Country Squire, Crown
Victoria & Mercury Colony Park ('75 thru '87);
Ford LTD Crown Victoria &
Mercury Gran Marquis ('83 thru '87)
36040 Granada & Mercury Monarch '75 thru '80
36044 Ford & Mercury Mid-size,
Ford Thunderbird & Mercury
Cougar ('75 thru '82);
Ford LTD & Mercury Marquis ('83 thru '86);
Ford Torino,Gran Torino, Elite, Ranchero
pick-up, LTD II, Mercury Montego, Comet,
XR-7 & Lincoln Versailles ('75 thru '86)
36048 Mustang V8 all models '64-1/2 thru '73
36049 Mustang II 4 cyl, V6 & V8 '74 thru '78
36050 Mustang & Mercury Capri incl. Turbo
Mustang, '79 thru '93; Capri, '79 thru '86
*36051 Mustang all models '94 thru '97
36054 Pick-ups and Bronco '73 thru '79
36058 Pick-ups and Bronco '80 thru '96
*36059 Pick-ups, Expedition &
Lincoln Navigator '97 thru '98
36062 Pinto & Mercury Bobcat '75 thru '80
36066 Probe all models '89 thru '92
*36070 Ranger/Bronco II gas models '83 thru '92
*36071 Ford Ranger '93 thru '97 &
Mazda Pick-ups '94 thru '97
*36074 Taurus & Mercury Sable '86 thru '95
36075 Taurus & Mercury Sable '96 thru '98
36078 Tempo & Mercury Topaz '84 thru '94
36082 Thunderbird/Mercury Cougar '83 thru '88
36086 Thunderbird/Mercury Cougar '89 and '97
36090 Vans all V8 Econoline models '69 thru '91
36094 Vans full size '92 thru '95
*36097 Windstar Mini-van '95 thru '98

GENERAL MOTORS
*10360 GM Automatic Transmission Overhaul
*38005 Buick Century, Chevrolet Celebrity,
Olds Cutlass Ciera & Pontiac 6000
all models '82 thru '96
*38010 Buick Regal, Chevrolet Lumina,
Oldsmobile Cutlass Supreme & Pontiac
Grand Prix front wheel drive '88 thru '95
*38015 Buick Skyhawk, Cadillac Cimarron,
Chevrolet Cavalier, Oldsmobile Firenza
Pontiac J-2000 & Sunbird '82 thru '94
*38016 Chevrolet Cavalier &
Pontiac Sunfire '95 thru '98
38020 Buick Skylark, Chevrolet Citation,
Olds Omega, Pontiac Phoenix '80 thru '85
38025 Buick Skylark & Somerset, Olds Achieva,
Calais & Pontiac Grand Am '85 thru '95
38030 Cadillac Eldorado & Oldsmobile
Toronado '71 thru '85, Seville '80 thru '85,
Buick Riviera '79 thru '85
*38035 Chevrolet Lumina APV, Oldsmobile
Silhouette & Pontiac Trans Sport '90 thru '95
General Motors Full-size
Rear-wheel drive - see BUICK (19025)

GEO
Metro - see CHEVROLET Sprint (24075)
Prizm - see CHEVROLET (24060) or
TOYOTA (92036)
*40030 Storm all models '90 thru '93
Tracker - see SUZUKI Samurai (90010)

GMC
Safari - see CHEVROLET ASTRO (24010)
Vans & Pick-ups - see CHEVROLET

HONDA
42010 Accord CVCC all models '76 thru '83
42011 Accord all models '84 thru '89
42012 Accord all models '90 thru '93
*42013 Accord all models '94 thru '95
42020 Civic 1200 all models '73 thru '79
42021 Civic 1300 & 1500 CVCC '80 thru '83
42022* Civic 1500 CVCC all models '75 thru '79
42023 Civic all models '84 thru '91
42024 Civic & del Sol '92 thru '95
Passport - see ISUZU Rodeo (47017)
*42040 Prelude CVCC all models '79 thru '89

HYUNDAI
*43015 Excel all models '86 thru '94

ISUZU
Hombre - see CHEVROLET S-10 (24071)
*47017 Rodeo '91 thru '97, Amigo '89 thru '94,
Honda Passport '95 thru '97
*47020 Trooper '84 thru '91, Pick-up '81 thru '93

JAGUAR
*49010 XJ6 all 6 cyl models '68 thru '86
*49011 XJ6 all models '88 thru '94
*49015 XJ12 & XJS all 12 cyl models '72 thru '85

JEEP
*50010 Cherokee, Comanche & Wagoneer
Limited all models '84 thru '96
50020 CJ all models '49 thru '86
*50025 Grand Cherokee all models '93 thru '98
*50029 Grand Wagoneer & Pick-up '72 thru '91
*50030 Wrangler all models '87 thru '95

LINCOLN
Navigator - see FORD Pick-up (36059)
59010 Rear Wheel Drive all models '70 thru '96

MAZDA
61010 GLC (rear wheel drive) '77 thru '83
61011 GLC (front wheel drive) '81 thru '85
*61015 323 & Protegé '90 thru '97
*61016 MX-5 Miata '90 thru '97
*61020 MPV all models '89 thru '94
Navajo - see FORD Explorer (36024)
61030 Pick-ups '72 thru '93
Pick-ups '94 on - see Ford (36071)
61035 RX-7 all models '79 thru '85
61036 RX-7 all models '86 thru '91
61040 626 (rear wheel drive) '79 thru '82
*61041 626 & MX-6 (front wheel drive) '83 thru '91

MERCEDES-BENZ
63012 123 Series Diesel '76 thru '85
*63015 190 Series 4-cyl gas models, '84 thru '88
63020 230, 250 & 280 6 cyl sohc '68 thru '72
63025 280 123 Series gas models '77 thru '81
63030 350 & 450 all models '71 thru '80

MERCURY
See FORD Listing

MG
66010 MGB Roadster & GT Coupe '62 thru '80
66015 MG Midget & Austin Healey Sprite
Roadster '58 thru '80

MITSUBISHI
*68020 Cordia, Tredia, Galant, Precis &
Mirage '83 thru '93
*68030 Eclipse, Eagle Talon &
Plymouth Laser '90 thru '94
*68040 Pick-up '83 thru '96, Montero '83 thru '93

NISSAN
72010 300ZX all models incl. Turbo '84 thru '89
*72015 Altima all models '93 thru '97
*72020 Maxima all models '85 thru '91
*72030 Pick-ups '80 thru '96, Pathfinder '87 thru '95
72040 Pulsar all models '83 thru '86
72050 Sentra all models '82 thru '94
*72051 Sentra & 200SX all models '95 thru '98
*72060 Stanza all models '82 thru '90

OLDSMOBILE
*73015 Cutlass '74 thru '88
For other OLDSMOBILE titles, see
BUICK, CHEVROLET or
GENERAL MOTORS listing.

PLYMOUTH
For PLYMOUTH titles, see DODGE.

PONTIAC
79008 Fiero all models '84 thru '88
79018 Firebird V8 models except Turbo '70 thru '81
79019 Firebird all models '82 thru '92
For other PONTIAC titles, see
BUICK, CHEVROLET or
GENERAL MOTORS listing.

PORSCHE
*80020 911 Coupe & Targa models '65 thru '89
80025 914 all 4 cyl models '69 thru '76
80030 924 all models incl. Turbo '76 thru '82
*80035 944 all models incl. Turbo '83 thru '89

RENAULT
Alliance, Encore - see AMC (14020)

SAAB
*84010 900 including Turbo '79 thru '88

SATURN
*87010 Saturn all models '91 thru '96

SUBARU
89002 1100, 1300, 1400 & 1600 '71 thru '79
*89003 1600 & 1800 2WD & 4WD '80 thru '94

SUZUKI
*90010 Samurai/Sidekick/Geo Tracker '86 thru '96

TOYOTA
92005 Camry all models '83 thru '91
*92006 Camry all models '92 thru '96
92015 Celica Rear Wheel Drive '71 thru '85
*92020 Celica Front Wheel Drive '86 thru '93
92025 Celica Supra all models '79 thru '92
92030 Corolla all models '75 thru '79
92032 Corolla rear wheel drive models '80 thru '87
*92035 Corolla front wheel drive models '84 thru '92
*92036 Corolla & Geo Prizm '93 thru '97
92040 Corolla Tercel all models '80 thru '82
92045 Corona all models '74 thru '82
92050 Cressida all models '78 thru '82
92055 Land Cruiser Series FJ40, 43, 45 & 55
'68 thru '82
*92056 Land Cruiser Series FJ60, 62, 80 &
FZJ80 '68 thru '82
*92065 MR2 all models '85 thru '87
92070 Pick-up all models '69 thru '78
92075 Pick-up all models '79 thru '95
*92076 Tacoma '95 thru '98,
4Runner '96 thru '98, T100 '93 thru '98
*92080 Previa all models '91 thru '95
92085 Tercel all models '87 thru '94

TRIUMPH
94007 Spitfire all models '62 thru '81
94010 TR7 all models '75 thru '81

VW
96008 Beetle & Karmann Ghia '54 thru '79
96012 Dasher all gasoline models '74 thru '81
*96016 Rabbit, Jetta, Scirocco, & Pick-up gas
models '74 thru '91 & Convertible '80 thru '92
*96017 Golf & Jetta '93 thru '97
96020 Rabbit, Jetta, Pick-up diesel '77 thru '84
96030 Transporter 1600 all models '68 thru '79
96035 Transporter 1700, 1800, 2000 '72 thru '79
96040 Type 3 1500 & 1600 '63 thru '73
96045 Vanagon air-cooled models '80 thru '83

VOLVO
97010 120, 130 Series & 1800 Sports '61 thru '73
97015 140 Series all models '66 thru '74
*97020 240 Series all models '76 thru '93
97025 260 Series all models '75 thru '82
*97040 740 & 760 Series all models '82 thru '88

TECHBOOK MANUALS
10205 Automotive Computer Codes
10210 Automotive Emissions Control Manual
10215 Fuel Injection Manual, 1978 thru 1985
10220 Fuel Injection Manual, 1986 thru 1996
10225 Holley Carburetor Manual
10230 Rochester Carburetor Manual
10240 Weber/Zenith/Stromberg/SU Carburetor
10305 Chevrolet Engine Overhaul Manual
10310 Chrysler Engine Overhaul Manual
10320 Ford Engine Overhaul Manual
10330 GM and Ford Diesel Engine Repair
10340 Small Engine Repair Manual
10345 Suspension, Steering & Driveline
10355 Ford Automatic Transmission Overhaul
10360 GM Automatic Transmission Overhaul
10405 Automotive Body Repair & Painting
10410 Automotive Brake Manual
10415 Automotive Detailing Manual
10420 Automotive Eelectrical Manual
10425 Automotive Heating & Air Conditioning
10430 Automotive Reference Dictionary
10435 Automotive Tools Manual
10440 Used Car Buying Guide
10445 Welding Manual
10450 ATV Basics

SPANISH MANUALS
98903 Reparación de Carrocería & Pintura
98905 Códigos Automotrices de la Computadora
98910 Frenos Automotriz
98915 Inyección de Combustible 1986 al 1994
99040 Chevrolet & GMC Camionetas '67 al '87
99041 Chevrolet & GMC Camionetas '88 al '95
99042 Chevrolet Camionetas Cerradas '68 al '95
99055 Dodge Caravan/Ply. Voyager '84 al '95
99075 Ford Camionetas y Bronco '80 al '94
99077 Ford Camionetas Cerradas '69 al '91
99083 Ford Modelos de Tamaño Grande '75 al '87
99088 Ford Modelos de Tamaño Mediano '75 al '86
99091 Ford Taurus & Mercury Sable '75 al '96
99095 GM Modelos de Tamaño Grande '70 al '90
99100 GM Modelos de Tamaño Mediano '70 al '88
99110 Nissan Camionetas '80 al '96,
Pathfinder '87 al '95
99118 Nissan Sentra '82 al '94
99125 Toyota Camionetas y 4-Runner '79 al '95

Nearly 100 Haynes
motorcycle manuals
also available

5-98

Haynes North America, Inc., 861 Lawrence Drive, Newbury Park, CA 91320 • (805) 498-6703